SCRIPTURAL TRACES
CRITICAL PERSPECTIVES ON THE RECEPTION AND INFLUENCE OF THE BIBLE

**9**



Published under

**Library of New Testament Studies**

563

*Formerly Journal for the Study of the Old Testament Supplement Series*

A section of Chapter 2 previously appeared as "Alice Guy Blaché and Gene Gauntier: Bringing New Perspectives to Film," in *The Bible in Motion: A Handbook of the Bible and its Reception in Film*: 543–55. Rhonda Burnette-Bletsch, ed. (Berlin: de Gruyter, 2015). Reprinted by permission of de Gruyter.

A section of Chapter 8 previously appeared as "Judas as Portrayed in Film," in *The Bible in Motion: A Handbook of the Bible and its Reception in Film*: 463–82. Rhonda Burnette-Bletsch, ed. (Berlin: de Gruyter, 2015). Reprinted by permission of de Gruyter.

# JUDAS ISCARIOT
# DAMNED OR REDEEMED?

## A Critical Examination of the Portrayal of Judas in Jesus Films (1902–2014)

Carol A. Hebron

Bloomsbury T&T Clark
An imprint of Bloomsbury Publishing Plc

BLOOMSBURY
LONDON • OXFORD • NEW YORK • NEW DELHI • SYDNEY

**Bloomsbury T&T Clark**
An imprint of Bloomsbury Publishing Plc

Imprint previously known as T&T Clark

50 Bedford Square
London
WC1B 3DP
UK

1385 Broadway
New York
NY 10018
USA

**www.bloomsbury.com**



First published 2016



**British Library Cataloguing-in-Publication Data**
A catalogue record for this book is available from the British Library.

ISBN: HB: 978-0-56766-829-5
ePDF: 978-0-56766-830-1
ePUB: 978-0-56766-831-8

**Library of Congress Cataloging-in-Publication Data**
A catalog record for this book is available from the Library of Congress

Series: Library of New Testament Studies, volume 563

Typeset by Forthcoming Publications (www.forthpub.com)
Printed and bound in Great Britain

*For my husband Philip Hebron who believed in me.*
*October 14, 1950 – July 21, 1995*

*For my PhD supervisor the Rev'd Canon Dr Nigel Leaves who guided and encouraged me.*
*September 27, 1958 – June 22, 2015*

*For my friend Sandra McNeill who shared this journey with me.*
*November 11, 1946 – November 4, 2014*

# Contents

# FIGURES

## ACKNOWLEDGMENTS

The article in *Ecclesia*, "Judas Iscariot to get Vatican makeover" (January 12, 2006), fed my curiosity and I began looking at what would need to be done to achieve a makeover or rehabilitation of the Judas character. My research resulted in a Masters' Thesis looking at the portrayals of Judas in the Arts. From this work, I wanted to find out why the portrayals of Judas changed, particularly in film. Hence, my PhD dissertation. My findings were interesting, and it was suggested that I "do" something with my dissertation. So here is the book.

There are several people to thank for their help in making this book possible. The Reverend Dr Gregory Jenks, Academic Dean of St Francis' Theological College, Milton, Queensland, started me on this journey. The presentation of work to my peers at Post-Graduate Seminars provided me with useful feedback and constructive comments. The aid of librarian Eve James and access to Charles Sturt's library provided me with a smorgasbord of resources. I want to acknowledge the support and scholarly banter provided by my PhD supervisor, the late Reverend Canon Dr Nigel Leaves. It was his guidance, interest, and eye for detail, that kept my work focused. The observations and suggestions made by my examiners, Professor W. Barnes Tatum, Dr John Lyden, and the Reverend Dr Richard Leonard, S.J., assured me that the years spent on studying the character of Judas Iscariot, were not in vain.

This book would not have reached this stage had not Dr Anthony Rees, a colleague and fellow Charles Sturt University PhD graduate, mentioned my "interesting thesis" to Dr Andrew Mein, editor of Bloomsbury T&T Clark's Library of Hebrew Bible/Old Testament Studies.

Miriam Cantwell, Biblical Studies Editorial Assistant of Bloomsbury was gracious with her time and ready assistance. The task of converting a dissertation to a book is just that, a task. I thank my sister, Lynette Hebron for her literary critique and her avid interest in the topic. Her questions, both challenging and insightful, provided the impetus for further research.

Finally, I want to acknowledge the role my late husband, Philip Hebron played in my early academic journey. He was my driving force and would often reaffirm my scholarly ability and reassure me by saying, "You can do it." I have done it! Thank you, Philip.

# Abbreviations

| | |
|---|---|
| *AB* | *Adoremus Bulletin* |
| *ATR* | *Anglican Theological Review* |
| *BI* | *Biblical Interpretation* |
| *BLFJ* | *Bright Light Films Journal* |
| *Cah Cinema* | *Cahiers du Cinéma* |
| *CAL* | *Christianity and Literature* |
| *CCEL* | *Christian Classics Ethereal Library* |
| *Chr Cent* | *Christian Century* |
| *Chr Tod* | *Christianity Today* |
| *Cross CURR* | *Cross Currents* |
| *Enc* | *Encounter* |
| *FC* | *Film Comment* |
| *FCm* | *Film Criticism* |
| *FaF* | *Films and Filming* |
| *JCPA* | *Jerusalem Center for Public Affairs* |
| *JETS* | *Journal of the Evangelical Theological Society* |
| *JMGS* | *Journal of Modern Greek Studies* |
| *JNE* | *Journal of Negro Education* |
| *JPSR* | *Jewish Political Studies Review* |
| *JRF* | *Journal of Religion and Film* |
| *JRPC* | *Journal of Religion and Popular Culture* |
| *Jud* | *Judaism* |
| *NTC* | *Nuevo Texto Crítico* |
| *NTS* | *New Testament Studies* |
| *PMS* | *Pro Musica Sana* |
| *Relig Life* | *Religion in Life* |
| *SMR* | *St Mark's Review* |
| *SCJR* | *Studies in Christian–Jewish Relations* |
| *TL* | *Theological Librarianship* |
| *TS* | *Theological Studies* |
| *VLT* | *Velvet Light Trap: A Critical Journal of Film & Television* |

# Introduction: Who Was Judas? Christianity's Evaluation of Judas

## *Introduction*

The film begins with a close-up of the actor (Howard Jacobson) placing a *tallit* (Jewish prayer shawl) around his shoulders, followed by the donning of a voluminous yellow satin coat. The actor lifts a wide leather belt from a hook and wraps it around his waist. Attached to it are a red kerchief and a small leather satchel. Next, two cloth moneybags are hung around his neck. His act of "weighing" them in his hands and the sound of clinking coins suggests that he is wealthy. The camera pans the dressing room, showing a nose-file kit, large jars of evil-eye drops, wart remover, menstrual blood, infant gentile blood and a pot of "Judas' Freckle Cream." The actor attaches a large rubber-nose. The close-up of a side-profile reveals an exaggerated hooked nose. He strategically places on his face three large black moles, one on his left cheek, one on the bridge of his nose and one on his forehead. The frame cuts to a close-up of two silver cups containing water and wine. The camera continues panning and stops at a small leather pouch: silver coins are scattered over and near it. He slips on a long-curly-auburn wig and begins to look closely at himself in the mirror. Something is missing. He reaches and takes from a hook a yellow-pointed-hat and carefully places it on his head.

Now that he is dressed, he reaches for the jar of infant gentile blood. He removes the lid and sniffs the contents in a similar manner to how a connoisseur would appreciate the bouquet of a vintage wine. The reflection in the large mirror shows him pouring the contents into a silver cup. Looking at the camera, he raises the cup as though making a toast, drinks and then with his hand, wipes his mouth. He has an air of smugness about him. Taking something from the dressing table, he slaps it onto his left breast: it is a circular cloth badge. Taking another cloth badge, he slaps it on to his right breast; a yellow Star of David with the name "Judas" printed in large black letters. The camera zooms in, magnifying his grotesque facial features. Looking directly into the camera, the actor asks, "Jewish enough for you?" He puckers his lips and kisses the air.

In this opening scene of the film *Sorry, Judas* (dir. Celia Lowenstein, 1993/2004), the audience sees a caricature of a manufactured Jew and that Jew was Judas Iscariot.

Throughout the history of Christianity Judas Iscariot has been usually regarded with deep suspicion and loathing. His notoriety began with the Gospel writers labelling him as "the one who betrayed Jesus" (Matt 10:4).[1] By the tenth century, Judas had become the incarnation of evil. The Middle Ages, with its flourishing of creative arts, was a time of morbid fascination with the figure of Judas, especially with the horrendous punishment that was meted out to him. Moreover, Judas' treachery came to symbolize the condemnation accorded to all Jews for their culpability in killing Jesus. Judaism was likewise implicated in being a religion that had not only failed to recognize Jesus as the Messiah but had murdered the Savior of the World. Texts such as "His blood be upon us and our children" (Matt 27:25) were interpreted literally to mean that Judaism was condemned forever.

Remarkably, Christianity's abhorrence towards Judas—and the Jewish people—continued until very recently. Indeed, it was not until the middle of the twentieth century that Judas was transformed from an object of scorn into someone who might have been misunderstood or misinterpreted by Christian commentators. This coincided with the rehabilitation of Judaism in the founding of the State of Israel (1948) after the horrendous incarceration and deaths of millions of Jews in the concentration camps in Europe, the direct result of Adolf Hitler's Final Solution. This had prompted many Christians to reconsider the relationship between their religion and Judaism. Had Christian anti-Semitism contributed towards the marginalization of European Jews that had provided the environment in which National Socialism could flourish? How much did the figure of Judas embody the hatred of all Jews?

Then there was a gradual reassessment by biblical theologians of the role of Judas in the crucifixion of Jesus with the use of new critical and hermeneutical tools such as form, source and redaction criticism. Moreover, the discovery of the "lost" Gospel of Judas and its publication in 2006 presented a new Christian understanding of the role of Judas.

1. Unless otherwise indicated, all biblical quotations are from the *New Revised Standard Version Bible*, copyright © 1989, by the Division of Christian Education of the National Council of the Churches of Christ in the United States of America. Published by Thomas Nelson, Inc., Nashville, TN 37214.

The development and impact of the Judas story can be traced in three stages. Using Manfred Gerstendfeld's three stages of the anti-Semitic process—demonization, isolation and elimination—demonstrates how the character of Judas has mirrored Christianity's attitude towards the Jews.[2]

### *The First Stage: Demonization*

The demonization stage plants the seeds for the vilification of Judas and the Jewish race. Animosity towards Judas Iscariot is evident in all four Gospels. The Gospel writers' depiction of his character and the role that he played in the Passion narrative can be easily summarized as follows.

Judas Iscariot, son of Simon Iscariot, was one of the twelve disciples chosen by Jesus (Mark 3:13–19a; Matt 10:1–4; Luke 6:12–16; John 6:64–71). Along with eleven other disciples, Judas had "authority over unclean spirits, to cast them out, and to cure every disease and every sickness" (Matt 10:1). He took advantage of his role as "treasurer" and pilfered from the common purse (John 12:6). He was conniving, greedy and a "thief." He is considered "a devil" (John 6:71) and "the son of perdition" (John 17:12). Judas may not have had any concern for the poor but his questioning of the amount spent on the special oil used by Mary in her anointing of Jesus (John 12:1–8) suggests that Judas was not afraid to challenge Jesus and was concerned that his leader might have been extravagant.

Jesus singled out Judas so that Jesus could fulfil what was written in the Scriptures (Luke 2:37). Judas' role was pre-ordained by God and known by Jesus (John 13:18): Judas was to hand over Jesus to the Jewish authorities. The Gospel accounts do not offer clear motives for Judas' actions. We read that his intention was to betray Jesus to the chief priests. He may have been seeking revenge, after being rebuked earlier by Jesus (Mark 14:6–7). Perhaps Judas was looking for financial gain. He did make a monetary deal with the chief priests and asked, "What will you give me if I betray him to you?" (Matt 26:15). There is no bargaining or haggling: the chief priests give him "thirty pieces of silver." At the Passover meal Judas is identified by various means as "the one who will betray Jesus" (Mark 14:20; Matt 26:23; Luke 20:21), and is instructed by Jesus to "do quickly" what needs to be done (John 13:27).

2. Manfred Gerstendfeld, "Anti-Israelism and Anti-Semitism: Common Characteristics and Motifs," *JPSR* 19, no. 1–2 (2007). http://jcpa.org/article anti-israelism-and-anti-semitism-common-characteristics-and-motifs/.

Judas was not only a disciple of Jesus but also his friend (Matt 26:49–50). Judas displayed respect for his "Master" and "Rabbi" but this could have been to mask an ulterior motive or to illustrate his duplicity. Judas' greeting of Jesus with a kiss at Gethsemane (Matt 26:49; Mark 14:45) was not seen to be unusual and did not raise any suspicion among the other disciples.

Judas is portrayed as having a conscience. Realizing that the Jewish authorities wanted more than to rebuke Jesus, Judas attempted to redress the situation (Matt 27:3–10). However, his attempts at returning the payoff money to the authorities stating that he had "sinned," in that he betrayed "innocent blood," came to no avail. Judas killed himself by hanging (Matt 27:5; Acts 1:18–19). Whether this was driven by remorse, guilt or repentance is impossible to know with any degree of certainty.

In conclusion, the Gospel writers' portrayal of Judas is that he is a "betrayer" and that even though he is contrite he deserves his fate—death by hanging—which mirrors the death of the innocent Jesus on a tree. It is these seeds of hatred for Judas' unforgiveable act of betrayal that provided the fuel for his demonization by the early Church Fathers.

Christian tradition recognized that the character of Judas provided an effective teaching tool so that his actions and fate could be used as warnings to the faithful. The blame for Jesus' death was placed on both Judas for handing Jesus over, and on the Jews whose shouts of "Crucify him" (Matt 27:22–23; Mark 15:13–14; Luke 23:21–23; John 19:6) branded them as "Christ killers." Judas and the Jews were seen as inter-changeable and Judas became representative of all Jews.[3] These two incidents within the Passion narrative provided the impetus for the early Church Fathers to produce many harsh polemical writings against Judas and the Jewish people. Known as the *Adversus Judaeos* (Against Jews) writings, they are primary sources for studying the attitudes towards the Jews.[4] The writings center on two themes: the rejection of the Jews by God and the election of the Gentiles, and, the nullification and spiritual fulfilment of the Law and the temple cult.[5]

3. Dan Cohn-Sherbok, *The Crucified Jew: Twenty Centuries of Anti-Semitism* (London: Harper Collins, 1992), 65.

4. Rosemary Ruether, *Faith and Fratricide: The Theological Roots of Anti-Semitism* (Eugene: Wipf & Stock, 1997), 117.

5. Wim Beuken, Seán Freyne and Anton Weiler, eds., *Messianism Through History*, Concilium (London: SCM, 1993), 127.

According to Ignatius of Antioch (35–108), the Jews killed Christ.[6] Tertullian (ca. 160–225) and his denigration of the Jews have continued to influence orthodoxy until today.[7] Origen (ca. 185–254) is conciliatory in his portrayal of Judas but links his betrayal to the fate of Jews forever: "The blood of Jesus falls not only on the Jews of that time, but on all generations of Jews up to the end of the world."[8] Jerome (ca. 345–420) in Tract Psalm 108 asks, "Whom do you suppose are the sons of Judas?" He answers, "The Jews (*Iudaeos*). The Jews take their name from the betrayer. From the former, we are spiritual Jews; from the traitor came the carnal Jews." Identifying Judas with the Jews comes from the popular perception that both Judas and the Jewish people refused to accept Jesus as the Christian Messiah. Thus, the Judas character became a paradigm for evil and provided preachers with an exemplar of corruption, treachery, deceit, disloyalty and betrayal. A sample of sermon excerpts illustrates how preachers manipulated biblical texts and thus exploited Judas' role.

John Chrysostom (347–407), a renowned orator who used humiliation and coarseness in order to fire the imagination of his hearers, describes Judas' actions as inexcusable and shameful: "Oh! What depravity had the traitor's soul received? For with what kind of eyes did he then look at his Master? With what mouth did he kiss Him? Oh! Accursed purpose. What did he devise? What did he dare?" (Homily 83 on Matt 26:36–38).

Abraham à Sancta Clara (1644–1709), a Discalced Augustinian friar, was instrumental in spreading anti-Semitism in Austria. In his *Judas der Ertz-Schelm* (Judas the Arch-Scoundrel), a didactic novel that took ten years to write, he examined the apocryphal life of Judas and wrote moral reflections on his actions. For example, Abraham declares that the married life of Judas' parents was unhappy, and makes this his point of departure for a long discourse—above forty pages—on conjugal infelicity. Judas became the epitome of the godless, wretched, virtueless, faithless and reasonless Jew. The dark side of the human soul is Judas incarnate.

6. Ignatius, "Epistle to the Philadelphians, Chapter 6: Do Not Accept Judaism," *Christian Classics Ethereal Library*. http://www.ccel.org/ccel/schaff/anf01.v.vi.vi.html.

7. William Nicholls, *Christian Antisemitism: A History of Hate* (Lanham: Rowman & Littlefield, 1993), 187.

8. Origen, *Contra Celsum*, trans. Henry Chadwick (Cambridge: Cambridge University Press, 1980), 76–77.

The early Fathers and homilists propagated the Judas myth by "finding instructive illustrations where they did not exist, as well as for appending morality that did not fit with extreme accuracy."[9]

Post-biblical gospels, legends and myths contributed to disparaging images of Judas and Jews. The *Gospel of Judas*,[10] dated to the middle of the second century, shares some similarities with the Judas of the canonical gospels. However, a significant difference is that Judas is given a new persona: he becomes an "instrument of salvation."[11] The theme of this gospel is expressed in the central line where Jesus tells Judas: "As for you, you will surpass them all. For you will sacrifice the human being who bears me" (15:3–4). Jesus needs to die so that he can escape the material trappings of his body and return to "the divine Pleroma" from which he has come.[12] Jesus' statement is significant in that it is contrary to the traditional Christian beliefs of the atonement and, unlike the canonical accounts of the betrayal, "Judas is not acting out of greed; he is not being driven by Satan; he is not himself a wicked man acting out the evil machinations of his heart."[13] Judas' act of betrayal is in faithful obedience to Jesus' will.

It is evident why Irenaeus (ca. 125–202), bishop of Lyons and theologian, branded this gospel as heretical. The *Gospel of Judas* provides a controversial portrayal of Judas that contradicts the canonical accounts of the handing over of Jesus. Judas "becomes a Gnostic paradigm of discipleship and faithfulness to Jesus."[14] It is important that this text be included here not just for its narrative but also to show how the Church, in suppressing this gospel, imposed censorship on what people should read and believe.

9. Paul Franklin Baum, *The Mediaeval Legend of Judas Iscariot (1916)*. Reprinted from the *Publications of the Modern Language Association of America* 31, no. 3 (Kessinger Legacy Reprints; Whitefish, MT: Kessinger, n.d.), 484.

10. Two translations of the text are referred to, Rudolphe Kasser, Marvin Meyer and Gregor Wurst, eds., *The Gospel of Judas* (Washington: National Geographic, 2006) and Karen King's translation in Elaine Pagels and Karen L. King, *Reading Judas: The Gospel of Judas and the Shaping of Christianity* (New York: Viking Penguin, 2007).

11. William Klassen, *Judas, Betrayer or Friend of Jesus?* (Minneapolis: Fortress, 1996), 6. Kim Paffenroth, describes Judas as "an agent of salvation." Kim Paffenroth, *Judas: Images of the Lost Disciple* (Louisville: Westminster John Knox, 2001), 142.

12. Bart D. Ehrman, *The Lost Gospel of Judas Iscariot: A New Look at Betrayer and Betrayed* (Oxford: Oxford University Press, 2006), 88.

13. Ibid., 97.

14. Marvin Meyer, *Judas: The Definitive Collection of Gospels and Legends About the Infamous Apostle of Jesus* (New York: HarperOne 2007), 52.

In judging Judas, the Church affirmed that the only just punishment for his action was condemnation to hell. The Coptic *Gospel of Bartholomew* (ca. 300–500) provides a glimpse of the place of torment. Christ's descent into hell was to free the just who had gone before him. Only three souls remain—Cain, Herod and Judas—all murderers and all biblical characters.

Fascination with Judas Iscariot was so widespread that even accounts of his childhood began to appear. A popular work was *The Arabic Gospel of the Infancy of the Savior* (fifth or sixth century), which recounted how the young Judas, tormented by Satan, would bite either himself or all who came near him. This portrayal as "a nasty Satan-inspired, biter of a child"[15] was an interpretation of the gospel's references to the devil's influence on Judas' decision to hand Jesus over to the religious authorities (Luke 22:3; John 13:27). It was a short bow to draw the conclusion that the devil and Judas were the same!

Satan and devils were an ever-present part of reality in a way that is difficult for modern Westernized people to understand. They were depicted by artists as "misshapen, hideous, and threatening, the embodiment of nightmares and half-expressed fears."[16] The representation of Jews and Judas as "tools of Satan"[17] deepened Christian hatred and added to the *Adversus Judaeos* catalogue of Jewish faults and crimes.

A Jewish biography of Jesus entitled *Toledoth Yeshu* (sixth/seventh century) provided an alternative to the highly negative Christian narratives. Combining material from the Talmud, the New Testament and pagan folklore, the character of Judah Iskarioto (Judas) has magical powers similar to those of Yeshu (Jesus). Instead of portraying Judas as a traitor, this fanciful folklore saga paints him as a formidable "defender of Jewish monotheism against Jesus' new idolatry"[18] and exonerates the Jews from the charge of Christ killers. That this text was written suggests a Jewish response to their treatment by Christians.

Dominican monk, Jacobus de Voragine, in his *The Golden Legend* (1265), draws on an earlier twelfth-century Latin version of a Judas biography, which is essentially identical to Sophocles' classical story *Oedipus.* Jacobus parallels the Judas story to events in the life of the Old Testament characters Adam, Cain, Moses and Joseph. This legend became the foundation of many Passion plays of the Middle Ages and of religious poems

15. Ehrman, *Lost Gospel*, 138.

16. Joseph H. Lynch, *The Medieval Church: A Brief History* (London: Longman, 1992), 262.

17. Cohn-Sherbok, *The Crucified Jew*, 65.

18. Hyam Maccoby, *Judas Iscariot and the Myth of Jewish Evil* (New York: Free Press, 1992), 99.

of latter times. The popularity of *The Golden Legend* was in the portrayal of Judas as "rotten to the core, from the very beginning and in every way: fratricide, patricide, incestuous thief and Christ-killer. Christian readers would understand full well the subject: this is Judas, the proto-typical Jew."[19] The suggestion that Judas was representative of Jews and Judaism was promoted in numerous types of religious dramas.

Mystery, Miracle and Passion plays were meant to entertain while also providing biblical and theological teaching. The dramatic performances of the Passion narrative also provided an opportunity to teach the audiences to hate the Jews. From the early tenth century, para-liturgies commemorating the feasts of the year were developed and presented in dramatic form on the town streets. Judas was portrayed as the stereotypical Jewish villain: his role defined by both his actions and his speech. Judas boasts that he is the purser "and whatever was trusted me till, the tenth part I stole, and would still."[20] Salacious salutations exaggerate Judas' hypocrisy. "Hail Master in faith, and fellows here. / With great gracious meeting on ground, you are graced. / I would ask you a kiss, master, and your will were / for all my love and my liking upon you is laid."[21]

When found guilty of treason, Judas is branded a traitor and is "damned to Hell's pit [where] / he shall have no rest, but evermore wake / burning in hot fire, in prison ever shut."[22] Judas is portrayed as the "most gentle of Jewry" and becomes the personification of the Jews who "have intent in their minds full of malice."[23] This identification of Judas with the Jews provided a "single *dramatis persona* who would act as a focus of hate."[24]

With the removal of the devil characters from the Oberammergau Passion Play in 1811—their popularity and the crowds' rowdy responses were seen as debasing to the Easter mystery—the focus of blame turned to the Jews and Judas. The audience's hatred was such that they were despised both on and off stage. Saul Friedman cites examples of how the actors portraying Jews were treated by visiting spectators. In 1900, two

19. Ehrman, *Lost Gospel*, 49.

20. Chester N. Scoville and Kimberley M. Yates, "The Cutlers' Play: The Conspiracy," *The York Plays: A Modernization*. http://www.rhaworth.myby.co.uk/pofstp/REED/York26.html.

21. Chester N. Scoville and Kimberley M. Yates, "The Cordwainers' Play: The Agony in the Garden and Betrayal," *The York Plays: A Modernization*. http://www.rhaworth.myby.co.uk/pofstp/REED/York28.html.

22. Ibid.

23. Ibid.

24. Maccoby, *Judas Iscariot*, 82.

English women refused to lodge in the home of Andreas Lang whose character was known as simply "Rabbi."[25] The character of Judas was particularly maligned. It is difficult today to imagine an actor being persecuted for playing the role of Judas but this happened to Gregor Lechner. Following his father, Lechner played the role for two decades. However, he refused to pass the role onto his son, claiming, "I love my child too much to bring the same sufferings upon him which I and my father before me have been obliged to endure."[26]

Judas Iscariot has been demonized for a variety of reasons. William Klassen suggests that when someone deserts a close fellowship "the motives of those who leave are often presented in a hostile light as others seek to interpret the reasons for their departure."[27] Judas also fulfils the need for a foil, contrasting evil with good. Moreover, there is the innate need to blame someone and Judas is the obvious target as Kim Paffenroth explains: "When later story-tellers looked at Judas, they saw the perfect cipher on which to practice their art, shaping him into the kind of man or monster that their individual stories needed."[28]

The importance of Judas as an historical character is not as important as the church's need to recount his story. It has been suggested that Judas is a fictitious dimension of the Passion narrative and was deliberately introduced into the biblical text by early Christian writers. Howard Jacobsen maintains, "Judas Iscariot appears in [the Christian story] not because there actually was such a person, but because a person is needed for the story to have maximum psychological and spiritual impact. Judas is entangled in the Christian story because [he] serve[s] the politics of the Church."[29]

Hyam Maccoby notes, "The mythic status given to Judas as the betrayer of the god-sacrifice gives his role an imaginative quality that takes it out of sober history." He adds, "Once this mythic aura has been analyzed and removed, it will be possible to ask who Judas actually is."[30]

25. Saul S. Friedman, *The Oberammergau Passion Play: A Lance Against Civilization* (Carbondale: Southern Illinois University Press, 1984), 103.

26. Joseph Krauskopf, *A Rabbi's Impressions on the Oberammergau Passion Play* (Philadelphia: Stern, 1901), 33.

27. Klassen, *Judas*, 11.

28. Paffenroth, *Judas: Images*, 15.

29. Howard Jacobsen, commenting on Hyam Maccoby's statement in the film, *Sorry, Judas.*

30. Maccoby, *Judas Iscariot*, 100.

The demonization of Judas and the consequent dehumanization of Jews are the foundation of anti-Semitism, which for two millennia has permeated political, social and religious structures of countries worldwide.[31] A major consequence of the demonization stage of anti-Semitism was the rise of Christian supersessionist theology, also known as replacement theology.

Christian supersessionism is the belief that the covenant between God and the people of Israel no longer exists, that Jesus is the new covenant and that Christianity is the "New Israel." Justin Martyr (ca. 100–165) is the first writer in the Church to claim that Christians are the "true spiritual Israel" and have replaced the Jews (*Dialogue With Trypho* 11). There are three major forms of supersessionism: (1) punitive supersessionism, (2) economic supersessionism and (3) structural supersessionism.

Punitive supersessionism argues that Israel's disobedience and consequent punishment by God is the prime reason for its displacement as the chosen people of God, as Kendall Soulen explains: "God abrogates God's covenant with Israel…on account of Israel's rejection of Christ and the Gospel."[32] An example of this is Martin Luther's belief that the destruction of Jerusalem was proof of God's permanent rejection of Israel.[33]

Economic supersessionism is the view that "carnal Israel's history is providentially ordered from the outset to be taken up into the spiritual church."[34] Israel is replaced because its role in the history of redemption expired with the coming of Jesus Christ. Even such a liberal theologian as Rudolf Bultmann argued that the Jewish nation is no longer an "empirical historical entity—it does not exist as a people requiring institutional ordinance for its organization."[35] Tom Wright put it more simply: "Israel's purpose had come to its head in Jesus' work."[36]

The third form is structural supersessionism. Soulen argues:

31. Marvin Perry and Frederick M. Schweitzer, eds., *Antisemitic Myths: A Historical and Contemporary Anthology* (Bloomington: Indiana University Press, 2008), 6.

32. R. Kendall Soulen, *The God of Israel and Christian Theology* (Minneapolis: Fortress, 1996), 30.

33. Martin Luther, *On the Jews and Their Lies, 1543*, trans. Martin H. Bertram. Part 1, para. 5. http://reactor-core.org/jewish-lies.html.

34. Soulen, *God of Israel*, 181 n. 6.

35. Rudolf Bultmann, "Prophecy and Fulfillment," in *Essays on Old Testament Hermeneutics*, ed. Claus Westermann, trans. James J. C. Greig (London: SCM, 1963), 71.

36. N. T. Wright, *The New Testament and the People of God* (Minneapolis: Fortress, 1992), 457.

> The problem of supersessionism in Christian theology goes beyond the explicit teaching that the church has displaced Israel as God's people in the economy of salvation. At a deeper level, the problem of supersessionism coincides with the way in which Christians have traditionally understood the theological and narrative unity of the Christian canon as a whole.[37]

Supersessionism affects the significance given to the Jewishness of Jesus and his Jewish designations. Originally such titles as Messiah, Son of Man and Lord were drawn from the Hebrew Scriptures to convey the significance of Jesus' life and ministry, but as the Church became increasingly Gentile, these titles came to emphasize his divine status. God is described in Scripture as "the God of Israel" and the "God of Abraham, Isaac and Jacob." In short, for the Jewish people and Judaism, supersessionism means, "Israel has been replaced or superseded by the Gentile Church."[38]

### *The Second Stage: Isolation*

It is significant that Gerstendfeld identifies the second stage in the anti-Semitism process as the "isolation stage." In describing the Holocaust, historians speak of "Five stages of Isolation": stripping of rights (Nuremberg Laws), segregation (ghettos), concentration (labor camps), extermination (Final Solution) and aftermath (displacement). Historically, the Jews were expelled from society, subject to restrictions and persecuted for their religious beliefs. The film *Sorry, Judas,* graphically explains this "isolation stage" and in the opening scene, introduces the concept of the manufactured Jew.

Apart from the *tallit*, the other items of clothing and props are representative of a number of Christian myths. Lowenstein's short-film is a satirical film that looks at centuries of negative stereotypes of Jews as greedy, ugly and corrupt. The correlation between anti-Semitism and the film's title is that it was Christianity's strong stance against Judas that helped plant the seeds of anti-Semitism.

The name Judas—paralleled with Judah (Jew)—provided a seed from which anti-Semitism could grow. Although Judas killed himself, it was asserted that he continued to live on in the Jew. Moreover, to help identify Judas in the Jew, Christian governments enacted laws that detailed what Jewish people should wear.

37. Soulen, *God of Israel*, 33.

38. Craig A. Blaising, "The Future of Israel as a Theological Question," *JETS* 44, no. 3 (2001): 435.

From as early as 1215 European Jews were forced to dress in a manner that would easily identify them as Jews. The Council of Arles (1234) passed a decree "that male Jews from the age of thirteen and up, when outside their homes, except when on a journey, must wear upon the outer garment, upon the breast, a round badge of three or four fingers in width."[39] Other distinguishing badges included one with the inscription "*Der Juden Zeichen / Welches Sie ihren Kleidern zu tragen schuldig*"—(The Jewish badge of guilt which is their tragedy to wear)—and a circular patch of yellow cloth with a red 'bull's eye' in the center, which Jews from Barcelona were forced to wear in 1397. The distinguishing badge resurfaced in 1941 when the wearing of a yellow Shield (Star) of David inscribed with J or *Jude*, *Juif*, or *Jood*, became mandatory in countries under Nazi rule. That the actor in *Sorry, Judas* wears a yellow star with "Judas" suggests Judas is representative of all Jews. Yellow is a color that is associated with Judas. In medieval art, yellow depicts treachery and ignominy. In latter times yellow became the symbol of cowardice and jealousy. Other distinctive clothing imposed on Jews included the cone-shaped *Judenhut* (Jewish hat), introduced in 1218 on the recommendation of the Lateran Council. There were even different colored kerchiefs that identified the nationalities of Jews. For example, the red kerchief worn on the actor's belt signifies he is a Venetian Jew. The main objective for introducing distinctive clothing was to erect a barrier between Jews and non-Jews and to restrict their movements. Distinctive clothing alerted Christians and thus avoided "carnal union with a Jew."[40]

The physical features of Jews were often accentuated—or belabored—to their detriment. In the art of the Middle Ages and Renaissance, Judas was portrayed with stereotypically Jewish characteristics, such as a large hooked nose, thick lips and dark or ruddy skin. The addition of warts, moles and other blemishes provided possible portals through which Satan could enter a body. Likewise, Jews were viewed as Satan's agents, who, armed with his superhuman powers, robbed and murdered Christians to fulfil their master's will. These exaggerated physical characteristics were exploited by Julius Streicher's *Der Stürmer* (The Attacker), an anti-Semitic tabloid-style newspaper published from 1923 almost continuously through to the end of the Second World War (1939–1945).

39. Maureen Fiedler and Linda Rabben, eds., *Rome Has Spoken: A Guide to Forgotten Papal Statements, and How They Have Changed Through the Centuries* (New York: Crossroad, 1998), 69. Jewish women from the age of twelve and up had to wear veils when outside their homes.

40. *Decretum*, Council of Auvergne (ca. 1140). Ibid., 68.

Another stereotypical Jewish characteristic was red hair. This feature was not a unique Jewish characteristic but became an identifying mark of Judas. The jar of "Judas' Freckle Cream" among the props of *Sorry, Judas* alludes to Judas' red hair and complexion.

Bizarre myths about Jews emerged during the Middle Ages. The jar of infant gentile blood is indicative of the libel of ritual murder: the accusation that Jews ritually murder a Christian child at the season of Passover and mingle the child's blood with the unleavened bread they eat at that time. The jar of menstrual blood is a criticism of the restrictive and punitive Talmud law of Niddah: the uncleanliness of a woman during menstruation. The inclusion of a bottle of evil-eye drops among the props reinforces Christian fear and suspicion of Jews having the ability to bring about evil results by a malicious gaze.

Myths of Jewish avarice, and the linking of this greed to the actions of Judas Iscariot and his betrayal of Jesus, feed Christian hatred of Jews and Judaism. Martin Luther attacked the Jews for their arrogance and financial greed, claiming: "Their breath stinks with lust for the Gentiles' gold and silver; for no nation under the sun is greedier than they were, still are, and always will be, as is evident from their accursed usury."[41] The moneybag and thirty pieces of silver became a popular iconography trope of avarice. However, the most recognizable trait of Judas is not greed but the kiss he gave Jesus in the Garden of Gethsemane.

The infamous kiss, popularized in art, literature and music, has become a standard metaphor for treachery. Where the opening scene in *Sorry, Judas* ends with Jacobson (Judas) pursing his lips and kissing the air, the Judas kiss marked the beginning of anti-Semitism and two thousand years of demonization, persecution, expulsion and eradication of Jewish people. This leads to the third stage in the process of anti-Semitism: elimination.

### *The Third Stage: Elimination*

Martin Luther played a major role in the vilification of the Jews. After the failure of his early missionary efforts to convert Jews to Christianity, his later writings were especially anti-Semitic.[42] By the sixteenth century, Luther took supersessionism to the next level, calling for the "elimination" of Jews. He advised Christians to burn synagogues, destroy Jewish homes and place Jews "under one roof or a stable," and "deprive them of their

41. Luther, *On the Jews*, Part 6, para. 18.
42. Cohn-Sherbok, *Crucified Jew*, 72.

prayer books, Talmuds, and rabbinic leadership."[43] Four hundred years later Adolf Hitler and the German Nazi Party, believing they had the Final Solution to the Jewish problem, set out to "exterminate" Jews and Judaism.

David Weiss Halivni begins his "Prologue: Between Sinai and Auschwitz" with:

> There were two major theological events in Jewish history; Revelation at Sinai and Revelation at Auschwitz. The former was revelation of God's presence, the latter a revelation of God's absence; the former indicated God's nearness to us, the latter God's distance. At Sinai, God appeared before Israel, addressed us, and gave us instructions; at Auschwitz God absented Himself from Israel, abandoned us, and handed us over to the enemy.[44]

In an attempt to reconcile these two events, Christian and Jewish theologians have wrestled to make sense and find meaning in the tragic events of the Shoah (Holocaust). Shoah theology is an attempt to reconcile various conflicting views about God's role in the Nazi Holocaust.

The Holocaust was the single most atrocious act of anti-Semitism. It was also the single act to turn around negative perception of the Jewish people and their faith. The Holocaust has influenced the ways in which filmmakers have portrayed the Jewish people and their culture. Significantly, the Holocaust affects the way in which the Judas story is translated onto the big screen, thus rehabilitating the Judas character.

In 2006, coinciding with the plans to publish the *Gospel of Judas*, the Vatican announced that it was time for a "re-reading" of Judas in the New Testament. Judas was to have a makeover. The rise of historical-critical methods, academic theology and biblical studies recognized that not only was a negative reading of Judas problematic but that the figure of Judas might have been a Christian construct that had little basis in history. Judas could be rehabilitated and Jewish–Christian relations placed on a friendlier footing.

The first significant Vatican announcement in healing Jewish–Christian relations was the 1965 "Declaration on the Relations of the Church to Non-Christian Religions—*Nostra Aetate* (In Our Time)," which exonerated the Jewish people for the death of Christ. In 1975, the Commission

43. Luther, *On the Jews*, Part 9.

44. David Weiss Halịvni, "Prologue: Between Sinai and Auschwitz," in *Breaking the Tablets: Jewish Theology After the Shoah* (Lanham: Rowman & Littlefield, 2007), x.

for Religious Relations with the Jews produced notes on the correct way to present the Jews and Judaism in preaching and catechesis in the Roman Catholic Church. Fifty-three years after the horrors of the Nazi concentration camps and the Holocaust were exposed to the world, the Commission for Religious Relations with the Jews published the document "We Remember: A Reflection on the *Shoah*,"[45] recognizing the relative inactivity and silence of many Roman Catholics during the Holocaust. The Church and academia had to re-think, re-assess and respond to the root cause of the Holocaust: anti-Semitism.

There have been constructive contributions towards rehabilitating Judas and the Jewish people. William Klassen provides conclusive literary and historical evidence that the mistranslation of the Greek word *paradidōmi* has resulted in the negative impact on Christianity's perception of Judas. Klassen states there is "no linguistic basis—in classical Greek, in Greek translation of the Hebrew Bible, in Josephus or patristic sources—for a translation of 'betray' to describe what Judas did."[46] The original Greek text, *paradidōmi*, meaning "handed over," has been erroneously translated as "betrayed." Klassen concludes that "handing over" does not make Judas a traitor or a betrayer, thus challenging traditional ideas about his role in Christ's crucifixion. Klassen reasons: "the absence of the Greek word *paradidōmi* or 'traitor' or 'betray' applied to Judas in the earliest sources is an unassailable witness to the fact that whatever Judas did, the earliest Christians did not view it as betrayal of Jesus or of their faith community."[47] Klassen argues Judas was a scapegoat instead of a participant in the action of saving history. Despite being the correct translation of "handing over" it did not suit the purposes of Christian writers who could see the value in conveying the treachery of a specific action by one person; and so it was not long before the word "betrayal" was used in its stead.

Anthony Cane questions the role of Judas in the economy of salvation. Cane reasons that because the doctrine of providence "asserts that all things are directed and ordered by God, from their beginning to their appointed end, all things are therefore subordinate to the knowledge and will of God."[48] This raises the question whether Judas was acting of his

45. Edward Idris Cassidy, Pierre Duprey, and Remi Hoeckman, "We Remember: A Reflection on the Shoah," *Commission for Religious Relations with the Jews* (March 16, 1998). http://www.vatican.va/roman_curia/pontifical_councils/chrstuni/documents/rc_pc_chrstuni_doc_16031998_shoah_en.html.

46. Klassen, *Judas*, 57.

47. Ibid., 57–58.

48. Anthony Cane, *The Place of Judas Iscariot in Christology* (Aldershot, Hampshire: Ashgate, 2005), 5.

own free will or whether he was governed by God's will. Cane rules out the view that Judas is "simply a necessary pawn in a celestial game"[49] or that he is a "tragic mistake."[50] He acknowledges Judas' role in "handing over" Jesus and that Judas "should be understood as caught up in the suffering and cost of salvation, not as one to be vilified and scapegoated."[51]

Gerald Forshey posits that in order to avoid claims of anti-Semitism and to solve their problems, filmmakers consulted modern biblical scholarship.[52] The development of biblical criticism and the quest for the historical Jesus in theology also contributed to the development of the revised Judas portrait.

Another medium for theological reflection and promotion of varying interpretations of Judas and his role in the death and Passion of Jesus is film. Filmmakers have the freedom to draw on a vast array of resources and can present them in any film genre. Scriptwriters use poetic license to adapt/rewrite the story and dialogue to fit a particular theme. Producers seek to hire a cast that will be convincing in their acting. Cinematographers scrutinize for the best shot. Directors then manipulate all of these filmmaking components to exhibit his or her ideology.

Although Judas is first mentioned in the Gospels, Kaile Shilling believes he is "best defined and best understood through mythic mediums," which include literature and films.[53] At the beginning of the twentieth century when Jesus films were first screened, the Judas figure was the epitome of evil, the villainous Jew. Filmmakers cast Judas in this way because this was the Judas audiences knew and recognized. Supersessionism influenced filmmakers. In the early Jesus films, filmmakers sanction Christian supersessionist ideas by promoting Jesus as the "new covenant," Judas as the vanquished Jew and by ignoring Jesus' Jewish ethnicity. Filmmakers separate Jesus from his Jewish roots and isolate Judas from Jesus. Judas is ostracized and quarantined. The implication is that God's mandate to the Jewish nation, as outlined in Jewish Scriptures, has been superseded by the gospel to Christians, which is manifested in the Church.

49. Ibid., 181.

50. Ibid., 182.

51. Ibid., 186.

52. Gerald E. Forshey, *American Religious and Biblical Spectaculars* (Westport: Praeger, 1992), 10.

53. Kaile Shilling, "Servant of the Story: Judas as Tragic Hero in Film," *JRF* 8, no. 2 (2004). http://www.unomaha.edu/jrf/Vol8No2/servant.htm.

In the following three decades, filmmakers looked beyond the Gospel accounts and gave Judas a more significant role in the film. His motive for betrayal became a sub-plot. By the middle of the century, filmmakers moved away from typecasting Judas as a villain for fear of accusations of anti-Semitism. Judas took on a cameo role so that filmmakers could focus on the ministry of Jesus. From the 1960s onwards, Judas became the protagonist whose role in the film was as important as that of Jesus. It is in these films that we begin to see the rehabilitation of Judas.

The development of the Judas character in film advances not only from Judas' words and actions, but also from his relationship with Jesus. Adele Reinhartz identifies Judas as one of the few Gospel characters who "undergoes emotional development" and as one who "carries the dramatic weight" of many of the Jesus films.[54] This is particularly evident in *The King of Kings* (1927), *El mártir del Calvario* (1952), *Jesus Christ Superstar* (1973) and *The Last Temptation of Christ* (1988).

William Telford, in "The Two Faces of Betrayal," begins with the premise that with respect to their relationship with Jesus, both Peter and Judas are "guilty of an act of disloyalty, treachery, or denial."[55] By juxtaposing the two disciples, Telford reveals

> one came to be *the* great apostle, the other *the* great apostate. One is seen as the proto-typical Christian, the other the stereotypical Jew. One has come to be the supreme example of Christian discipleship, the other the universal symbol of Jewish perfidy. The one became a Pope, the other a pariah. Peter was given the keys to the kingdom of heaven, Judas was sent to eternal damnation in hell… One was *rehabilitated* after his denial of Jesus, the other *vilified* in consequence of his treachery.[56]

## *Summary*

Søren Kierkegaard's assertion that, "One will get a deep insight into the state of Christianity in every age by seeing how it interprets Judas" is surely correct.[57] Throughout two thousand years, the Judas character and

54. Adele Reinhartz, *Jesus of Hollywood* (Oxford: Oxford University Press, 2007), 152.

55. William R. Telford, "The Two Faces of Betrayal: The Characterization of Peter and Judas in the Biblical Epic or Christ Film," in *Cinéma Divinité: Religion, Theology and the Bible in Film*, ed. Eric C. Christianson, Peter Francis, and William R. Telford (London: SCM, 2005), 215.

56. Ibid. Emphasis in the original.

57. Søren Kierkegaard, *Journals and Papers*, Vol. 2, *F–K*, trans. and ed. Howard V. Hong and Edna H. Hong (Bloomington: Indiana University Press, 1970), 512.

his story have been embellished. He has been recast to demonize the Jewish race. From a small role in the Gospels,[58] Judas Iscariot evolved into a major and leading character in the Passion and death of Jesus of Nazareth. This book traces a similar development in Judas' role in film. As well as exploring and evaluating the changing portrayals of Judas and their influence on the emergence of new theologies, reasons for these changes are identified and discussed.

58. He is mentioned twenty-two times in the Gospels. By comparison, fellow disciple Peter is mentioned 154 times.

# Chapter 1

# STUDYING THE FILMIC JUDAS CHARACTER

## *Introduction*

Film is a powerful, influential and far-reaching medium, which reflects social and cultural beliefs, values and practices. The prevailing *Zeitgeist* similarly affects religion and theology. In short, how does film and theology interact in its understanding of Judas? This study of the filmic Judas character addresses the following three questions:

1. How is Judas portrayed in film?
2. Why does the Judas character change?
3. What are the theological implications of these changes?

The central focus of enquiry in each of these questions is on change. One approach to studying and measuring change in film is to follow a chronological framework in which films are viewed and studied in the order of their production. I adopt this approach. These changes point toward differences in trends in attitudes to the Bible, religion, theology and authority of the Church.

## *Question 1: How Is Judas Portrayed in Film?*
### *Film Studies*

Any analysis of Jesus films necessitates both understanding of scriptural texts and the medium of film. George Aichele and Richard Walsh propose that there is no inherent connection between Scripture and film and that the viewer provides any correlation that they wish.[1] Similarly, Margaret Miles suggests that often, religious motifs are in "the eye of

1. Introduction to George Aichele and Richard Walsh, eds., *Screening Scripture: Intertextual Connection Between Scripture and Film* (Harrisburg, PA: Trinity Press International, 2002), ix.

the beholder," but in order to recognize them, the viewer requires a theological perspective and theological language.[2] What is self-evident is that films transform the scriptural texts in question, re-writing and re-conceptualizing them.[3]

Jesus films are adaptations of literary texts. Joseph Boggs and Dennis Petrie identify two types of adaptations from text to film. Faithful adaptations "translate nearly every character and scene from page to screen" whereas looser adaptations omit many elements from the original work and add others.[4] In order to convey the Jesus story on the big screen, some filmmakers have harmonized the often-contradictory Gospel accounts, "melding them all together, so that Jesus says and does *all* the things that each of the Gospel writers identify."[5] Bart Ehrman criticizes this hermeneutical methodology:

> Anyone who interprets the Gospels this way is not letting each author have his own say; anyone who does this is not reading what the author wrote in order to understand his message; anyone who does this is not reading the Gospels themselves—he or she is making up a new Gospel consisting of the four in the New Testament, a new Gospel that is not like any of the ones that have come down to us.[6]

Ehrman's criticism is valid for the study of the Gospels but is not applicable in the context of filmmaking. The filmic Jesus (and Judas) stories in most instances are biographies in that they tell the story of Jesus as told in the Gospels. The Gospels do not record the same Jesus events. In order to produce a Jesus film that begins with an angel telling Mary that she is to bear a son, his birth in Bethlehem, a visit to the Temple in Jerusalem when he was twelve and then his years of ministry and miracles, culminating in his death and resurrection, filmmakers need to draw from the four Gospels.

Arie Zwiep notes, "The tension between biblical scholarship and theological interests comes into sharp focus with the figure of Judas Iscariot: 'Tell me what you think of Judas and I will tell you what your exegetical

2. Margaret R. Miles, *Seeing and Believing: Religion and Values in Movies* (Boston: Beacon, 1996), 19.

3. Aichele and Walsh, *Screening Scripture*, ix.

4. Joseph M. Boggs and Dennis W. Petrie. *The Art of Watching Films*, 7th ed. (Boston: McGraw-Hill, 2008). 430.

5. Bart D. Ehrman, *Misquoting Jesus: The Story Behind Who Changed the Bible and Why* (New York: HarperSanFrancisco, 2005), 214.

6. Ibid., 215.

method and your theological convictions are.'"[7] Clearly, a study of the biblical Judas and the filmic Judas is complex.

To answer the question "How is Judas portrayed in film?" I undertook a systematic approach, which included the following steps: selection of films, viewing films and analyzing films for close study.

*Step 1: Selection of Films*

The selection of films is obviously of prime importance. My decision to look beyond Hollywood Jesus films—which merely reflect American culture and values—and to include foreign films, was based on their wide diversity of Judas portrayals. French, Danish, American, English, Italian, Mexican and Indian productions are addressed with reference also to Iranian and German films. Criteria for the selection of films included availability of the film, year and country of production, genre and the number of appearances made by Judas. To narrow the study and to guarantee a relatively accurate comparison of the Judas portrayals, decision was made to focus on one incident in the Jesus/Judas narrative: the Last Supper. This scene was chosen for the following four reasons. First, the Last Supper is included in most Jesus films. Second, the Last Supper scene is pivotal to the Passion narrative and is of fundamental importance to Christian theology. Third, the Last Supper scene is restricted to one location, enabling deeper focus in a mise-en-scène analysis. Fourth, the diverse representations of the Last Supper in these films raise significant theological questions.

In deciding which Jesus films would be suitable for analysis of the Last Supper scene, a number of factors were considered. These included the length of the scene, the presence of Judas at the meal, embellishment of Gospel narratives and harmonizing of the Gospel texts, the meal's composition and setting, Judas' response to, or refusal of, receiving the cup and the bread and the naming of Judas as "the betrayer." This elimination process resulted in the selection of the following twenty-four films:

- *La Vie et la Passion de Jésus Christ* (France, Ferdinand Zecca and Lucien Nouquet, 1902–1905)
- *La Vie du Christ* (France, Alice Guy, 1906)
- *From the Manger to the Cross* (USA, Sidney Olcott, 1912)
- *Christus* (Italy, Giulio Antamora, 1916)
- *Blade af Satans Bog* (Denmark, Carl Theodor Dreyer, 1921)
- *The Kings of Kings* (USA, Cecil B. de Mille, 1927)

7. Arie W. Zwiep, *Christ, the Spirit and the Community of God: Essays on the Acts of the Apostles*, WUNT 2/293 (Tübingen: Mohr Siebeck, 2010), 98.

- *Golgotha* (France, Julien Duvivier, 1935)
- *Maria Magdalena, pecadora de Magdala* (Mexico, Miguel Contreras Torres, 1946)
- *I Beheld His Glory* (USA, John T. Coyle, 1952)
- *El mártir del Calvario* (Mexico, Miguel Morayta Martinez, 1952)
- *Day of Triumph* (USA, John T. Coyle and Irving Pichel, 1954)
- *King of Kings* (USA, Nicholas Ray, 1961)
- *Il Vangelo Secondo Matteo* (Italy, Pier Paolo Pasolini, 1964)
- *The Greatest Story Ever Told* (USA, George Stevens, 1965)
- *Jesus, Nuestro Señor* (Mexico, Miquel Zacarias, 1972)
- *Godspell: A Musical Based on the Gospel According to St. Matthew* (USA, David Greene, 1973)
- *Jesus Christ Superstar* (USA, Norman Jewison, 1973)
- *Gospel Road: The Story of Jesus* (USA, Robert Elfstrom, 1973)
- *Jesus of Nazareth* (UK, Franco Zeffirelli,1977)
- *Karunamayudu* (India, A. Bheem Singh and Christopher Coelho, 1978)
- *The Last Temptation of Christ* (USA, Martin Scorsese, 1988)
- *Jesus* (USA, Roger Young, 1999)
- *Color of the Cross* (USA, Jeane-Claude Le Marre, 2006)
- *Son of God* (USA, Christopher Spencer, 2014).

Brief descriptions of three additional films, which did not meet the criteria for the Last Supper mise-en-scène analysis, are also included. Mel Gibson's *The Passion of the Christ* (USA, 2004) is a valuable study and includes an interesting interpretation of Judas Iscariot. Similarly, the Iranian film, *The Messiah* (Iran, Nader Talebzadeh, 2007) portrays Judas—and Jesus—in an incredible way. Made as a response to Gibson's film, it too is worthy of comment. Reference is also made to the 2008 BBC miniseries, *The Passion* (UK, dir. Michael Offer). It includes significant and revealing dialogue between Jesus and Judas, supporting Judas' progression from damnation to redemption.

*Step 2: View Films for Close Study*

The process of viewing films comprises watching films as film, noting filmic features, analyzing the movies as theological texts with implicit and explicit statements about God and Jesus, and appreciating that films are cultural artefacts.[8] This is the foundation of film criticism.

8. Richard Stern, Clayton N. Jefford, and Guerric Debona, *Savior on the Silver Screen* (New York: Paulist, 1999), 3 and 5.

Film reviewing and film criticism were formalized in 1913 with the recognition that film was a factor of culture and not just a matter of entertainment. Film criticism and critics gained importance and influence in the 1950s and early 1960s, notably with the contribution of the *Cahiers du cinema* group in France and its critic André Bazin.

Ambros Eichenberger identifies five approaches to film criticism.[9] The first is a *formalist* position where focus is primarily on internal evidence. This approach concentrates on the film's use of *mise-en-scène*; the effect of photographic composition; the use of sound and editing choices; and how the viewer perceives and interprets these cinematic techniques. Second is the *realist* approach, which considers film merely as a "window to reality." Third is the *auteurist* approach in which interest is in the complete works of a director and how he or she attempts to persuade audiences of his/her "personal visions, themes, and motifs." Fourth is *social science criticism* that studies "the effects of films on viewers' behavior, emotions, and attitudes" and discerns "how far films and filmmakers are determined by the socio-cultural ground they are rooted in." The fifth critical approach to film is the *humanist* approach, which accepts that films are a product of an industry, which is constrained by financial pressure, and, through vast advertisement campaigns, sells and distributes its product worldwide. This approach also accepts that films, like other forms of art, are "expressions of deliberate human activity by an individual artist." The *humanist* approach also looks at films as a "representation of universal values, of the truths of human experience, of insights that will help us to understand better the complexity of human life and human society."

Analysis from a variety of approaches assists the viewer in realizing the function and intent of the film. Each of these five approaches has been used in the study of the role of Judas in the selected Jesus films. Although this study concentrates on the film's use of mise-en-scène in the Last Supper, discussing the authenticity of the settings and characterizations, interpreting directorial nuances and stressing value and content, attention is given to how all these five approaches work together to produce meaning and relevance. This multi-analytical approach "allows us to reach valid conclusions on a movie's meaning and value; helps us to capture the experience of a film in our minds; sharpens our critical judgments overall, and opens up new channels of awareness and new depths of understanding."[10]

9. Ambros Eichenberger, "Approaches to Film Criticism," in *New Image of Religious Film*, ed. John R. May (Franklin: Sheed & Ward, 1997), 4–8.

10. Boggs and Petrie, *Art of Watching Film*, 7–8.

How does one study a film? Richard Stern, Clayton Jefford and Guerric Debona propose that one should first "let the movie be a movie."[11] That is, view the movie without any preconceptions and expectations. It is only after seeing the movie that a deeper analysis should be undertaken. There are different approaches to studying films. Roy Kinnard and Tim Davis use a decadal chronological ordering of films, commencing with "Early Silents (1897–1919)" and concluding with "The Nineteen Eighties." It becomes apparent that Jesus has been portrayed in a "striking way."[12] Although film production began in 1897, changes to the portrayal of Jesus did not come about until the 1960s. Kinnard and Davis propose the reason for these changes is the impact of the social, political and religious changes since the 1960s. To keep the Gospel relevant to society's changing values, the filmic Jesus also needs to change.[13] Similarly, it can be argued that there would also be changes to Judas' portrayal.

Lloyd Baugh notes the radical difference between the nature and function of the genre "sacred Scripture and the genre cinema."[14] To join the two genres, a number of methodologies can be applied. Christopher Deacy and Gaye Ortiz utilize H. Richard Niebuhr's five models of the interrelationship between *Christ and Culture* as a frame of reference.[15] While this is an appealing hermeneutic, it is not a useful one for this study. Niebuhr's five models: Christ against Culture, Christ of Culture, Christ above Culture, Christ and Culture in Paradox and Christ Transforms Culture, are christocentric, focusing on the sole authority of Christ, the messianic Jesus, God's supremacy and God as creator. Of the five models, only Niebuhr's fourth category, Christ and Culture in Paradox, contributes to an understanding of the portrayals of Judas Iscariot in film. The fourth model is a dualist position, which recognizes the corrupt nature of human culture and pronounces it godless, but realizes that we cannot remove ourselves from it. Niebuhr suggests that a film character does not need to be either a "blameless hero" or a "seamless villain" to be theologically valuable.[16] This

11. Stern, *Savior*, 3.

12. Roy Kinnard and Tim Davis, *Divine Images: A History of Jesus on the Screen* (New York: Carol Publishing Group, 1992), 13.

13. Ibid., 14.

14. Lloyd Baugh, *Imaging the Divine: Jesus and Christ-Figures in Film* (Franklin: Sheed & Ward, 1997), 4.

15. Details of Niebuhr's five models are provided in Christopher Deacy and Gaye Williams Ortiz, *Theology and Film: Challenging the Sacred/Secular Divide* (Malden: Blackwell, 2008), 26–65.

16. Sara Anson Vaux, "Unforgiven: The Sentence Death and Radical Forgiveness," *C&L* 47, no. 4 (1998): 445.

suggestion points to the possibility that the Judas character can be rehabilitated. I will show how Judas' actions point to rehabilitation.

According to William Telford, viewing film in a systematic, critical and insightful way is not an easy task and suggests the use of common lenses. For film reflection, the common lenses are the moral lens, the theological lens, the textual lens, the cultural lens, the sociological lens and the psychoanalytic lens.[17] To use Telford's methodology I would need to omit the psychoanalytic lens that approaches the film with a view to what it discloses about the human psyche. The Jesus films in general do not lend themselves to such an analysis because the characters are so thinly described and lack commonality in their respective representations. An exception to this is the Jesus character in Martin Scorsese's *The Last Temptation of Christ*.

Stern, Jefford and Debona, in exploring how representations of Jesus are constructed in each film, use three lenses. Lens One examines the sources and how they are used by filmmakers to construct their film of the historical Jesus. Lens Two analyzes how the filmmaker creates and communicates the content of the film. Lens Three explains how the portrait of Jesus in the film can be used as an entry point for examining the culture of the time in which the film was produced.[18] This is a useful method for an analytical approach to studying film in that it covers textual sources, cinematic features and cultural history. The three lenses is my preferred method for analysis and is applied to each of the selected films.

Lens One seeks to answer four questions. (1) How does the film compare to the Gospel accounts? (2) What sources did the screenwriters use to recreate the narrative? (3) Has the story been altered or embellished to enhance the plot? (4) What purposes do these additions and changes serve?[19] Lens One provides an overview of the historical setting of the film, and of significant events and influences of the particular period. Details of the film director and of his/her particular contribution to the film are also included.

Most of Lens Two can be understood under the term mise-en-scène. This refers to everything in the frame or view that is under the film director's control, and includes setting, costume, lighting, camera techniques, editing, sound and music. Close attention to these elements of film production and critical analysis enable the viewer to see how the filmmaker

17. William Telford, "Through a Lens Darkly: Critical Approaches to Theology and Film," in Christianson, Francis, and Telford, eds., *Cinéma Divinité*, 16–17.

18. Stern, *Savior*, 14–24, provides succinct explanations of these lenses.

19. These questions are adaptations of those proposed by Stern in ibid., 15.

manipulates the audio-visual vocabulary to achieve the purpose(s) of the films. The viewer's perception is influential in this process.

Lens Three deals with contextualizing the films. Stern, Jefford and Debona suggest that "one can follow particular issues through the sweep of the movies" and that "a broader set of values is also implicit in the film."[20] Film is not a static medium, neither is filmmaking a vacuous craft. Films do not evolve solely from imagination, nor are they devoid of external influences. For example, filmmakers sometimes reflect changing societal attitudes or they may shape them. To understand and appreciate why there have been such dramatic shifts in film content, context and presentation of Judas, it was necessary to analyze the prevailing cultural and world events at the time of the film's production.

To assist in this investigation it was helpful to ask the following four questions (1) "What questions does this film raise?" (2) "What answers does it propose?" (3) "Is this film consistent with or in contrast to the prevailing mood of the time of production?" 4) "What does the film reveal about the filmmaker?"[21] These questions kept me focused, stimulated and enthused with the topic.

*Step 3: Analyze Films for Close Study*

Analyzing twenty-four films could be seen as a daunting experience, running the risk of films merging into each other. To avoid this, two analysis sheets were devised, one for the Judas character in film and the other for the Last Supper scene. The Judas sheet facilitated in the recording of vital information ranging from the character's physiology, his interaction with other characters, significant actions and behavior, as well as key phrases and dialogue. The Last Supper scene grid provided an overall picture of the way in which the Last Supper has been translated into film. It was surprising that the fifty-four seconds Last Supper scene in the 1905 silent film, *La Vie et la Passion de Jésus Christ*, revealed more about the Judas character than the twelve minutes and thirty-three seconds scene in the 1964 epic, *The Greatest Story Ever Told.*

### *Question 2: Why Does the Judas Character Change?*<br>*Cultural Studies*

In each film's analysis, a section "The Portrayal of Judas" is included summarizing Judas' appearances in the film, his costume, significant details and insights into his behavior. Although the focus in this study is

20. Ibid., 21.
21. Ibid., 21–24.

the Last Supper scene, it is important to develop an understanding and overall picture of the Judas character as presented in each film. Judas' actions at the Last Supper were influenced by previous events. Therefore, it is necessary to be aware of these for plot and character development.

Boggs and Petrie outline eight techniques in which a character is developed.[22]

1. *Characterization through appearance*. When a character first appears, we tend to make certain assumptions based on their appearance, how they speak and particular mannerisms. Often, our first impression is incorrect, as in the case of Frances McDormand's role as Marge Gunderson in *Fargo*.
2. *Characterization through dialogue*. A character's dialogue and delivery can reveal a great deal about themselves by the words used and how they are said. Clint Eastwood's character as the ageing veteran Walt Kowalski in *Gran Torino* is an example.
3. *Characterization through external action*. Actions best depict the important traits to any character. There should be a clear relationship between a character and his or her actions. Thus, the actions should evolve naturally out of the character's personality. Gregory Peck's role as Atticus Finch in *To Kill A Mockingbird* reflects this mode of character development.
4. *Characterization through internal action*. Being privy to a character's thoughts and his or her point of view is the most obvious way in which the filmmaker reveals inner reality. In *Brokeback Mountain* we watch Ennis Del Mar (Heath Ledger) struggle with his homosexuality.
5. *Characterization through reactions of other characters*. Hearing the story of Andy Dufresne (Tim Robbins) told by fellow inmate Ellis Boyd "Red" Redding (Morgan Freeman) in *The Shawshank Redemption*, not only gives the audience insights into Andy's character but also Red's.
6. *Characterization through contrast—dramatic foils*. To highlight the main character, filmmakers include contrasting characters whose behavior, attitudes, opinions, lifestyle, physical appearance and so on, are the opposite to those of the main character. Jake Gyllenhaal as Donnie Darko in *Donnie Darko* illustrates characterization through contrast.

22. Boggs and Petrie, *Art of Watching Films*, 59–67. These pages have been paraphrased. To illustrate the techniques, I include my own film examples.

7. *Characterization through caricature and leitmotif.* To etch a character quickly and deeply into the audience's mind and memory, actors often exaggerate or distort one or more dominant features or personality traits. Consider the memorable characters Walter Sobchak (John Goodman) and "The Dude" (Jeff Bridges) in *The Big Lebowsky*. That is caricature. Leitmotif is the repetition of a single action, phrase or idea by a character until it becomes almost a trademark. An example of leitmotif is Travis Bickle's (Robert De Niro) "You talkin' to me?," as he repeatedly questions his mirror image in *Taxi Driver*.
8. *Characterization through choice of name—name typing.* One important method of characterization is the use of names possessing appropriate qualities of sound, meaning, or connotation. Bill Cutting "The Butcher" (Daniel Day Lewis) in *Gangs of New York* is a notable example.

These eight ways to study characterization can be applied to the filmic Judas. For example:

1. Judas' appearance, particularly in the earliest films, clearly conveys a negative impression.
2. From his meeting with the Jewish authorities in *The Greatest Story Ever Told* we meet a portrayal of Judas that is not evident in the Gospels.
3. Judas' determination to see Jesus crowned as Messiah in *The King of Kings* reflects the disciple's belief in Jesus.
4. In *Blade af Satans Bog*, Judas evokes sympathy as the audience witnesses his internal struggle.
5. That Judas was an outsider is established by the disciples' reaction to him and his actions, although a fellow disciple holding a knife to Judas' throat in *Color of the Cross* is perhaps an overstatement.
6. Judas in most of the selected Jesus films is a dramatic foil.
7. Judas can be caricatured as a lover of money, the leitmotif being a moneybag. Tradition influenced Judas' characterization.
8. The name Judas is synonymous with betrayal and treachery. Intertitles in silent films reinforce this image. In sound films, the other Judas named as a disciple in the Gospels (Luke 6:16) is called Thaddaeus (Matt 10:3; Mark 3:18) to avoid any confusion.

This eight-fold method of characterization proved too unwieldy in developing a summary of the portrayal of Judas Iscariot. The process and structure were too fractured, and consolidating the details was difficult. The method was abandoned and the chronological method was adopted instead.

A chronological examination of the Judas character as presented in the twenty-four Jesus films, and specifically in adaptations of the Last Supper, shows a progressive change in the ways in which Judas is portrayed. This progressive change can be divided into two distinct eras and separated by a period of transition. The first fifty years of Jesus films present Judas in a negative light and bearing traditional characteristics. The 1950s, a period of transition, saw the emergence of Judas as a Zealot striving for freedom from Roman oppression. From the 1960s, Judas is no longer recognized by Jewish traits but by his zealous pursuit in ending Roman oppression. What influenced these major changes in the Judas filmic portrayals?

*Cultural and Social Changes*

Jesus films are products of culture and ideology. Barnes Tatum identifies a four-stage process in the history of Jesus films: reluctance, reverence, diversity and scandal.[23] In the formative years of moving pictures, filmmakers were reluctant to film the Jesus story lest they drew opposition and condemnation from the Church and the viewing public. They were careful to present the Jesus of the biblical texts and used intertitles with Gospel quotes to authenticate the story. The American Production Code of 1930 and the Catholic Legion of Decency set up in 1933, enforced strict guidelines in the casting of Jesus in particular. The character had to impart holiness. From the 1960s onwards, the divine Jesus was replaced by one both displaying divinity *and* humanity. This opened the way for diversity in characterization. In a classic film from this period, *Godspell*, Jesus shed his traditional long caftan for a clown suit. With the easing of censorship and the decline of Church influence, filmmakers since the 1980s had free rein as to how they could portray Jesus. The filmic Jesus had become so humanized that his divinity was lost to violent outbursts (*Jesus Christ Superstar*), self-doubt and a love affair with Mary Magdalene (*The Last Temptation of Christ*).

The tracing of the portrayal of Judas Iscariot in film shows a *reversal* of Tatum's four-stage process in the history of Jesus films. It is worth noting that restrictions were not imposed on filmic representations of

23. W. Barnes Tatum, *Jesus at the Movies: A Guide to the First Hundred Years* (Santa Rosa, CA: Polebridge, 1997), 2–5, 195–97.

Judas, or other Gospel figures. Why not? If Judas' filmic debut was one that scandalized, what transpired that resulted in the Judas character being exonerated and revered from the late 1990s on? This study provides possible explanations for this evolution in the representation of Judas.

Robert Sklar's *Movie-Made America: A Cultural History of American Movies* provides some answers. As a study of cultural changes and the influence historical events have had on the film industry's production, the book offers valuable insights.[24] Sklar posits, for example, that the Holocaust has made a dramatic impact on the way in which Jews and Judaism are portrayed in film. It is therefore feasible to assume that the Holocaust also influenced the post-war filmic portrayals of Judas. To test this assumption, particular attention is paid as to how Judas, Jews, Jesus and Jewish culture are portrayed in the selected films.

Cultural changes and historical events influence the film industry. Terry Lindvall maintains that "how we understand the context of the film, both in its historical setting and its creative and economic productions, shapes how we see."[25] Maarten Pereboom, who states that film reflects "[t]he ways we respond to historical evidence and how we interpret that evidence," supports this concept.[26]

*Audiences and Viewer Response*

Viewing a film is a unique experience: "no-one sees a movie, reads a book, or hears a song in the same way."[27] As a viewer exercising critical subjectivity, I acknowledge that my pre-Vatican II Roman Catholic background influences any interpretation of the filmic Judas. Like Richard Walsh, I too believe that Judas "got a raw deal."[28] I acknowledge this sentiment and am reminded that one cannot view a film with total objectivity. To view a film we need to be aware of our beliefs, opinions and values "so

24. Robert Sklar, *Movie-Made America: A Cultural History of American Movies* (New York: Vintage, 1994), 173.

25. Terry Lindvall, "Hollywood Chronicles: Toward an Intersection of Church History and Film History," in *Reframing Theology and Film: New Focus for an Emerging Discipline*, ed. Robert K. Johnston (Grand Rapids: Baker Academic, 2007), 131.

26. Maarten Pereboom, *History and Film: Moving Pictures and the Study of the Past* (Boston: Prentice Hall, 2011), 5.

27. Rose Pacatte, "Shaping Morals, Shifting Views: Have the Rating Systems Influenced How (Christian) America Sees Movies?" in Johnston, ed., *Reframing Theology and Film*, 282.

28. Richard Walsh, preface to *Three Versions of Judas* (London: Equinox, 2010), vii.

that we control them and not they us."[29] Every viewer approaches a film with his or her preconceptions. I am not only a viewer, but also one who is critically analyzing films. I am not a viewer who watches the film once but a viewer who watches the same film a number of times and who examines individual frames. These viewing practices provide me with a clear advantage over someone (e.g. a film-critic) who views the film only once. It is highly probable that aspects of a film are noticed that would probably be missed in only one viewing.

Cultural and historical criticism is not without problems. These problems are not only distinctive to film studies but to other forms of literature, including the Bible. Apart from the audience not making the connection with the historical event, there is a danger of reading into the film something that is not there, or making tenuous links. Aichele and Walsh explain:

> All readers read from concrete social and material locations, and no reader has privileged access to some site of authoritative, univocal meaning, such as the mind of the text's author, the social context of the text's production, or even "what really happened." There is no proper or correct exegesis of any text. All readings are eisegeses, biased expressions of one ideology or another, and the conflict of readings is often a conflict of ideologies.[30]

This explanation is helpful in that it is a reminder that obstacles to objectivity, created through our prejudices and preconceptions, can affect the way in which a film is viewed and analyzed.

### *Question 3: What Are the Theological Implications of These Changes? Theological Studies*

The knowledge that there are a multiplicity of viewer responses and that "no two theologies will ever be the same"[31] is reassuring and encouraging. This multiplicity is made possible because of what Clive Marsh calls "the suspension of belief" which many viewers willingly undertake as they enter "the house of illusions."[32] Illusion is only one of several elements in the reception process according to Marsh. Other elements include

29. Stern, *Savior*, 23.

30. Aichele and Walsh, eds., *Screening Scripture*, vii–viii.

31. Deacy and Ortiz, *Theology and Film*, 81.

32. Clive Marsh, *Cinema and Sentiment: Film's Challenge to Theology* (Waynesboro: Paternoster, 2004), 84.

emotion, embodiment, visuality and attentiveness.[33] Marsh explores the theological significance of not only what the film does to the audience, but also what the audience does with the film.[34]

Films are more than reflections of culture, history, and filmmakers' ideologies: they also can be theological testimonies. Films "provide a bridge between consideration of what the films can do to-and-for viewers and the theological reflections that then follow."[35]

Theology through film can be a method of reading the dialogue between film and Western culture, as well as a relevant and contemporary theology. Marsh's theory is important in that instead of reducing the theological analysis of culture to an imposition of theological concepts onto culture, he proposes that theology develops in critical engagement with popular culture. The interaction between a theological tradition and life's activities is a constant process. Watching films, according to Marsh, "contributes to the way in which theology is constantly evolving."[36]

As a theological method, Marsh shows the use of film as an example of the way in which any aspect of culture can become a critically received theological resource. He notes the following five consequences of using film in theology. First, film is a "key way" in explaining theology's major themes. Second, film is a "reminder" of the public dimension of any Christian theology. Third, Marsh views film as inviting theological reflection to begin through an "emotional channel" and fourth, because of its accessibility and popularity, film provides "the potential raising of theological questions." A fifth consequence of using film in theology is that theology which takes film seriously is reminded of its own temporary nature and, one could add, its contemporary dynamics.[37]

The films selected for close study support Marsh's argument. The filmic character of Judas does not change theology but, rather, changes in theology reflect the way in which the filmic Judas is portrayed. Marsh's five consequences offer a point of entry into examining theological aspects of the Last Supper, identifying changes in theological thought, and determining the implications of those shifts within one specific example.

33. Ibid. See pp. 87–103 for explanation.

34. Ibid., 1.

35. Clive Marsh, *Theology Goes to the Movies: An Introduction to Critical Christian Thinking* (London: Routledge, 2007), 44.

36. Ibid., 166.

37. Clive Marsh, "Film and Theologies of Culture," in *Explorations in Theology and Film*, ed. Clive Marsh and Gaye Ortiz (Malden: Blackwell, 1997), 32–33.

## *Summary*

Film is not just about 'the story.' Barry Taylor argues that for any given film, the text comprises at least three intersecting issues: "image, story, and sound, all working together both to create context and to give meaning to the tale being told."[38] It is evident that the study of film is a complex discipline and that the major factor in studying film is analysis. The analytical approach is essential to the art of watching film because it enables the viewer to form a deeper understanding and appreciation of the film. The film is no longer just a collection of images and sounds but a conveyor of some profound message or thought. Without film analysis, understanding of the film's meaning and value would be lacking, and there would be a failure to accept mentally the filmic experience.

This work addresses three focus questions. (1) How is Judas portrayed in film? (2) Why does the Judas character change? (3) What are the theological implications of these changes? Answering these questions requires an inter-disciplinary approach relating to film, cultural and theological studies. The goal of using this approach is to develop an appreciation of "the nature and functions of film 'texts' operating within—and constructing—particular contexts."[39]

I approach the selected films using Eichenberger's five approaches to film criticism and adopt the Stern, Jefford and Debona "three lens" method to examine critically the portrayal of Judas Iscariot in Jesus films across twelve decades. In particular, I extrapolate the theological implications of the variety of Judas portrayals and argue for the rehabilitation of Judas from damnation to redemption.

38. Barry Taylor, "The Colors of Sound: Music and Meaning Making in Film," in Johnston, eds., *Reframing Theology*, 51.

39. Melanie Wright, *Religion and Film: An Introduction* (London: I. B. Tauris, 2007), 75.

Chapter 2

# THE SILENT ERA (1902–1927)

## *Introduction*

The Jesus story was popular in silent films. Between 1897 and 1930, thirty-seven Jesus films were produced in France, Austria, United States of America, Great Britain, Italy, Denmark and Germany.[1] Films ranged from five minutes in length (*La Passion*, 1897) to 155 minutes (*The King of Kings*, 1927). *The Passion Play*, both as narrative and film title, was the most popular with ten films. Other common titles were *The Life of Christ* and *Jesus of Nazareth*. These early Jesus films fascinated audiences who marveled at seeing the life of Christ on the "big screen."

Viewing silent Jesus films, especially those from the first decade of the twentieth century, can be a challenging undertaking. Poor quality film, as well as modest lighting, hinders the viewing experience, while acting, costumes and props can be likened to those often used in children's Sunday school plays. With no dialogue, apart from title cards introducing a new scene, a few intermittent and selective intertitles, and possibly a narrator—provided by the cinema—who contributes "descriptive readings,"[2] the narrative is reliant on the moving image. Nevertheless, "the cinema is a dynamic, evolving art form, always capable of providing us with new films that won't fit the old rules."[3] Therefore, to watch an early silent Jesus film demands the viewer's entire attention if he or she is to make new discoveries in an old film. The following six silent films are indicative of the evolving nature of film, and how the Jesus and Judas stories are portrayed and developed.

1. Richard H. Campbell and Michael R. Pitts, *The Bible on Film: A Checklist: 1897–1980* (Metuchen: Scarecrow, 1981), 73–110.

2. Richard Abel, *The Red Rooster Scare: Making Cinema American 1900–1910* (Berkeley: University of California Press, 1999), 114.

3. Boggs and Petrie, *Watching Films*, 423.

## *La Vie et la Passion de Jésus Christ (1902/1905)* *(The Life and Passion of Jesus Christ)*

Director: Ferdinand Zecca and Lucien Nonquet. Screenwriter: unknown. Country: France. Production Company: Pathé Frères. Length: 44 minutes. Length of Last Supper scene: 54 seconds. Color: black and white/four color tinting. Filming locations: Paris. Cast: Judas (uncredited), Jesus (uncredited).

### *Lens One*

The French cinema industry was founded during the *Belle Époque* (1890–1914), an era of artistic and cultural refinement that characterized French life at the beginning of the twentieth century. French film company Pathé, produced three of the earliest Jesus films: *La Vie et la Passion de Jésus Christ* (1902), *La Vie du Christ* (1906), and an extended version of *La Vie et la Passion de Jésus Christ* (1905).[4] The latter was filmed in three stages: eighteen tableaux in 1902, an additional ten tableau in 1904 and finally completed in 1905 with an extra three tableaux directed by Lucien Nonquet.[5] Each of the thirty-one tableau is a complete story, varying in length and number of scenes, and has an introductory title card to identify the scene. A 1908 Pathé advertisement describes the film as superseding all others in photographic quality, "excellency [*sic*] in staging," "steadiness and durability" in "5 parts," and with "39 pictures all hand colored."[6] There are no intertitles within the scenes because the assumption was that 1902 audiences would be familiar with the Bible or at least the Jesus story.

The film is innovative not only because of such "special effects" as the introduction of camera movement and super-imposing images, but also because many of the scenes were in color. This was achieved by using Pathécolor, a four-strip color process where each frame of film is individually hand-colored. This use of color heightens the visual impression of scenes as animated religious paintings. Many of the scenes, including the annunciation, Jesus' baptism and the transfiguration, replicate well-known works of art. Engravings on Christian themes by the nineteenth-century French illustrator Gustave Doré (1832–1883) were a principal influence on both settings and costumes. Doré created hundreds of drawings in realistic style, which were used in numerous translations of the Bible.

4. The 1905 version of the film is referred to in this study.

5. Philip Strick, "The Greatest Stories Ever Told," *The Movie: The Illustrated History of the Cinema* 103 (1981): 2051. The film is known by a number of other names, including *Passion and Death of Christ*, *The Passion Play*, *The Life and Passion of Christ*, and *Vie et Passion du Christ*.

6. Abel, *Red Rooster Scare*, 473.

Director Ferdinand Zecca (1864–1947) draws from all four Gospels with no single Gospel taking precedence. The dominant scriptural theme according to Geoffrey Staley and Richard Walsh is "the angelic proclamation, '*Gloria in excelsis deo*' (Luke 2:14)."[7] Zecca's frequent use of angels in a number of scenes attests to that statement. Zecca and Nonquet draw heavily on Roman Catholicism, which was France's state religion up to 1905. It is self-evident that a Roman Catholic perspective would be *de rigeur* especially as the majority of the audience would embrace that faith. Two examples of pandering to Catholic tradition are the images of Veronica wiping the face of Jesus as he carries the cross to Calvary and St Michael the archangel escorting the Holy Family to Egypt. Although non-biblical, the inclusion of these scenes would have reinforced popular piety and Church teaching. In the nativity scene, Zecca endorses the Catholic dogmas of the virgin birth and the perpetual virginity of Mary. Joseph and Mary kneel beside an empty manger and while both pray, a baby Jesus mystically appears, much to the surprise of Joseph and a relieved looking Mary.

Early silent films were relatively short. To recount as much of the story as possible, filmmakers often blended two separate incidents into one scene. In the nativity scene, for example, the magi and shepherds kneel together before the manger. Although this is inconsistent with Gospel nativity accounts (Matt 1:18–2:12; Luke 2:1–20), it was a popular artistic portrayal of the birth of Jesus and one easily recognized by audiences. In the resurrection scene, a *deus ex machina* device is used enabling Jesus to rise up out of the bowels of the earth. This is biblically incorrect. Perhaps the scriptwriter drew from the Apostles' Creed which states "[Jesus] descended into hell; the third day He rose again from the dead." The same mechanical device is used again in the ascension scene—"He ascended into heaven, is seated at the right hand of God the Father Almighty." This final scene is quite dramatic in that the disciples watch Jesus rise into the heavens. What the disciples (and audience) see are the Father (old, with white hair and a long beard) and the Son seated on a billowing cloud with the Holy Spirit (in the form of a white dove) hovering above them. As an angelic orchestra plays and with effective imagery, we can almost hear the audience responding with "*Gloria in excelsis deo*."

7. Jeffrey L. Staley and Richard Walsh, *Jesus, the Gospels, and Cinematic Imagination: A Handbook to Jesus on DVD* (Louisville: Westminster John Knox, 2007), 8.

*Lens Two*

Figure 1. Judas is deciding whether to drink the wine.


The title card "The Last Supper" introduces the film's nineteenth segment, which follows Jesus' "Clearing of the Temple." The height of the room implies that it is large. Heavy cloth-drapes cover the back brick-wall suggesting that the owner of the house is wealthy. Openings above the wall provide natural lighting. It is evident that filming of the scene took place during the day: the large oil lamp hanging from the center of the ceiling is unlit. This may be an editing oversight or perhaps the recapturing of an evening atmosphere was not important for the director. There is nothing to indicate that a meal has taken place. A rectangular table covered with a voluminous draping white tablecloth is the scene's focal point. The table is set with two matching clay jugs, goblets and a round-flat loaf of bread. In front of the table stand two different sized ewers. These allude to the anointing of Jesus and the foot-washing incidents (Matt 26:6–13; Mark 14:3–9; John 12:1–8; 13:1–11). Couches are in front of the table and at each end.

Jesus and eleven disciples enter in single file from both sides of the room to take their places at the table. Only seven disciples are in the frame when Jesus gestures for them to sit down. Jesus, still standing, bends over to pick up the loaf of bread while the remaining disciples take their seats. It is unclear what words Jesus is saying but his gestures suggest that he is explaining the significance of the bread. Jesus breaks the loaf in half and while passing the halves to the disciple on either side of him, Judas enters the room from the screen's right. Without any acknowledgment of Jesus or the other disciples, Judas takes his place in front of the table and at the right side. As the last disciple to enter, he naturally attracts the attention of the viewing audience. Is this Zecca's subtle reference to Judas being the last-named in the Gospel listing of the apostles (Matt 10:4; Mark 3:19; Luke 6:16)? Alternatively, is it to indicate that Judas had already separated himself from the other disciples, perhaps bargaining with the Jewish religious authorities (Matt 26:14–16; Mark 14:10–11; Luke 22:3–6)? Reaching over the table, Judas takes a piece of bread given to him by one of the disciples and turns to face the camera. Jesus and the other disciples eat the bread. Although Judas appears to put the bread in his mouth, he surreptitiously places it beside him on the couch. Jesus then pours two cups of wine, one for himself and the other for Peter sitting at his left.

Taking a similar jug of wine, Jesus fills John's cup and then passes the jug to him. While all this is taking place, Judas has his back to the table and is deep in thought. He continues looking forward, increasing the audience's animosity. Suddenly he turns towards John who is pouring the second jug of wine. Judas leans over, takes the cup and turns to face the camera again so that his actions are in full view of the audience. When Jesus and the other disciples stand to drink their goblet of wine, Judas remains seated. Having pretended to drink the wine, Judas tips the contents onto the floor. Taking their seats again, John leans into Jesus and appears to be asking him a question. Could John be expressing his concern for Jesus' visible uneasiness? Jesus is resting his head on his hand and is looking steely-eyed at Judas. Likewise, Judas, replicating Auguste Rodin's *The Thinker* pose, is deep in thought. For no apparent reason, Jesus suddenly stands and with his right arm outstretched, points his index finger to the sky. This gesture denotes Jesus' divinity and his relationship with God the Father.

The disciples' reaction indicates that Jesus has revealed that one of those gathered is to betray him. Expressing their alarm, some stand while others turn to question each other. Judas recoils in shock: his conspiracy is exposed. Judas reluctantly turns to face Jesus who, together with John, is staring intently at him. Jesus points directly at Judas and like a magician waving his wand sweeps his arm across his chest and away from himself. The directive is clear: Judas is the betrayer and no longer welcome at the table. Judas has to leave immediately.

With his left arm across his chest, Judas hastily rises from his seat and moves to center-screen. Having looked to his left he then quickly glances at Jesus. Judas extends his left arm; fingers splayed as if to question Jesus' directive. All eyes are on the betrayer. Like a petulant child, Judas raises his arm, waves it over his head, mouths an inaudible comment, and then quickly leaves. Immediately following Judas' melodramatic exit, Jesus and the disciples rise and leave the room. Their departure is less theatrical: they process out in pairs.

A standard cinematographic technique in early films is that the actors move about within the frame while the stationary camera observes the entire stage. Zecca employs the long shot enabling full view of characters and their surrounds within a single frame. A problem with this technique is that the camera is so far away from the actors that it is impossible to absorb all that is happening within the frame. For example, in the Last Supper scene, one presumes that the focus of the audience would be on Jesus. This being the case, the audience might not notice Judas tipping out the wine, thereby missing a significant facet of Judas' character. The long shot is problematic because the distance makes seeing the characters' emotions difficult. To overcome this, actors use extreme gesturing. Bruce Babington and Peter Evans note that in the silent Jesus film, there is

> a consistent repertoire of transparent gestures that in immediately accessible terms mediate between the authoritative and consolatory, the constantly pointing index finger, the characteristic consolatory gestures of arms spread out, palms outward, and eyes constantly lifting heavenwards to credit their eternal source of inspiration.[8]

Clearly, the film reflects both the audience's and the film director's Christian cultural bias. The term "Last Supper" does not appear in the Gospels but it is a popular term in both art and Christian writings to describe the final meal on the evening of Jesus' arrest. There is little to suggest that the scene portrays a Jewish Passover meal (Seder supper). Wine and bread are the only nourishment evident and there are no utensils apart from individual pottery cups and jugs. Historically, the white tablecloth looks out of place for a first-century Middle Eastern table.

8. Bruce Francis Babington and Peter William Evans, *Biblical Epics: Sacred Narratives in the Hollywood Cinema* (Eugene: Wipf & Stock, 1993), 119.

Perhaps Zecca intended it to be an altar cloth. This suggests two possible reasons influencing Zecca's representation of the Supper: Zecca wanted to make the Last Supper into a Catholic mass and did not want to equate the supper with a Jewish religious meal.

*Lens Three*

The first decade of the twentieth century witnessed the rise of anti-Semitism in Europe together with religious and political upheaval in France. When Captain Alfred Dreyfus, a Jewish officer in the French army, was unjustly accused of treason in 1894, open expressions of anti-Semitism escalated. The Dreyfus Affair became one of the determinants in the genesis of Political Zionism founded by Theodor Herzl.

In 1905, under the pressures of the Dreyfus Case, the three socialist parties merged into a unified parliamentary party. This new party aimed to transform a capitalist society into a collectivist or communist society.[9] Irrespective of their differences, political parties of both left and center shared an anti-clericalism that promoted a steady "de-sacralization of French society."[10]

The same year saw the separation of the Church from the State in France: Roman Catholicism was no longer considered the official religion. With the papal encyclical "*Vehementer Nos*—On the French Law of Separation," the Church's influence diminished with the laicization of schools and hospitals, clergy were subjected to military service and religious congregations dispersed. These changes affected much of French culture, especially cinema.

*La Vie et la Passion de Jésus Christ* re-asserted Christian values, principles and Catholicism. Catholic missionaries used the film to introduce the Gospels to new cultures as an effective way of propagating the Christian faith. Between 1907 and 1908, more people in the United States saw the film than any other single film.[11] The Vatican recognized the film's success and achievement in bringing the life of Christ to both the faithful and the general populace. On the 100th anniversary of cinema in 1995, the Vatican compiled a list of forty-five "great films." *La Vie et la Passion de Jésus Christ* made the list under the Religion category.

9. David Thomson, *Europe Since Napoleon* (Harmondsworth: Penguin, 1982), 398–400.

10. Richard Abel, *Ciné Goes to Town: French Cinema 1896–1914*, updated and expanded (Berkeley: University of California Press, 1998), 3.

11. Abel, *Red Rooster Scare*, 61.

*The Portrayal of Judas*

Judas appears in three scenes. The first is a walk-on with three other disciples in the "Jesus and the woman of Samaria" tableau. This particular scene is only thirteen seconds in duration. Judas, along with John, Peter and an unidentified disciple react with horror that Jesus has been talking with a Samaritan woman. With exaggerated arm movements, Judas sends the woman away. What is significant in this scene is that when they leave the well, John turns to Judas, takes his arm and together they walk away. Clearly, at this earlier stage the other disciples accept Judas.

The "Last Supper" is the second scene where Judas appears. This scene is an excellent illustration of the assumption that audiences would be familiar with the biblical narrative.

The third scene is "Jesus on the Mount of Olives. The Kiss of Judas." Leading a group of Roman soldiers, Judas looks for Jesus. When he sees him, Judas promptly kisses Jesus on the cheek and steps back. Peter draws his sword to defend Jesus, while Judas, showing signs of cowardice, takes cover near a tree. When Jesus has been securely bound, a Roman soldier throws a moneybag onto the ground. Like a dog scavenging for food scraps, Judas excitedly picks up the bag making sure that no one sees that he has the money. It is only when Jesus is taken away that Judas realizes what he has done. He places his hand on his head, quickly turns, runs away, and is not seen again.

Judas' excitement upon receiving payment for "identifying" Jesus suggests that his motive for betrayal was greed. What is significant is that payment for the deed is carried out by a Roman centurion and not by the Jewish chief priests (Matt 26:14; Mark 14:10; Luke 22:3–6). As the clandestine meeting between Judas and the religious authorities is not shown in the film, Zecca in effect has negated Jewish blame for the capture of Jesus. It would be easy to conclude that Zecca was avoiding being accused of anti-Semitism but the ensuing Passion scenes do not support this observation. Jesus is brought to trial before Caiaphas although there is little to identify Caiaphas as a Jewish chief priest. The crowds, present at the trial before Pilate and at the release of Barabbas, influence Pilate's decision. They are very angry, animated and (soundlessly) vocal. When Jesus carries his cross to Calvary, the crowd is hostile towards him.

Judas is not easily recognized but blends easily within the group of disciples. His thick dark hair, full beard and stocky physique are not distinctive. Likewise, neither is his attire: a dark cloak clasped at the shoulder and draped over a light colored caftan. Two other disciples are similarly dressed at the Last Supper. Although the other disciples have costume changes throughout the film, Judas' costume remains unchanged.

This helps establish Judas' identity. What does distinguish Judas from the other eleven disciples is his body language. At the Supper, he sits with his back to the table, which places him in full view of the audience. Judas appears disinterested or distracted. Whatever the reason, Judas' body language suggests that he does not want to be there. Judas has separated himself from the group and his pretense of eating the bread and drinking the wine highlights his aversion to share in the Supper. It is only when Jesus points to Judas and calls him by name that Judas' attention is gained. His feigned shock emphasizes his duplicity. His grandiose departure reveals Judas' contempt for Jesus.

The three appearances of Judas in *The Life and Passion of Jesus Christ* amount to two minutes and thirty-five seconds. In this short time, Zecca shows Judas as Middle Eastern in appearance, who as a disciple is seemingly disinterested yet also preoccupied with a dark secret. He is presented as full of anger, a lover of money and one who, with a kiss, betrays Jesus. Although Judas' motive for betrayal is unclear, his actions cast him as a villain.

### *La Vie du Christ (1906) (The Life of Christ)*

Director: Alice Guy. Screenwriter: unknown. Country: France. Production Company: Société des Etablissements, L. Gaumont. Length: 33 minutes. Length of Last Supper scene: 1:23 minutes. Color: black and white. Filming locations: Paris. Cast: Judas (uncredited), Jesus (uncredited).

*Lens One*

Alice Guy (1873–1968) was a founding figure of the French and American film industries who at the age of 23 became the world's first female film director and the first woman to build her own motion picture studio. Between 1897 and 1907, she was involved in either the production or direction of 403 films.[12] Guy's contribution to the film industry includes experimentation with sound technology in films, masking off parts of the film picture, using double exposures and running film backwards to achieve certain desired effects. She was the first director to use facial close-ups and reaction shots to heighten dramatic effects,[13] and was "a pioneer of early narrative development."[14]

12. Anthony Slide, ed., *The Memoirs of Alice Guy Blaché* (Lanham: Scarecrow, 1986), Appendix 1, 143–62.

13. Gwendolyn Audrey Foster, "Performity and Gender in Alice Guy's *La Vie du Christ*," *FCm* 23 (1998): 7.

14. Alison McMahan, *Alice Guy Blaché: Lost Visionary of the Cinema* (New York: Continuum International, 2002), 42.

Guy had a strict Roman Catholic upbringing. Although she described her six years of schooling at the Convent of the Sacred Heart in Viry on the Swiss border as "years of imprisonment,"[15] she remained committed to her faith. This is apparent in her 1906 film *La Vie du Christ.* Guy drew on the Gospels for the narrative and the watercolors of the Tissott Bible for inspiration.[16] She incorporated the traditional fourteen Stations of the Cross and employed two Jesuit priests as consultants. Guy's depiction of the Passion, however, differs in many significant ways from the established genre of Passion plays.

Guy brings a new dimension to the portrayal of the Passion story, notably her "insistence on privileging women in relation to Jesus."[17] By including the Stations of the Cross, Guy was able to highlight the presence of Mary the mother of Jesus, weeping women and the iconic Veronica with her veil. The attendance of a large group of women around the foot of the cross implies their faithfulness in contrast to the male disciples' absence and lack of fidelity. Although the Gospels differ in the number of women who return to the tomb to anoint Jesus' body, Guy draws on Luke's account: "Now it was Mary Magdalene, Joanna, Mary the mother of James, and the other women with them" (Luke 24:1–5).[18] She has eight women return to Jesus' tomb. Mary Magdalene does not enter the tomb but walks left and out of frame leaving her actions open to various suggestions. Was Mary following the angel's instruction, "Go quickly and tell his disciples" (Matt 28:7) or was Guy setting the scene where Jesus appears to Mary Magdalene (John 20:11–18)? Whatever is the correct answer; the implication is quite profound and anticipates feminist theologians' insistence almost a century later, that Mary Magdalene was the first to see the risen Christ. Elisabeth Schüssler Fiorenza, for example, argues that as Mary Magdalene not only discovers the empty tomb, but is also the first to receive a resurrection appearance, in a "double sense she becomes the *apostola apostolorum*, the apostle to the apostles."[19]

15. Ibid., introduction, xxxviii.

16. Slide, *Memoirs*, 45.

17. Abel, *Ciné Goes to Town*, 66.

18. Matthew cites "Mary Magdalene and the other Mary" (28.1). Mark names "Mary Magdalene and Mary the mother of James, and Salome" (16:1), while John mentions only Mary Magdalene (20:1).

19. Elisabeth Schüssler Fiorenza, *In Memory of Her: A Theological Reconstruction of Christian Origins*, 10th Anniversary ed. (New York: Crossroad, 1994), 332.

Gwendolyn Foster notes that in *La Vie du Christ*, "women are foregrounded as central characters and witnesses to the spectacle of Christ's birth. Christ himself is feminized and eroticized… Characters are suffused with familiarity, carnality, and corporeality… Scenes of family life are intercut with scenes of pageantry."[20] Foster's analysis of the *La Vie du Christ* is through a postmodern reconstruction lens. She observes that white men are not prominently featured and that black men are portrayed negatively.[21] Black men beat Jesus while he is being flogged and two black men hold the cross while Jesus is being nailed to it. Foster also construes that the film is "distinctly homophobic. Pontius Pilate is clearly effeminate, flamboyant, gay-coded for evil."[22]

While Guy uses painted tableau, a staple for Passion plays, she also added location scenes, which include the Samaritan woman at the well, Gethsemane and the Via Dolorosa scenes. These outdoor scenes draw the audience into the experience rather than being onlookers of a staged performance.

Guy was one of the first directors to use deep-focus photography where the entire image—foreground, midground and background—is in sharp focus. She designed this film to emphasize the use of deep focus and to fill the frame with movement along diagonal lines.[23] The latter heightens or emphasizes drama and action by providing an easy path for the eye to follow to the main subject, while deep focus achieves a more accurate representation of space. These camera shots are equally evident in "The Last Supper" segment.

*Lens Two*

"The Last Supper," as the title card heralds, takes place in an imposing building. The stonewalls are draped with heavy curtains, making the space less pretentious. Five large stone pillars tower over Jesus and his disciples, seated around the white-clothed rectangular table. In keeping with the Tissot and Doré illustrations, long couches provide seating. Judas is in front of the table and to the right of the frame. He has his back to Jesus and the others and is deep in thought, with legs astride and his chin resting in his hand.

20. Foster, "Performity and Gender," 8–9.

21. Gwendolyn Audrey Foster, *Performing Whiteness: Postmodern Re/Construction in the Cinema* (Albany: State University of New York Press, 2003), 58.

22. Ibid.

23. McMahan, *Alice Guy Blaché*, 104.

Jesus raises his right arm signifying that he is speaking, looks to his left and then to his right. His announcement results in the disciples' shock and questioning gestures. Judas remains stationary, still brooding. Jesus again raises his right arm and points heavenward. The disciples become very animated. Rising from their seats and leaning towards Jesus, they point to themselves. "Is it I?" Jesus makes no response. Recovering their composure, the disciples return to their seats while Jesus appears to be waiting for something to happen. He does not have to wait long. Judas rises from his couch and reaches across the table. He dips both his hands into the bowl that is in front of Jesus and then slinks back to his couch, all the while under the scrutiny of the disciples.

Jesus stands, takes the bread, breaks off two pieces, and gives these to the disciple on either side of him. He puts the remaining bread on the table. Extending his right hand over the large silver chalice that is in front of him, Jesus speaks. He picks up the chalice and hands it to John. At this point Judas turns to face Jesus. What Judas sees terrifies him, and he recoils in fear. Guy, using the dissolve technique, has Jesus transform into a vision of the Suffering Servant (Isa 53:3–5). The half-naked Jesus is wearing a crown of thorns, holding a reed scepter, and bears the marks of crucifixion. A dark cloak drapes across his shoulders. Behind Jesus are three angels, one on either side, and one slightly above him. Judas approaches the table as though he wants to speak to Jesus but the apparition is too frightening. Judas tries to block it out by covering his eyes with his arm but to no avail. The disciples, who are not privy to the vision, watch in bewilderment at Judas' behavior. A terrified and confused Judas backs away from the table and hurriedly leaves the room. The scene returns to Jesus breaking the bread in half again and distributing pieces to the disciples. Each of the disciples takes and eats the bread. The screen blackens and the title card "The Olive Garden" appears.

*Lens Three*

Filming in the same historical context as Ferdinand Zecca and Lucien Nonquet, Guy's film suggests two additional historical and cultural influences. The first is the gathering momentum of the French feminist movement. The second is the publication in 1906 of Pope Pius X's encyclical, "*Vehementer Nos*—On the French Law of Separation."

Was Alice Guy a feminist? Viewing the film through a postmodern reconstruction lens suggests that she was. That she was a female filmmaker in a male domain adds weight to the suggestion. Foster contends that some critics "unfairly dismissed" the innovative director as "a non-feminist."[24] Her portrayals of women in the film *La Vie du Christ*, their inclusion in miracle scenes such as "The Samaritan" and "The Miracle of Jairus's Daughter" and the prominent characterizations of Jesus' mother and Mary Magdalene, were to propagate traditional family values and social mores. Guy labors the point to distraction by including women and children in nearly every scene. One questions the value of having children witness the flogging of Jesus, walking with Jesus along the Via Dolorosa and being present when Jesus is nailed to the cross. Could Guy's inclusion of children be her interpretation of the blood curse, "His blood be on us and on our children" (Matt 27:25)? Foster offers an uncomplicated reason: the women and children encourage audience identification with the film and open up the film to a wider viewing audience.[25] Whether Guy was a feminist or not did not detract from her artistic genius. It simply influenced the ways in which she filmed the Jesus story.

Guy's faith stance as presented in the film raises the question, "Was she defending Catholicism or stretching the boundaries of belief?" I believe that for Guy, family and Catholicism were stabilizing forces and when they were threatened, she used her films to promote that stability. An example of this is the unique inclusion of the Suffering Servant vision at the Last Supper. McMahon describes it as "a masterful expression of Judas' dilemma: to not betray Jesus and therefore prevent salvation for the rest of humanity, or to betray him, let Jesus save the world, but be damned himself."[26] Given the tension between the French State and the Church, I would argue that Guy also uses the vision to symbolize the consequence of the Separation of the State and Church Law in 1906. Judas represents the State's betrayal of the French people while the Suffering Servant symbolizes the Roman Catholic Church.

In his encyclical "*Vehementer Nos*—On the French Law of Separation," Pius X writes, "That the State must be separated from the Church is a thesis absolutely false, a most pernicious error. Based, as it is, on the principle that the State must not recognize any religious cult, it is in the first place guilty of a great injustice to God."[27] It can be assumed that the two Jesuit priests acting as Guy's consultants had knowledge of the encyclical and therefore acted upon the Pope's directive. Indeed, Pius X continues:

24. Foster, "Performity and Gender," 15.

25. Ibid., 12.

26. McMahan, *Alice Guy Blaché*, 103.

27. Pius X, "*Vehementer Nos*," Encyclical of Pope Pius X on "The French Law of Separation." http://w2.vatican.va/content/pius-x/en/encyclicals/documents/hf_p-x_enc_11021906_vehementer-nos.html. Italics in the original.

as long as oppressive persecution continues, the children of the Church, *putting on the arms of light*, must act with all their strength in defense of Truth and justice—it is their duty always, and today more than ever… Meanwhile continue the salutary work you are doing; strive to kindle piety among the people as much as possible; promote and popularize more and more the teaching of Christian doctrine.

Guy's *La Vie du Christ* was meant to promote and popularize the teaching of Catholic doctrine. Guy's respect for and awareness of the responsibility of filming the life of Christ are evident in the manner in which she handles the subject matter: with paralyzed reverence. The film became a huge success—a nickelodeon spectacular and a "credible precursor of the studio blockbuster."[28]

### *The Portrayal of Judas*

Judas appears in only two scenes, "The Last Supper" and "Judas's Betrayal." Both scenes total less than two and a half minutes, which makes analysis difficult. Judas does not have any special features that distinguish him from those around him. His costume, according to the illustrations of James Tissot, is typically Middle Eastern and is similar to the costumes of many of the cast. He has black hair and a short full beard, as do a number of the disciples.

At the Last Supper, we see Judas separated from the group in that he has his back to the table and to Jesus. Dipping his hand into the bowl suggests a willingness to be identified as the one who is to betray Jesus. Slinking back to his seat conveys a sense of shame, guilt and resignation. The Suffering Servant vision, while a masterful expression of Judas' dilemma, also suggests that Judas has a conscience and struggles with the decision he has to make. Leaving the Supper before the wine is shared could be interpreted in one of two ways. First, Judas is just doing what Jesus has told him to do and, "doing what he has to do quickly" (John 13:27). Second, it is possible that Judas believes he can no longer be a part of the group.

The second scene in which Judas appears is in the "Olive Garden." Judas leads a small group of what appears to be peasants and shepherds armed with lanterns, staffs and hayforks. He has the group hide behind the trees while he stands in full view of Jesus who is walking towards him. Lifting his head and raising his arms in salutation, Judas moves to greet

28. J. Hoberman, "First Lady of Film Alice Guy Blaché at the Whitney," *Village Voice* (November 3, 2009). http://www.villagevoice.com/2009-11-03/film/first-lady-of-film-alice-guy-blanch-eacute-at-the-whitney/.

Jesus. Taking hold of Jesus' right hand, Judas kisses Jesus on the cheek and then steps back to enable the men access to Jesus. It is difficult to determine whether it was because of shame, guilt or cunning that Judas lowered his head. Perhaps Judas was trying to avoid witnessing Jesus' capture. As Jesus is led away by the angry group, Judas turns and runs in the opposite direction, passing a large group of frantic women trying to catch up with Jesus and the arresting party. Again, there is a contrast between the faithfulness of women and the infidelity of a man.

Guy's interpretation of the betrayal by Judas is lacking in one crucial respect: a motive. No deal is struck with the religious authorities and no money is mentioned. There are no Roman or temple guards present at the arrest, and there is no indication that Judas is disillusioned with Jesus or that he hates Jesus. What was Guy's reasoning for these omissions?

Paffenroth suggests that these omissions could be Guy alluding to Judas as being merely the instrument of betrayal and thus "an agent of salvation."[29] If this is the case, Guy introduces in this film a modern, radical interpretation of Judas. However, I am not persuaded, as an alternative explanation could simply be the limiting factors of the film's budget and length. This is substantiated by Guy's omission of Judas' bargaining with the Jewish priests. For this particular event to have worth, Guy would also need to include the exchange of thirty pieces of silver, Judas' return of the coins, and possibly Judas' suicide. By not including these scenes in her film, Guy relies on the audience's knowledge of the story.

The omission is however, still intriguing. By not showing Judas' collusion with the Jewish religious authorities, Guy presents a Judas character whose only noticeable "sin" is that of identifying Jesus at Gethsemane. However, it is undeniable that the audience would exit the film with an understanding that, Judas' actions identify him as "Judas Iscariot, the one who betrayed [Jesus]" (Mark 3:19).

## *From the Manger to the Cross (1912)*

Director: Sidney Olcott. Screenwriter: Gene Gauntier. Country: USA. Production Company: Kalem Company. Length: 71 minutes. Length of Last Supper scene: 5:35 minutes. Color: black and white. Filming locations: Jerusalem, Bethlehem, Palestine, Egypt and Syria. Cast: Judas (Robert G. Vignola), Jesus (Robert Henderson-Bland).

29. Paffenroth, *Judas: Images*, 135.

*Lens One*

America's earliest attempt at a biographical Jesus film was Sidney Olcott's 1912 production *From the Manger to the Cross*, also known as *Jesus of Nazareth*. The film is important for two reasons. It is the first Jesus film shot on location with, as the title card informs, "Scenes filmed at JERUSALEM, BETHLEHEM and other authentic locations in PALESTINE." Without the confines of stage sets, Olcott was able to add plenty of action and movement. It was also the first American film about Jesus to achieve enormous success not only in America but also in the United Kingdom and Europe. Box-office popularity was in part a response to the authentic locations shots. Cinema audiences were taken on a virtual tour of places previously seen only in print and the inclusion of intertitles narrated the events.

Like Alice Guy before him, Olcott drew inspiration for the sets, furnishings and costumes from Tissot's *Illustrated Bible*. Many of the scenes are replicas of the illustrations, for example, Judas' bargaining with the high priest. Olcott not only copies the costumes and the setting, he also mimics the exact number of characters and their positions within the sketch. Fra Angelico's *Annunciation* and Raphael's *Transfiguration* are easily recognized as the major artistic inspirations for these two scenes.

For the narrative, Olcott draws on all of the four Gospels, thus representing the "harmonizing trajectory of the Jesus film tradition."[30] The Last Supper scene includes accounts of Jesus' washing of the disciples' feet; his foretelling of Judas' betrayal; his words over the bread and wine; and Judas' exit into the night. Steven Greydanus, film reviewer for the *National Catholic Register*, notes that the film relies extensively on the King James Bible for title cards for narration and dialogue. "Perhaps *too* extensively, reflecting a Protestant tendency, rooted in *sola scriptura*, to want the text to be self-explanatory, over against the Catholic expectation that sacred art exists and has meaning within a social and cultural context."[31]

The intertitles are so faithful to the biblical text that ellipses are included where words are omitted from the quote. The film's theological sub-text is John's Gospel, especially his contrasting theme of light versus darkness.[32] This manifests in Olcott's use of lighting and by contrasting the pure white attire of Jesus with Judas' black costume.

30. Tatum, *Jesus at the Movies*, 24.

31. Steven D. Greydanus, "From the Manger to the Cross (1912)," *National Catholic Register*. http://decentfilms.com/reviews/fromthemangertothecross.

32. Staley and Walsh, *Jesus, the Gospels*, 13. For examples of light and darkness symbolism, see John 1:36; 3:20–21; 8:58; 9:5; 20:1.

*Lens Two*

The Last Supper scene commences with the title card, "He poureth water into a basin, and began to wash the disciples' feet. John 30:5." This is a crowded montage with only ten of the disciples, Jesus (Robert Henderson-Bland) and furniture fitting within the long shot frame. Olcott replicates Tissot's *The Washing of the Feet* sketch with one major difference: the scene is not in a room but is *al fresco*, perhaps on a balcony. Lighting difficulties could have dictated the setting. The swaying of the decorations and hair wafting in the wind can be a distraction. Some viewers however will appreciate the air of authenticity. There is nothing to suggest that it is evening, no burning oil lamps and not even the use of blue tint to denote night.

Seated and reclining disciples watch Jesus as he begins to wash the feet of one of the disciples. Judas (Robert G. Vignola) is turned side-on to the proceedings and is engaged in a conversation with a fellow disciple. He holds one of his sandals in his hand. Could this be in preparation of having his feet washed or to suggest a quick departure? His attention is roused when Peter gestures that Jesus should not only wash his feet but his hands and head as well (John 13:8–9). However, when Jesus replies with what one imagines is "Unless I wash you, you have no share with me" (John 13:9), Judas turns away, shaking his head and mumbling under his breath.

The narrative continues: "And they sat and did eat. Mark 14:18." The scene remains outdoors. The re-positioned couches make space for the rectangular table covered with a white cloth. The tableau is again crowded, with Jesus and twelve disciples in the frame. Those sitting behind the table, and in the center of the frame, include John, Jesus and Peter. Three disciples in front of the table recline on couches. Judas is also in front of the table and is almost opposite Jesus. Judas is leaning with his back against the table and his right arm rests on it.

In response to a question asked by John, Jesus spreads his arms drawing the attention of those gathered. "Verily I say unto you, one of you which eateth with me shall betray me. Mark 14:18." This raises concern among the disciples. Judas is quick to respond by looking at Jesus and joining with the others in questioning as to who that person could be. Jesus dips a morsel of bread into a large bowl situated in front of him. Significantly, Judas has already reached to take the sop before Jesus has finished dipping it. Judas takes the sop and in clear view of the disciples—and the audience—takes a bite. Realizing the implications of what he has done Judas drops the sop, draws back in horror, and hunches over. Jesus stands, drawing attention to himself. The other disciples are staring adoringly at

Jesus and seem unaware of Judas slowly rising from the couch. Gathering his outer garment and looking directly into the camera, Judas bends down and picks up his sandals. The scene changes to the next intertitle interrupting Judas' departure from the room.

The audience reads the intertitle "The First Communion. And he took bread, and gave thanks, and brake it. Luke 22:19." Olcott reproduces another Tissot illustration, *The Communion of the Apostles*, but with a significant omission. Where Judas is present in the Tissot drawing, he is absent in Olcott's scene. Clearly, Olcott did not want to offend audiences by having the "sinner" Judas partaking in communion. However, Olcott includes a female figure, which is prominent in the Tissot illustration. The assumption is that the figure is Mary Magdalene. She was not visible at the preceding feet-washing scene nor was she seated at the table. Those shots were too close, which made it impossible to include the entire group. The frame could fit only ten disciples. However, in the reception of bread and wine, she crouches at the extreme right of the frame. It is highly likely that the audience would not notice her because Jesus is the focus of the shot. The disciples are kneeling, some with their hands clasped in prayer, others with their heads covered.

Jesus proceeds to distribute the bite-sized pieces of bread to the open hands of one of the disciples. The intertitle takes the place of dialogue. "This is my body which is given for you. Luke 22:19." Another disciple reverently receives the bread from Jesus. "Likewise also the cup after supper. Luke 22:20." John hands the chalice back to Jesus. The others are still deep in prayer and with heads bowed. Jesus turns face on to the camera and raises his head heavenwards. "This cup is the new testament in my blood, which is shed for you. Luke 22:20." Holding the chalice at shoulder height, Jesus turns to the disciple on his right. For no apparent reason (perhaps it is poor editing) Jesus turns to John on his left and gives him the chalice again. Jesus steps back and places his hand on his breast. He takes the chalice from John and passes it to another disciple. Again, Jesus places his hand on his breast. "The First Communion" ends abruptly and changes to a street scene. The blue tint suggests that it is night. Judas, cloaked in black, is hurrying and looking for the chief priest's house. When he finds it, the screen fades to black. Judas is about to enter the realm of darkness: conspiracy, greed and betrayal.

*Lens Three*

In his direction of this film, Olcott takes into consideration three faith traditions: Protestantism, Roman Catholicism and Judaism. Opinions vary as to the make-up of the targeted audiences. Richard Walsh suggests that the film emerged from a "Protestant American culture" influenced by "tradition" and "reluctance to portray religion in film."[33] However, Herbert Reynolds opines that *From the Manger to the Cross* was made "with an eye to exclusively Catholic audiences."[34] A number of scenes support this claim particularly in the Last Supper event where many actions derive from distinctively Catholic liturgical practices. In the foot-washing scene only one foot is placed in the bowl, a practice that is carried out at the Maundy Thursday service. Catholic tradition is augmented further at the First Communion with Jesus distributing bread and wine in a priestly manner and the disciples kneeling, head bowed, and hands clasped in silent prayer. Pamela Grace argues that Olcott "showed an unusual sensibility…avoiding the most anti-Semitic moments that sometimes appear on screen."[35] Grace observes that Caiaphas does not question Jesus and although there is a cry to "Crucify him," when Pilate presents Jesus to the crowd, the contentious blood libel curse, "His blood be on us and on our children" (Matt 27:25) is omitted. Grace adds that Roman soldiers usher Jesus to the cross, without the involvement of Jewish priests.

Olcott promotes Jesus' Jewishness by having Jesus as a young boy wearing a *yarmulka* (skullcap), yet paradoxically in the scene where the twelve-year-old Jesus is in the temple "sitting among the teachers, listening to them and asking them questions" (Luke 2:41–51) his head is uncovered. Olcott's inclusion of a *yarmulka* is anachronistic in that wearing this Jewish head covering was instituted in Talmudic times, approximately the second century CE.

Similarly, in endeavoring to maintain Jewish religious practices, the boy Jesus wears the *payot* (long side-locks), yet Joseph does not. One would expect that both father and son would wear the distinguishing side locks. Was Olcott being sensitive to Roman Catholic dogma in alluding to Joseph not being Jesus' birth father and thus upholding the virgin birth (Matt 1:18–25; Luke 1:26–38) and the perpetual virginity of Mary?

33. Richard Walsh, *Reading the Gospels in the Dark: Portrayals of Jesus in Film* (Harrisburg, PA: Trinity International Press, 2003), 4–7.

34. Herbert Reynolds, "From the Palette to the Screen: The Tissot Bible as Source-book for *From the Manger to the Cross*," in *An Invention of the Devil? Religion and the Early Cinema: Une Invention du Diable? Cinéma des Premiers et Religion*, ed. Roland Cosandey, Andre Gaudreault and Tom Gunning (Sainte Foy, Canada: Les Presses de l'Université Laval, 1992), 276.

35. Pamela Grace, *The Religious Film* (Chichester: Wiley-Blackwell, 2009), 22.

Olcott may have deflected blame for the death of Jesus from the Jews to the Romans but he still perpetuated the myth of Jewish avarice, a vital component in anti-Semitism. This is most evident in the scene where Judas and the Jewish priests are haggling over the betrayal fee.

Olcott's "sensibility" to Jews and Judaism was not enough to curb public criticism. Robert Henderson-Bland, the Jesus character in the film, recalls:

> No film that was ever made called forth such a storm of protests, as did the announcement of "From the Manger to the Cross." Criticism, like an avalanche literally poured down upon it from every quarter of the globe. The newspapers were full of it; the public talked of it; the clergy raved about the blasphemy of it.[36]

The disparaging response to the film in England was so damning that it is said to be directly responsible for the establishment of film censorship in that country.[37] The main objection was the inappropriateness of showing a full figure of Jesus on the screen. There was little in the film that warranted accusations of blasphemy. The main reason why clergy were incensed was that the Jesus story had been taken out of the church—God's house and place of worship—and into cinemas—seen to be places of ill repute. Nevertheless, with a reported budget of US$100,000, *From the Manger to the Cross* was a huge success, drawing thirty times the cost of its production and making millionaires of the studio executives.[38] To cater for both Protestant and Catholic audiences, the film was distributed in two versions— one containing and one without the scene of the miracle of Veronica's veil. The film was re-issued in 1916 as *Jesus of Nazareth* and included a resurrection scene. In 1932, the film was re-issued again including sound.

*The Portrayal of Judas*

Judas has a significant role in the film. Although he is not part of "The Calling of the Disciples" segment, Judas is present at a number of miracles. It is here that we can detect a deterioration of Judas' relationship with Jesus. At the marriage at Cana (John 2:1–11) Jesus sits between

36. R. Henderson-Bland, *Actor–Soldier–Poet* (London: Heath Cranton, 1939), 70.

37. Lewis Jacobs, *The Rise of the American Film: A Critical History* (New York: Teachers College Press, 1968), 124.

38. Marc Wanamaker, "The Kalem Trailblazers," *The Movie: The Illustrated History of the Cinema* 102 (1981): 2033.

Judas and John at the head table. At the healing of the paralytic (Mark 2:1–12) Judas again is seated close to Jesus and is listening intently to him. Judas is agitated when Jesus responds to the scribes' accusation of blasphemy. Judas stands behind Jesus when Jesus calls, "Lazarus, come forth. John 11.43." While the "sinful woman" anoints Jesus' feet (Luke 7:36–50), Judas sits on the floor at the feet of Jesus. Judas does not speak but it is apparent that he disapproves of the woman's actions. When Jesus, his disciples, and "a great multitude" of followers leave Jericho and are walking towards Jerusalem, Judas is at the rear of the group and by himself.[39]

At the anointing at Bethany (Matt 26:6–13), we see Judas' manner change. Although Judas is reclining next to Jesus at a table, Judas has his back to him. (In the Tissot illustration, Judas is facing Jesus.) The perfume of the anointment pricks his attention. He becomes very animated when he condemns the use of the oil and the waste of money. "To what purpose is this waste? For this ointment might have been sold for much and given to the poor" (Matt 26:8–9). When Jesus chastises him, Judas reacts with exaggerated gestures of anger and frustration, leaves the room and goes to meet with the chief priests (Mark 14:10) where he haggles for the betrayal fee. The negotiator discreetly gestures with his open hands: his offer is twenty pieces of silver. Judas responds by clenching and opening his hands three times: Judas wants thirty. There is much discussion among the priests. The price must be considered a bargain because the negotiator is also rubbing his hands together in delight. The price is settled. A very sinister looking Judas rubs his chin, his eyes dart wildly, and he wrings his hands together, expressing both his pleasure and his greed. In a matter of seconds, however, Judas' emotions change from delight to uncertainty, then to confusion and, finally, guilt.

Identified by Jesus as his betrayer (Matt 26:25), Judas leaves the supper to lead the arresting party of temple guards and priests to the Mount of Olives. Jesus notices Judas and the group in the distance and, waking the sleeping disciples, instructs, "Rise let us be going: behold, he is at hand that doth betray me (Matt 26:46)." Judas greets Jesus with a kiss (Matt 26:49). There is no physical contact apart from Judas' lips on Jesus' cheek. The intertitle card reads, "Then Judas, which had betrayed him… repented…himself."

Judas runs to the chief priests and attempts to return the thirty pieces of silver. When they refuse, Judas tosses down the bag of coins, throws up his arms, and then falls to his knees sobbing. The priests laugh at Judas,

39. Olcott erroneously cites Mark 20:29 instead of Matt 20:29.

displaying their lack of interest and cold-heartedness. A visibly distraught Judas rises and with his hands holds his head, runs off, "and went and hanged himself" (Matt 27:5).

Judas is clearly the villain in *From the Manger to the Cross.* His unkempt black hair and beard, the heavy black eye-shadow and his black clothing add to his sinister appearance. Olcott singles out Judas as the one who complained of the price of the anointing oil when according to the Gospel text cited the complaint came from "the disciples." The intertitles include the word "betray" and its derivatives four times. This not only identifies Judas as the one who betrayed Jesus but underpins his role in the narrative and film.

## *Christus (1916)*

Director: Giulio Antamoro. Screenwriters: Giulio Antamoro and Ignazio Lupi. Country: Italy. Production Company: Societá Italiana Cines. Length: 105 minutes. Length of Last Supper scene: 3:09 minutes. Color: black and white. Filming locations: Egypt. Cast: Judas (Augusto Mastripietri), Jesus (Alberto Pasquali).

### *Lens One*

This Italian silent film follows a long tradition of visual narrative in Italy. The genre, which ultimately marked "the high-water mark in Italian production,"[40] was the historical or costume film. From 1907–1915, the average yearly output was 500 films. During this time, three great epic stories of faith were made: *Quo Vadis?*, *Spartacus* and *The Last Days of Pompeii*. One of the reasons for the success of the early Italian film industry was that it had Vatican support as Philip Strick reports:

> In 1897, Pope Leo XIII nodded graciously from his elegant horse-drawn carriage at one of the world's first motion picture cameras. It was a historic moment. Intrigued at the idea of this new method of communicating with devout audiences around the world, Pope Leo allowed himself to be persuaded to wave a benediction at the lens, mopping his venerable brow with the effort. The cinema, within months of it birth, had been granted its baptism.[41]

40. Peter Bondanella, *A History of Italian Cinema* (New York: Continuum, 2009), 5–6.

41. Strick, "*Greatest Stories*," 2050.

*Christus* is a pictorial dramatization of Fausto Salvadori's 1916 poem of the same name. The film has three distinct parts, "Annunciation and Nativity," "Life and Works" and "Death and Resurrection of Jesus Christ." Intertitles with explanatory passages show that the film includes accounts from all four Gospels. A *New York Times* (May 1, 1917) film reviewer notes that the number of intertitles detract from the film's artistic value but suggests that filmmakers "feared to trust the biblical knowledge of Manhattan audiences." Another distraction, albeit an attention-grabbing one, is that a number of the intertitles are in three languages: Italian for the original audience, Latin for the words of Jesus, and English for foreign markets.

Director Giulio Antamoro (1877–1945) is faithful to the Gospel texts in his intertitles but also includes non-biblical scenes and alters the chronology of Jesus' ministry. These differences include an adult Jesus returning to Egypt to preach his message, and his temptation in the wilderness (Mark 1:12–13) occurs after his teaching on the mount (Matt 5–7) and before his baptism (Mark 1:9–11). While previous Jesus films promoted the miracles of Jesus, Antamoro has only one: Jesus walking on water (Mark 6:45–52). However, the resurrection segment contains scenes not previously shown in Jesus films. These include "the light of the risen Christ in the maternal eyes" (non-biblical); Jesus' appearance to Mary Magdalene in the garden (John 20:11–17); "the gathering of the disciples in Peter's house," and Thomas' touching the side of the risen Christ (John 20:27–29). These additional scenes appear as testimonies verifying the resurrection of Jesus and encouraging audiences to join in with the disciples' declaration, "We have seen the Lord!" (John 20:25).

Early producers and artistic directors saw art and literature as "magical helpers in their quest for cinema's complex artistic legitimacy."[42] *Christus* is a gallery of artwork. Giulio Antamoro brings to life masterpieces, which include Fra Angelico's *The Annunciation*, Correggio's *The Nativity*, de Champaigne's *The Good Shepherd*, da Vinci's *The Last Supper*, Quarton's *Pietà of Villeneuve-lès-Avignon* and Raffael's *The Transfiguration*. Freeze-framing the images gives the audience time to make the connection and to marvel at the iconography.

Antamoro, following Olcott's lead, filmed *Christus* on location in Egypt. Brunetta explains: "[T]he use of open space gave life to a policy of virtual power. It could transmit energy and convey vitality to a static,

42. Gian Piero Brunetta, *The History of Italian Cinema: A Guide to Italian Film from Its Origins to the Twenty-first Century*, trans. Jeremy Parzen (Princeton: Princeton University Press, 2003), 32.

monumental, and repetitive conception of time. As the action space began to expand on the screen, so did the space in the theatre and in the audiences' imagination."[43]

The scenes of the entourage of the magi (Matt 2:1–12) are quite spectacular. Some two thousand extras dressed in authentic costumes, an unknown number of camels—provided by Lord Kitchener—and obligatory goats and sheep make their way across the Egyptian desert.[44] One marvels at how Antamoro was able to direct and position such a huge cast considering Cecil B. DeMille was the first director to use the megaphone a decade later. Communication would have been extremely difficult as the cast was multi-lingual.

*Lens Two*

The title card reads "Passover—The Last Supper—The Table Spread by Angels."

A long shot of the room shows a long rectangular table covered with a white cloth and utensils. The next frame is quite extraordinary. Although the intertitle states the table is set by angels, the twelve youthful girls dressed in long white robes look more like altar servers dressed in liturgical garments. However, as females were not permitted to serve at Roman Catholic altars until 1994, early audiences would have accepted them as being angels. The angels dissolve into the frame. They process ceremoniously towards the table, both from the front and back of the table. Some are holding aloft what looks like bread, and a chalice, while the remainder clasp their hands in prayer-like fashion. After placing all the items on the table, the angels cross their arms across their chests and process in single file, forming a cruciform shape: a single line in front of the table while others flank the table. Slowly turning to face the table and in synchronized fashion, the angels genuflect. With the angels still on their knees, Jesus (Alberto Pasquali) leads the dining party into the room and takes his place at the center of the table. The disciples process in a liturgical manner to their seats. Some have staffs and resemble bishops. When all are in their places, the angels rise from their knees and fade out of the shot.

The title card "The Last Supper of Leonardo da Vinci" announces the next scene followed by a freeze-frame showing the group replicating the Italian masterpiece. The overall plan of the supper room corresponds in all respects to da Vinci's fresco with drapes hanging on the side-walls, doorways in the background and a coffered ceiling all reinforcing the *tableau vivant* (living picture) impression.

43. Ibid., 33.

44. Campbell and Pitts, *The Bible on Film*, 93.

Another title card "speaks" for Jesus. "*Sumite, hoc est corpus meum. Mangiate, questo é il mio corps.* Eat, this is my body." Although the text corresponds closely to the biblical texts (Matt 26:26; Mark 14:22; Luke 22:19; 1 Cor 11:24), no citation is given. A mid-shot shows John, Jesus, Peter (standing) and another disciple at the table. Jesus breaks off a piece of bread and gives it to Peter. Jesus places his hand on Peter's head. Although nothing is said, the action implies a blessing. Peter proceeds to eat the bread as though he is gnawing at a bone. Judas (Augusto Mastripietri) enters into the frame from the left and stands behind Jesus. Again, Jesus breaks off some bread and hands it to Judas. Reluctantly Judas receives the bread and in a sinister fashion slides the bread into his cloak. Judas cowers to avoid Jesus' blessing. The outstretched arm and look on Jesus' face express his sadness at his disciple's rejection. Returning to the long shot, Jesus pours wine from a large metal ewer into an ornate silver chalice. An intertitle informs, "*Hic est sanguis meus. Questo é il mio sanguine.* This is my blood."

The next scene is a long shot of the table and room. Judas is seated at the table and appears to be eating the bread. Jesus raises his hands in an *orans* posture (praying hands extended) and then takes the chalice in both hands. Standing up, Jesus raises his head heavenward and elevates the chalice. A large white dove (a symbol of the Holy Spirit) hovers above the chalice. Although slight movement is detected among those gathered, the dove miraculously remains stationary. A mid-shot is used to draw attention to the expressions on the faces of John, Jesus and Peter, who are gazing up at the chalice. A white light from above bathes Jesus. The camera changes to a long shot of the table to include the group and the dove. While the others are engrossed in what is happening, a barely visible (poor lighting) Judas sneaks out of the room. The scene ends.

*Lens Three*

Italy experienced an industrial boom between 1896 and 1915. Northern Italy in particular was the beneficiary, raising the living standards of many ordinary Italians, while southern Italy remained rural, poor, and backward. In 1912, Italy expanded their colonial territories by conquering Libya. When the First World War began in 1914, Italy took a neutral stance, but was persuaded by Britain and France to join the Allied cause by offering Italy territory from Austria-Hungary. Italy declared war on Austria on 26 April 1915.

During the making of *Christus*, Italy was entrenched in the war. Films became a depository of Italy's national identity, its history and memory, while the cinema "served as an ambassador of its culture and creativity."[45]

45. Brunetta, preface in *History of Italian Cinema*, ix.

*The Portrayal of Judas*

Figure 2. Satan goads Judas. © Societa Italiana Cines.

The title card, "The Hatred of Judas who now sought the opportunity to betray him [Jesus]" introduces Judas to the audience. Jesus has just made his triumphant entry into Jerusalem with Judas watching the event from a side street. His costume suggests that he is a man of wealth. The satin turban and wide cummerbund, from which a moneybag hangs, are studded with gems. Judas appears to be aged thirty, of ruddy complexion, with a prominent nose, thick dark hair and full beard; heavy black eye-shadow circles his eyes. The voluminous black overcoat adds to his sinister appearance. He is holding a staff.

Continuing with the image of the disciples resembling bishops, their staffs symbolize their traditional role of shepherding the faithful. So when Judas, filled with hatred and anger—the audience is not privy to reasons for these emotions—breaks his staff over his knee he is symbolically severing his allegiance to Jesus and the Church. Judas throws the two pieces to the ground and is shocked to see that the pieces land in a cruciform. He deliberately stamps on the pieces to destroy the image. With arms crossed and shoulders slouched, Judas glares defiantly at the camera.

After the Last Supper and in the dark of the night, "Judas goes to the Sanhedrin." As he comes to the door of Caiaphas' house, Judas turns and looks directly at the camera. This is so that the audience can identify him. Judas pushes his way through the throng of priests to tell Caiaphas how the betrayal will take place: "Whosoever I shall kiss, that same is he." Receiving the coins and carefully counting them, Judas places them in his moneybag, and leaves. Outside, an apparition confronts Judas: it is Satan goading him on. Judas reaches into his purse and pulls out a handful of coins. While he looks at the coins, they turn into droplets of blood, presenting a unique pictorial representation of the metaphoric "blood money." Regaining his senses, Judas returns the coins to the bag, turns, and steals off into the night. It is highly significant that Satan appears *after* Judas' agreement with Caiaphas. This suggests that Judas' actions are self-motivated and not because "Satan entered into him" as the Gospel according to John records (John 13:27a).

Judas is next seen leading a member of the Sanhedrin and a cohort of Roman guards to Gethsemane. The intertitle states, "Said the man, who betrayed him, 'Hail, Master'." Judas kisses Jesus on the cheek, quickly turns, and rushes to a nearby tree, making room for Peter to cut off a guard's ear. Jesus' healing of the guard and the warning, "They that take the sword shall perish by the sword" (Matt 26:52) stun Judas. Jesus breaks the sword in two. This action is unique to Jesus films and suggests that Antamoro might have included this as an anti-war statement. Prior to the war Italy was a member of the Triple Alliance along with Germany and Austria-Hungary. It was not until 26 April 1915 that Italy entered the war but on the side of the Triple Entente—Britain, France and Russia. The reason for Italy's changing sides was Britain's offer of large sections of territory in the Adriatic Sea region. Italy's action parallels those of Judas' betrayal. Jesus' show of strength frightens Judas. The guards lead the bound Jesus away, followed by only one disciple, Judas, who seeks anonymity at the back of the mob.

Judas makes an unforeseen and non-biblical appearance at "The Flagellation." He stands in front of those gathered around the whipping pillar. Again, this is to make Judas' presence visible. Upon seeing Jesus, he turns to flee but two guards seize him and push him closer to the one he betrayed. Pointing towards Jesus, the guards seem to be saying, "Look at what you have done." Judas reels back in horror, only to be pushed towards Jesus. Judas falls to his knees. A guard bends down to question Judas. He responds by kissing the guard on his cheek. By this action, Judas admits to what he has done and accepts the blame for Jesus being flogged at the whipping pillar. Pushed aside by an angry guard, Judas fights his way through the crowd who have turned their fury away from Jesus and toward Judas.

Filled with regret and guilt "Judas returns the Sanhedrin's blood money." The Sanhedrin responds by mocking Judas and having him thrown out onto the street. Satan appears for the second time tempting Judas to join him. Confusion traps Judas. Seeing the blood still on his hands fills him with terror and he flees to escape Satan's goading.

The next intertitle informs the audience of Judas' fate: "Judas goes to a desolate death." Chased by Satan, Judas makes his way to a wooded area and finds a large tree. He frantically removes his turban and overcoat and throws a long rope over a branch. Judas hangs himself while Satan waits for him to enter "into the darkness, where there will be weeping and gnashing of teeth" (Luke 13:28).

Antamoro re-kindles anti-Semitic myths in his interpretation of the Judas character. Judas clearly represents the Jewish race and their rejection of Jesus as the Messiah. A number of Judas' actions express a theology of rejection. His stamping on the cruciform-shaped broken staff represents the Jews rejection of Christianity. His deliberate hiding of the bread in his cloak at the Last Supper brings to mind the thirteenth-century host desecration incident where a Christian retained a host from mass and took it to a synagogue where the Jews "subjected it to every indignity."[46] His shying away and refusal of Jesus' blessing at the Supper suggests that Judaism did not recognize the divinity of Jesus and considered his claim of messiah to be anathema. The three interactions between Satan and Judas reinforce the Middle Ages *foetor judaicus* myth that Jews were in collusion with the devil.[47] Finally, the crowd turning their fury away from Jesus and towards Judas symbolizes global anti-Semitism.

### *Blade af Satans Bog (1921) (Leaves from Satan's Book)*

Director: Carl Theodor Dreyer. Screenwriter: Edgar Høyer and Marie Corelli. Country: Denmark. Production Company: Nordisk Films Kompagni. Length: 151 minutes. Length of Last Supper scene: 4:14 minutes. Color: black and white. Filming locations: Unknown. Cast: Judas (Jacob Texiere), Jesus (Halvard Hoff).

#### *Lens One*

It is not widely known that Denmark was an early pioneer in the film industry. It reached its peak in World War 1, only to fade slowly away in the 1920s.[48] Carl Theodor Dreyer (1889–1968), considered to be the greatest figure in the Danish cinema, had a cinematic career spanning almost

46. Nicholls, *Christian Antisemitism*, 239–40.

47. "The Jew showed his association with the devil in part by the *foetor judaicus*, the Jewish stink, the sulphurous smell of the devil himself." Ibid., 241.

48. Peter Cowie, "Silents of the North," *The Movie: The Illustrated History of the Cinema* 112 (1982): 2242.

six decades.[49] He made nine films in the last decade of the Silents. The story of Dreyer's second film, *Blade af Satans Bog*, is allegedly based on Marie Corelli's 1895 novel *The Sorrows of Satan*, although Morten Egholm claims it is a fairly loyal adaptation of an original screenplay by the successful Danish playwright Edgard Høyer. Inspired by the thematic structure of D. W. Griffith's 1916 epic film, *Intolerance*, Dreyer presents four historical episodes where Satan, a tragic figure in the style of John Milton's *Paradise Lost*, condemned to earth by God, must fail in his tempting of men to do evil in order to be delivered from God's curse. The first episode is the story of Judas' betrayal of Jesus.

For artistic inspiration, Dreyer referred to late Renaissance artwork. *The Last Supper* paintings by Jacapo Bassano, Juan de Juanes and Andre del Sarto provided suggestions for the film's settings and costumes. For the narrative Dreyer draws on all four Gospels but most notably John's Gospel which is the impetus for the episode: "The devil had already put it into the heart of Judas son of Simon Iscariot to betray [Jesus]" (John 13:3). Intertitles without Gospel citations relate the story.

Although Dreyer borrowed ideas for the plot, characterization and settings, his filming technique is both creative and unique. In particular, to create a sense of concentrated expression, Dreyer incorporates a series of distinctive experimental techniques and stylistic devices. These include the singular focus close-ups and application of austere *kammerspiel* film elements.[50] The shot used to achieve this is a vignette effect, where the camera aperture or a masque is used to put a black round or square shadow around the face as a way of calling attention to it. Dreyer frequently uses this type of shot in the film.

*Lens Two*

The Last Supper appears in the first of the four sections and encompasses three scenes: "The Festival of the Unleavened Bread," "The Last Supper," and "The Hymn." The Supper is interspersed with clandestine meetings between Judas (Jacob Texiere) and Satan (Helge Nissen) who is in the guise of a Pharisee. He plays the part convincingly even to the point of kissing the *mezuzah* on the door lintel before he enters the high priest's house. By pretending to be a Pharisee and by hiding his real identity, Satan is able to deceive both Judas and the Sanhedrin and to persuade them to be a part of his plan to arrest Jesus (Halvard Hoff).

49. Jack Lodge, "Carl Theodor Dreyer," *The Movie: The Illustrated History of the Cinema* 113 (1982): 2252.

50. *Kammerspiel* is categorized by its focus on character psychology, lack of intricate set design and its frequent depiction of the working class.

Figure 3. Jesus hands Judas the bread. © Image Entertainment.

The intertitle sets the scene: "And when the hour had come, He sat down to eat, and the disciples with Him." The scene shows the group sitting at the table and within the group, Jesus and the disciples are engaged in conversation, with the exception of Judas who is seated at the left end of the table. He is side-on to the camera, facing towards Jesus, slumped over as though he is bearing the weight of the world on his shoulders. Judas is staring vacantly—deep in thought.

The narrative continues: "And when they were eating, He said: 'Verily I say unto you—one of you will betray me.'" A mid-shot of Jesus uses a vigneted effect. He is facing towards the direction of Judas. Jesus slowly turns his head in the opposite direction and when facing the front, he lifts both his arms and begins to pray. He raises his head, closes his eyes and has an ecstatic look on his face. Four elderly and bearded disciples look intently at Jesus. One of them questions Jesus, "Master, is it I?" followed by a crosscut to a sorrowful looking Jesus, slowly shaking his head implying "No." Jesus places one hand on his chest signifying that he is heavy-hearted while he places his other hand on the table. In front of his hand is a large knife pointing in the direction of Judas. Drawing closer to Jesus, the disciple John asks the same question, and again Jesus shakes his head. Jesus turns and looks towards Judas. A close shot of Judas' hands shows him pre-occupied, nervously crumbling the matzot between his fingers.

Jesus leans forward and appears to be calling Judas by name. Judas slowly raises his head and looks at Jesus. At the opposite end of the table, three disciples stand and stare accusingly at Judas. Jesus breaks off a piece of matzot, dips it in the large metal chalice, and looking towards Judas, moves to pass the bread to him. The intertitle informs, "And he brake the bread dipped it and gave it to Judas, saying: 'That thou doest, do quickly!'" Without looking up, Judas edges his way to Jesus and avoiding eye contact with him, Judas takes the matzot. The disciples watch Judas' every move: some are even standing to gain a better view. Judas does not eat the matzot but places it on the table. Slowly he rises and turns to face the camera. With head lowered, shoulders drooped, Judas slowly and laboriously steps away from the table and moves towards the door. A mid-shot of John and Jesus shows Jesus looking straight ahead while John keeps his eyes on Judas. John turns to Jesus and pointing to Judas asks, "Is he the betrayer?" Jesus with down cast eyes nods, "Yes."

The next scene, shot from a camera point-of-view, highlights the subject's perspective. Judas opens the door and steps into the night. The blue tint conveys the illusion of darkness. The disciples are craning their necks to see where Judas is going. Without looking behind him, Judas quietly closes the door, slips on his sandals that are near the door, and makes his way down the stone-steps.

Four crosscuts follow showing Satan waiting for Judas and Judas walking to the assigned meeting place. The scene returns to the Supper. John and Jesus sit while the others stand and look toward Jesus. Dreyer freezes the frame to allow the audience time to make the connection between what they see and a section of da Vinci's *The Last Supper*. Jesus takes the chalice and places his right hand over it, then raises both his head and his hand and gives thanks (Matt 26:27).

A further four crosscuts show Satan and Judas arriving at the rendezvous point. The panning shot shows Jesus and the remaining eleven disciples ending their last supper together by standing and singing "The Hymn" (Matt 26:30). Of all the Last Supper scenes analyzed, *Blade af Satans Bog* is the only film to include the hymn. Although hymn singing is an integral part of Christian liturgy, perhaps directors thought singing might detract from the somber moment prior to leaving for the Garden of Gethsemane. However, Dreyer could include the hymn in *Blade af Satans Bog* because it is a silent film. Daniel Harrington notes that the Passover meal traditionally concluded with Pss 113–118, "the so-called great *Hallel* (Praise), which proclaim God's power to redeem and his faithfulness in leading Israel to freedom."[51] However, there is nothing to suggest that the hymn being sung is a psalm.

51. Daniel J. Harrington, ed., *The Gospel of Matthew*, Sacra Pagina 1 (Collegeville: Liturgical Press, 1991), 368.

*Lens Three*

Europe was still recovering from the First World War when *Blade af Satans Bog* was produced. Germany had huge reparation debts that could not be paid due to the collapse of the German mark. Russia was in a similar economically precarious situation. The Fascists, under Benito Mussolini, seized control of Rome and formed a new government. Pope Benedict XV died and the College of Cardinals elected Pope Pius XI (Achille Ratti) as his successor. It was an era when Europe lacked political, economic and religious stability.

Reactions to the film were heated with criticisms from two widely different fronts: conservative Christians and the labor movement. Censures included the inappropriateness of presenting Jesus as a "profane actor" and that the film "bordered on blasphemy."[52] A critic from the Christian daily *Kristelig Dagblad* condemned the film: "We have but one word to describe this show. We call it 'revolting'."[53] No explanation was given. The labor newspapers *Solidaritet* and *Arbejdet* reviewed *Blade af Satans Bog* under the respective headlines of "A Brazen Agitation Film" and "Danish Upper-Class Propaganda." Both papers note the film's portrayal of workers and revolution, claiming that during both the French and the Finnish Revolutions, Satan is on the side of the Reds. In both these periods, "the Reds are furnished with the foulest possible and criminal attributes, while the Whites conversely are represented in such a way that they inevitably compel sympathy from the viewer who is unable to reflect on the matters himself."[54] These comments exemplify passive reception and the way film is received or interpreted differently by viewers.

Processing or challenging images can provide viewers with various connotations. Take for example the image of Jesus placing his hand near the knife on the table. The knife could be seen as simply a utensil to carve the lamb that is also on the table. However, when one notices that the blade of the knife is pointing towards Judas, it takes on a different meaning: Judas is about to stab Jesus in the back. Of course, the viewer

52. Jes Nysten, "An Unrealized Lifelong Dream—Dreyer's Jesus Film," *Carl Th. Dreyer—The Man and His Work*. Danish Film Institute. http://english.carlthdreyer.dk/AboutDreyer/Themes/An-Unrealized-Lifelong-Dream.aspx.

53. Lisbeth Richter Larsen, "Shoot," *Carl Th. Dreyer—The Man and His Work*, Danish Film Institute. http://english.carlthdreyer.dk/Films/La-Passion-de-Jeanne-dArc/Shoot.aspx.

54. A. D. Henriksen, review of "Blade af Satans Bog," in *Arbedjet*, cited by Lisbeth Richter Larsen, "Reception," *Carl Th. Dreyer—The Man and His Works*. http://english.carlthdreyer.dk/Films/Blade-af-Satans-Bog/Reception.aspx.

would need to be aware of Judas' pending betrayal of Jesus in Gethsemane to be able to make that connection. Could Dreyer's inclusion of the knife pointing towards Judas be representative of betrayal?

A possible answer is the *Dolchstoßlegende* (Dagger-Stab-In-The-Back) legend that circulated after the First World War.[55] The legend claims that socialists, communists, Jews and Catholics had not supported the war and had played a role in "selling out" Germany to its enemies. The loss of the war was blamed on these minority groups. However, it is unlikely that Dreyer intended to endorse the legend. He zealously fought against anti-Semitism even to the point of directing *Die Gezeichneten* (Love One Another), a 1922 film depicting Russian persecution of the Jews.

Dreyer's inclusion of the close-up of the knife on the table remains a mystery. It is made even more enigmatic when one takes into consideration a similar shot of a knife on a table in Marie Antoinette's cell in the French Revolution episode of *Blade af Satans Bog.*

*The Portrayal of Judas*

Although the first section of *Blade af Satans Bog* is entitled "The Last Days of Jesus" and includes recognizable Gospel episodes such as the anointing, preparation for the Passover meal, the Last Supper and betrayal, the Judas character is significantly different to previous filmic portrayals.

Jesus and the disciples are "Guests in the home of Simon, the leper." Jesus is speaking while the others listen. A nameless woman of the household comes forward and anoints Jesus' head and feet. Judas, middle-aged, clean-shaven, with a very high receding hairline, is concerned, and asks Jesus, "Why was this ointment not sold for three hundred pence, and the money given to the poor?" Jesus' response offends Judas. "Let her alone. For the poor ye have always with you, but me ye have not always." Judas stands up, walks across and in front of the group, and leaves the room.

The scene changes to Judas sitting on a low stone wall outside on the street. It is apparent that Judas is disillusioned, disappointed and despondent. Feigning concern for the troubled Judas, Satan stops to talk to him. Satan asks, "Why do you believe in Him? God's son is what He calls himself—the devil's son is what He is, and you have been snared by the power of the devil." Judas is agitated and rises to leave. Satan grabs his arm and continues, "We shall meet tomorrow at noon-tide outside the Golden Gate." It is significant that Dreyer chose the Golden Gate as their

55. William Carr, *A History of Germany 1815–1985*, 3rd ed. (London: Arnold, 1987), 263–64, 323.

rendezvous point. This gate faces the Mount of Olives on the eastern side of the Old City. According to Jewish tradition, the Messiah will enter Jerusalem through this gate. In order to prevent this, the gate was sealed by Muslims during the rule of Suleiman (1520–1566). Satan's words, "I know you will come" could be interpreted as confirmation that the Messiah will indeed come. Disgusted by Satan's demands, Judas pulls his arm free of Satan's grip.

During the Last Supper we see Judas, despite being troubled by inner thoughts, willingly take the piece of dipped bread from Jesus and passively respond to his directive, "That thou doest, do quickly!"

Judas' final appearance is at Gethsemane where a cohort of Roman soldiers meets him and Satan. "How am I to know Jesus?" asks the Roman leader. Satan thinks. Then with a smirk on his lips, glances at Judas and declares, "The kiss of friendship shall be the sign." Judas is horrified. Walking further into the woods, Satan and Judas stop. Satan places his right hand on Judas' shoulder as a gesture of encouragement and points forward. Judas' look is incredulous: it is as though he has no control over his actions.

Having told his disciples to stay put, Jesus walks out into a clearing to meet the soldiers. When Jesus extends his arm, the soldiers mysteriously reel back in fear (John 18:6). The leader orders Judas to identify Jesus. A compliant Judas nods, moves towards Jesus, and kisses him on the cheek. Jesus responds, "Judas, betrayest thou the Son of Man with a kiss?" Judas, filled with shame, covers his face with his arm and departs the scene. There is no melee: the bound Jesus is willingly led away.

Judas stops further into the woods. Satan walks up behind him and again places his hand on Judas' shoulder startling him. Satan nods his approval and hands Judas a leather purse. Curious of its contents, Judas undoes the drawstring, puts in his hand and draws out a fistful of coins. Judas is disgusted. He throws the coins to the ground and, overwhelmed with sorrow, drops to his knees and sobs. The first section of *Blade af Satans Bog* ends with a cut back to Satan and "the Lord's command, 'Continue thy evil doings'."

Dreyer's portrayal of Judas is distinct in that unlike the Gospel accounts, there is nothing to indicate that Judas is a thief or even the group's treasurer. Judas makes no contact or bargain with the Jewish religious authorities. Satan, who is disguised as a Pharisee, initiates the events and is the liaison between the Jewish authorities and Judas. This disguise sub-consciously links Satan with Jewishness for the viewer. Satan does not tempt Judas but rather he manipulates him. Judas has integrity and shows that he is repulsed by Satan's payment for identifying Jesus with "the kiss of friendship." Judas' remorse is not because he betrayed Jesus but because Judas was chosen by God "to deliver the Son of God into the hands of human tormentors."

Dreyer has created a Judas character who is representative of humanity. He suffers from indecisiveness, struggles with decision-making, seeks approval and acceptance, succumbs to temptation, and baulks at his lot in life. Judas is not in control of his life or his destiny. He does not claim responsibility for his actions: he blames God for his wretchedness.

### *The King of Kings (1927)*

Director: Cecil B. DeMille. Screenwriter: Jeanie Macpherson. Country: USA. Production Company: DeMille Pictures Corporation. Length: 155 minutes (premiere version); 112 minutes (alternate version). Length of Last Supper scene: 11:39 minutes. Color: black and white. Filming locations: California. Cast: Judas (Joseph Schildkraut), Jesus (H. B. Warner).

*Lens One*

Cecil B. DeMille, in 1925, explained to financier Jeremiah Milbank his "impossible dream." He elaborates, "I wanted to make a film on the life of Christ. I wanted simply to take the four Gospels and tell the story of Jesus of Nazareth as He appeared to those around Him, a figure no less human than divine, to tell that story in a way that might bring millions of people throughout the world to know Him better, might bring many to know Him for the first time."[56]

Cecil B. DeMille achieved this aim of bringing to the screen the Jesus story with *The King of Kings*. He also established "the style of the reverent epic."[57] Like other directors before him, DeMille does not draw on a single Gospel but "creates a homogenized Gospel, blending passages, stories, and themes."[58] His reverence for the Bible is such that when Jesus speaks, DeMille adheres strictly to the scriptural text. However, for the sake of story-telling and character development, he creatively paraphrases those passages spoken by other characters. Bill Jenkins claims DeMille's radical revision was carried out for at least two compelling reasons: "to make money and to make the narrative about Jesus work on the screen."[59]

56. Cecil B. DeMille, *The Autobiography of Cecil B. DeMille*, ed. Donald Hayne (Englewood Cliffs: Prentice-Hall, 1959), 267.

57. Walsh, *Reading the Gospels*, 2.

58. Stern, *Savior*, 36.

59. Bill Jenkins, "Jesus Christ Superstar? Why the Gospels Don't Make Good Movies," *JRF* 12, no. 2 (2008), http://www.unomaha.edu/jrf/vol12no2/Jenkins_Passion.htm.

DeMille sought advice from a variety of religious sources, including Protestant and Catholic clergy, as well as Jewish consultants. According to Felicia Herman, this was "to infuse his film with religious legitimacy."[60] DeMille also uses two characters to verify Gospel authorship. An early title describes, "Young Mark…healed by the great physician, and destined to become one of the FOUR to write the immortal Gospels." Later during the Last Supper, we see Matthew writing in a notebook and again at Gethsemane. How Matthew would be able to write in the dark apparently was not considered problematic! DeMille implies that the Gospels of Matthew and Mark were eyewitness accounts. Babington and Evans explain:

> This emotionally unwritten transmission is extremely significant in its reassurance at a time when the ravages of "Higher," "Form" and "Tendency" criticism were breaking down the transparent integrity of the Gospels into the impersonality of traditions and sources about which it was becoming difficult to hold ideas of absolutely certain derivation.[61]

DeMille also looked to religious art for inspiration. Cameraman Peverall Marley studied three hundred biblical paintings by the European masters with two hundred and sixty-seven of them making it into the film.[62] While Renaissance paintings are indeed apparent, the most significant influence is Victorian art.

*Lens Two*

The Last Supper scene begins with the intertitle "Now when Jesus knew that His hour was come, desiring to eat Passover with His Disciples—He sat down, at eventide, for the Last Supper." No biblical reference is given because the intertitle is not a direct scriptural quotation.

The scene opens with a dissolve revealing Jesus (H. B. Warner) and the twelve disciples seated on stools around a rectangular shaped wooden table. Though the entire group fits into the frame, the scene is not crowded but suggests intimacy. The large arched-wall behind the group achieves this and appears to embrace the group. The long shot shows the depth of the room and includes the stone floor in front of the table and another open

60. Felicia Herman, "The Most Dangerous Anti-Semitic Photoplay in Filmdom: American Jews and *The King of Kings* (DeMille, 1927)," *VLT* 4 (2000): 15; DeMille, *Autobiography*, 279.

61. Babington and Evans, *Biblical Epics*, 118.

62. Jon Solomon, *The Ancient World in the Cinema*, rev. and expanded ed. (New Haven: Yale University Press, 2001), 182.

space beyond the arch. The table is set with cups, a cup that looks like a chalice, a jug and bread. There is no evidence of burning lamps and yet Jesus is bathed in white light. This promotes his divinity.

Figure 4. An attentive John looks up at Jesus, while a disinterested Judas looks down at the table. © The Criterion Collection.

Jesus sits between John (Joseph Striker) and Judas (Joseph Schildkraut). John and Jesus are in deep conversation while Judas is seated, staring forward. His chin is resting in his hands and he appears bored. The other disciples are looking at Jesus who turns his head as if signaling the start of the meal. A disciple sitting in front of the table lifts a jug and fills the cups of those near him. Jesus stands and takes the matzot in both his hands. Judas raises his head and looks at what Jesus is doing. Jesus lowers the bread and raises his eyes heavenward. He breaks the matzot and passing half to John and half to Judas, says, "Take, eat—this is My body which is given for you. This do in remembrance of Me. Luke 22:19." John breaks his gaze and looks down at Jesus' hand with the bread. In contrast, Judas looks up at Jesus and then looks suspiciously at the bread. John receives the bread in both hands while Judas casually takes the bread in his fingers, snaps off a piece and without lifting his elbows off the table passes the remainder to the disciple next to him. John's actions are opposite to those of Judas. John carefully breaks off a piece and with deliberate intent passes the remainder of the bread to the disciple next to him. Jesus, still bathed in white light and with hands clasped, looks prayerfully toward heaven.

Judas considers what to do with the bread: should he eat it or not? Covering his mouth with both hands, Judas pretends to eat the bread but lets the piece drop behind his fingers. With eyes darting left and right checking that his deception went unobserved, Judas returns to resting his chin on his hands. John has yet to consume the bread: he is still looking adoringly at it. Peter raises the bread with both hands to his lips and gazes in wonderment at Jesus. Peter places the bread in his mouth, clasps his hands together, and with eyes closed, he prays. Judas passively watches the others receive the bread.

The mood of Judas changes when he notices Jesus elevating the chalice of wine and hears his words, "This is My blood of the new testament which is shed for many unto the remission of sins. Drink ye all of it! Matt 26:27–28." Jesus passes the chalice to John while Judas, looking straight ahead, appears to be nervously biting his nails. As John looks up to Jesus, Judas looks down at his own hands. The contrasting actions between John and Judas suggest that John has his eyes on that which is good while Judas has his eyes on evil. Peter reverently receives the chalice ensuring not to spill a drop, and, looking at Jesus, takes a sip and then presses the chalice to his heart. The chalice continues to be passed around. When it comes nearer to Judas, a look of panic comes over him and his hand clutches his throat. The intertitle informs the group (and the audience), "Little children, yet a little while I am with you. A new commandment I give unto you—that ye love one another, as I have loved you. John 13:33–34." This timely insertion heightens the tension. Can Judas willingly drink from the chalice knowing that he has broken this new commandment because he has already betrayed Jesus? Or, will Judas drink from the chalice to show his contempt for this new commandment?

Judas' facial expression is now one of contempt. By Judas' summation, Jesus had let him and the revolutionary cause down. Deep in thought, Judas does not notice the chalice held out to him but a disciple draws his attention to it. Judas takes the cup in his right hand but he hesitates putting it to his lips. Looking to see if anyone is watching him, he quickly places the cup in front of him and with eyes wide with panic continues to stare at it. Jesus continues, "Behold the hand of him that betrayeth Me is with Me on the table! Luke 22:21." Judas immediately releases his grip on the chalice. The others check to see where their hands are. John has a smug look: his hands are folded across his chest. Peter quickly lifts his hands from the table and tucks them in his waistband. Disagreement erupts as to who has their hands on the table. A wily Judas rises from the table and with open hand on his chest gestures, "Surely you don't mean me, Jesus?" When Jesus turns and stares at him, Judas' composure is unsettled. Even more so when Jesus says to him, "That which thou doest—do quickly! John 13:27."

Judas is rendered speechless and after lengthy eye contact with Jesus, he backs away from the table. His departure goes unnoticed because the disciples are still anxious to know, "Lord, is it I? Is it? Matt 26:22." Judas slinks out the door, making what he thinks is a clean retreat only to turn and find Mary (Dorothy Cumming,) the mother of Jesus, sitting near the doorway. Judas stops abruptly. Shocked at seeing Mary, he tries to avert her stare by pulling his cloak across his face and hurries down the steps. Meanwhile back inside the room Peter is stating emphatically, "Lord, I am ready to go with Thee—both into prison, and to death! Luke 22:33." Peter is mortified when Jesus tells him, "The cock shall not crow this day, before thou shalt THRICE deny that thou knowest Me! Luke 22:34."

The bickering ends when Jesus raises his hands and remorse overcomes the disciples. To placate them Jesus says, "My peace I give unto you. In the world ye shall have tribulation, but be of good cheer, I have overcome the world. John 16:33." Jesus points to the door and the disciples prepare to leave. Jesus leads the way. Peter, brandishing a large sword, is the last to leave the room. He hesitates, turns towards the chalice, places his hand over it, and overcome with emotion he hugs his sword—implying that he will defend Jesus—and then departs. The room darkens but a white aura surrounds the chalice. A white dove flies in through an open window and settles at the base of the chalice. The room fades to black leaving only the chalice and dove visible. The Supper has ended.

*Lens Three*

*The King of Kings* was released in an era of great social change. Douglas Linder summarizes American society in the 1920s:

> The early 1920s found social patterns in chaos. Traditionalists, the older Victorians, worried that everything valuable was ending. Younger modernists no longer asked whether society would approve of their behavior, only whether their behavior met the approval of their intellect. Intellectual experimentation flourished. Americans danced to the sound of the Jazz Age, showed their contempt for alcoholic prohibition, debated abstract art and Freudian theories. In a response to the new social patterns set in motion by modernism, a wave of revivalism developed.[63]

The 1920s also saw the reprise of the Ku Klux Klan; increasing numbers of World War I immigrants; hysteria fueled by the Red Scare;

63. Douglas O. Linder, "State v. John Scopes ('The Monkey Trial')." Speech on the 75th anniversary of the Scopes Trial, July 10, 2000. http://law2.umkc.edu/faculty/projects/ftrials/scopes/scopes.htm.

and the debate of "creation versus evolution" was famously put on trial. Anti-Semitism and the identification of Jews as 'Christ killers' intensified.

Paul's claim that the Jews, "who killed both the Lord Jesus and the prophets" (1 Thess 2:14–15) and affirmed repeatedly by Augustine of Hippo (354–430), became the core of anti-Semitic vitriol.[64] DeMille was cautious in not portraying Jews as "Christ killers." Instead, he placed the blame solely on the high priest, Caiaphas. Standing at the foot of the cross, Caiaphas declares, "Lord, God, Jehovah, vent not thy wrath on thy mighty people Israel. I alone am guilty." DeMille's liberal interpretation shifted a generalized racial blame to one person.

Prior to public release, DeMille made some significant changes to and eliminations from the film. An introductory title was added, numerous modifications were made to the Pilate scene, intertitles were added that placed sole responsibility for the crucifixion onto Caiaphas and there was "considerable toning down of details in the scourging and crucifixion scenes."[65] Even with these changes the Jewish service organization, the B'Nai Brith (Sons of the Covenant) protested and urged its members not to see the film because it "treated historic Jewish authorities with hatred and contempt."[66] Caiaphas' character, played by Rudolph Schildkraut (father of Joseph/Judas), himself a Jew, is the archetypical medieval caricature of the avaricious Jew. He is the principal antagonist in this Jesus story and represents all that is evil about the rigidity of first-century Judaism as described in the later church. Significantly, the release of *The King of Kings* not only changed the way the B'Nai Brith would relate to Hollywood and film content, but it also changed their influence on society.[67]

Films provided an escape from the difficulties of the era. By 1926, the United States had 20,000 theatres and weekly attendances of 100 million. In attempting to estimate the number of viewers since the film's opening in 1927 to the year of his autobiography, 1959, DeMille calculated "that probably more people have been told the story of Jesus of Nazareth through *The King of Kings* than through any other single work, except the Bible itself."[68] The same can be said about the story of Judas Iscariot.

64. Jeremy Cohen, *Christ Killers: The Jews and the Passion from the Bible to the Big Screen* (Oxford: Oxford University Press, 2007), 75–76.

65. Richard Maltby, "*The King of Kings* and the Czar of All the Rushes: The Propriety of the Christ Story," in *Controlling Hollywood: Censorship and Regulation in the Studio Era*, ed. Matthew Bernstein (London: Athlone, 2000), 81.

66. Charles Higham, *Cecil B. DeMille* (New York: Da Capo, 1973), 180.

67. Herman, "Most Dangerous Anti-Semitic Photoplay," 2.

68. DeMille, *Autobiography*, 281–82.

*The Portrayal of Judas*

Stern, Jefford and Debona note that DeMille is not concerned with the historical Jesus as presented in the Gospels but "for the life of Jesus as it has become synthesized into the faith memory of the modern believing Christian."[69] The same cannot be said about DeMille's visual rendering of the Judas figure. Judas as presented by DeMille is "safely outside Christian orthodoxy."[70]

DeMille opens the film with Mary Magdalene (Jacqueline Logan), a "spectacularly draped whore"[71] who is concerned that her favorite client, Judas Iscariot, has left her to follow Jesus of Nazareth. DeMille included the love relationship, inspired by a little known German legend of the Middle Ages, because he was not completely convinced that thirty pieces of silver was Judas' only motivation for betrayal. However, the imagined affair was edited out before the film's final release—"for considerations of length, not accuracy, or taste."[72] The intertitle introduces him as "Judas Iscariot, the Ambitious, who joined the Disciples in the belief that Jesus would be the Nation's King, and reward him with honor and high office."

Judas is so different to the other disciples that he is easily identified and singled out. He is young, suave and sophisticated, extremely handsome, clean-shaven with neatly groomed hair. His clothes when compared with those of the group could be described as "designer labels." Judas also likes jewelry. He wears a large gold signet ring on the third finger of his right hand. Wrapped around his right wrist is a five-stranded gold-beaded bangle. Judas looks the part of a rich young man—one who could afford the company and services of a high-class courtesan such as Mary Magdalene. The traditional image of Judas has become a "foppish blue-blood, rising politico."[73]

Judas expresses embarrassment and uneasiness when Mary Magdalene comes to the house looking for the "vagabond carpenter." This disquiet could also be his fear of Mary exposing their love tryst to Jesus. Judas is full of self-importance and confidence when he attempts to cure a boy of epilepsy (Matt 17:16). His failure to do so prompts him to ask Jesus, "Master, why could not I cast out the devil? Matt 17:19." Jesus replies, "Because of your unbelief. Matt 17:20": a simple statement but a powerful

69. Stern, *Savior*, 36.

70. Walsh, *Reading the Gospels*, 35.

71. Gordon Thomas, review of *The King of Kings*, "A Tale of Two *Kings*," *BLFJ* 51 (February 2006). http://brightlightsfilm.com/51/51king.php.

72. Solomon, *Ancient World*, 183.

73. Peter Matts, "Showman of Piety," *The King of Kings*, DVD booklet, 9.

condemnation of Judas' character. When Peter asks Judas for a coin to pay taxes to Caesar, Judas shows his empty purse. This identifies Judas' role as keeper of the common purse and that he either stole from it (John 12:6–7), or mismanaged the group's finances.

Both Peter and Judas open the gates to the Temple so that the jubilant crowd, shouting "Hosanna in the highest," can enter. Judas is ecstatic. Using a pot's lid—that conveniently looks like a crown—Judas holds it high and shouts, "He is our King. Let us crown him!" Jesus miraculously disappears from the crowd's midst. When he looks for Jesus in the temple, Judas comes face to face with Caiaphas who warns the "King maker" that Judas, his master and fellow "knaves" will pay with their lives.

Judas standing at a distance overhears Jesus addressing the crowd, "Do ye not understand? My kingdom is not of this world!" (John 18:36). This is the turning and breaking point for Judas. "And so it was that Judas, bitter…panic stricken…desperate…all hope of earthly kingdom gone, betrayed his Lord for thirty pieces of silver." Judas' motive for betrayal is clearly stated—he will not become the privileged person of power he had hoped to be. Instead, he resorted to find wealth in betraying Jesus.

The next scene is evocative: a close up of Caiaphas' left hand, filled with coins which he drops one by one onto a table. A disheveled and edgy Judas watches the coins drop. Reluctantly he nods in agreement to Caiaphas' demand that Judas takes them to Jesus so that they can destroy Jesus. Judas leads the arresting party comprising temple priests, Roman soldiers and Jerusalemites. Having identified Jesus with a kiss, Judas retreats to the safety of some rocks to observe. He appears troubled and confused.

To develop further the character of Judas, DeMille places him at the flagellation scene. Hiding behind a large pillar and looking as though he is demon possessed, Judas flinches with the sound of each lash. When a crown of thorns is placed on the head of Jesus, a terror-filled Judas places his hands on his head and drops to the floor. Looking up he sees his defeated king draped in a cloak, crowned with thorns, and holding a reed scepter.

Guilt ridden, Judas attempts to return the thirty pieces of silver to Caiaphas. This is not a clandestine meeting but a very public encounter with Caiaphas, a large group of priests, accusers and Jesus. Judas clutching his purse confesses, "I have sinned, in that I have betrayed innocent blood! Matt 27:4." Caiaphas is not interested, ignoring Judas' plea. In a fit of desperation, Judas raises his arms and the coins drop from his moneybag. For one brief moment, Judas stands in a crucified position, the coins falling like droplets of blood—an allusion to "blood money."

Who betrayed whom? Judas' attention turns to the soldiers untying Jesus. The rope is tossed and lands among the coins at Judas' feet. He picks up the rope. Has Judas already thought of suicide or is DeMille preparing the audience for what is about to take place? Judas watches a cross being carried through the crowd. This is more than he can bear. Pulling his cloak up over his head, blocking the sight, he makes a hasty exit.

While Jesus is being nailed to the cross, Judas runs up a rocky slope. He covers his ears to block out the sound of hammering. Stopping at a tree, Judas turns to look at Calvary, and with his eyes fixed on the crucified Jesus, he slowly ties the rope around his neck. The moment Jesus dies, Judas looks heavenward, his arms outstretched, pleading. Tempest and lightning fill the screen and the scene changes to Judas' limp body swinging from the branch.

The juxtaposition of the Judas figure with Peter and Jesus highlights their differences. DeMille elevates Judas' position in the apostolic rank to higher than that of Peter, traditionally Jesus' right hand man. This is evident by the number of scenes in which Judas appears and the part he plays in the narrative. DeMille also contrasts the Judas and Jesus figures. Judas' role as "king maker" is counter to that of Jesus the King. Where Jesus is the protagonist, Judas is the antagonist.

Combining the image of Judas as lover, ambitious loyalist and faithful follower, DeMille attempts "to make the actions of Judas understandable."[74] Paffenroth is correct, but there is surely a difference between an audience's understanding and biblical accuracy. The traditional interpretation of Judas' motive for betrayal is that of avarice. DeMille expands this by "situating greedy Judas between equally greedy Caiaphas and the ethereal Jesus."[75]

### *Summary*

It will have become evident in the six films analyzed— two French, two American, one Italian and one Danish—that the portrayals of Judas were extremely diverse in the thirty years of silent Jesus films. The length of the film and the perceived role in betraying Jesus often governed the development of the Judas character. Iconic images of the Last Supper scene and Judas' kiss were included in each of the films. In contrast, his suicide appeared in only two (*Christus* and *The King of Kings*). Judas' actions are

74. Kim Paffenroth, "Film Depictions of Judas," *JRF* 5, no. 2 (2001). https://www.unomaha.edu/jrf/judas.htm.

75. Walsh, *Reading the Gospels*, 35.

for the most part influenced by greed—reinforcing stereotypical images of avaricious Jews. A new idea is introduced in *Christus* when Satan tempts Judas. Similarly, in *Blade af Satans Bog*, Satan manipulates Judas. Although there was a reluctance to portray religion in film, specifically in the person of Jesus, this did not carry over to the character of Judas. Where most of the films attempted to remain faithful to the Gospels, DeMille embellished Judas' role by including a romantic entanglement with Mary Magdalene. Dreyer's Judas (based on a novel), provided psychological insights into his character, while Guy's vision-seeing Judas raised theological questions such as the providence of God and the doctrine of predestination. The filmic character of Judas Iscariot provided filmmakers with an opportunity to explore and develop further the role of Judas in Jesus films. Where Jesus' role and portrayal were sacrosanct and governed by censorship codes, Judas was the "villain" of the story and open for interpretation and embellishment.

## Chapter 3

# BETWEEN THE BIBLICAL EPICS (1930–1960)

### *Introduction*

It is often argued that there was a hiatus in the production of Jesus films from 1927 to 1961. However, that assessment is flawed. Rather it should be stated that films advanced in two new directions. First, with the advent of television, American Christian film companies, such as Family Films, continued to produce Jesus films for this new medium. Second, with Hollywood "moth-balling" Jesus film productions, other countries such as France, Spain, Germany, Mexico, Italy and Brazil seized the opportunity to fill the void. Indeed, the net was spread far and wide with Carlos Vander Tolosa in 1952 directing the first Filipino-produced Jesus film, *Kalbaryo ni Hesus* (The Passion of Jesus Christ). Three global events, the Great Depression (1929–1933), the Second World War (1939–1945) and the perceived threat of Communism (the "Red Scare": 1946 onwards) dominated the years 1930–1960. European and American film companies reacted differently to these events. Will Hayes, first president of the Motion Pictures Producers and Distributors Association of America, claimed:

> No medium had contributed more greatly than the film to the maintenance of the national morale during a period featured by revolution, riot and political turmoil in other countries. It has been the mission of the screen, without ignoring the serious social problems of the day, to reflect aspiration, optimism, and kindly humor in its entertainment.[1]

Hollywood produced more than five thousand feature films during the 1930s but surprisingly none contained a biblical theme. Prior to the First World War, there were only seventy biblical films. This lull carried on into the 1940s. Hollywood films on the life of Christ did not return to the big screen until 1961with the release of Nicholas Ray's *King of Kings*.

1. Quoted in Steven Mintz and Randy Roberts, eds., *Hollywood's America: United States History Through Its Films*, 2nd ed. (St. James: Brandywine, 1999), 92.

There are five reasons for Hollywood filmmakers' reluctance to produce Jesus films in these decades. First, it was thought that a benchmark in that genre has already been set. Tatum notes that Cecil B. DeMille's 1927 production of *The King of Kings* "set the standard by which his successors in the era of sound often judged themselves."[2] Even though the film was claimed to be a box-office success, studio heads saw it as a "novelty."[3]

Second, was the adoption in 1930 of the Motion Picture Production Code by the Motion Picture Producers and Distributors of America (MPPDA). The Code was a means to rein in the excesses of violence, sex and perceived immorality in films. Thus, if the Code, for example, had been in force at the time of the release of DeMille's *The King of Kings*, the seductive prowess of Mary Magdalene would have been censored,[4] the crucifixion scene would have been modified[5] and the villainous portrayal of Caiaphas and other Jewish religious figures would have needed a radical make-over. Indeed, Sections 1 and 2 of the Code's "Religion" section prohibited the ridiculing of any "religious faith *honestly maintained*," and that "*ministers of religion* in their characters of ministers should not be used in comedy, as villains, or as unpleasant persons."[6]

Censorship at this stage did not involve ratings according to age but merely an approval for release of the film. Major studios would not release a film without the Code's seal of approval. This was not because of any legal obligation, but to satisfy the American viewing public's increasing hostility to the screening of immorality, of what was deemed morally corruptible to the vast majority in a conservative society.

A more prescriptive classification of films came in 1934 with the establishment of the Roman Catholic Legion of Decency. Organized under the leadership of John Timothy McNicholas, Archbishop of Cincinnati, the Legion of Decency became "the most feared of all the private protest groups bedeviling Hollywood."[7] The Legion's Pledge encapsulates its objectives.

2. Tatum, *Jesus at the Movies*, 165.

3. Terry Lindvall and Andrew Quicke, *Celluloid Sermons: The Emergence of the Christian Film Industry, 1930–1986* (New York: New York University Press, 2011), 26.

4. Section 3 (e) of the Code's "Plot Material" states, "The *methods* by which seduction, essential to the plot, is attained should not be explicit or represented in detail where there is likelihood of arousing wrongful emotions on the part of the audience." Mintz and Roberts, eds., *Hollywood's America*, 147.

5. Section 6 (b) states "*Brutal killings* should not be presented in detail." Ibid., 148.

6. Ibid., 151. Emphasis in the original.

7. Thomas Doherty, "A Code Is Born," *Reason*, December 4, 2007. http://reason.com/archives/2007/12/04/a-code-is-born/print.

> In the name of the Father and of the Son and of the Holy Ghost. Amen. I condemn all indecent and immoral motion pictures, and those, which glorify crime or criminals. I promise to do all that I can to strengthen public opinion against the production of indecent and immoral films, and to unite with all who protest against them. I acknowledge my obligation to form a right conscience about pictures that are dangerous to my moral life. I pledge myself to remain away from them. I promise, further, to stay away altogether from places of amusement, which show them as a matter of policy.[8]

Copies of the Pledge were made available to Roman Catholics queuing outside cinemas as well as to all in Catholic schools and churches.

Tatum posits a third reason for the absence of Bible films. He suggests that the popularity of the sub-genre of the biblical epic, the Roman/Christian epic, provided "a particular alternative approach to Jesus on film: telling the Jesus story in association with, but in subordination to, another story or other stories."[9] Films such as *Quo Vadis* (1951), *The Robe* (1953) and *Ben-Hur* (1959) are examples of films that included scenes from the Jesus story.

A fourth reason was economic. It was costly to produce a film and box-office success was not always assured. Matthew Bernstein in *Controlling Hollywood: Censorship and Regulation in the Studio Era* contests the oft-quoted notion that DeMille's *The King of Kings* was a huge box-office success:

> Only one film based on a Biblical story, Warner Bros.' *Noah's Ark* (1928), which was in production at the same time as *The King of Kings*, was released by a major company over the next eight years, until RKO's *The Last Days of Pompeii* in 1935. Had *The King of Kings* demonstrated the existence of a market, it would certainly have been imitated.[10]

Bernstein's assessment is correct. A film's financial success is gauged by the film's profit and ticket sales. Although *The King of Kings* was seen by large audiences, many tickets were complimentary and production was plagued by "budget troubles."[11] That DeMille and financier Jeremy Milbank "had not taken a penny of profit" from the film but gave their "share of the earnings" to charity corroborate poor box-office returns.

8. "The Pledge of the Legion of Decency," *Catholic Apologetics*. http://www.catholicapologetics.info/morality/general/decent.htm.
9. Tatum, *Jesus at the Movies*, 62.
10. Bernstein, ed., *Controlling Hollywood*, 79.
11. DeMille, *Autobiography*, 284, 274.

I would argue that a fifth reason was audience sophistication. Audiences may have outgrown the excitement of watching moving pictures about the life of Jesus. The Jesus story was all too familiar and predictable. Producers could not rely on audiences going to see a film "as a sort of sacred duty."[12] Moreover, the breadth of movie genres meant that the public had a wide variety of movies from which to choose. Although Jesus films might be inspirational, they could not compete with people's need for escapism, especially in a period of deep uncertainty.

## *The 1930s*

Perhaps surprisingly, despite the turbulent times, there was no decline in film production, especially in America. The 1930s were Hollywood's heyday, with studios producing films of high quality and in huge quantities. American moviegoers, still marveling at moving pictures with sound, continued to frequent cinemas. In 1933 when the economy reached its lowest point, sixty to eighty million people still attended cinemas weekly! Movie going was pure escapism from the realities of the Depression, and as Maury Klien notes, "film became the fantasy life of a nation in pain."[13]

In the 1930s there began to emerge distinctive film genres. Each genre reflected the changes that were taking place within American society. Gangster films, such as *Little Caesar* (1930) and *Scarface* (1932), were popular because they "embodied both the triumph of the individual and the failure of the system."[14] The Screwball Comedy such as Frank Capra's *It Happened One Night* (1934), was topical and "born of a vision intent on healing the wounds and divisions of a dispirited nation."[15] Other genres to emerge from this decade were Musicals (*42nd Street*, 1933), Westerns (*Destry Rides Again*, 1939) and Cartoons (*Snow White and the Seven Dwarfs*, 1937).

American and European filmmakers' reluctance to invest in Jesus films is evident: the only major Jesus film made in the 1930s, which depicts the events from Jesus' entry into Jerusalem to his resurrection, was the 1935 French production *Golgotha.*

12. Harry Medved and Michael Medved, *The Hollywood Hall of Shame: The Most Expensive Flops in Movie History* (New York: Perigree, 1984), 141.

13. Maury Klien, "Laughing Through Tears: Hollywood Answers to the Depression," in Mintz and Roberts, eds., *Hollywood's America*, 87.

14. Ibid., 88.

15. Ibid., 91.

### *Golgotha aka Ecce Homo (1935) (Behold the Man)*

Director: Julien Duvivier. Screenwriter: Julien Duvivier. Country: France. Production Company: Ichtys Film. Length: 95 minutes. Length of Last Supper scene: 7 minutes. Color: black and white. Language: French, English dubbed. Musical score: Jacques Ibert. Filming locations: Algeria, Paris Studios Cinéma. Cast: Judas (Lucas Gridoux), Jesus (Robert Le Vigan).

*Lens One*

Outside of Hollywood, the 1930s belonged to the French cinema.[16] Julien Duvivier (1896–1967) together with Jean Renoir, René Clair, Jacques Feyder and Marcel Carne make up the 'Big Five' of classic French cinema. Duvivier began his movie career in 1918 but it was not until his 1931 adaptation of Irène Némirovsky's 1929 novel *David Golder*, about a self-made Jewish businessman, that his filmmaking talents were recognized. Aided by the advent of sound in motion pictures, Duvivier's subsequent efforts in this decade established him as one of the leading forces in world cinema. One of Duvivier's greatest achievements was his 1935 film *Ecce Homo* (Behold the Man). In 1937, the film was dubbed in English and released in the United States of America under the title of *Golgotha*. It is to this 1937 dubbed version reference is made.

*Golgotha* is significant because it is the first sound-picture ever made about Jesus. It is not a conventional Passion story in that there is no attempt to develop Jesus' (Robert Le Vigan) distinctive personality. The film also demonstrates a maturing of cinematic styles. Duvivier, a pioneer of poetic realism, not only relies on actors to tell the story but also uses the camera and a variety of shots to develop characters. The camera work in the opening scene is notable. A point-of-view shot is used for Jesus as he walks through the crowd. When he comes into view it is at a distance, and shot from a low angle. There is a moment of confusion when trying to discern who Jesus is because he is partially obscured by his disciples. Remarkably, the effect is to give the viewer the impression of actually being there, and "discovering Jesus for the first time."[17]

*Golgotha* begins with Jesus' entry into Jerusalem and focuses on the immediate events leading up to his death. Consequently, most of the dialogue centers on the political machinations within the Sanhedrin and between Pontius Pilate (Jean Gabin) and the Jewish leaders. Duvivier

16. Roy Armes, "Images of France," *The Movie: The Illustrated History of the Cinema* 16 (1980): 301.

17. Matt Page, review of Golgotha, "One of the Finest Films Ever Made," *Golgotha. IMDb*. http://www.imdb.com/title/tt0025191/?ref_=fn_tt_tt_2.

favors these non-scriptural conversations and ignores much of the biblical teachings of Jesus, including parables and the Sermon on the Mount. The audience experiences Jesus principally in the way Pontius Pilate, along with Herod Antipas (Harry Bauer), Caiaphas (Charles Granval) and Judas Iscariot (Lucas Gridoux) would view him.

Although the screenplay draws from all four Gospels, it prioritizes Mark's Gospel. Duvivier uses two styles of dialogue: the language of the *King James Bible* and contemporary language. The former is used for the words spoken by Jesus or when biblical texts are being quoted; the latter is used for script written exclusively for the film. This is problematic for the viewing audience as Danel Griffen notes:

> It is difficult to switch gears, especially considering that most of the dialogue is freshly written material from the Pharisees as they contemplate what to do with Christ. Just as we are engaged with what is happening, a character straightens up and says, "Verily, verily I say unto thee…" and the conflict and suspense previously generated in the scene deflates.[18]

Duvivier introduces an unusual interpretation of the twelve disciples and Pilate. The disciples are somewhat detached from Jesus, seem to barely know him, and are convinced that Jesus' mission is politically motivated to overthrow the Roman rule. Pilate's role is more complex and deviates from the Gospels' accounts. Agreeing first to arrest and condemn Jesus, Pilate double-crosses the Jewish leaders and claims Jesus' innocence. This turn-around is not only to show the Jewish leaders that he is in charge, but also that he and Rome do not make deals with Jews.

It is highly significant that Duvivier also draws on two apocryphal gospels: the *Gospel of Peter* and the *Gospel of Nicodemus*. The *Gospel of Peter* maligns the Jews, exonerates Pilate, and Herod, the Jewish king, orders Jesus' execution. The blame for Jesus' death is clearly placed on the Jews.

Duvivier promotes the divinity of Jesus and his supernatural powers. Unlike previous filmic depictions of Jesus' suffering and crucifixion, Duvivier's Jesus is scourged and nailed to the cross, but he seems to feel no pain. This is in accordance with the *Gospel of Peter*, which records: "They brought forward two evildoers and crucified the Lord between them. But he was silent, as if he had no pain" (Fragment 4:10). This silence raises doubt about the reality of Jesus' sufferings and by consequence upon the

18. Danel Griffen, "Film as Art," *Danel Griffin's Guide to Cinema*. http://uashome.alaska.edu/~dfgriffin/website/golgotha.htm.

reality of his human-body. It is difficult to imagine that a 1935 audience would doubt Jesus' humanity. On the contrary, it is likely that they would marvel at Jesus' courage and composure at a time of suffering.

After the crucifixion, the Jewish leaders question whether Jesus really was the Messiah (*Gos. Nic.* 13; 14). Duvivier's addition to the Passion account is important. By planting the seeds of doubt into the minds of the Jewish leaders, Duvivier magnifies the barbarity of Jesus' condemnation and reinforces the notion that even though Jews were presented with evidence, they still chose not to believe in the divinity of Jesus and rejected him as the messiah. It thus becomes a very anti-Semitic film.

*Lens Two*

The mother of Jesus introduces the Supper scene by telling her female companions that Jesus is upstairs, celebrating the Passover. The scene changes to a shot of half of the room and two men bringing in jugs of water. The eye is drawn to a large inverted U-shaped table in the center of the room. It is covered with a fringed white cloth and is set for a meal. Cushioned benches surround the table, and although the room is sparsely decorated, the patterned carpet on the floor suggests that the owner of the house is wealthy. Three lamps hanging from the ceiling provide light.

The camera pans to outside the room showing Jesus and all the disciples standing on an open-air balcony, which overlooks Jerusalem. Jesus, looking pre-occupied, is leaning against the balcony wall. He is bareheaded, in sharp contrast to the disciples whose heads are covered with shawls. One could almost believe that Duvivier wanted to separate Jesus from Jewish practices and to drive a wedge between Judaism and Christianity. A close up of Jesus shows him looking to the sky and deep in thought. Peter and John look at Jesus waiting for him to say something. The camera pans in front of Jesus who then turns and addresses those gathered, "With desire I have desired [*sic*] to eat this Passover with you before I suffer. For I say unto you I will not eat any more there-of until it be fulfilled in the Kingdom of God" (Luke 22:15–16). A close-up of Judas shows him listening intently to Jesus' words. He makes eye contact with Jesus but quickly looks away: he is uncertain whether Jesus knows what he has planned.

Jesus leads them into the room where two male servants are preparing the table. After a roasted lamb is placed on the center of the table, the servants depart. Jesus and the disciples come into view, and make their way to the table.

The scene dissolves to show all the disciples and Jesus seated around the table. They are eating, except for Jesus who appears anxious. Someone asks, "What troubles the master?" A disciple facing diagonally across from

Jesus also asks, "What troubles you Master?" All eyes turn toward Jesus, intent to find out. Jesus answers, "Verily I say unto you that one of you shall betray me" (Matt 26:21). There is an outbreak of questions: "Who can it be? Surely, it is not I. Surely he doesn't think that…" Peter, with frustration in his voice, leans towards Jesus and bluntly asks him, "Who is it?" It is only when John repeats the question that Jesus acknowledges it. He turns to look at John and then at Judas. To avoid eye contact Judas leans towards those near him, pretending to be deep in conversation. Judas is visibly uncomfortable: his fingers are twitching nervously. Jesus answers, "One of the twelve that dippeth with me in the dish" (Matt 26:23). No one, except Judas, seems to be interested in what Jesus is saying. Having dipped the bread Jesus passes it to Judas. By this time, Judas has turned and is staring at Jesus. Judas reaches out and takes the bread. The disciples are oblivious to what is taking place: they are deep in conversation.

A close-up of Jesus heightens the tension. Jesus orders Judas, "That thou doest do quickly" (John 13:27). He looks long and hard at Judas and then turns away with closed eyes, accepting that his fate is sealed. Judas looks at Jesus and, almost as an act of defiance, boldly rises from his seat, tosses his outer garment over his shoulder, and struts out of the room. Three disciples notice his departure but pay little attention.

Nearing the steps of the balcony, Judas stops and looks back at those around the table. Slowly he moves to a position where he can observe the proceedings without the others noticing him. The point-of-view shot enables the audience to look into the room and see what Judas is witnessing. Although Judas is within earshot, the audience do not hear what is being said but the choral religious music indicates that this is a hallowed moment and a sanctified scene.

A long-diagonal-shot gives a clear view of what is happening in the upper room. The disciples stop eating and look at Jesus when he offers what appears to be a blessing over the bread. As he elevates the bread, Jesus is bathed in light. He breaks the bread and gives a half to the disciples on either side of him. A crosscut to Judas standing outside shows his attention firmly fixed on Jesus' actions and words. A close-up of Judas' eyes widening in amazement followed by a look of profound disappointment evokes pathos. Judas is clearly an outsider, no longer part of Jesus' select group. The shot returns to the room. Jesus blesses the chalice and passes it to John who drinks and then reverently passes it on. The implication is that Judas is excluded from the Eucharist.

Judas by now has returned to the balcony and is slowly walking towards the steps. With an anguished look on his face, Judas bows his head. Pausing for a moment, he wrestles with his thoughts and then as if to escape them, Judas hurries down the steps and onto the empty street.

He stops, looks back once more, and with resolve strides briskly to Caiaphas' house to collect his thirty pieces of silver.

The disciples gather around Jesus who does a visual full sweep of the circle of friends. He does not speak and moves onto the balcony. Peter follows and declares his faithfulness to Jesus. Solemnly Jesus responds, "Verily I say unto you that this day, even this night, before the cock crows, thou shalt deny me thrice" (John 22:31). Peter defensively replies, "But if I should have to die with you Master, I'll never deny thee." Hearing Peter's declaration of loyalty, the anxious disciples express their own willingness to die also for their Master. Jesus, with the single directive, "Come," urges that his disciples leave for Gethsemane.

*Lens Three*

The 1930s was a decade of socio-economic and political crisis in France. The decade began with the Great Depression of 1929–1933. Disputes were still raging regarding reparations for World War I. Although immigration was encouraged in these post-war years to create a workforce to compensate for the thousands of men who died on the battlefields, the status of refugees from Central and Eastern Europe became an important public issue.[19] In response to the threat of fascism, the Socialist Popular Front coalition emerged in France and went on to win the elections in 1936. Vicki Caron, in *Uneasy Asylum, France and the Jewish Refugee Crisis, 1933–1942*, identifies the French refugee policy in the 1930s as a factor in political unrest, noting that the French Jewish community was sharply divided over the handling of the refugee crisis.[20] Some Jewish leaders pressed for a hardline refugee policy, while others sought relief for the refugees and the adoption of more liberal refugee policies. These factors reflect the xenophobic policy that developed in France, the end of tolerance of the Jews and the rise of anti-Semitism.

*Golgotha* was filmed when widespread attention was being drawn to the rise of German anti-Semitism. In 1933, the *NS Studentenbund* (National Socialist German Students' League) burnt books by Jewish writers on Berlin's Odeonplatz. A concordat assuring the Roman Catholic Church full religious freedom was negotiated between Monsignor Pacelli and Chancellor Franz Papen. The following year witnessed the Night of the Long Knives purge by the *Sturm Abteilung* (Storm Section), also

19. Michael R. Marrus and Robert O. Paxton, *Vichy France and the Jews* (Stanford: Stanford University Press, 1995), 35.

20. Vicki Caron, *Uneasy Asylum, France and the Jewish Refugee Crisis 1933–1942* (Stanford: Stanford University Press, 1999), 94–116.

known as storm-troopers or brown-shirts, that resulted in the slaying of several hundred Germans whom Hitler saw as a threat to his authority. In the same year, he amalgamated the offices of Chancellor and President and assumed the new title of *Führer* and *Reichskanzler*.

The release of Duvivier's *Golgotha* took place in August 1935, the same month of enactment of the Nuremberg Laws. The first law, The Law for the Protection of German Blood and German Honor, prohibited marriages and extra-marital relations between Jews and Germans. German females who were under the age of forty-five were forbidden to work in Jewish households. The second law, The Reich Citizenship Law, stripped Jews of their German citizenship and introduced a new distinction between Reich citizens and nationals.[21] The film was screened throughout Europe but in a twist of historical fate was not seen in Germany. The nationalistic fervor of Nazi Germany banned foreign artists and promoted "Buy German," ironically depriving the Nazis of an opportunity to reinforce anti-Semitism.

*Golgotha* was subsequently not released in Germany until 1954, and only then in West Germany. By that time, East Germany was under direct Soviet rule, which did not endorse religious films! *Golgotha* was also released in Britain but with deletions. The British Board of Film Censors, established in 1912 by the film industry to bring a degree of uniformity to censorship standards, compiled a list of forty-three grounds for deletion laid down for the guidance of examiners. When British audiences viewed *Golgotha*, close shots of Jesus were edited out because the forty-third ground for deletions was "Materialisation of the conventional figure of Christ."[22] The sanctity of the Jesus figure and the "perceived" image of Christ—white, Anglo-Saxon and Protestant—were upheld by not showing the actor's face and frontal view.

A post-holocaust viewing of *Golgotha* affects and influences one's interpretation of the film and especially its representation of Judas. There can be no denying the blatant anti-Semitism in Duvivier's film. Moreover, the endorsement of fascism is evident, as the political side of the story is not passed over in silence. The Sanhedrin, in protecting its position, rids itself of any threat to its power, just as Hitler removed opposition in the Night of the Long Knives purge. In a number of scenes, Roman soldiers acknowledge Pilate and his orders with a "Nazi-style" salute. Pilate's use

21. Jeremy Noakes and Geoffrey Pridham, *Documents on Nazism 1919–1945* (New York: Viking, 1974), 463–67.

22. "1916—T. P. O'Connor," *Students' British Board of Film Classification*. http://www.sbbfc.co.uk/Assets/documents/sbbfc_online_new.pdf.

of this salute is particularly provocative because when he presents Jesus to the gathered crowd, the scene is reminiscent of a Nuremburg Nazi rally. The people, paid by Temple guards to come to the square to show anger at Jesus, allude to the abusive and persuasive actions of Hitler's "brown shirts." More importantly, the scene reinforces popular mythology that Jews were money-lovers and could easily be procured for the right price. When a voice shouts from the crowd, "His blood be upon us" the crowd's response is a deafening, "Yes! Yes!" It is self-evident that Duvivier is identifying the Jews as "Christ killers."

Duvivier's choice of Robert Le Vigan to play the role of Jesus re-emphasizes the film's hostility towards the Jews. Le Vigan was openly racist, being a member of the *Parti Populiste Français*, a right-wing pro-Fascist party. He advocated collaboration with the German authorities, and supported anti-Semitic propaganda on Radio Paris. After the war, he was brought to trial in November 1946 for treason. He was eventually stripped of his French citizenship, his assets were confiscated and he was sentenced to ten years hard labor, of which he served three. Like many other Fascists, he spent the rest of his life in Argentina, a country that after World War II harbored many Nazi sympathizers.

*The Portrayal of Judas*

Judas is first seen buying a drink from a vendor in the Temple precincts. He takes a coin from inside his cummerbund and not a moneybag—a familiar accessory and leitmotif for depicting Judas. Following Judas is a Sanhedrin informant, who considers that Judas might help deliver Jesus to them. The informant is aware that Judas is disillusioned with Jesus and suggests offering him money to coax him into delivering Jesus. Judas does not seek out the Jewish authorities to hand over Jesus: the Sanhedrin seeks him. Nor does Judas seek payment: it is offered to him. Judas' betrayal of Jesus is not initiated by Judas, nor is it a response to Satan's manipulative powers. By re-interpreting the Gospel accounts Duvivier deliberately transfers responsibility for the betrayal to the Jewish religious authorities.

Judas is next seen that evening sitting alone on a low wall outside the Temple. One of the Sanhedrin approaches him and warns that Judas is in danger and that he could help them if he is need of "a little money." Judas has a quizzical look on his face and turns to look at the man. Feigning friendship the man puts his arm around Judas' shoulders and together they wander away from the Temple. They remain silent. After a short distance the priest leaves and Judas keeps walking.

The mention of money in this brief encounter seems out of place but again it alerts the audience to a commonly held belief that Jews were lovers of money and that their "object of worship" was usury and huckstering.[23] Duvivier was exploiting this negative sentiment to heighten tension.

The next scene shows Judas in the woods, sitting at the base of a tree and resting his head in his hands. We hear his thoughts and see his torment. Jesus' commands such as loving your enemies, selling your house and giving to the poor, and take up your cross, ring in Judas' ears. Judas becomes distressed as the voices develop into a loud babble and warnings of what is ahead. They shall spit on you, persecute you and put you to death. It is quite reasonable to conclude that Duvivier is endorsing the Nazi persecution of Jews because of their betrayal of Jesus. The voices become too much for Judas and again he hurries off as if to escape them. However, the sound of the priest's voice lingers and warns Judas, "You are in danger. There is nothing more to expect from this." Judas realizes that his following Jesus is pointless and makes his fateful decision.

Inside the Temple, Judas sits on a chair surrounded by members of the Sanhedrin. Feeling the heat of the moment Judas opens his cloak and quietly agrees to deliver Jesus to them. Assuring the Sanhedrin that there is nothing to fear, Judas asks the question, "How much will you give?" He tries to increase the price by explaining how he gave up his trade for Jesus and is now ruined because he was so gullible. Thirty pieces of silver is the price offered, an amount Judas finds "satisfactory." However, when he stands to leave, Judas' facial expression shows that he is reveling in the thought of thirty pieces of silver. So as not to taint their own hands, the Sanhedrin has a servant deliver the purse to Judas. Judas leads the Temple guards, Roman soldiers and members of the Sanhedrin to Gethsemane. He greets Jesus with a very insincere "Hail, Master" and attempts to kiss Jesus on his cheek. Jesus asks, "Friend. Is it with a kiss that you betray me?" Judas draws away and stands behind Jesus. Once arrested, Jesus is taken to Caiaphas' house and Judas makes his way to the Temple.

Duvivier's direction masks the machinations influencing Judas and so the impetus that prompted him to return to the Temple is not clear. It might be possible that Judas wanted to rid himself of the inner voices by confessing to the Sanhedrin that he had "sinned in selling the blood of the just." In disgust, Judas throws down the thirty coins and wanders off in a dazed state.

23. From an excerpt of Karl Marx's 1843 essay, "The Jewish Question," in Perry and Schweitzer, eds., *Antisemitic Myths*, 79.

As Jesus and two criminals ascend Calvary with their crosses, a crosscut shows a close-up of hands frantically untying a rope girdle. It is Judas preparing to hang himself. He makes a noose but before he puts it around his neck, the scene goes back to Calvary. Duvivier chose not to show Judas hanging from a branch thus leaving Judas' suicide in doubt and thereby implying that evil—Judas is the epitome of evil—cannot be eradicated.

Duvivier's Judas is an enigma. Many questions about the person, his motives and actions remain. Why was he at the disposal of the Sanhedrin? Was his motive for delivering Jesus because he feared for his own life? How did Judas come to the realization that he had "sinned in selling the blood of the just"? Duvivier's Judas does not provide answers to these questions. The viewer is led to believe that Judas is shallow, dishonest, two-faced, a resentful coward and an outsider. It is no coincidence that these were some of the characteristics with which Hitler branded the Jews in his anti-Semitic propaganda.

However, was Duvivier in fact sanctioning anti-Semitism? The assumption is that his Jesuit education would reinforce the traditional Christian antipathy towards the Jews. Indeed, Duvivier's choice of having the Jesus character played by a card-carrying anti-Semite adds to the quandary. Moreover, the lack of published biographical details and absence of any mention of the director in seminal cinema texts suggests that Duvivier was something of an embarrassment to the film industry and that his name was erased from the records. It is certain that his departure from France during the years of German occupation (1940–1944), and his return after the war, resulted in his fall from fame. Likewise, those directors who had remained in France during the occupation displaced Duvivier's popularity.[24] The mystery heightens with Duvivier's 1940 film *Untel pére et fil* (The Heart of the Nation). This is the story of three generations of the Froment family and how the inhabitants of Paris survive three wars—the Franco-Prussian War of 1871, the First World War (1914–1918) and the invasion by the Germans in World War II. This "classic of wartime resistance" was declared forbidden by Joseph Goebbels, the Reich Minister of Propaganda,[25] and was not released in France until 1945.

24. "Julien Duvivier 1896–1967," *filmsdefrance.com*. http://www.filmsdefrance.com/biography/julien-duvivier.html.

25. Michael Atkinson, "Time Regained: Remembering Julien Duvivier, a Casualty of Auteurism," *Moving Image Source*. http://www.movingimagesource.us/articles/time-regained-20090504.

It seems beyond any reasonable doubt that Duvivier was sanctioning anti-Semitism in his film *Golgotha*. Its production in 1935 was highly suggestive of the mood of the times with the dark days of the Holocaust on the horizon.

### *The 1940s*

The Second World War raged for the first half of the decade. German military expansion into most of Europe presented the German film industry with a ready-made market. As a result, German films dominated European screens.[26] The Propaganda Minister, Joseph Goebbels, who was responsible for film content, set the necessary guidelines to which the film industry had to adhere. Two of the stipulations were that the film had to "feature clear-cut heroes and villains, and, for the most part, happy endings."[27] Likewise, film producers in the United States of America were heavily regulated.

Hollywood's film studios still managed to mass-produce films despite being stifled by the unprecedented control over film content by the Office of War Information (OWI). Message films that questioned underlying American social problems and issues were scarce. Examples of message films made in the 1940s include Elia Kazan's *Gentleman's Agreement* (1947) that tackled bigotry and anti-Semitism; Billy Wilder's *The Lost Weekend* (1945) exposed the horrors of alcoholism; and King Vidor's *The Fountainhead* (1949) expressed the struggle to maintain an individual's integrity in a society that demanded conformity. In contrast, romances, musicals, murder mysteries and westerns were in the majority being promoted as "*pure* entertainment."[28] Combat films, produced to rally public support for the war effort, became allegories of a democratic nation at war.[29] Films were even touted as good propaganda. The OWI director Elmer Davis asserted quite openly, "the easiest way to inject a propaganda idea into most people's minds is to let it go through the medium of an entertainment picture when they do not realize that they are being propagandized."[30]

26. Stephen Brockman, *A Critical History of German Film* (Suffolk: Camden House, 2010), 138.

27. Ibid.

28. Clayton R. Koppes and Gregory D. Black, "What to Show the World: The Office of War Information and Hollywood, 1942–1945," in Mintz and Roberts, eds., *Hollywood's America*, 159. Emphasis in the original.

29. Ibid., 155.

30. Ibid., 157–58.

Hollywood did not produce Jesus films in the period 1930–1960, but an independent Christian company, Cathedral Films, made a number of religious serials and films for television primarily for the Christian education of children. Established by James K. Friedrich (1903–1966), an Episcopalian priest, the film company's main rationale was "to serve Christ with [the] instrument of films."[31] Friedrich also acknowledged Thomas Edison's "fear of misuse of the moving picture" and the possible detrimental effects of its contemporary use on young people, but by building a Christian production studio he hoped to "influence American and international lives" and to bring people to the Christian faith.

Friedrich's first film, *The Great Commandment*, directed by Irving Pichel, was produced in 1939, but not released until 1941. The film narrates the story of a Jewish Zealot who has his life turned upside down after his brother is killed by Longinus, a Roman centurion. In response to concerns, expressed by Joseph Breen from the Production Code Administration (PCA), about an onscreen representation of Jesus, producer John T. Coyle eliminated Jesus as an on-screen character and used the camera's point-of-view to represent him instead. Director Irving Pichel provided the voice of the off-screen Jesus. *The Great Commandment* was reviewed as "good propaganda" in its effective telling of "the Gospel story of forgiveness."[32] However, the film was not released nationally because the theme "love your enemy" was not deemed appropriate with a nation reeling from the recent Japanese bombing of Pearl Harbor on December 7, 1941.

Mexican cinema enjoyed its Golden Age in the 1940s and 1950s. It was the primary producer of Spanish-language films and had one of the most successful industries in the world.[33] One reason for its success was that Mexican audiences disregarded Hollywood films, preferring instead films in their own language, and "dealing with issues specific to national cultural identity."[34] Religious films were also a popular genre for a country steeped in Roman Catholicism.

31. Paraphrased from Frances L. Brocker and J. Nasgowitz, "Interview of James Kempe Friedrich—Collection 327," *Billy Graham Centre Archives*, Wheaton, IL. Accession 85–100, July 30, 1986. http://www2.wheaton.edu/bgc/archives/GUIDES/327.htm.

32. Lindvall and Quicke, *Celluloid Sermons*, 29.

33. Seth Fein, "From Collaboration to Containment: Hollywood and the International Political Economy of Mexican Cinema After the Second World War," in *Mexico's Cinema: A Century of Film and Filmmakers*, ed. Joanne Hershfield and David R. Maciel (Wilmington: SR Books, 1999), 128.

34. Andrea Noble, *Mexican National Cinema* (London: Routledge, 2005), 91.

### *Maria Magdalena, pecadora de Magdala (1946)* *(Mary Magdalene, Sinner of Magdala)*

Director: Miguel Contreras Torres. Screenwriter: Medea de Novara. Country: Mexico. Production Company: Hispano Continental Films. Length: 114 minutes. Length of Last Supper scene: 3:29 minutes. Color: black and white. Language: Spanish. Musical score: Miguel Bernal Jiménez. Filming locations: Azteco Studios, Mexico. Cast: Judas (Tito Junco), Jesus (Luis Alcoriza).

*Lens One*

In 1946, Hispano Continental Films (Mexico) produced *Maria Magdalena, pecadora de Magdala* (Mary Magdalene, Sinner of Magdala) directed by Miguel Contreras Torres (1899–1981). Torres is a notable Mexican director whose filmic talents also included being producer, writer, actor, cinematographer and editor.[35] Easily adapting to the introduction of sound, Torres became the first filmmaker to address the challenges of emigration to the United States in *El Hombre sin Patria* (The Man Without a Country, 1922). This film was also the first Mexican film shot on location in the United States. Torres directed only one other religious film: *Reina de Reinas: La Virgen Maria* (Queen of Queens: The Virgin Mary, 1948).

The film's focus is Mary Magdalene's conversion from a wealthy and promiscuous courtesan to a faithful follower of Jesus. The film includes "popular" miracles, two anointing scenes, the Sermon on the Mount, all the events following Jesus' entry into Jerusalem, and adaptations of the Stations of the Cross. Torres draws from all four Gospels and from Cecil B. DeMille's *The King of Kings*. The film reflects pre-Vatican II Roman Catholic piety and iconography. Mary, the mother of Jesus, is dressed like a nun, Jesus' right hand is in a perpetual "blessing" configuration and religious choral music accompanies miracles, the Last Supper and perceived moments of deep reverence.

*Lens Two*

The Last Supper setting is a reproduction of Leonardo da Vinci's painting of the same name. A freeze-frame lasting eight seconds familiarizes the audience with the occasion while the extreme long shot suggests the watching of a staged Passion play.

In this adaptation of the Last Supper, Jesus (Luis Alcoriza) blesses the wine first and then the bread. It is uncertain as to whether Judas (Tito Junco) receives the bread and wine because the camera stops panning

35. Frederico Dávalos Orozco, "The Birth of the Film Industry and the Emergence of Sound," in Hershfield and Maciel, eds., *Mexico's Cinema*, 21.

at John who is sitting next to Judas. Jesus then identifies the betrayer by handing Judas a piece of the blessed bread dipped in the consecrated wine—obviously Holy Communion! This could be a directorial oversight or perhaps an occasion to show Judas' rejection of Jesus and by implication the (Catholic) Church. Judas takes the bread but we do not see him eat it. So that there is no mistaking the betrayer, Jesus calls him by name, "Judas. Do what you have to do."

*Lens Three*

Hollywood imports to Mexico dropped to their lowest level in 1945. Only eighty-six films out of one hundred and fifty-two were released[36] while Mexico itself produced eighty-two feature films. Moreover, there were fourteen hundred cinemas in the country and movie-going had become "the most popular form of entertainment amongst the subaltern classes."[37] There were three identifiable social classes in Mexico: the proletariat, the working class and the wealthy. These divisions also carried into practices of film audiences and different categories of movie theatres. At one end of the scale, and catering for the masses, were *cines de piojitos* (flea pits)—a term of affection rather than a description—while at the other end were "first-run cinemas," luxurious, with expensive admission tickets and which premiered major films.[38] Disregarding the classes, Paranaguá argues, "There was one public. No matter how different the spectators might be from one another in social or economic terms, from the days of the Nickelodeon, film exhibition and production address themselves to a mythical, unique, and homogenous mass audience."[39]

How then would this "homogenous mass audience" respond to *Maria Magdalena, pecadora de Magdala*? The wealth and extravagant lifestyle of Maria Magdalena would gratify the upper class while tantalizing the working class and poor. Judas' declarations of love to Maria suggest that a person's financial status should not discriminate against their eligibility for a romantic liaison. Love transcends social class. Moreover, turning her back on her status and wealth may seem drastic but Maria's reasons are inspired by Jesus' words in the Sermon on the Mount, "the poor in spirit are blessed and theirs is the kingdom of heaven…the meek are blessed and they will inherit the earth" (Matt 5:1–12; Luke 6:20–23). Hearing

36. Paulo Antonio Paranaguá, ed., *Mexican Cinema*, trans. Ana M. López (London: British Film Institute, 1995), 35.

37. Noble, *Mexican National Cinema*, 74.

38. Ibid. See Chapter 3, "The Formation of a National Cinema Audience," 70–94.

39. Paulo Antonio Paranaguá, "Of Periodizations and Paradigms: The Fifties in Comparative Perspective," *NTC* 10, no. 21/22 (1998): 33.

these familiar words, and seeing them put into action, bolstered the spirits of the poorer class and cultivated the seeds of what later would be known as liberation theology.

*The Portrayal of Judas*
Judas has third billing in the cast list—Jesus is first, followed by Mary Magdalena (Medea Novara, the director's wife). Whereas the other disciples are listed with *San* (Saint) before their names, Judas is not given that appellation. From the outset, Judas is condemned to being separated from the group.

Mary Magdalene's characterization alerts the audience to the director's portrayal of Judas. He is smitten by Mary Magdalena's beauty when he notices her listening to Jesus' Sermon on the Mount. Judas visits her in her sumptuous house and vies for Mary's affection. However, Mary is more interested in Jesus and his words, unlike Judas who, according to Mary, is not a true and loyal friend or a disciple. She rejects Judas' advances and demands that he leave.

Judas is a likeable character. He is charming, sophisticated, well attired, courteous and handsome. Even when Judas is brought to the Sanhedrin—we assume it is to betray Jesus—Judas' only action is biting his knuckles when Caiaphas counts out the thirty pieces of silver. It is uncertain whether Judas is trying to contain his excitement or whether he is struggling with the enormity of what he has done. At Gethsemane, Judas' identifying kiss is tender and his face reveals remorse. Realizing that he has been double-crossed by the Sanhedrin, Judas returns and angrily throws down the coins. He is distraught when watching Jesus struggle on the way to Calvary and, after Jesus falls a second time, Judas hurries away. Filled with regret, Judas hangs himself from a tree.

## *The 1950s*

The 1950s was a decade of invention, social upheaval and political intrigue. The American economy boomed, with credit cards competing with bank notes, "fast food" becoming fashionable with the burger chain McDonald's opening for business (1953) and "sex" hitting the streets with the publication of *Playboy* magazine (1953). Youth danced to Rock and Roll, frequented Drive-In theatres and milk bars and imitated Hollywood stars such as Marlon Brando, James Dean and Grace Kelly. To counter this new cultural and sexual wave, television programs such as *Father Knows Best*, *Leave It to Beaver* and *The Adventures of Ozzie and Harriet* responded by promoting "family values."

Film studios introduced Cinerama, which required three separate copies of the 35mm film with sound carried on a fourth 35mm magnetic film with seven soundtracks. *How the West Was Won*, a 1962 MGM release, is the best-known cineramic film of this era. B-grade science-fiction and horror-films entertained audiences. *Forbidden Planet* (1956) and *The Creature from the Black Lagoon* (1954) provided welcome distractions in a seemingly unsettled and chaotic world. The demobilization of returning service men, the radical re-defining of the role of women, along with Cold War suspicion and nuclear bombs, deeply affected American society. Stuart Samuels explains that responding to "the threats of social banality and universal annihilation, three concepts dominated the decade: (1) conformity, (2) paranoia, and (3) alienation."[40]

It was in this turbulent social climate that the Reverend James Friedrich (Cathedral Films) left the Episcopalian parochial ministry to concentrate on producing films in order to satisfy four goals: "to edify and educate the church; to enhance interest in civic affairs; to promote mission work around the world; and to evangelize."[41] He produced eight films of which two, *I Beheld His Glory* (1952) and *Day of Triumph* (1954), were of such high quality that they were released to television and cinemas.

## *I Beheld His Glory (1952)*

Director: John T. Coyle. Screenwriter: John Evans and Arthur T. Horman. Country: USA. Production Company: Cathedral Films. Length: 53 minutes. Length of Last Supper scene: 7:06 minutes. Color: Color. Language: English. Musical score: uncredited. Filming locations: Vasquez Rocks Natural Area Park, Agua Dulce, California, Westlake Entertainment Studio. Cast: Judas (uncredited), Jesus (Robert Wilson).

### *Lens One*

*I Beheld His Glory* was originally produced for the religious television series *Family Theatre.* The screenplay draws from the four Gospels and fiction. The Passion is told from the point of view of the Roman centurion who is reported to have declared at Jesus' crucifixion, "Truly this Man was the Son of God" (Mark 15:39; Matt 27:54). He is given the name Cornelius (George Macready). Through the disciple Thomas, he learns the details of the Last Supper and other events and relates these though the use of flashbacks.

40. Stuart Samuels, "The Age of Conspiracy and Conformity: *Invasion of the Body Snatchers* (1956)," in Mintz and Roberts, eds., *Hollywood's America*, 223.

41. Lindvall and Quicke, *Celluloid Sermons*, 31.

*Lens Two*

According to Cornelius, Jesus (Robert Wilson) and his disciples were gathering to celebrate "the feast of the unleavened bread" in an upper room. Its décor is sparse. They sit on individual wooden stools around a wooden rectangular table. Plates, cups, a round loaf of bread and a silver chalice are on the table. All the disciples are present for the supper. Judas (un-credited) is seated at the right of Jesus and John sits at Jesus' left. Framing the three men are two lit oil lamps, which look similar to candle sticks used on a Christian altar.

The meal begins with Jesus saying that he "earnestly desired to eat this Passover with [them]" (Luke 22:15). The scriptwriter has incorporated verses from all four Gospels,[42] 1 Cor 11:23–26 and both Jewish and Christian blessings over the bread and wine. Jesus, taking a round loaf of bread in his hands, prays, "Blessed art thou O Lord God King of the world who hath brought forth bread from the earth." This blessing is very similar to the *Hamotzi*, the Jewish blessing over bread: "Blessed are You, O Lord our God, Ruler of the universe, who brings forth bread from the earth." An analogous prayer is also offered at the presentation of the gifts in the Catholic mass where the priest prays: "Blessed are you, Lord, God of all creation. Through your goodness we have this bread to offer, which earth has given and human hands have made. It will become for us the bread of life." Jesus breaks the bread in two, gives one-half to John, and says, "Take. Eat. This is my body given for thee. This do in remembrance of me." The bread is passed among them.

Jesus then takes the silver chalice and prays, "Blessed art thou O Lord of the world who hath created fruit of the vine." This is almost identical to the *Kiddush*, the Jewish blessing over wine, "Blessed are You, O Lord our God, Ruler of the universe, creator of the fruit of the vine." In the Catholic mass the priest prays, "Blessed are you, Lord, God of all creation. Through your goodness, we have this wine to offer, fruit of the vine and work of human hands. It will become our spiritual drink." It is uncertain whether most audiences would know the Jewish origin of these prayers. Before handing John the chalice, Jesus says, "Drink ye all of this for this is my blood of the new testament which is shed for you and for many for the remission of sins."

The disciples pass the bread and chalice to each other. The camera captures each of them reverently breaking off a piece of bread, eating it, and then drinking from the chalice. The shot abruptly changes before the bread and wine reach Judas. Jesus looks at Judas whose arms are resting on the table. Without any provocation Jesus states, "Behold the hand of

42. Matt 26:17–30; Mark 14:12–26; Luke 22:7–39; John 13:21–30.

him who betrays me is on the table." Judas slowly withdraws his hands from the table and places them in his lap. Jesus continues, "For the Son of Man is going as it has been determined, but woe to that one by whom he is betrayed" (Luke 22:21–22). The disciples begin to question Jesus as to what he means and how can he doubt their loyalty. Judas rises and without acknowledgment from Jesus or the other disciples, heads towards to the door. He stops to look at the disciples and Jesus but they are all pre-occupied, arguing over who made the greatest sacrifice in order to follow Jesus. The voiceover adds, "While they were affirming their loyalty, there was one who slipped out to betray him." No name is mentioned.

Jesus calms the dispute by explaining, how the greatest among them must become like the youngest and the leader like one who serves (John 22:24–28). Then having informed Peter of his imminent denial, the Last Supper ends with Peter's declaration, "Not I. Never would I deny you."

*Lens Three*

This film does not endorse a particular Christian denomination nor does it show evidence of anti-Semitism. The enemy is Roman oppression. This is evident in the manner in which Roman centurions treat the Jewish populace. The Romans are feared by the Jews. Caiaphas, the chief priest, assumes all Roman soldiers can be bribed. When Cornelius and fellow centurion Longinus discuss the extent and the status of the Roman Empire, Longinus claims, "We can't rule through crushing power anymore." For astute viewers the "crushing power" is reference to the might of the Soviet Union and the perceived threat of communism. The United States, in an age inspired by the "Cold War" and suspicion of the "Red Scare" and "domino effect" that would see the erosion of American democracy by communist countries, needed films (especially religious ones) to reinforce the belief that America was the "land of the free" and that the Christian Gospel was on their side. This will become even more evident in the film *Day of Triumph* (see below).

*The Portrayal of Judas*

Judas has a minimalist role in this film. The name Judas Iscariot is never mentioned, and Judas is mentioned only twice. The first reference to him is in the opening scene when Cornelius reports on the welfare of the disciples after Jesus' crucifixion, "All but one is well: Judas of Kerioth who died by his own hand." Kerioth, a town in Judah (Jer 48:24, 41; Amos 2:2), was thought to be Judas' birthplace.[43] The audience could easily have

43. John R. Donahue and Daniel J. Harrington, *The Gospel of Mark*, Sacra Pagina 2 (Collegeville: Liturgical Press, 2002), 125.

missed the connection between Kerioth and Iscariot. When Judas leaves the Supper, Cornelius describes him as "the one who slipped out to betray Jesus." No motive for the betrayal is given but when questioned by those listening to his story as to why "the one" was not stopped, Cornelius explains how the very thought of betrayal seemed impossible as each man loved Jesus. It was assumed that the one who went out was going to pay for the food they had eaten or to give alms to the poor. After all, he was so well trusted that he had been chosen as the keeper of the communal purse.

Judas plays such a minor role in the film that even the actor is not credited. Judas is seen only at the Last Supper and at Gethsemane, where he speaks his only word in the film, "Master." This is when he identifies Jesus. It is in Jesus' response that we hear "Judas is it with a kiss that you betray the Son of Man?" (Luke 22:48).

Although Judas plays a small part in the film, his role is highly significant and has enormous theological implications. His role is not that of a sinner but of one who is acting out the task assigned to him by God. He is faithfully fulfilling God's plan and thus cannot be condemned by his actions.

There is little to identify Judas or to distinguish him from the other disciples. By not identifying Judas specifically, it is thus possible for Judas to have been a welcome and active participant of the Lord's Supper. It is significant that it is only when Jesus declares that the hand of the betrayer is on the table that Judas removes his hands from the table—identifying himself as the betrayer—and rises from his seat. Jesus' declaration is the signal for Judas to leave the room. It is as if Judas and Jesus had pre-planned the event. Judas had no need to ask if he was the betrayer or feign ignorance. The implication of these omissions or changes to the Gospel accounts is that Judas was not acting alone but with the assent of Jesus. This is reinforced by Jesus' claim that "the Son of Man is going as it has been determined." Judas is a mere pawn in a greater theological drama.

## *Day of Triumph (1954)*

Director: John T. Coyle and Irving Pichel. Screenwriter: Arthur T. Horman. Country: USA. Production Company: Century Films Inc. Length: 110 minutes. Length of Last Supper scene: 4:10 minutes. Color: Eastman Kodak Color. Language: English. Musical score: Daniele Anfitheatro. Filming locations: Hal Roach Studios, Southern California. Cast: Judas (James Griffith), Jesus (Robert Wilson).

*Lens One*

*Day of Triumph* (also known as *Jesus and the Great Betrayal*) was the first feature-length English language sound film in which the audience saw and heard an actor playing Jesus (Robert Wilson). It is considered as Cathedral Film's "apotheosis of sincere filmmaking."[44] Friedrich had to contend with controversial aspects of the Gospels, such as the miracle at Cana where Jesus turns the water into wine (John 2:1–11). To appease "teetotaling denominations," Friedrich responded by "visualizing such miracles with a sense of ambiguity…and mystery. Miracles, however, were recorded with a literal sense of realism, eschewing special effects for 'just the facts'."[45]

*Lens Two*

Figure 5. Jesus and Judas share a reflective moment. © Century Films, Inc.

A point-of-view shot ascends stone steps and stops at a slightly ajar wooden door. It conveys the impression of welcoming the viewer inside. Once there we hear Jesus saying, "Servants are not greater than their master" (John 13:16) and the ominous prediction, "The one who ate my bread has lifted his heel against me" (John 13:18). Jesus adds, "Very

44. Lindvall and Quicke, *Celluloid Sermons*, 37.
45. Ibid., 36.

truly, I tell you, one of you will betray me." When asked by the disciples, "Lord, who is it?" Jesus bows his head and shakes it as if to say, "I do not want to say." Jesus then discretely leans over to Judas (James Griffith) seated next to him. Judas, looking straight ahead asks, "Is it I Master?" Jesus takes a piece of bread, and says, "It is he to whom I shall give this morsel when I have dipped it." Jesus dips the bread in the golden chalice. Neither looks at each other as Jesus places the morsel in Judas' hand. It is only then that they look at each other. Jesus is full of anguish: Judas shows no emotion. Jesus says, "That you are going to do, do quickly." He turns to face the camera, pinching the bridge of his nose and bowing his head. Judas places the morsel on the table and rises from his stool. As he nears the door, one of the disciples asks him where he is going. A disciple chides, "Shhh! The Master"—Jesus was about to speak. "Now is the Son of Man glorified and in him, God is glorified." Judas closes the door behind him.

Jesus tells his disciples that that he is leaving them (John 13:31) and gives them a new commandment to love one another (John 13:34). The camera pulls back as Jesus rises from his stool. He takes a round loaf of bread, holds it in both hands, raises his head towards heaven and prays. "Blessed art thou O Lord God, King of the world…" Breaking the bread in two and handing it to John, Jesus commands, "Take. Eat. This is my body. This do in remembrance of me." As the bread is passed around, Jesus takes the chalice in both hands and looks heavenward as the scene closes.

*Lens Three*

As reported in a *New York Times* news item of July 27, 1952, the producer James K. Friedrich claimed the film was produced as "a stronger spiritual counter-attack on Communism in America." An analysis of the film's introduction, which is both textual and spoken, shows that one of the aims of the film is to contrast the oppression of the "Western Civilization" to the oppressive Communist regime in the Soviet Union. The off-screen narrator sets the scene by explaining Imperial Rome's oppression in the land of Israel and how the Zealots—men who struck back at their oppressors—planned unceasingly to cast off the yoke of slavery.

Most of the narrative has a documentary tone and is without the usually added familiar embellishments to the Jesus story. Perhaps the documentary genre added to the story's authenticity. The film did not escape criticism from The National Catholic Legion of Decency, claiming that the film's "representation (in part fictional) of a period in the life of Christ is based upon a modern interpretation of the Protestant version of the New Testament. While presented in a reverent and inspirational manner, it contains variances from and omissions of spiritual and theological truth."[46] These observations by the Legion of Decency highlight theological and biblical divisions between the Protestant and Roman Catholic denominations.

*Day of Triumph* was not a financial success because the film was withdrawn from distribution in the United States after objections to its treatment of Jewish themes in the New Testament. It is significant that Friedrich believed that certain members of the secular Jewish community stonewalled him due to what they perceived as an anti-Semitic portrayal of Judas. These "secular Jews"—Friedrich was not specific in naming his opponents—claimed Judas looked "more Jewish than the other disciples" and as the "villain," they feared his portrayal would perpetuate anti-Semitic stereotypes. These concerns proved effective with newly independent theatre chains, who, fearing a backlash, withdrew the film before it had played on even twenty per cent of screens. Consequently, the film failed even to recoup its US$700,000 production cost.

*The Portrayal of Judas*

Judas is a close friend of the Zealot Zadok (Lee J. Cobb) and together they seek a leader for the forthcoming religious uprising. The enthusiastic Judas suggests Jesus and believes that "Jesus' quest for spiritual freedom could be advantageous to their cause if they spread the word that Jesus is the Messiah." Zadok vetoes the suggestion: his primary interest is political freedom. His preference as leader is fellow Zealot named Barabbas.

The Jesus story is not the focus of the film. The plot revolves around the political intrigue and plotting of the Sanhedrin and the Zealots. The film presents a different and sympathetic interpretation of Judas contrary to the secular Jewish community's criticism. His role as a disciple is less important than his role as a Zealot. He identifies Jesus' mission as bringing about "spiritual freedom" but believes that Jesus could be "manipulated into political activism." Judas sells out Jesus for thirty pieces of silver only to provoke Caiaphas' arrest of Jesus and the anticipated protests from the people.

Judas is not the villain in this film as the following dialogue between Caiaphas and Judas reveals. Caiaphas asks Judas why he is betraying Jesus. Judas admits, "I trusted him. I thought he was the Messiah. Now I see him for what he is." When asked by Caiaphas if he would repeat that to the Procurator, Judas was adamant, "No!" Judas believed Pilate would

46. For a full text of "Motion Pictures classified by National Legion of Decency," see https://archive.org/stream/motionpicturescl00nati/motionpicturescl00nati_djvu.txt.

"slaughter" Jesus and his followers. Caiaphas guarantees Judas' safety but Judas is more concerned for the safety of the others. He explains, "They're good men: just fooled by him as I was. He [Jesus] alone is your threat. Arrest him, imprison him, and the threat is ended." Judas asks that his terms be met: "Full secrecy and enough money to see me to Egypt." Judas is paid thirty pieces of silver.

Judas reluctantly leads the Temple guards to Jesus in Gethsemane but when he sees that Jesus is taken to the Romans, instead of to the Sanhedrin as planned, he becomes distraught. Judas is concerned for Jesus' safety. Judas is among the riotous crowd when Pilate offers freedom to either Jesus or Barabbas. In an unprecedented move, Judas shouts, "Free the Nazarene" placing himself at odds with the crowd by defending Jesus. His shouts are stifled when a fellow Zealot places his hand over Judas' mouth and knocks him unconscious.

Unable to change Jesus' fate, Judas goes to the Sanhedrin, confesses that he has "sinned and betrayed innocent blood," and throws the coins onto the floor. As he leaves, he begins to unwind the sash from around his waist. It is only at the cross on Calvary that we find out what has happened to Judas. Zadok asks a fellow Zealot, "Has Judas been found?" The man hands over Judas' sash: it has been tied into a noose.

The suicide of Judas evokes sympathy. Unlike the previous two thousand years of history where Judas represented the Jews, his character as a Zealot in *Day of Triumph* personified the mood of the United States in the 1950s: patriotism and anti-Communism, courage in the face of adversity, rallying for justice and the overthrow of oppression. Judas was no longer portrayed as the epitome of evil but as an innocent victim in the world of political intrigue.

### *El mártir del Calvario (1952) (The Martyr of Calvary)*

Director: Miguel Morayta Martinez. Screen writer: Gonzalo E. Sanchez Aparicio. Country: Mexico. Production Company: Oro Films. Length: 113 minutes. Length of Last Supper scene: 4:27 minutes. Color: black and white. Language: Spanish. Musical score: Gustavo Césaro Carrión. Filming locations: Forums Tepeyac Studios, Mexico. Cast: Judas (Manolo Fábregas), Jesus (Enrique Rambal Jr).

#### *Lens One*

Mexican cinema, from its beginnings in the late 1890s to its Golden Age (1935 to 1959), was consistently the largest and most important of all the Spanish-speaking countries. At its peak, the Mexican film industry produced one hundred films annually and supplied screen entertainment to both domestic audiences and international markets in Latin America, the United States and Europe.[47] Their films dealt with Mexican social issues such as poverty, the struggles of urban life and social injustices, together with the idealization of values like love and happiness. Between 1946 and 1950, a period of violent political demonstrations, national economic crises and "the resurgence of Hollywood film production,"[48] Mexican films focused on city life and the deficiency of moral values:[49]

> [L]ife in the city was presented with accuracies and errors, there appeared films of "easy" women and poor neighborhoods, highlighting the loss of moral values, where the city and the search for a better future, fashion and fun, had lost women and men, turning them into negative beings for society. The emblematic films of this era are "Los Tres Garcia" (*The Three Garcias*) from 1946 and "Nosotros los Pobres" (*We the Poor*) from 1947.[50]

Film producers relied on both audience opinion and the film star system, satisfying the audience's cravings for both drama and entertainment.[51] The director, Miguel Morayta Martinez (1907–2013), was one of the most distinguished directors of the Mexican cinema, with over 200 films to his credit. This large number can be attributed to the short length of filming—many were made in just two weeks—and that a film was generally only exhibited for a period of three weeks. Martinez participated in the founding of Film City of Mexico (Churubusco Studios) as well as in the creation of the Union of Writers and Film Directors. A pioneer of color films, Martinez is noted for his creative independence and narrative talent.

*El mártir del Calvario* is a Roman Catholic film intended for a Roman Catholic audience. The film commences with a frame citing a quotation from Jesus, "*Id por todo el mundo; predicad el evangelio a todas las criaturas* (*San Marcos* 16:15)" (Go into all the world and proclaim the good news to the whole creation). The film continues with opening credits on backgrounds of religious paintings depicting events from the annunciation to the baptism of Jesus. Manuel Fábregas (Judas Iscariot) shares

47. Fein, "From Collaboration to Containment," 128–29.

48. Eduardo de la Vega Alfaro, "The Decline of the Golden Age and the Making of the Crisis," in Hershfield and Maciel, eds., *Mexico's Cinema*, 165.

49. Herbert W. Piekow, "The Golden Age of Mexican Cinema," *El Ojo del Lago*. http://www.chapala.com/elojo/index.php?option=com_content&view=article&id=77: mexcinema&catid=59:aprilissue.

50. "Mexican Cinema," *Mexico Explorando*. http://www.explorandomexico.com/about-mexico/5/105/.

51. Carl J. Moro, *Mexican Cinema: Reflections of a Society 1896 to 2004*, 3rd ed. (Jefferson: McFarland & Co., 2005), 75.

equal billing with Enrique Rambal (Jesus) and Consuelo Frank (Mary, mother of Jesus). The narrative begins with Jesus gathering four disciples, John, James, Andrew and Peter, at the Sea of Galilee.

The film substantially utilizes the Gospel of Mark with additional elements drawn from Matthew and John. Martinez also draws on images from the Cecil B. DeMille 1927 epic *The King of Kings* as is evident in the embellishments of the Mary Magdalene and Judas Iscariot characters. The walk to Golgotha is a pictorial "Way of the Cross" which includes recognizable stations, such as Veronica and her veil, Simon of Cyrene helping with the cross and Jesus falling three times.

The film can be neatly arranged into two parts. The first seven chapters illustrate miraculous events such as the multiplication of the loaves and fishes, the healing of the blind man, and the raising of Lazarus. These popular miracle stories would capture the audience's attention but more importantly, they demonstrate the divinity of Jesus. The second part—with nine chapters—traces Jesus' journey, beginning with his entry into Jerusalem and culminating with his crucifixion on Golgotha. As the sub-plots begin to mesh and materialize into the arrest of Jesus, the characters become more developed and convincing while the events leading to Jesus' death are more confrontational. This dramatically alters the tone of the film.

*Lens Two*

A first impression of the Last Supper scene is that it is a typical representation. A long shot encompasses the width of the room. Within the frame are Jesus and his twelve disciples seated at the inverted U-shaped table. Jesus sits at the center of table with Judas sitting at his left and John at his right. On the white tablecloth are pottery mugs with handles, a pottery ewer, individual plates, a number of bowls and a large oval plate in front of Jesus. It is difficult to discern what is on the plate but it is evident that some food has already been eaten. A large, shiny metal chalice is also in front of Jesus.

A more analytical and ordered study of the room reveals a large open window on the back wall behind the table. Through the window are stone houses and a larger building. Some of their windows emit dim light suggesting that it is evening. We cannot see the doorways and paths of these buildings indicating that the Last Supper is taking place in an upper room. Another suggestion that it is early evening is the inclusion of three dimly flickering oil lamps hanging above the table. It is during the progress of the meal and up to the disciples' departure that we see the flames of these lamps intensify, implying that the evening has turned into night.

The relaxed atmosphere of the meal changes when Jesus declares that one of them is going to betray him: one whose hand is on the table. Immediately there is a flurry of activity as the disciples lift their hands off the table. All the disciples are shocked; some stand, others look questioningly at each other. Judas' nervous response is evident by his clutching of his throat and turning to look at Jesus. A clean-shaven and youthful John nestles up to Jesus and asks who will betray him. The betrayer is identified as "one of the twelve, one who is dipping bread into the bowl with me." Jesus breaks off a piece of bread and dips it in the large chalice in front of him. He turns to give the morsel to Judas who willingly takes it in his fingers but does not eat it. The disciples have not made the connection that Judas is the betrayer. A mid-shot shows Judas leaning close to Jesus and asking him, "Master, is it I?" Jesus responds, "Thou hast said it. You are him." The long shot shows Judas turning away from Jesus, his slumping body revealing his despair. The other disciples are oblivious to this exchange of words.

Jesus stands and holds in both hands a large, round flat bread, which looks similar to a priest's large host used in Holy Communion. Jesus says, "Take; this is my body." He breaks the bread into two, giving one-half to Judas and the other half to John. Breaking off a piece, they pass the bread on. Jesus takes in both hands a large metal chalice, elevates it and says, "This is my blood of the covenant." A crosscut to Judas shows that he is still holding the bread. He is deliberating whether to eat it or not and makes two aborted attempts to consume it. Judas then looks to see what the other disciples are doing. Finally, concealing the fact that he will not eat the bread, Judas lets it fall from his fingers and into his lap.

Judas is the first to receive the chalice. He holds it to his lips, but at an angle that makes sipping the wine impossible. His abstaining from drinking the wine goes unnoticed by the disciples but Jesus who was standing next to him and watching would have been aware of the ruse. There is a subtle hint of sadness on Jesus' face when Judas returns the chalice to Jesus. The chalice is then passed to John.

Jesus sits down and turns to speak to Judas, "Go and do what you have to do." There is a look of resignation on Judas' face as he rises from the table. As he goes to leave, he remembers his moneybag and snatches it off the table. The disciples watch Judas leave but they make no comment.

The evening is progressing. The oil lamps are burning brightly and only the lights of the neighboring houses can be seen. The supper continues with Jesus declaring, "Now the Son of Man has been glorified" (John 13:31). Peter asks, "Lord, where are you going?" Thomas poses another question, "Lord, we do not know where you are going. How can we know the way?" Jesus responds, "I am the way, and the truth, and the life" (John 14:6). After a lengthy discourse, the supper concludes with Jesus offering the disciples "the peace." As they leave the table, the scene dissolves into their strolling in Gethsemane.

*Lens Three*

The 1952 release of *El mártir del Calvario* seems inconsistent with the Mexican audiences' desire for escapist movies and yet the film was nominated for best film in 1954 at the Cannes Film Festival. This reinforced the notion that Jesus films were still a viable genre. Moreover, Martinez's directing skills contributed significantly to this nomination.

During the Spanish Civil War (1936–1939), Martinez was a Republican Lieutenant General. Although he did not actively promote his Republican ideals in his films, it seems self-evident that his wartime experiences influenced his filmmaking. Through the role and voice of Judas, Martinez echoed his own disillusionment and frustrations with unfulfilled promises of a better kingdom. Martinez was to comment after the war, "There was no Republican side, only people who rose up and people who did not."[52] Judas' enthusiastic rallying of the people of Jerusalem and their their non-committal attitude to the cause substantiates Martinez's comment.

Despite being a nephew of General Francisco Franco—leader of the Nationalists and dictator of the new fascist regime—Martinez was exiled from his birth country, Spain, for his part in the Civil War. His reputation was tarnished because of this relationship with Franco and his support for the Republicans. Judas Iscariot's reputation is also tarnished. His relationship with the Jewish religious authorities and his desire to overthrow Roman oppression makes him an unwelcome supporter.

*The Portrayal of Judas*

Judas stands out in the group, not only for the major role he plays in this Passion narrative but also for his good looks and flamboyant costume. Judas is in his mid-twenties, clean-shaven and handsome. Appearance is important to him as is evidenced by his hairstyle. His short black hair is beautifully styled with "kiss curls" and is always neat. The clothing he wears is quite different to that of the other disciples. He wears a knee-length patterned tunic of a light color and a large leather belt with two ornate metal discs. Over the short-sleeved tunic, he wears a long sleeveless cloak of a darker color. The large gold chains around his neck, the three garish gemmed rings and two gold bangles suggest that Judas has wealth

52. Antonio Regaldo, "Miguel Morayta: A Forgotten Film," *ABC.es* (October 30, 2009). http://www.abc.es/hermeroteca/historico-30-10-2009/abc/Toledo/miguel-moroayta-un-olvido-de-cine_1131083948429.html.

and expensive tastes. One startling feature that distinguishes Judas from the other disciples is that he wears a large gold hoop earring. An actor wearing this style of earring would not have raised much attention in the late 1940s/50s because of the popularity of pirate films. A gold hoop earring was part of the pirate's costume. The dissimilarity, however, is that pirates wore their earring in their left ear: in this film, Judas wears the earring in his right ear, suggesting that he is being portrayed as homosexual.

This portrayal raises a number of pertinent questions. Was Martinez using Judas to make a statement about what he considered deviant sexuality? During the 1950s there was a strong social and religious stigma attached to anyone regarded as homosexual. Indeed, the Roman Catholic Catechism teaches "homosexual acts are intrinsically disordered… Under no circumstances can they be approved."[53]

It is Judas who introduces Jesus to Mary Magdalene when she comes looking for the Nazarene. This begs another question, "How did Judas know her?" If Judas were homosexual, one would assume that he would be privy to the Jerusalem sexual sub-cultures and socialize among them. However, if he had been one of Mary's "clients," does this dismiss the implication that Judas was gay? Certainly, the way in which Judas leers at Mary's half-naked body suggests that he was heterosexual. Perhaps the director was hedging his bets by implying homosexuality and then allowing one lascivious moment. Another possible explanation is that Judas is bisexual—an even more heinous sin. The images of a leering Judas are fleeting and would probably go unnoticed by the audience because their focus would likely be on Mary. However, the gold earring in Judas' right ear remained throughout the film, a constant reminder to the viewers of his possible marginal sexual respectability.

The Judas character in *El mártir del Calvario* is multifaceted. With each of his appearances in the film, we learn of another trait that can be added to his profile. Judas first encounters Jesus in a town when a paralytic seeks healing. Having witnessed the miraculous healing, Judas approaches and greets Jesus with "*Maestro*!" This salutation shows Judas' awe and respect for Jesus and his desire to serve him. He introduces himself as "Judas, Judas Iscariot" and takes his place as the twelfth disciple. From this point on Judas takes precedence over the other disciples. He does not push his way into this leadership position. He is constantly seen standing at Jesus' side, has the most to say and has the closest relationship with Jesus. This is evident by Jesus giving Judas the chalice before he passes it to John—traditionally "the beloved disciple."

53. Article 2357, "Chastity and homosexuality," *Catechism of the Catholic Church* (Dublin: Veritas, 1994), 505.

Figure 6. Judas, wearing a gold hoop earring, and Jesus talking.
© Laguna Films.

Judas understood the meaning of Jesus' mission and could see ways in which to exploit it. He first recognized Jesus as the one who could lead the revolt against Rome when he saw the crowd's response to Jesus' teaching them how to pray the Lord's Prayer (Luke 11:1–13). From that moment on, Judas only saw Jesus as the "King of Israel" and took every opportunity to campaign for the Jewish overthrow of the Roman occupation of Israel. For example, when a Roman centurion asks Jesus to heal his slave, Judas suggests to Jesus that he should charge for "these healings" to build up the communal purse of which Judas was in charge. Judas is a shrewd business manager! Judas is the one who informs Jesus of the death of Lazarus and, at the rising of Lazarus, he is first to acknowledge that Lazarus is alive and "has been set free." Judas' shouting was not because he was amazed at the miracle, but that he was trying to generate mourners' support for Jesus. The more supporters Jesus has, the stronger the influence he will have in ousting the Roman oppressors—or so Judas believes.

Judas continues with this enthusiasm into Jerusalem where he leads Jesus' entry. Waving an olive branch Judas shouts, "*Viva Rey de Israel*!" (Long live the King of Israel!) This image would resonate with Spanish and Mexican audiences who witnessed a number of demonstrations and calls for revolutions in their recent turbulent histories. When Jesus dismounts his donkey and does a "walk-through" to heal the sick, Judas becomes disgruntled that Jesus is not focusing on political objectives. A frustrated Judas throws down his olive branch alluding to his desire for rebellion not peace. Yet Judas does not lose faith in his *Maestro*.

The cleansing of the Temple by Jesus allays any concerns Judas may have had. Indeed, Judas is reassured when he hears Jesus tell the Temple priests, "In three days I will destroy the Temple, and in three days I will re-build it" (John 2:19). When Jesus is telling the disciples what to do and where to go to prepare for their Passover meal, Judas listens carefully. When they leave, Judas stays behind so that he can commence his plan to force Jesus' hand by turning him over to the Sanhedrin.

There is nothing to support traditional accusations that Judas was greedy, a thief and that he betrayed Jesus for money. We do not see Judas striking a bargain with the priests but we do see him checking and counting the thirty pieces of silver doled out by one of the priests. His actions are perfunctory and he appears confident and in control. Judas is the one giving instructions as to who, when, where and how Jesus will be identified. Clearly, the meeting with the priests is a means to an end: Judas is forcing Jesus' hand.

The betrayal goes to plan. This is an arrest made solely by Jewish guards led by Malchus. Having kissed Jesus on the cheek Jesus asks, "Judas is it with a kiss that you betray me?" Judas raises his lantern, making Jesus more visible, and then steps away. Judas cannot watch Jesus' arrest: troubled by what he has had to do, he buries his head in his chest.

Judas' loyalty to Jesus is evident in the next scene: Jesus' trial before the Sanhedrin. This scene is particularly volatile. Judas is standing in the crowd watching the proceedings and is visibly upset by the people's animosity towards Jesus and their damning testimonies. Caiaphas finds Jesus guilty of blasphemy and orders that he be sent to Pilate to be tried as a criminal. Judas cannot contain himself and shouts, "Wait!" He pushes his way through the guards, runs towards Caiaphas, grabs him by his cloak, and spins him around. A distraught Judas pleads his case and dramatically empties his money purse, but to no avail. Two guards forcibly remove the still shouting and struggling Judas. As they make their way through the crowd, the people punch Judas and jeer at him. Their anger turns away from Jesus and is now directed at Judas.

Judas' role in this Jesus film is of such significance that his final appearance is shown in a parallel scene with Jesus. A bloodied and exhausted Jesus carries a cross out of the city to the sound of a beating drum. A crosscut to Judas shows him running through an olive grove, his hands covering his ears trying to block out the sound of the drumbeats. A large rope dangles from his arm. Another crosscut returns us to Golgotha and Jesus' crucifixion. Jesus cries out his last words, "Father, into your hands I commend my spirit." A storm breaks, and a crosscut shows Judas hanging from a tree, his lifeless body swaying in the wind.

Miguel Morayta Martinez presents a Judas who breaks the stereotypical filmic Judas Iscariot mold: Judas actually looks the part of a 1950s hero. There is little to show that his character is questionable, apart from the gold earring and the issue of his sexuality. He marvels at Jesus' miracles and listens intently to his teachings. He is Jesus' avid supporter and confidante and is the first of the disciples to recognize Jesus' mission. Judas is the only disciple who attends Jesus' trial before the Sanhedrin and the only person to defend Jesus' actions.

In presenting Judas in this way, Martinez highlights the real villain of narrative: the Jews. The Star of David is a significant—and anachronistic—symbol differentiating the Romans and the Jews. A large Star of David is displayed behind Caiaphas' chair whereas a large eagle statue is behind Pontius Pilate's throne. The shields of the Roman army are unadorned whereas a large Star of David decorates the shields of the Jewish Temple guards. Caiaphas and his two associate priests, in their lavish priestly robes, feigning piety, are the ones who demand Jesus be crucified and stand at the foot of the cross heckling Jesus. Pilate in contrast appears to be the mediator in an internal religious matter. By omitting Pilate's washing his hands of the whole affair, Martinez dilutes Pilate's responsibility, and any blame pointed at him.

*El mártir del Calvario* was post-Holocaust and yet the film still promoted anti-Semitism and anti-Judaism, although this may have had more to do with Mexico's Roman Catholic religious conservatism, anti-Semitic history and immigration policies. Mexico admitted only 400 Jewish refugees between 1933 and 1945, but issued at least 16,000 immigration visas to Spanish loyalist refugees between 1938 and 1945, and over 1,400 visas to Catholic Polish refugees between 1939 and 1941.[54]

## *Summary*

It is in the 1930s–1950s that we see dramatic changes in the traditional portrayals of Judas. *Golgotha* (1935) depicted Judas as the exemplar of Jewish behavior as propagated by Nazi anti-Semitic propaganda. *Maria Magdalena, pecadora de Magdala* (1946) introduces "the twelfth

54. "Refuge in Latin America," *Holocaust Encyclopedia*, United States Holocaust Museum. http://www.ushmm.org/wlc/en/article.php?ModuleId=10007824.

disciple" as middle class, handsome and sophisticated and who is double-crossed by the upper echelons of Jewish society, the Sanhedrin. Another Mexican film, *El mártir del Calvario* (1952), breaks the mold of the stereotypical Jew and presents Judas as having traits of a 1950s' hero. Judas' role in *I Beheld His Glory* (1952) is so small that his name is mentioned only twice, and he only says one word, "Master." However, two years later in *Day of Triumph*, we see Judas' role as disciple superseded by his political activism and position within the Zealots. American filmmakers in the 1950s did not have the unbridled creative freedoms afforded to directors in the first three decades of filmmaking. They were governed by Production Codes and sought the "Seal of Approval" for their films. They were cognizant not only of how film could sway public opinion and denigrate sub-cultures in society but how the success—or otherwise—of a film was dictated by the response of an audience. Would they pay to enter the movie theatre? Still recovering from the Second World War and Nazi Holocaust, explicit anti-Semitic content was avoided and more nuanced portraits of Jesus were filmed. It is in this historical and economic environment that similarly the Judas portrayal began to be transformed.

## Chapter 4

# THE BIBLICAL EPICS: THE SIXTIES

### *Introduction*

The 1960s was a decade of "isms": afro-centrism, feminism, environmentalism, terrorism, mysticism, materialism, minimalism, racism, communism, socialism, anti-Semitism, colonialism and liberalism. It was a decade of "New Left" uprisings from Prague to Peru, and of "wars": the Vietnam War, the Six-Day War and even the "Space War" (the race to the moon). The 1960s also witnessed a number of "revolutions": the Chinese Cultural Revolution, the sexual revolution and the emergence of "gay" liberation. Fashion underwent radical change with the introduction of mini-skirts and bell-bottomed pants, while medicine marveled at the revolutionary first heart transplant performed by South African, Christiaan Barnard. The Roman Catholic Church responded to this perceived decadence by issuing fifteen Papal Encyclicals that addressed issues, such as the doctrine and worship of the Holy Eucharist (*Mysterium Fidei*—Mystery of Faith), the Church's traditional teaching of marriage, parenthood and the continuing proscription of most forms of "unnatural" birth control (*Humanae Vitae*—Of Human Life).[1]

Together with sweeping changes in society came transformations of cinema and the re-shaping of the commercial cinema of Hollywood and of Europe's art of cinema. Film-making in this era was characterized by "a dominance of the subjective point of view, a critical view of society—sometimes even with a strong political motive—and a conscious and critical use of conventional narrative and genre structures."[2] European directors such as Ingmar Bergman, Luis Buñuel, Federico Fellini and

1. "Papal Encyclicals," *Papal Encyclicals Online*. http://www.papalencyclicals.net/all.htm.

2. Peter Hasenberg, "The 'Religious' in Film: From *King of Kings* to *The Fisher King*," in May, ed., *New Images of Religious Film*, 43.

Pier Paolo Pasolini, promoted their films as a medium to express their own understanding of religion/Christianity and to offer discussions of theological questions. Hollywood director Nicholas Ray used his films as social commentaries and as expressions of his leftist views. His protagonists were usually troubled loners unable to fit in with society, and his films sympathized with them. One notable exception is his epic film, *King of Kings*.

### *King of Kings (1961)*

Director: Nicholas Ray. Screenwriter: Philip Yordan. Country: USA. Production Company: Samuel Bronston Productions. Length: 168 minutes. Length of Last Supper scene: 5:47 minutes. Color: Technicolor. Language: English. Musical score: Miklós Rózsa. Filming locations: Chinçon, Madrid, Spain. Cast: Judas (Rip Torn), Jesus (Jeffrey Hunter).

#### *Lens One*

A publicity poster for *King of Kings* describes the film as an "intelligent" telling of "the life of Christ," "beautifully filmed" and "full of deeply moving moments." It is uncertain as to what the advertisers meant by "intelligent." Perhaps it would have been more accurate to advertise the film as an unusual interpretation of the telling of the life of Christ. When compared to Cecil B. DeMille's *The King of Kings*, there are significant differences in the plot and characterization. The treatment of the Christ story varies significantly from the 1927 silent film of the same name. Producer Samuel Bronston attempted to frame the biblical story of Jesus within the context of ancient and contemporary history, and notably post-Holocaust Jewish history.[3]

Although screenwriter Philip Yordan telescopes many of the Gospels' events and statements, he "totally ignores a wealth of potentially dramatic material."[4] Lloyd Baugh notes that to make *King of Kings* into an epic-spectacular style and to attract the largest possible viewing public, the production team had to effect two major transformations on their basic source-text, the Gospels. On the one hand, they had to transform the sparse, elliptical, linear, non-dramatic text of the Gospels into a full, organic narrative, characterized by dramatic action and movement, character interest and suspense, in order to grab and hold onto the attention of the audience. On the other hand, they had to transform the tough

3. Babington and Evans, *Biblical Epics*, 127.
4. Kinnard and Davis, *Divine Images*, 131.

radical, uncompromising, prophetic content and tone of the Gospel text into a form that continued to edify, of course, but in a softer, safer manner, without offending or alienating any member of the viewing public.[5]

The result is that the film contains many historical, biblical and theological distortions. Thus, we view Jesus (Jeffrey Hunter) visiting John the Baptist (Robert Ryan) in prison! Then there is a supposed close relationship between Pilate (Hurd Hatfield) and Herod Antipas (Frank Thring). Likewise, maintaining the spectacle and excitement of the "sword and sandal" films of the 1950s, *King of Kings* has two battle scenes: one at the beginning of the film and the other when Jesus enters Jerusalem. There is an additional character to the Gospel accounts with the inclusion of the Roman centurion, Lucius (Ron Randal). He appears at all of the following events: the "massacre of the innocents," the Sermon on the Mount, the trial before Pilate and the crucifixion.

*King of Kings* presents a very human Jesus. Although Jesus' words are largely scripturally faithful, there is little to suggest that he is divine. Therefore, important biblical events such as the transfiguration, Jesus' foretelling of his death and resurrection, the "cleansing" of the Temple and the miracles are missing from the film. Edward O'Connor in reviewing *Kings of Kings* points out that Jesus never claims to be divine and that "some scenes are constructed [so] that he seems to be disclaiming it."[6]

There are six reasons for the film's reluctance to portray the divinity of Jesus. Keeping Jesus' humanity dominant over his divinity was to accommodate pluralism and to give the least possible offense to the religious sensibilities of all audiences—believers and non-believers.[7] Parts of the Gospel message ran counter to certain contemporary values and needed to be synchronized with these.[8] Jesus for example spoke of peace and did not seek freedom from Roman oppression. Whereas, President John F. Kennedy's inaugural address had warned, "Those who make freedom impossible made revolution inevitable."[9] A third reason for the reluctance to portray Jesus' divinity was that the miracles would not go down with a modern audience. For them, experience was the only way of knowing, seeing is believing, and they would try to rationalize miraculous events such as the five thousand sharing their lunches as opposed to Jesus multiplying the five loaves and two fish (Matt 14:13–21; Mark 6:31–44;

5. Baugh, *Imaging the Divine*, 18–19.

6. Edward O'Connor, "King of Kings," *Films* 12, no. 9 (November 1961): 549.

7. Ibid.

8. Forshey, *American Spectaculars*, 92–93.

9. Mark Hawkins-Dady, *Speeches That Changed the World* (London: Quercus, 2010), 132–35.

Luke 9:10–17; John 6:5–11). There were also Hollywood constraints such as budget.[10] Lang suggests that Ray had no real religious motive for directing the film,[11] and the producer, director and writer viewed the subject of Christ solely as hot box-office property. It was hoped that *King of Kings* would be an economic success. There was no intention of producing a Christian evangelistic movie.

I would also add another reason. Due to additional and inter-connecting narratives involving Barabbas (Harry Guardino), Lucius, John the Baptist, Pontius Pilate, Herod Antipas and Judas Iscariot (Rip Torn), there is simply not enough screen-time to expand Jesus' role. For a film about the life of Jesus, it seems extraordinary that not even half the film's screen-time (77 minutes) centers on Jesus himself. An omniscient narrator (Orson Welles) connects episodes by quoting Scripture, explaining an event and tying together story lines involving the main characters.

There are various screenplay sources for the *King of Kings*. The film draws mainly from the Synoptic Gospels, with only three references to John's Gospel; Jesus' teaching about the Good Shepherd, the woman caught in adultery and Mary Magdalene's appearance at the tomb. These reinforce the humanity of Jesus because to have used John's "high Christology" would have elevated Jesus' status to divine. Non-scriptural sources include Josephus' *The Antiquities of the Jews* and *The War of the Jews*, which provide the necessary details of Roman colonial oppression. The Stations of the Cross are used sparingly: for example, a woman (Veronica) wipes Jesus' bloodied face with her veil but no facial imprint is shown. The apocryphal tradition of identifying Mary Magdalene as the woman caught in adultery is to contrast her as a "woman of sin" to the Virgin Mary who is a "woman of grace."

*Lens Two*

Nicholas Ray's interpretation of the Last Supper is very different to the corresponding scenes in earlier and later Jesus films. The most striking variance is that the table is a Y-shape. Ray did not want to replicate Leonardo da Vinci's *Last Supper* but to design a table whereby Jesus could distribute the broken bread to each of the disciples. Ray explains in an interview: "I took a cross and broke it in such a way that the horizontal arms did not meet. Then I placed Jesus at the head of the cross."[12]

10. Babington and Evans, *Biblical Epics*, 127.

11. Stephen J. Lang, *The Bible on the Big Screen: A Guide from Silent Films to Today's Movies* (Grand Rapids: Baker Books, 2007), 159.

12. Jean Douchet and Jacques Joly, "*Nouvel entretien avec* Nicholas Ray," *Cah Cinema* 22, no. 127 (January 1962): 10.

Looking at the table is a reminder of Jesus' body nailed to the cross and his arms extended. Moreover, the table is wooden and uncovered adding to the impression of a cross. The Y-shape is also similar to the 1960s Hippy "Peace" symbol suggesting that the table/cross is a metaphor for Jesus' message of universal peace.

Figure 7. Judas is hesitant to take the bread from Jesus.
© Metro-Goldwyn-Mayer.

The Last Supper scene commences with the disciples setting the table with suitable utensils and various bowls of food suggesting that it is to be a Jewish Seder meal. During the setting of the table, a disciple washes Jesus' hands. This is the *urchatz* (washing the hands without a blessing). To a Christian audience the action is similar to the priest washing his/her hands before the Great Thanksgiving in the Mass. Jesus and the disciples are standing at the table when Judas hurries into the room. He removes his sandals and places them with the others. A close-up of the sandals suggests that the foot washing has already taken place, thus inferring that Judas is ritually unwashed. Judas, with head lowered so as not to look at Jesus, makes his way to his seat. Judas' late arrival is noticed. The disciples look questioningly at him but Jesus' expression is like that of a teacher glaring at a student coming late into class. They remain sitting in silence. Judas is situated diagonally opposite Jesus. The disciple's nervousness is evident from his body language: his hand is clutching his throat.

The Seder meal continues with Jesus placing his fingers in a bowl of green herbs and offering the *maror* (traditional blessing), "Blessed are you O Lord our God, King of the universe who bids us eat bitter herbs." This is followed by *karpas*, the dipping of parsley into salt-water and eating it. Jesus then informs them, "Tonight one of you will betray me." The camera cuts to Judas and an extreme close-up of his face: he is staring at Jesus. There is no anger or fear in his eyes but he has a resolute look. The camera cuts to Jesus and again an extreme close-up shot is used. Jesus too has a look of acceptance. He rises from the table, leans over to Judas, and orders, "What you must do, do it quickly." A compliant Judas leaves the table, collects his sandals and hurries down the stairs. His early departure means that he does not share in the bread or the cup.

There follows a discussion about Jesus being with the disciples for only a short time, the disciples' declaration that they will "follow Jesus to the ends of the earth," Jesus' prediction that Peter will deny him three times, that their grief will be like that of a woman giving birth and that "tonight you will all lose courage." Jesus concludes with, "My last wish is that you love one another as I have loved you. The greatest gift a man can give to his friends is to lay down his life for his friends."

To create a solemn Jewish ambience as well as hinting at Jesus' own Jewish heritage, background music of a male Hebrew *a cappella* chorus is singing a *piut* (a form of Hebrew poetry). The lyrics recount how foreign armies had conquered Israel, but God will eventually redeem the nation. This song is strategically placed between the end of the Jewish Seder meal (Matt 26:30) and the beginning of the Christian Eucharist.

Jesus stands and takes flat bread in both hands and with eyes closed, prays the Jewish blessing, "Blessed are You, Lord our God, King of the Universe, who brings forth bread from the earth." He breaks the bread in two and then breaks off a morsel to give to John sitting on his right. Jesus says, "Take," continues to break the bread and hands it to three of the disciples. Jesus then instructs them to "eat" and resumes distributing the bread. He explains, "For this is my body. Do this in remembrance of me" (Luke 22:19).

The supper now includes elements of a Christian Eucharist. Jesus removes the white veil from the silver chalice, already filled with wine. Taking the chalice, he elevates it with both hands and with eyes closed, Jesus again prays, "Blessed are you O Lord our God, King of the universe who creates the fruit of the vine." The placing of his open hand on the chalice reflects the Christian priestly act of consecration. Jesus continues, "Drink, for this is my blood of the covenant which is shed for you and for many for the remission of sins." Jesus does not include the word "new" when describing "covenant" (Luke 22:20; 1 Cor 11:25). Omitting "new" before "covenant" avoids the suggestion of Christian supersession of Judaism.

*Lens Three*

Babington and Evans note that although *King of Kings* presents itself as a Christ narrative and that the film "asserts orthodoxy," it also offers allusions to contemporary historical events.[13] These include the Nazi Holocaust of World War II, the Arab/Jewish conflict following the establishment of the State of Israel in 1948 and then the post-Suez (1956) consolidation of the Jewish State. There was the Russian threat and Communism, the Hungarian uprising in 1956, America's unwillingness to risk war with the Soviets and President John F. Kennedy's failed attempt to liberate Cuba and the failure of the Bay of Pigs invasion in 1961. Although *King of Kings* would have been in post-production for at least a year prior to its premiere on 11 October 1961, any connection to the Bay of Pigs incident would need to be inferred by the viewing audience. Nicholas Ray uses *King of Kings* as a social commentary on post-1948 American and Jewish history.

*King of Kings*, with its explanation of Barabbas, Judas and even to some degree Jesus, in terms of historical contexts, nationalism, and colonialism, explores Jewish victimization under Roman rule. This idea is paralleled with the Nazis' systematic extermination of European Jews.

The horrors of the Nazi concentration camps were exposed during the Nuremberg Trials of 1945–1946, where the documentary film entitled *Nazi Concentration Camps* was shown as evidence of the atrocities of the Holocaust and provided indelible images of crimes against humanity. Ray utilized a number of these images in his film to simulate Roman conquest of Jerusalem. The opening narration recounts the Roman pro-consul and General Pompey (Conrado San Martin) who in 63 BCE, and after a three-month siege that resulted in the slaughter of thousands of Jews,

13. Babington and Evans, *Biblical Epics*, 130.

took possession of Jerusalem. The corresponding scenes show Roman troops throwing the bodies of murdered Jews over the city walls onto a pile of burning corpses. This is clearly a grotesque re-enactment of what happened in Nazi concentration camps.

A further Holocaust reminder is a scene where Pompey, riding a black stallion, has his access to the Court of the Priests blocked by a line of resolute white-robed Temple priests. At Pompey's signal, soldiers hurl spears, killing the priests. Juxtaposed in our minds is the image of a black car entering a ghetto and from which emerges a Gestapo officer who dispassionately orders the shooting of innocent Jews.

It can be argued that it was out of sympathy for the tragedy of the Jews and a sincere but misguided effort to correct the sins of the past that *King of Kings* deliberately omits significant elements of the Passion narrative. The script absolves the Jewish authorities from *any* involvement in the death of Jesus. There is no confrontation between Jesus and the Jewish authorities represented by the scribes and Pharisees. The "cleansing of the temple" is omitted thus maintaining the image of Jesus as the "Messiah of Peace." There is no conspiracy to arrest Jesus and to have him executed and there is no trial of Jesus before the Sanhedrin. An obvious omission is that there is no mob shouting "Crucify him!" and no "His blood be upon us" curse. Babington and Evans note that imputed Jewish guilt is also diminished because it is the Romans who control the Jewish priesthood.[14]

Just as the blame for the death of Jesus was placed solely on Judas Iscariot, the responsibility for the execution of Jesus is placed entirely on the shoulders of Pilate, who proclaims before Jesus, "I and I alone, have the authority to sentence you to crucifixion." Missing from the film is Pilate's washing of his hands and declaration, "I am innocent of this man's blood" (Matt 27:24). Instead, Pilate oversees the scourging of Jesus and smiles in approval as the guards mockingly anoint Jesus as King with a crown of thorns.

Ray's films are considered to be social commentaries, yet *King of Kings* debates more than the upheavals of a revolutionary decade. By using symbolic images and a narrative that transcends the traditional version of biblical events, the film attempted to educate a post-Holocaust audience about the persecution of the Jewish people by an oppressive regime. It is uncertain whether audiences in 1961 made this connection as reviews of the film from that time lack any mention of the Holocaust. It seems that the audience's attention was fixed on how Jesus was portrayed. Incredulously, at one preview, the crucifixion scene offended the audience because Jesus'

14. Ibid., 106.

chest and armpits were considered too hairy! Indeed, Jeffrey Hunter was forced to shave them and then re-shoot the scene. Significantly, the two bare-chested criminals crucified with Jesus escaped criticism and thus having to shave!

*King of Kings* received mixed reviews. Although the film was praised for the vast technical resources of the modern cinema, and acknowledged as the crowning achievement in the portrayal of Christ on the screen, the Legion of Decency was compelled to give *King of Kings* a "Separate Classification." The explanation was, "While acknowledging the inspirational intent of this motion picture, the poetic license taken in the development of the life of Christ renders the film theologically, historically, and scripturally inaccurate."[15] With an estimated production budget of just over five million dollars and the world-wide gross box-office takings up to January 1989 of only twenty-five million dollars, the film can be considered a box-office failure.

### *The Portrayal of Judas*

There are significant differences between Judas in *King of Kings* and Judas in the Gospels. The filmic Judas is a key player in the narrative. His actions and motives are governed by his desire to rid Judea of Roman rule. He has two options available to him: to "run with Barabbas, the messiah of war, or to walk with Jesus, the new messiah of peace." Judas becomes a disciple of both.

Judas is an intermediary, liaising between Jesus and Barabbas. He is advisor and part of the patriots' inner circle, and, having fought side by side with Barabbas, knows that violent insurrection is ultimately futile. Initially swayed by Jesus and his message of peace, Judas unsuccessfully attempts to convert Barabbas to non-violent resistance to Roman rule.

Jesus does not call Judas to be a disciple but rather Judas asks if he can follow him. Having witnessed an angry mob's attempt at stoning a woman caught in adultery—erroneously identified as Mary Magdalene—Judas believes that Jesus' message of peace could be a better way to free Judea of Roman tyranny. However, Judas' understanding of the messianic role of Jesus is tragically twisted, and he becomes disillusioned with the refusal of Jesus to do anything about the Roman occupation.

Judas becomes impatient with Jesus and rejects Jesus' more difficult "way"—that of establishing the Kingdom of God. Instead, Judas chooses a more direct route, one that is more aligned with Barabbas' vision. Judas wants Jesus to declare his kingship openly and to use his miraculous

15. Moira Walsh, "Christ or Credit Card?" *America* 106, no. 3 (October 21, 1961): 72.

powers to topple the Romans. To achieve this, Judas plans to put Jesus to the test and force his hand because "once [Jesus] feels the Roman sword at his throat, he will strike them down with the wave of one arm."

George Komar suggests that by contrasting Judas' plan with Jesus' rebuttal to the Devil in the final temptation in the desert[16] ("You cannot force me to put the Lord my God to the proof!" Matt 4:7), "Judas has assumed the role of the Tempter."[17] Komar's observation is corroborated with the background music reminiscent of the Devil's theme heard during the previous temptation in the desert scene.

Barabbas and his accomplices' failed attempt to overthrow the Romans at the Temple forces Judas to act on his plan to have Jesus acknowledge that he is the Messiah. The film's narrator explains that Judas runs to Caiaphas "to betray Jesus to the chief priests and the captains" and goes on to say how "Jesus and Barabbas were the left and the right hands of the same body, thus Judas thought to test and prove forever the divine power of the Messiah." This act of betrayal is not portrayed on screen and the audience is left to imagine that it was carried out. There is no meeting between the Jewish authorities or Temple guards and no discussion of payment or the counting out of thirty pieces of silver. Judas in the Gospels is described as acting out of selfish gain and monetary greed, whereas in *King of Kings*, he betrays Jesus for patriotic reasons: for the benefit of Judea. This film offers a credible reason for Judas' act of betrayal by "wrapping the motivations up in a plausible package."[18]

Apart from the subtle musical paralleling of Judas with the "Tempter," there is nothing to suggest that Judas is evil or that he is the stereotypical Jew. Rather he is a confused and tormented patriot whose failure is that he "cannot chose between what are diametrically, opposed perspectives."[19] Judas' only "sin" is that of presumption: thinking that he knows better than Jesus as to what Jesus should be doing.[20] There is no malice in Judas when he approaches Jesus in the Garden of Gethsemane. His eyes are fixed upon Jesus and his betrayal by a kiss is to force Jesus' hand.

Judas has absolute faith in Jesus' ability to bring about peace and has no qualms in telling Barabbas and his followers of the "Messiah of

16. Matt 4:1–11; Mark 1:12–13; Luke 4:1–13.

17. George Komar, "*King of Kings:* Rediscovering the Film and Score," *PMS* 60 Series 2, 4, no. 2 (Winter 2002): 11. http://www.mrs.miklosrozsa.info/pmsfiles/PMS60.pdf.

18. Forshey, *American Spectaculars*, 92.

19. Paul V. M. Flesher and Robert Torry, *Religion and Film: An Introduction* (Nashville: Abingdon, 2007) 106.

20. Paffenroth, "Film Depictions," 2.

Peace." When the disciples scatter at Gethsemane, Judas follows Jesus. With horror, he witnesses the scourging of Jesus and collapses when he sees carpenters assembling crosses. Judas follows the progress of the way of the cross by running on the roof-tops. In witnessing Jesus' struggle, the loyal disciple still expects Jesus to make his messianic declaration. As Jesus nears the place of execution, a matte-shot of the walled city of Jerusalem reveals Judas making his way up to Golgotha. He picks up a stone reminding the audience of when he picked up a discarded stone on first meeting Jesus who was defending the adulterous woman. The stone that Judas now holds has blood on it. He realizes that his plan to force Jesus' hand has resulted in the shedding of innocent blood.

A confused Barabbas, who has also been following Jesus to Golgotha, joins Judas, and attempts reconciliation, but Judas, who is now beyond consolation, spurns him and together they watch the crucifixion. When Judas finally comes to the realization that Jesus is not going to perform a miracle he turns and runs away.

Later, Barabbas, walking through Gethsemane, comes across Judas' lifeless body hanging from a tree. The snapping of the branch from which Judas is suspended intensifies the scene. Judas falls to the ground, his head twisted by the cord of his money purse. It is noteworthy that Judas used his purse cord as the instrument of death. Even though Ray chose not to portray Judas as a lover of money, Judas' death reminds us of Jesus' earlier warning to Judas: "No man can serve two masters, either he will hate the one and love the other, or he will cling to the one and despise the other, you cannot serve God and Mammon [money]" (Matt 6:24; Luke 16:13).

Judas has a stronger belief in Jesus' temporal power than do the other disciples and this partially redeems him. Gerald Forshey notes:

> [Judas'] faith serves two functions—to show that Christ was not wrong to choose the disciple who later would betray him (thereby keeping intact his deity), and to allow the audience to identify Judas as one who believed, and therefore was worthy of eventual salvation—the popular American conviction that everyone will finally be saved.[21]

*King of Kings* presents a different interpretation of previous filmic Judases in that it overlooks Judas' motives and portrays him as a "bewildered scapegoat."[22] It also presents a Judas who bears no stereotypical Jewish traits. *The Jewish Daily Forward* wrote at the time of the New York world premiere of *King of Kings*: "Judas gives over Jesus to the

21. Forshey, *American Spectaculars*, 92.
22. Kinnard and Davis, *Divine Images*, 132.

Roman Governor of Judea, hoping that when He would be tortured He would prove his powers and would overthrow the Roman Governor and Judea would be free—were it that the Christian world would accept this interpretation…for this everyone who is associated with this picture deserves thanks and compliments."[23]

Judas has become the one who sets in motion Jesus' salvific act—his death on a cross. Judas is moving towards redemption!

### *Il Vangelo Secondo Matteo (1964)*<br>*(The Gospel According to Saint Matthew)*

Director: Pier Paolo Pasolini. Screenwriter: Pier Paolo Pasolini. Country: Italy/France. Production Company: Titanus Distribuzione S.p.a. Length: 137 minutes. Length of Last Supper scene: 2:45 minutes. Color: black and white. Language: Italian. Musical score: Luis Enriquez. Filming locations: Apulia and Calabria, Italy. Cast: Judas (Otello Sestili), Jesus (Enrique Irazoqui).

*Lens One*

Pier Paolo Pasolini's second major film, *Il Vangelo Secondo Matteo*, endorsed by the Vatican and dedicated to the memory of Pope John XXIII, is perhaps the least traditional of Jesus films. This reflects the persona of the late John XXIII, who "usurped notions about the Church and introduced Vatican II."[24]

Compared to Ray's *King of Kings* blockbuster production, Pasolini's dramatization of Jesus is, according to Chris Dashiell, "more like a home movie that happened to be about Jesus."[25] The film was shot in black and white, dislodging the narrative from its specific geographical context,[26] with much of the photography being carried out by a hand-held camera, and the cast made up of non-professional actors. By setting the film in rural southern Italy, Pasolini was able to switch from the ancient to the modern world without needing to recreate it either "archaeologically or philologically."[27] Maurizio Viano notes:

23. Komar, "*King of Kings*," 5.

24. Seth Studer, review of "*Il Vangelo Secondo Matteo*," *Vagrant Café*. http://www.vagrantcafe.com/christiancinema/2004_02_24_archive.htm.

25. Chris Dashiell, "Loaves and Fishes: Pasolini's Gospel and the Depiction of Jesus on Film," *CineScene.com*. http://www.cinescene.com/dash/gospel.htm.

26. Adele Reinhartz, "Jesus in Film: Hollywood Perspectives on the Jewishness of Jesus," *JRF* 2, no. 2 (1998): 3. http://www.unomaha.edu/jrf/JesusinFilmRein.htm.

27. Maurizio Viano, *A Certain Realism: Making Use of Pasolini's Film Theory and Practice* (Berkeley: University of California Press, 1993), 137.

> Free of expensive sets and technicolor embellishments, Pasolini's *Il Vangelo* is a low-budget production that eschews the idea of faithful historical reconstruction and opts for analogical rereading. Whereas reconstruction forgets the present and aims at an absolute past, analogy translates the past into the present and suggests a series of relations of resemblance and difference for the audience to recognize and to judge. If reconstruction ultimately abuses history, holding it up to the paranoid myth of discovering "what really happened," analogy *uses* personal and historical knowledge to gain insights for the present.[28]

Pasolini's cinematic techniques characterize the features of neo-realism, which André Bazin called a cinema of "fact" and "reconstituted reportage." Neo-realism in film began in 1943 during the anti-Fascist movement and ended in 1952.

*Il Vangelo* was the first Jesus film to be based solely on one Gospel, with no non-biblical material, and no consultation made with scholars about who the historical Jesus might have been.[29] The script is a literal translation of Matthew's Gospel. Pasolini considered this Gospel the most "revolutionary" of the four and that it presented Christ having "an oxymoronic love/hate relationship with the Law."[30] This is highlighted in the Sermon on the Mount scene—it is actually a number of scenes of Jesus traveling through different towns. Jesus berates the scribes and Pharisees with seven "Woe unto you" criticisms (Matt 23:25–35). Pasolini omits some of the Gospel's scenes and re-arranges others. He includes the messianic prophecies of Isaiah—Matthew's text has a number of Isaiah citations—and leaves out most of the parables and miracles. Pasolini's actions were not without reason: his intentional omissions of political and social characteristics, which add to a historical portrayal, were to re-consecrate and re-mythicize Jesus.[31] However, by "lifting" the whole story from the New Testament and quoting the Gospel literally, Pasolini in fact ignores the canon, desecrating and isolating it from the rest of the New Testament.[32]

28. Ibid., 136–37. Emphasis in the original.

29. Oswald Stack and Pier Paolo Pasolini, *Pasolini on Pasolini: Interviews with Oswald Stack* (London: Thames & Hudson, 1969), 83.

30. Ibid., 141.

31. Tatum, *Jesus at the Movies*, 112.

32. George Aichele, "Translation as De-canonization: Matthew's Gospel According to Pasolini," *Cross CURR* 51, no. 4 (Winter 2002): 524.

*Il Vangelo* is in two parts: the first deals with Jesus' rise to popularity while the second relates the story of the Passion. To achieve the film's quasi-documentary quality, Pasolini was inspired by two directors. First, fellow Italian director, Virgilio Sabel (1920–1989) and his 1954 film, *Il figlio dell 'uomo* (The Son of Man) in which he portrayed Jesus through the eyes of ordinary Galilean fishermen and farmers.[33] Second, Danish director Carl Theodor Dreyer (*Blade af Satans Bog*, 1921 and *The Passion of Joan of Arc*, 1928) replicating his use of many sharp-cuts, extreme close-ups and black-framing.

Pasolini attempted an entirely new approach when filming the John the Baptist scene. Discarding all his technical preconceptions, Pasolini started using the zoom, new camera movements and new frames, which were not reverential, but almost documentary. He employed the zoom-shot twenty-one times, extreme close-ups of characters to reveal their "social physiognomy"[34] and extreme wide angles of Jesus' face. Viano interprets these cinematographic techniques as a means to "depersonalize the Redeemer."[35] One could argue that these techniques actually do the reverse and make Pasolini's Jesus appear more personable. The two trials of Christ are filmed in long shot *cinéma vérité* style, giving the audience a sense of participation and spectatorship.[36]

Pasolini also breaks with traditional Jesus film costuming: the non-descript costumes succeed in eliminating the "social and ethnic context."[37] A lover of Renaissance art, Pasolini and costume director Danilo Donati referred to a number of recognizable Renaissance paintings for inspiration. They favored the work of Piero della Francesca whose paintings inspired a number of scenes. Thus, for example, the costumes of the Roman soldiers and the Pharisees are directly influenced by figures in his *Legend of the True Cross*. Moreover, a heavily pregnant Mary standing before Joseph is a copy of his *Madonna del Parto* and the baptism scene corresponds to his *Baptism of Christ*. Giotto's frescoes provided inspiration for the scenes of the flight into Egypt and Jesus' entry into Jerusalem, while the art of Mantegna and Giovanni Bellini is evident in the Garden of Gethsemane scene. Jesus (Enrique Irazoqui) has been likened to Byzantine art as well

33. Viano, *Certain Realism*, 136.

34. Ibid., 137.

35. Ibid., 139.

36. *Cinéma vérité* is a technique of documentary filmmaking in which the camera records actual persons and events without directorial control. The technique was introduced in France in the 1950s.

37. Reinhartz, "Jesus in Film," para. 12.

as the work of El Greco and expressionist artist, Georges Rouault. Enrique Irazoqui bears an uncanny resemblance to the Christ in Rouault's *Christ Scourged* and *La Sainte Face*.

The film's soundtrack is another divergence from neo-realism. The musical score is eclectic and includes a range of musical genres. The pulsating "Gloria" from the Congolese *Missa Luba* introduces the film. Odetta's haunting spiritual "Sometimes I Feel Like a Motherless Child," which is sung both at the magi's visit and at Jesus' baptism, is prophetic of Mary's knowing that she will have to give up her son according to God's will. Traditional Christian music includes J. S. Bach's "Mass in B Minor and Saint Matthew Passion." Jim Clark suggests "this polyglot score is an attempt to create subtle and shifting, tensions between the world of ancient Judea and our own."[38] Seth Studer proposes that by not limiting itself to one genre or era, "the music invokes afresh the transcendence of Christ across the ages, across cultures."[39] I agree with Studer.

In breaking with the traditional Jesus film genre, Pasolini presents Jesus, who is both human and divine; who in revolutionary tones challenges the *status quo*; and who has much to accomplish in a limited time—three years of ministry. By portraying Jesus as a peasant and setting the narrative against a backdrop of poverty and religious hypocrisy, Pasolini's film mirror's Jesus' concern for the poor without exaggerating it, or "reducing the Gospel to a political tract."[40]

*Lens Two*

Pasolini presents a simple and rustic staging of the Last Supper, a "gathering of a tired, disquieted group."[41] The Last Supper takes place outdoors. As there are no visible oil lamps and blanket-like shawls are wrapped around each member of the group, it can be assumed that it is late afternoon or early evening. The palm branches decorating the doorway remind us of the branch-waving crowds that greeted Jesus when he entered Jerusalem, riding on a donkey (Matt 21:1–10). The rectangular wooden table is

38. Jim Clark, "The Films of Pier Paolo Pasolini," *Jim's Reviews/Pasolini*. http://jclarkmedia.com/pasolini/pasolini05.html.

39. Studer, "*Il Vangelo Secondo Matteo.*"

40. Stephen D. Greydanus, review of "*The Gospel According to St. Matthew* (1964)," *Decent Films*. http://www.decentfilms.com/reviews/gospelaccordingtoMt.html.

41. Bosley Crowther, "The Life of Jesus: Pasolini's Film Opens at the Fine Arts," *New York Times* (February 18, 1966). http://movies.nytimes.com/movie/review?_r=1&res=9800E2D9143CE53BBC4052DFB466838D679EDE.

uncluttered, adding to the simplicity of the scene. The disciples sitting on floor mats have spread themselves around the table. Jesus appears to be sitting on a stool because his body is higher than the others are. Two other disciples to the extreme right of the frame sit on stools, as there is no room for them at the table. Judas sits second from left of Jesus.

The Last Supper scene commences with a close-up of a hand, dipping matzot into a bowl of lamb stew. The camera follows the action of the hand and reveals that it belongs to Judas (Otello Sestili). Immediately Jesus tells the disciples that one of them is to betray him. Matthew describes the apostles as becoming "greatly distressed" (Matt 26:22) but Pasolini presents five separate mid-shots of different apostles who appear calm and somewhat disinterested in Jesus' response to their question, "Is it I perhaps?" Waiting until Jesus is finished identifying the betrayer—"one who has dipped his hand into the bowl"—and saying, "It would have been better for that one not to have been born," Judas asks, "Is it perhaps I Lord?" His emotionless reaction to Jesus' response, "You have said it," is puzzling. Judas had already struck a deal with Caiaphas. One would expect a response of alarm or at least surprise that Jesus was aware of what Judas had done. It seems that Judas and Jesus are just going through the motions of what they knew had to be done.

A close-up of matzot held by two hands fills the screen. The camera lingers on the matzot, highlighting its resemblance to the "bread of affliction" eaten by Jews at their Passover Seder. Again, the camera follows the movement of the hands. The Jewish song "Kol Nidre" is heard. Jeremy Cohen notes that "Jewish memory typically associates this song with Jews of the Middle Ages,"[42] which was a time when Jews were forced to convert to other religions by their oppressors. He also posits, "[P]erhaps Pasolini found some room for [the Jews], too, in the messianic kingdom that Jesus came to establish."[43] Pasolini was thus signifying that all are welcome at the table: including all who are marginalized by society and the Church.

Jesus gives the command, "Take, eat; this is my body," breaks off pieces and gives a piece to each disciple. This distribution is different from other Last Supper scenes where Jesus breaks the bread in halves and the disciples break and pass it on. By having Jesus give bread to each disciple, Pasolini reinforces his Marxist ideals of feeding the hungry and sharing. Judas eats the bread without hesitation. The background music comes to a crescendo as the remaining bread is placed on the table. A close-up of an earthen amphora fills the screen. Jesus takes the jug, pours

42. Cohen, *Christ Killers*, 235.
43. Ibid.

wine into a clay cup and directs the disciples to "Drink from it, all of you; for this is my blood of the covenant." Although the Matthean text does not include the word "new" and refers to "covenant," English subtitles cite "new testament" while Spanish subtitles keep the original "covenant." Perhaps the subtitle creators were simply using familiar words said in their particular Eucharistic services. The cup is passed around the table. Only four of the disciples are shown drinking from the cup; Judas is not one of them. The background song ends in synchrony with the end of the scene.

Figure 8. Judas, on the left, watches Jesus break bread.
© Legend Films, Inc.

*Lens Three*

In 1962, Pasolini contended that "Italy is rotting in a prosperity that is selfishness, stupidity, ignorance, gossip, morals, coercion, and conformity: somehow part of this process is now fascism."[44] In examining to what extent the portrayal of Jesus—and indeed all the characters—as well as the film's setting, are consistent with or in contrast to the cultural mood of the day in which *Il Vangelo* was produced, we see that the film is very much a reflection of Pasolini's political perspective. Pasolini was a Marxist and in *Il Vangelo* he endeavors to find "the contemporary relevance of Jesus' message by seeing it from the perspective of a Marxist interpretation of society."[45] It is no coincidence that Jesus is a working-class Messiah speaking with passion, anger and frustration. As Pasolini clearly explains:

44. Giuseppe Bertolucci, "Pier Paolo Pasolini's Anger," *New Ways* 36 (September 6, 1962), *WUZ*. http://www.wuz.it/articolo-film/2498/rabbia-pasolini-bertolucci.html.

45. May, ed., *New Image of Religious Film*, 46.

> For a Frenchman *Il Vangelo Secondo Matteo* may be a religious film. For an Italian proletarian, there is no ambiguity. Christ is a member of the sub-proletariat and is involved with others of this class. An historical relationship exists between Christ and the Proletariat; he would not have done anything if he had not been followed by the proletarians. The Pharisees would not have killed him. And the proletariat would have remained immersed in an unhearing darkness without the revolutionary teaching of Christ.[46]

For Pasolini, Jesus is a social outcast working on behalf of the struggling masses. Pasolini was an atheist who claimed to be an unbeliever, but "an unbeliever who has nostalgia for belief."[47] One of his aims in producing *Il Vangelo* was to promote understanding between Christianity and Communism. Even though he considered that the miracles of Jesus were "disgusting pietism,"[48] he included a few of them to remain loyal to the text. Unfortunately, by promoting Christian-Communism dialogue he denigrated Judaism. He does not emphasize Jesus' Jewish heritage and the Jewish leaders are portrayed in an extremely negative light. He focuses especially on the religious establishment, the Pharisees and scribes. Pasolini portrays the Jewish religious leaders as conspirators and promoters of their own position and well-being. His message is clear: "the religious authorities are the villains of the Christ story, and have remained villains ever since."[49] Pasolini's observation is proven when one considers the Catholic Church's influence on his life. The Jewish priests are physically unappealing and are made to look preposterous in their anachronistic Renaissance headgear. Some priests' hats bear a striking resemblance to bishops' miters.

Pasolini was (a practicing) homosexual. In the 1960s, Italy discriminated against those of a homosexual orientation, and the state religion, Roman Catholicism, censured such practices. It is significant that Pasolini openly expressed and endorsed his sexual orientation in this film because it helps to explain some of his directorial choices. All twelve of the disciples, as well as Jesus, are aesthetically pleasing to the eye while the rest of the cast—for the most part, and excluding Mary, the young mother of Jesus—are a collection of wrinkled faces, crooked teeth and disproportioned bodies. Jesus' relationship with a youthful John has homosexual

46. Pasolini cited in Naomi Greene, *Pier Paolo Pasolini: Cinema and Heresy* (Princeton: Princeton University Press, 1990), 77.

47. Lang, *Bible on the Big Screen*, 180.

48. Stack, *Pasolini on Pasolini*, 87.

49. Studer, "*Il Vangelo*."

connotations. Jesus takes John's hand as the group leaves for Gethsemane. John is the only disciple who receives a passionate embrace before Jesus goes off to pray.

Maurizio Viano argues that the film discloses another aspect inside Pasolini's Jesus' story: "its phallocentrism"[50]—the privileging of the masculine in understanding meaning or social relations. Unlike other Jesus films, Pasolini does not develop the role of women. The characters of Mary Magdalene and Salome are examples of the desexualization of women. Viano comments, "The absence of sexual connotations in both Salome and Mary Magdalene, together with their minimal roles, exposes the extent to which we rely on the representation of woman as sex and just how much the founding text of Christianity is at a loss to provide her with another meaningful function."[51]

Pasolini was excommunicated from the Catholic Church because he was a Communist and expelled from the Communist Party in 1949 for being homosexual.[52] While his decision to make a film using only the Matthean text was met with some cynicism, the film received awards and accolades including best director, foreign film, costume and cinematography. Pasolini's intention for *Il Vangelo Secondo Matteo* was to present the life of Christ plus two thousand years of Christianity.[53] Pasolini portrays Jesus as a passionate revolutionary, critical of the religious authorities, and an outsider. In fact, Pasolini created Jesus in his own image: Marxist, atheist and homosexual.

### *The Portrayal of Judas*

If it were not for Jesus carrying out a "roll call" of his twelve disciples, and Pasolini's close shot of each of them as they are named, the viewer could not identify Judas until the anointing at Bethany scene. Even though Judas "carries the dramatic weight"[54] of many of the Jesus films, this is not the case in *Il Vangelo*. Judas has no distinguishing features. He is strong in stature, ruggedly handsome with dark unkempt hair, facial stubble and is in his early thirties. His costume of a light colored tunic and a lighter colored wrap is similar to that worn by other characters. What we can determine is that Judas is the group's treasurer: not because he has a visible moneybag but in that he counts out money to pay for food.

50. Viano, *Certain Realism*, 142–45.
51. Ibid., 144–45.
52. Ibid., 8
53. Stack, *Pasolini on Pasolini*, 83.
54. Reinhartz, *Jesus*, 152.

Tension rises when Jesus and his disciples are having a meal in the courtyard of Mary and Martha's house in Bethany. Judas sits at the very end of the table, staring into a cup, deep in thought. Mary anoints Jesus' head with oil. Judas turns towards them and angrily asks, "Why this waste? For this ointment could have been sold for a large sum and the money given to the poor." Although the text corresponds with Matthew's Gospel (26:8–9), Matthew cites "the disciples" as asking the question. Pasolini, in this instance, borrows from John's Gospel (12:4–6). By having Judas pose the question, Pasolini acquires a motive for Judas' later actions.

Judas, scorned by Jesus' response, runs off and is next seen leaning against a wall in the Temple courtyard. Upon being seen by Caiaphas, Judas cautiously approaches him and asks, "What will you give me that I deliver him?" Judas enthusiastically greets Caiaphas' answer of "Thirty pieces of silver." The scene ends with the return of the melody of "Kol Nidre" from the Jewish liturgy of Yom Kippur, the Day of Atonement.

This scene is significant for three reasons. First, Matthew records that Judas went to the chief priests but in the film, Caiaphas is the sole priestly representative. Second, Pasolini chooses the word "deliver" over Matthew's "betray" (Matt 26:15). English and Spanish subtitled versions of the film translate "betray" as "hand over." Pasolini in using the original Greek translation of *paradidōmi* (hand over) avoids demonizing Judas by not labelling his action as "betrayal." Third, according to Matthew, Judas was paid "thirty pieces of silver" and yet no money changes hands in this scene. Although these might be considered minor changes, they effectively weaken any motive of betrayal by Judas. Moreover, the inclusion of the "Kol Nidre" melody adds another dimension to the gravity of Judas' actions.

Kol Nidre means "all vows" and is a prayer offered on the evening of Yom Kippur (the Day of Atonement) where Jews ask God to annul all personal vows they may make in the next year. Although the prayer refers only to vows between the person making them and God, Pasolini also includes Judas' arrangement to "hand over" Jesus to the chief priests. Judas accepts that he has a significant role in bringing to fulfilment Jesus' prediction of his own death as atonement "for the forgiveness of sins" (Matt 26:28). Pasolini is comparing Judas to a scapegoat and the ritual described in Lev 16:1–34. Read in synagogues on Yom Kippur, the rite of the scapegoat is the high point of the Yom Kippur temple service. The high priest selects two male goats. One is sacrificed to God, and the other is sent to *Azazel* (a supernatural being) in the wilderness, bearing the sins of the people of Israel.

Judas' movements from the conclusion of the Last Supper to Gethsemane are not revealed in the film. His absence from the group walking to Gethsemane is particularly noticeable.

The praying of Jesus in the Garden of Olives is disturbed by the sound of an angry melee: the disciples are trying to fend off Temple guards. Four high priests are set apart from the fighting but close enough to observe what is happening. Jesus hurries to the scene shouting for the soldiers to lay down their swords. Judas sees Jesus, breaks through the mob, runs to him and with deep sincerity says, "Greetings, Rabbi!" Jesus looks relieved to see Judas and responds with "O friend, you have come." By calling Judas "friend," Jesus holds no animosity against him. It is as though Jesus was waiting for him and he pulls Judas into a passionate embrace. As Adele Reinhartz notes, "the intensity of the relationship between Judas and Jesus positively smolders."[55] The scene is moving and evokes sympathy for both Judas and Jesus: together they are trapped in a preordained plan that is beyond their control.

Next, Judas is seen in the crowd watching the trial proceedings. His furrowed brow and look of disbelief indicate his concern for Jesus and the verdict. Later, Judas attempts to intervene by returning the thirty pieces of silver. Where he was apprehensive in his first meeting with Caiaphas, Judas is now more confident. He strides up to the group of high priests, interrupting their discussion with the confession; "I have sinned by betraying innocent blood" (Matt 27:4). Rebuked by Caiaphas, Judas takes the silver coins from his moneybag and hurls them at the priests. As it was unlawful to return blood money to the treasury, the priests turn their backs on Judas and discuss using the money to purchase the potter's field. A distraught and defeated Judas turns away. The American blues song, "Dark Was the Night, Cold Was the Ground" written and performed by Blind Willie Johnson adds to the pathos. The evocative lyrics of "debt" and "crime" and the rhetorical questioning of why "the Savior could die to save a soul like mine" suggest that Judas is contrite.[56]

Pasolini's choice of this particular song for this specific scene introduces new insights into Judas and his actions. The song, while reinforcing

55. Ibid., 167. The "Judas kiss" has been edited out of the restored, colored and English dubbed version of the film, the two disc DVD Legend Films 2007 version distributed by Genius Products. I received no response from the distributers to my query regarding the omission.

56. "Dark Was the Night, Cold Was the Ground." Music and lyrics by Blind Willie Johnson. The 1927 song, one of twenty-seven tunes from around the world, was included on a golden record affixed to the 1977 star bound Voyager space probe. http://www.peripheralfocus.net/bwj/musicList.html.

Judas' culpability in bringing about Jesus' death, also includes Judas' admission of guilt and recognition that Jesus is his "Savior." More importantly, the lyrics of the song allude to Judas' redemption because Jesus died to save his (Judas) soul, clearing his "debt" (sin).

Judas' remorse and guilt drive him to suicide. Panic-stricken, Judas is seen running through trees and discarding his clothes. He ties the strap of his moneybag around his neck and climbs a tree. The shape of the tree is highly significant in that the trunk and two branches form a Y-shape. The shape could symbolize the parting of the way between Jesus and Judas, or a disjointed cross as in the Last Supper table in *King of Kings*. The Y-shape could also represent the omophorion, a stole worn by Eastern Orthodox bishops. In the Roman Catholic Church, this stole is called the pallium. Made from sheep's wool, the omophorion metaphorically symbolizes the role of Jesus as the Good Shepherd who leaves the ninety-nine sheep to search for the one lost and carries it home wrapped around his shoulders (Matt 18:12–14). Judas is the lost sheep. Judas immediately releases his grip and his body drops. The image is both provocative and atypical: Judas is clothed only in a loin-wrap. Previous filmic depictions of the suicide of Judas show him fully dressed. So, what might be Pasolini's reasoning for a semi-naked Judas?

If it was his intention to shock his audience, then Pasolini succeeded. The resultant image reminds one of the semi-naked Jesus hanging on a cross. Pasolini now significantly links Judas' suicide to the death of Jesus, with a second representation of an atoning sacrificial death. Judas becomes a Christ-like figure by obeying God's will. Jesus has to die and Judas was facilitating the fulfilment of God's plan.

### *The Greatest Story Ever Told (1965)*

Director: George Stevens. Screenwriter: Henry Denker, J. L. Barrett, George Stevens. Country: USA. Production Company: Metro Goldwyn Mayer. Length: 199 minutes. Length of Last Supper scene: 12:33 minutes. Color: Technicolor. Language: English. Musical score: Alfred Newman. Filming locations: Utah, Arizona, California, Illinois, Nevada. Cast: Judas (David McCallum), Jesus (Max von Sydow).

#### *Lens One*

George Stevens's primary motivation for making this epic film was Fulton Oursler's best-selling 1949 novel *The Greatest Story Ever Told*, a fictitious and romanticized life of Jesus. Stevens, a devout Roman Catholic, recognized the importance of the sacred text and the enormous responsibility of bringing the Gospels to the big screen: "I wouldn't have felt comfortable in going into the production of the film without the kind of study we did. Not only historic study, but more importantly Gospel studies. We had to approach our research with humility, reverence and a good deal of energy."[57]

Stevens went to extraordinary lengths in order to be assured that he had the correct historical and biblical Jesus story. He commissioned French artist André Girard to prepare 352 oil paintings illustrating biblical scenes as a facet of further study.[58] He consulted thirty-six Protestant ministers, had an audience with Pope John XXIII, and even discussed the script with David Ben-Gurion. Medved posits that Stevens was "taking care to cover absolutely all of his bases…though it remains unclear what, precisely, the Israeli prime minister could contribute to a project on the life of Jesus." The screenplay took two years to write. The film's opening credits indicate the huge amount of study that was put into the screenplay: "Screenplay by James Lee Barrett and George Stevens, based on the Books of the Old and New Testaments, Other Ancient Writings, the Writings of Fulton Oursler and Henry Denker, and in Creative Association with Carl Sandburg." Medved sarcastically suggests that Stevens had all these sources listed so that any blame levelled at the script could be widely shared!

Gospels include ellipses: omitting words or dialogue that are superfluous or that are understood from contextual clues. Often the details that connect separate incidents are lacking, resulting in a lack of continuity and gaps in the narrative. The most obvious gap is the lack of details from Jesus' infancy to when he began his ministry some thirty years later. The only recorded incident in any of the Gospels is where the twelve-year-old Jesus is conversing with the teachers in the Jerusalem Temple (Luke 2:41–51). Perplexingly, Stevens opted to omit this pericope, thus making an even longer historical leap from the return of the Holy Family from their exile in Egypt to the preaching of John the Baptist (Charlton Heston). Stevens, like the Synoptic Gospel accounts, chose to focus more on Jesus' ministry rather than his early years. The filmmaker's creation of sub-plots helps to fill in the elliptical gaps in the Gospel accounts and introduce additional characters.

57. From an interview Stevens gave to Bruce Petri in 1973. "George Stevens Biography," *Movie Movie*. http://www.moviemoviesite.com/People/S/stevens_george/biography_page_1.htm.

58. Medved and Medved, *Hollywood Hall of Shame*, 135.

Stevens introduces a new and non-biblical character in the film, the Dark Hermit (Donald Pleasence) who represents Satan. His primary purpose is to "reveal the demonic character of Jesus' opponents and of the road not taken by Jesus."[59] The Dark Hermit plays an integral role in the film. He is the first to identify Peter (Gary Raymond) and question him on his knowledge of Jesus. He is one of the accusers at the Jewish trial and at the trial before Pilate, and he incites the crowd by shouting, "Crucify him."

In Jesus films there are generally no surprises, no sense of tension and suspense, as the story is one that has been circulating for twenty centuries. A Jesus film-ending normally corresponds with that portrayed in the Gospels without the need for a "Hollywood" climax. The audience's knowledge of the story is clearly a disadvantage for a medium like cinema that requires dramatic structure. To counteract this negative aspect, filmmakers have been able to tantalize the audience's interest with the use of advertising, special effects, grandiose sets and a cast of well-known Hollywood stars.

The cast of *The Greatest Story Ever Told* attracted audiences in large numbers, with it being "impossible for those watching the film to avoid the merry game of 'Spot the Star'. The road to Calvary in particular resembles the Hollywood Boulevard 'Walk of Fame'."[60] Yet paradoxically in casting Jesus, Stevens chose a relatively unknown Swedish actor, Max von Sydow, so that he "would remain free of secular and unseemly associations in the mind of the public."[61] By using an unknown actor it was hoped that the audience would be caught up in the story rather than fixating on a superstar. Similarly, Pier Paolo Pasolini and Mel Gibson used this technique in choosing unknown actors to play the leading role in their Jesus films. Conversely, Nicholas Ray had used the "teenage idol" Jeffrey Hunter for his Jesus in *King of Kings*, which, as noted earlier, failed at the box-office!

There can be no denying Stevens had a sense of reverence for a divine Jesus in his direction of *The Greatest Story Ever Told*. He went to extraordinary lengths to suggest that Jesus was "fully God." To convey this, the actions of Jesus are slow and deliberate. He has a "melancholy demeanor"[62] and speaks "God's language" as recorded in the King James Version of the Bible, setting him apart from other characters who speak in contemporary American English.

59. Walsh, *Reading the Gospels*, 149.
60. Medved and Medved, *Hollywood Hall of Shame*, 137.
61. Ibid., 138.
62. Stern, *Savior*, 145.

*Lens Two*

A cursory viewing of the Last Supper scene suggests that Stevens based the table arrangement on a reproduction of Leonardo da Vinci's masterpiece. There are, however, a number of significant discrepancies. There is little to suggest that a meal is taking place. The long stark wooden table has only a few dishes, a cup and a jug. Jesus and his disciples wear similar-colored clothes and look more like a contemporary liturgical church sanctuary group than first-century Jews gathering for a meal.

One notable difference is that of the Judas figure. Da Vinci's Judas is dark haired, bearded and has a darker complexion than the other figures. Judas, positioned second to the left of Jesus, is leaning on the table, his right hand clutching a moneybag and his left hand reaching for bread. Stevens's Judas (David McCallum) is blonde-haired and has a neatly trimmed beard framing his "wholesome, almost boyish face."[63] There is no evidence of a moneybag, and he appears isolated from the group. He sits at the right end of the table and is straight-backed while the others lean toward Jesus.

Judas arrives late. He had been speaking with Caiaphas (Martin Landau) while the disciples and Jesus were preparing for the meal. He shuts the door and takes his place at the end of the table. His tardiness goes unnoticed by the disciples but Jesus is more observant. A close-up of Jesus suggests that he knows where Judas has been. The meal begins with Jesus' declaration, "Father, the hour has come." He continues by acknowledging the disciples giving up everything in order to follow him, but warns, that although they have been his friends, one with his hand on the table would betray him. When asked who it could be, Jesus gives a simple answer "One who is eating bread with me tonight." As though testing Jesus, Judas asks, "Is it I?" Jesus does not answer but stands up and looks at Judas.

Still standing, Jesus informs the group that in a little while he will be leaving them and where he is going they cannot come (John 13:33). This is met with Peter's (Gary Raymond) declaration of faithfulness and Jesus' response that Peter will deny him three times. Jesus continues, "In my Father's house" but Thomas (Tom Reese) interrupts him, "Speak plainly and speak no proverbs, Master."[64] Jesus answers Thomas' question as to how they will know where Jesus is going with the explanation, "I am the way, the truth, and the life. No one comes to the Father but by me" (John 14:1–8).

63. Forshey, *American Spectaculars*, 101.

64. The word "proverb" is out of place here. Jesus is noted for speaking in parables.

The scene changes to a long shot of the table and the disciples. Jesus picks up a plate, places his hand over the round pita bread and looks heavenward. One assumes that Jesus is offering a blessing or giving thanks to the Father. Jesus tears the pita bread in two. With one half in each hand Jesus says, "Take it and eat. This is my body, which is being given for you. Do this in remembrance of me" (Luke 22:19). Stevens's addition of the word "being" is noteworthy. The verb suggests what is happening in the present and yet it can point to what will happen in the future: Jesus' death on the cross. Bread is passed along the disciples who each in turn tears off a piece and eats. Although Judas looks undecided, he assertively takes the bread and tears off a piece. This boldness masks his duplicity. Just as Judas places the bread to his mouth, the camera crosses to a mid-shot of Jesus, leaving the audience to decide for themselves whether Judas will consume the bread.

Jesus then pours wine from a large pottery jug into a cup. He places an open palm over the cup, and looks heavenward and again silently prays. Another crosscut shot shows Judas looking at the piece of bread that he is still holding in his fingertips. The remainder of the bread is in his right hand. We hear Jesus say, "Drink this" and Judas lowers his hand. Judas has not eaten the bread!

Again, the camera moves from a crosscut to a long shot of Jesus. He continues, "For this is my blood of the new testament which shall be shed for many for the forgiveness of sins." At this point Jesus turns his head and looks towards Judas. Jesus hands the cup to Andrew (Burt Brinckerhoff) who is on his left. After drinking, the cup passes along for all to drink. Jesus tells the group how he desired to eat the Passover with them (Luke 21:15) and told them that he would not drink "the fruit of the vine" until he drinks it new with them in his Father's Kingdom (Mark 14:25; Matt 26:29). A close-up of Judas shows him holding the cup and looking at Jesus. The crosscut to Jesus shows him looking directly at Judas. Jesus declares, "A new commandment I give to you; that you love one another just as I have loved you" (John 13:34). The declaration of love heightens the tension between Jesus and Judas and in the audience. Following a short silence, Jesus orders Judas, "Do quickly what you have to do."

Without taking his eyes off Jesus, Judas rises quickly, knocking over his bench. The sound is like that of a nail hammered into wood. Judas steps backwards to the door, his eyes fixed on Jesus. He stops at the door and slightly raises both his arms in supplication. Is Judas pleading to be released from what he "has to do" or is he begging forgiveness for what he is about to do? The sound of the door shutting—another reminder of nail, hammer and wood—returns the viewer to a mid-shot of Jesus, and his self-satisfied declaration, "Now is the Son of Man glorified" (John 13:31). It seems that Jesus was just waiting for Judas to leave because he informs those gathered that he is going to the Garden of Gethsemane to pray.

*Lens Three*

George Stevens was not only director, but also producer and co-writer of the screenplay. This gave him complete authority over the entire production and permitted him to put his own stamp on the film. One of his aims was that *The Greatest Story Ever Told* would have "great ecumenical value" in that the film would not offend Catholicism, Protestantism or Judaism.[65] Raymond Durgnat explains how this was achieved. "Jesus has no brothers or sisters (because that would offend the Catholics), the miracles are kept to a minimum (so as not to put a strain on the agnostics [secularists]), [and] the crowd is very half-hearted about crucifying Jesus (because that might look like anti-Semitism)."[66]

Noticeably absent from the film is Jesus' Jewish tradition and culture. The opening and closing shots of the film are both of a painted Max von Sydow Christ icon on the inside of an Orthodox church, framing the film and placing it in the context of Christian faith and the Church. Stevens draws on his Catholic background as is evident in the Last Supper scene. "[W]hen Stevens has Jesus extend his right hand over the bread and the chalice of wine, in the liturgical gesture of epiclesis; he seems anachronistically to be presiding at a Catholic Eucharist service instead of a Hebrew Passover meal."[67]

Jesus refers to the wine as "my blood of the new testament" in place of the word "covenant." Stevens appears to have forfeited Jesus' Jewishness for the sake of promoting his own Christian ideals. The implication, according to Tatum, is that "Christianity was in the process of superseding Judaism—at least superseding the Judaism centered in the sacrificial cult of Jerusalem."[68] This is echoed in the repeated citations throughout the film: "For I desire steadfast love and not sacrifice, the knowledge of God rather than burnt offerings" (Hos 6:6). Yet ironically, the film actually promotes replacing Jewish Temple sacrifice with the Christian sacrifice of the Mass. How does the director, who was both personally and profoundly sensitive to anti-Semitism, reconcile the supersessionist liturgy?

65. F. Thomas Trotter, "The Church Moves Toward Film Discrimination," *Relig Life* 38, no. 2 (1969). http://www.religion-online.org/showarticle.asp?title=3474.

66. Raymond Durgnat, "*The Greatest Story Ever Told*: Raymond Durgnat on the Images of Jesus," *FaF* 11, no. 9 (1965): 25.

67. Baugh, *Imaging the Divine*, 29.

68. Tatum, *Jesus at the Movies*, 97.

Stevens had been an official photographer for the United States Army and was present at the liberation of Dachau concentration camp in Germany in the spring of 1945. His experience helps explain the portrayal of Jews in *The Greatest Story Ever Told*. He attempts to resolve the question of the culpability of the Jews for the death of Jesus by dividing the Sanhedrin into two factions—Caiaphas (Martin Landau) and company favor Jewish orthodoxy while Nicodemus (Joseph Schildkraut) and Joseph of Arimathea (Abraham Sofaer) support Jesus. At the trials, and when Pilate (Telly Savalas) offers Barabbas (Richard Conte) in place of Jesus, the crowd also is divided as to whether to "Release him!" or to "Crucify him!" Forshey explains Stevens's reasoning for the divisions: "[The] responsibility for Christ's death was an individual decision rather than a collective responsibility. By leaving an ambiguous impression, Stevens suggests that Jesus' main offence was that he was the Messiah and that it was the unbelievers who put him to death."[69]

The "unbelievers" are those who chose not to follow Jesus, who did not believe that he was the Messiah and put him to death. These could therefore include Caiaphas and company, Barabbas and his Zealots, and Pilate and his Roman cohort. Judas therefore cannot be blamed for Jesus' death because Judas believes in Jesus!

Despite making *The Greatest Story Ever Told* on an estimated budget of twenty million dollars, it was a commercial failure. Reasons given for the film's failure included the overall length of the film (199 minutes), the slow and drawn out scenes and the inappropriate portrayal of Jesus. A skulking, pan-faced, and emotionless Jesus did not connect with 1960s' audiences. The film was such a box-office disaster that film producers were reluctant to invest in future biblical epics.

*The Portrayal of Judas*

Judas' character in *The Greatest Story Ever Told* lacks depth because the reasons for his behavior and emotions remain obscure. Judas is the first disciple Jesus calls and in an early scene with Mary, Martha and Lazarus, he sits closest to Jesus, suggesting that he is part of the inner circle. He is baptized by John in the Jordan River. Judas is outraged at the anointing at Bethany, but no explanation is given for his protest.

Contrary to the Gospel's insistence that it is only Peter who "confesses" Jesus is the Messiah (Matt 16:15–16), Judas makes his own profession of faith at Caesarea Philippi exclaiming: "You [Jesus] are a great leader and the greatest teacher I have ever known." When Judas first goes to Caiaphas, Judas offers "to give" Jesus to him but only if Caiaphas can

69. Forshey, *American Spectaculars*, 102.

promise that no harm will come to Jesus. Up to this point, Stevens has carefully avoided the word "betray." However, it is in Caiaphas' response that Stevens plants the seed of Judas being the stereotypical betrayer. Caiaphas tells Judas, "If you are willing to *be* [stops himself] to give him to us, why do you care what happens to him?" Judas responds with a testimony of Jesus' qualities: "Jesus is the purest and kindest man I have ever known. I have never seen him do anything but good. His heart is so gentle I have seen him cry over little things that would go unnoticed by other men. Old people worship him. Children adore him. I love him."

How could a disciple who loved Jesus "give" him to the Sanhedrin? The answer lies in a blemish in Judas' character. Judas succumbs not to greed but to his own dark voices. When Caiaphas tells Judas to hold out his hand, and thirty pieces of silver are placed in it, Judas is repulsed and declares; "I don't want the money." Thus, his motive is not disillusionment, anger or hatred. Judas gives Jesus over to the Sanhedrin because the Dark Hermit seduces him. Judas succumbs to Satan. By transferring the blame onto the Dark Hermit, Judas—and the Jews—are acquitted of being "Christ killers."

Stevens juxtaposes the actions of Judas with those of Jesus. When Judas is making arrangements with Caiaphas to hand Jesus over, Jesus is in Gethsemane, praying to be delivered from what is ahead. As Jesus struggles with the cross through the pressing crowd, Judas walks along empty streets to the deserted Temple courtyard. While Jesus makes his way up to Calvary, Judas ascends the steps to the Temple's sacrificial fire. At the same moment that a nail is hammered into Jesus' hand, Judas stretches out his arms in cruciform style and falls headlong into the sacrificial fire.

There have been various explanations as to why Stevens chose for Judas to end his life in that way. One explanation is that Judas is condemned to the fires of hell. Forshey contends, "[The] Buddhist style of [Judas'] death suggests the depth of his alienation from Jesus' message."[70] Stern argues that the action is an adaptation of Acts 1:18: "On the one hand, this action may be taken as self-sacrifice of distress made to God in the moment of a sinner's repentance. On the other hand, perhaps it is the ultimate reprisal for the betrayal of God's Son, the hurling of the deceiver into the fires of hell."[71] Tatum proposes that when Jesus dies on the cross, "all temple activity has ceased and the courtyard stands empty—except for Judas who sacrifices himself on that altar, the efficacy of which has been replaced by the sacrifice of the one he betrayed."[72]

70. Ibid.

71. Stern, *Savior*, 139–40.

72. Tatum, *Jesus at the Movies*, 97.

I would argue that Judas' falling into the Temple's sacrificial fire symbolizes two things. The first is the Jewish sacrifice of the burnt offering. The ritual of the burnt offering is explained in Lev 1 and is the oldest and most common sacrifice that represented submission to God's will. Because the offering represents complete submission to God's will and the entire offering is given to God then it cannot be used after it is burnt. So, Judas has to die as a burnt sacrifice. Second, and perhaps most pertinent, is that Judas was the perceived representative of Jewish people. His sacrificial death in the Temple fire symbolizes the six million Jews exterminated in the Nazi Holocaust. This contributes to an emerging sympathy for the Jews and the growing abhorrence of anti-Semitism.

### *Summary*

The analyses of these three films support Jeffrey Well's observation that *The Greatest Story Ever Told* is the Protestant version, Pasolini's *Il Vangelo Secondo Matteo* is the Marxist version and *King of Kings* is the Zionist version.[73] However, the Judas character in these three films cannot be so easily categorized. Contrary to the film-poster billing, Judas is the major character in *King of Kings* (1961). His inner conflict of choosing between running with Barabbas—the messiah of war—or to walk with Jesus—the new messiah of peace—is a major theme in the film. Judas no longer represents the Jews but a twentieth-century world in the grip of a new and potentially world-ending calamity: the Cold War. In *Il Vangelo Secondo Matteo* (1964), Judas accepts that his role is to precipitate the handing over of Jesus. He is like the scapegoat represented in the Hebrew Scriptures sent into the wilderness, bearing the sins of the people of Israel. The concept of Judas as sacrifice is confirmed in *The Greatest Story Ever Told* (1965). Judas' weakness is that he succumbs to the Tempter and temptation, and instead of hanging, Judas falls headlong into the Temple's sacrificial fire. Judas, still representing the Jews, now symbolizes, not those who "betrayed" Jesus with cries of "Crucify him! Crucify him!,"[74] but those Jews who were victimized and murdered in the Holocaust. The representation of Judas as a damned sinner is undergoing a radical metamorphosis.

73. Wells also describes Zeffirelli's *Jesus of Nazareth* as the Catholic version. Jeffrey Wells, "Red and White," *Hollywood Elsewhere*. http://www.hollywood-elsewhere.com/2008/07/five_things.php.

74. Mark 15:13; Luke 23:21; John 19:15.

## Chapter 5

# The Seventies

### *Introduction*

The 1970s stands in great contrast to the 1960s. The communitarian values of the hippy generation were replaced by the "Me Decade." The rallying call of hope for a better future for humankind became the neurosis of an atomized individual. Psychological and behavioral studies displaced the study of sociology.

The West's most powerful nation, the United States of America, suffered the humiliation of a President, Richard Nixon, having to resign (the Watergate scandal) along with the first "defeat" in a war (Vietnam). Acts of terrorism such as those perpetrated by the Baader-Meinhof Group and the Palestinian Liberation Organization raised awareness of political causes. However, Pol Pot's "Killing Fields" in Kampuchea (Cambodia) and Alianza Anticomunista Argentina death squads went unchallenged. The entire industrialized world suffered the consequences of its alarming dependence on fossil fuels—rising energy costs. While humankind continued to despoil the environment, scientists in England created new life with the birth of "Louise," the first test tube baby.

In response to the disillusionment, dissatisfaction and perceived decay of Western society, a Christian religious uprising emerged which came to be known as the Jesus Revolution.[1] The slogan "Jesus loves you" and the message "the Bible is true, miracles happen, God really did so love the world that he gave it his only begotten son,"[2] attracted many young Americans who were searching for "meaning in their lives." This was a very individualistic message of personal salvation—Jesus loves and saves

1. James Drane, *A New American Reformation* (New York: Philosophical Library, 1973), 108. The movement is variously classified as the Jesus Revolution, Jesus Movement, Jesus People and the Jesus People Movement.

2. "The Alternative Jesus: Psychedelic Christ," *Time Magazine* (21 June 1971). http://www.time.com/time/magazine/article/0,9171,905202,00.html.

YOU—that reflected the "Me" decade. The movement drew from three spiritual streams. The first group were "Jesus People," also known as "Street Christians" or "Jesus Freaks," who blended counter-culture with conservative Christian religion. The second group were the "Straight People," the largest of the groups, who were mainly active in inter-denominational youth movements. The third group, "the Catholic Pentecostals," drew inspiration from the Pentecostal movement that attempted to re-introduce the gifts of the Spirit into the lives of believers and the Church. This latter group remained loyal to the Roman Catholic Church despite being viewed with suspicion by its hierarchy.

Gerald Forshey, referring to the United Sates, claims that:

> In the 1970s, the theme of the "righteous nation" became an examination and indictment of the "unrighteous" nation. In large-scale films, such as *Hawaii* and *The Sand Pebbles*, Americans were portrayed as abrasive and destructive elements in a foreign culture. There was little room left for the "grand style," and even the biblical spectaculars that had shakily survived in the 1960s began to speak with a less assured voice.[3]

It was into this cultural mix that a vast variety of Jesus films was produced in Mexico, USA, Italy, England and India. There were traditional Passion play productions such as *Jesús, Nuestro Señor* (dir. Miquel Zacarias, 1971) together with musicals such as *Jesus Christ Superstar* (dir. Norman Jewison, 1973), *Gospel Road* (dir. Johnny Cash, 1973) and *Godspell: A Musical Based on the Gospel According to St. Matthew* (dir. David Greene, 1973). Then there was Roberto Rossellini's *Il Messia* (1975) that portrayed a human vision of Jesus, while *Jesus of Nazareth* (dir. Franco Zeffirelli, 1977) introduced the television religious miniseries genre. Creative visual and unique Indian cultural influences set apart *Karunamayudu* (dirs. A. Bheem Singh and Christopher Coelho, 1978). *Jesus* (dirs. Peter Sykes and John Kirsh, 1979), like *Karunamayudu*, aimed to convert people to Christianity. Based on the Gospel of Luke, the *Jesus* film has been translated into more than 1,160 languages.[4] *The Life of Brian* (dir. Terry Jones, 1979) was even banned in some parts of Europe and the United Kingdom. For example, in Aberystwyth the ban was not lifted until 2009 as the film was considered to be blasphemous.

3. Forshey, *American Spectaculars*, 52.

4. "The Jesus Film Project," *Jesusfilm.org*. http://www.jesusfilm.org/. The site claims, "Since 1979 more than 200 million men, women, and children worldwide have indicated decisions to follow Jesus after viewing the film."

### *Jesús, Nuestro Señor (1971) (Jesus, Our Lord)*

Director: Miquel Zacarías. Screenwriter: Miguel Zacarías, Alfredo Zacarías (story). Country: Mexico. Production Company: Panorama Films. Length: 115 minutes. Length of Last Supper scene: 4:24 minutes. Color: Eastmancolor. Language: Spanish. Musical score: Enrico Cabiati. Filming locations: Guanajuato, Mexico. Cast: Judas (Juan Gallardo), Jesus (Claudio Brook).

*Lens One*

The first commercial film on the life of Jesus for the 1970s was *Jesús, Nuestro Señor* (Jesus, Our Lord). The scarcity of online reviews and information about this film indicate that it was either largely forgotten or ignored. Miguel Zacarías (1905–2006), a Mexican of Lebanese descent, was a pioneer of sound-film and produced, directed and wrote some 103 films over a fifty-two year film career.[5] Included in his filmography is a series of three films on the life and Passion of Jesus Christ: *Jesús, el Niño Dios* (Jesus the Christ Child, 1970), *Jesús, María y José* (Jesus, Mary and Joseph, 1970) and *Jesús, Nuestro Señor* (1971), as well as the 1969 biblical epic, *El Pecado de Adán y Eva* (The Sin of Adam and Eve). Zacarías' directorial success was aided by his uncanny ability to make films that were of superior quality that appealed to large audiences, and were thus very profitable.

*Jesús, Nuestro Señor* was based primarily on the Gospels. The narrative is in sixteen chapters with an off-screen narrator telling the audience the initial scenes of Joseph and Mary and the entire nativity sequence. There is a blending of all four Gospel accounts, inclusion of legendary material and influences from previous Jesus films. For example, Mary Magdalene's transportation to see Jesus is a chariot similar to that in DeMille's *The King of Kings*. However, where zebras pulled DeMille's chariot, Zacharias settled for a single horse. The conversion of Mary Magdalene (Nélida Bottini) scene is another example of Zacarías' "borrowing" of sources. Instead of exorcizing seven sinful translucent spirits from Mary, Jesus names them using the traditional categories of the "seven deadly sins": wrath, greed, sloth, pride, lust, envy and gluttony. Although the Via Dolorosa episode is relatively short, various Stations of the Cross are included. Veronica's veil scene is particularly significant. Instead of an immediate transference of the image of Jesus' face onto the cloth, Zacarías

5. Julio Alejandro Quijano, "Murió Miguel Zacarías el creador de estrellas," *El Universal* (April 21, 2006). http://www.eluniversal.com.mx/espectaculos/69505.html.

has the image gradually appearing to show a replica of the face of Jesus as shown in the film's advertising poster, thus emphasizing the miraculous nature of the event.

Zacarías understood the art of great theatre and was not afraid to innovate and experiment with photographic shots. For example, at his baptism by John, Jesus (Claudio Brook) is transformed into a white dove. It soars off to the top of a mountain only to take on human shape again. The crucifixion sequence depicts all the "supernatural" events including the opening of tombs and the raising of many bodies of the saints who had fallen asleep (Matt 27:52–53). However, surprisingly, Jesus' burial and tomb sequence are not shown. When we do see the resurrected Jesus meeting a "doubting" Thomas, Jesus is wearing the same tattered and bloodied gown that he wore on the way to his crucifixion. Although he does not have the crown of thorns, rivulets of blood are evident on his forehead and the bloody marks of crucifixion are still evident.

Zacarías is not presenting a low-cost representation of the resurrection but an event that is in accord with the doctrines of his Roman Catholic faith. The resurrected Jesus looks the same as when he died on the cross, thus being in agreement with the Gospel accounts that has Jesus rise before his body could be washed and anointed with oil. Jesus has not been transformed into an ethereal figure who cannot be touched because he has not ascended to the Father (Matt 28:1–10; Mark 16:1–8; Luke 24:1–12; John 20:1–10). When the disciples claim, "Jesus is alive," the audience too sees the one who died and rose again.

Zacarías' inclusion of many of the most familiar miracles—the feeding of the five thousand; turning water in wine; walking on water; healings and raising people from the dead—reinforce Jesus' divinity. Zacarías also endows Jesus with an additional and non-scriptural miraculous talent: that of extra-sensory perception. When defending the woman caught in the act of adultery, Jesus confronts six of the male accusers and instead of writing with his finger on the ground (John 8:1–11), he "names and shames" the accusers' sins using mental telepathy. As Jesus approaches each of the accusers, he simply looks at them and a voiceover narrator identifies their sin!

*Lens Two*

A familiar artwork introduces the Last Supper scene. The room is stark, lacking decorations and furnishings apart from a long table covered with a white cloth. There is one window situated immediately behind the middle of the table. A long shot reveals a typical da Vinci *Last Supper* image. The freeze-frame allows the audience to make the link with the painting and to enter into what is, for Roman Catholics, "a sacramental moment."

Peter and John flank Jesus. Eight other disciples sit behind the table so that they are all facing the camera. Judas (Juan Gallardo) and another unidentified disciple are the exceptions. Judas sits at the right and at the end of the table, side-on to the viewing audience: a typical positioning of Judas in art. This position indicates isolation from the group, enables the artist to include Judas wearing a moneybag, and the side-on portrait suggests Judas is hiding something. The table is set with brass-colored goblets, pottery jugs, small bowls and plates for individual use. There are round loaves placed at intervals along the table and platters of fruit. In front of Jesus is a large metal tray with three whole fish, a recognizable Christian symbol of the Trinity.

The meal commences with a mid-shot of Jesus predicting that someone is going to betray him, someone who is eating with him. The camera cuts to Judas who, with a slight smile on his face, asks, "Surely not I, Lord?" The camera then crosses to Jesus who identifies his betrayer as having his hand on the table. The camera cuts to Judas and zooms in to an extreme close-up of Judas' eyes: he is looking straight at Jesus. Jesus makes further declarations: "the Son of Man goes as it is written of him. But woe to that one by whom the Son of Man is betrayed! It would have been better for that one not to have been born" (Matt 26:24).

The camera pans from the right but does not include Judas in the frame. This is not poor cinematography but to signify that Judas has left the Supper. Jesus raises his hand to summon a servant who quickly approaches the table and is carrying a large bowl of water. Jesus rises from his seat and prepares to wash the feet of the disciples. The scene cuts to Judas talking to three priests and then cuts back to the Supper scene. We know the Supper has ended because the fish tray has gone. All that is in front of Jesus now is a large goblet and a large loaf of bread. His open hands rest on the goblet and bread. Background music of a religious solo chant creates an atmosphere of reverence and awe. The camera zooms in to the cup and bread. Jesus breaks the loaf and takes half and, with his other hand, he takes the cup. The camera zooms out to show a popular Catholic Holy Communion image: Jesus standing and holding the bread and the cup. He states, "This is my body. This is my blood of the new testament."

The distribution of the bread and wine is particularly startling, and within the parameters of this filmic research, is unique to this film. Jesus stands and calls each disciple by name who in turn approach Jesus. Each breaks off a morsel of bread and then dips the bread into the cup. Peter is the first to be called, then John, Andrew, James son of Zebedee, Thomas, Matthew, James son of Alphaeus, Phillip, Bartholomew, Simon and Thaddeus. Only eleven disciples are called. Why Zacarías chose to order the disciples in this manner is uncertain, but individually calling the disciples highlights Judas' absence from the "Institution of the Lord's Supper." The scene ends with a mid-shot of Jesus looking heavenward while still holding the bread and wine. The shot fades marking the end of the Supper.

*Lens Three*

Although referred to in Mexican cinema as "the 70s Thaw"—a period following the latter days of great cinema—the decade also experienced a revival with the founding of *Cine Independiente* by three major directors: Arturo Ripstein, Felipe Cazals and Rafael Casternado. Other catalysts for film revival were increased government funding for film productions and a relaxation of the growing tendency toward restrictive overview of film content. New filmmakers "confronted contemporary issues head-on; class conflict, racism, machismo, and Cold War politics were all subjected to their critical gaze."[6]

A major event that brought about change in Mexican cinema was the massacre by government troops of student protestors at La Plaza de las Tres Culturas at Tlatelolco, Mexico City, on October 2, 1968. Kate Doyle, analyst and director of the Guatemala and Mexico Documentation Projects for the National Security Archive, writes:

> The extent of the violence stunned the country. Although months of nationwide student strikes that preceded October 2nd had prompted an increasingly repressive response from the Díaz Ordaz regime, no one was prepared for the bloodbath that Tlatelolco became. When the shooting stopped, hundreds of people lay dead or wounded, as Army and police forces seized thousands of surviving protesters and dragged them away. More shocking still was the cover-up that kicked in as soon as the smoke cleared. Eyewitnesses to the killings pointed to the President's "security" forces, who had entered the plaza bristling with weapons, backed by armored vehicles. But the government pointed back, claiming that extremists and Communist agitators had initiated the violence. Who was responsible for Tlatelolco? The Mexican people have been demanding an answer ever since.[7]

6. Don M. Coerver, Suzanne B. Pasztor and Robert Buffington, *Mexico: An Encyclopedia of Contemporary Culture and History* (Santa Barbara: ABC-CLIO, 2004), 94–95.

7. Kate Doyle, "The Tlatelolco Massacre US Documents on Mexico and the Events of 1968," *The National Security Archive*. http://www.gwu.edu/~nsarchiv/NSAEBB/NSAEBB99/.

Three film scenes in *Jesús, Nuestro Señor* identify with this massacre. The first scene condemns the abuse of power and oppressive rule. The main antagonists in the film are the Pharisees while the Roman presence is not evident, nor encountered until the Passion scenes. Pilate is not the sympathetic figure presented in other Jesus films but appears ineffective and indifferent. The iconic "washing his hands of the blood of Jesus" is probably a reminder of the repressive regime of President Ordaz and his refusal to acknowledge the government's involvement in the Tlatelolco massacre.

The second reference is the spilling of innocent blood. At the Last Supper scene, the disciples receive the bread and wine by intinction (dipping the bread into the wine). This is highly unusual and is forbidden in the Roman Catholic rite. Only the priest can intinct. Although the General Instruction of the Roman Missal states, "The Blood of the Lord may be received either by drinking from the chalice directly, or by intinction, or by means of a tube or a spoon,"[8] "the practice is rare, largely because liturgists oppose it."[9] This is due to a fear that the consecrated wine might be accidentally spilt. Thus a parallel could be made between this spilling of the sacred blood of Christ and the sacrificial spilling of the students' blood in the Tlatelolco massacre. However, once it is understood that Zacarías was a Lebanese Maronite, the reason for intinction becomes less controversial. In the Maronite Church, communion is received by intinction, after the priest dips the bread in the chalice. This is the only form prescribed for reception of the Body and Blood of Christ. Thus, the director was following his own religious tradition.

A third parallel between the film and the Tlatelolco massacre is the bloodied resurrected body of Jesus. Like Jesus, the students spoke out against injustices and corruption. Like Jesus, these innocent victims were killed by an oppressive regime. Their death was not futile; it brought about political change. Their sacrifice is significant and continues to live on in Mexican historical memory through the Monument to the Tlatelolco massacre, which stands in the Plaza de las Tres Culturas.

*The Portrayal of Judas*

Judas is a liberationist, representing Mexican students who sought freedom from an oppressive government. Judas' role is significant in this film as the following reasons explain.

8. GIRM 245. David Lysik, ed., *The Liturgy Documents: A Parish Resource*, Vol. 1, 4th ed. (Chicago: Liturgy Training Publications, 2004), 81.

9. Susan Benofy, "Communion by Intinction: A 'New' Way of Receiving Communion in Both Kinds," *AB* 9, no. 6 (2003). www.adoremus.org.

First, there is the manner in which Judas joins the other disciples. Judas is present in the synagogue when Jesus is handed a scroll and reads from the prophet Isaiah (Luke 4:16–21)—"The Spirit of the Lord is upon me, because he has anointed me to bring good news to the poor. He has sent me to proclaim release to the captives and recovery of sight to the blind, to let the oppressed go free, to proclaim the year of the Lord's favor." This text was pivotal for South American liberation theologians who argued for an armed struggle against unjust regimes. Thus, its inclusion when Judas first appears suggests that he is on the side of armed resistance. His wearing a large sword wedged in the rope around his waist reinforces this. Upon hearing Jesus say, "Today this scripture has been fulfilled in your hearing," the camera pans towards Judas and the zoom-shot shows that he is pleased with what Jesus says. Rubbing his beard with one hand while the other hand rests on his sword suggests that Judas is contemplating whether Jesus is the one who will bring about armed resistance to the Roman occupiers. Unlike the other disciples, who are called individually by Jesus to follow him, Judas actively pursues Jesus. He introduces himself and asks to join the group. Jesus is pleased to have Judas join as the twelfth and last addition to the group of disciples (Matt 10:14; Mark 3:13–19a; Luke 6:12–16). Judas can be of use to Jesus and to his mission. Mexican students would have been inspired and moved to action by this "revolutionary" film. They would have looked to the Church, which promoted these Jesus ideals.

Second, Judas has a significant position within the disciples. At the marriage at Cana, Jesus and the twelve disciples sit at a separate table from the other guests, including Mary, the mother of Jesus. This image is like a dress rehearsal for their Last Supper together. Judas sits next to Jesus alluding to Judas' position of privilege. When Jesus miraculously—although the action is depicted as being more magical than miraculous—changes the water into wine, both Judas and Peter look on with wonder. After Jesus cleanses the temple, and is questioned by the priests, Judas holds Jesus' red cloak while Peter nurses a white dove. In Christian art, color operates on two basic levels: its inherent characteristics (red as the color of fire) and its emotional connotations (red equals heat, therefore passion or suffering). Here, in the two characters of Peter and Judas, and with what they are holding, we can see a divergence in personalities and behavior. Peter holds a white dove, a harbinger of peace that also symbolizes innocence and gentleness (Gen 8:8, 10). The image of Judas holding Jesus' red cloak is almost a prophecy of what is about to happen. Red is associated with passion, blood and fire, and is the color of love and hate, sin and suffering. The Tlatelolco massacre too was about suffering, passion and blood.

Third, there is a lack of motive for Judas handing over Jesus to the Sanhedrin. When Judas is paid for his information, he holds out his tunic to catch the coins, counted out singularly and tossed by a temple priest. It is almost as though Judas does not want to touch this "blood money." He shows neither signs of greed nor remorse. The conundrum for Judas is that he has to do wrong to bring about right. Students knew that in protesting they would be breaking the law but this was necessary to bring about political change.

A fourth reason that Judas' role is important, is the plea Judas makes just before he hangs himself. Looking towards Calvary and the crucified Jesus, a penitent Judas prays, "Lord, don't have pity on my soul, because I don't deserve it." This plea is significant because it pre-empts Jesus' pity for, and forgiveness of Judas. That Judas claims he is not deserving of pity suggests that he acknowledges his wrongdoing, that he regrets his actions and that the magnitude of his sin cannot merit forgiveness. We are left wondering whether Jesus in fact forgives Judas. Although Judas recognized his sin and asked for forgiveness, he failed to make restitution by returning the thirty pieces of silver to the Sanhedrin. Perhaps his grief was such that he simply forgot the money. Many protesting students would have been unprepared for the unexpected violence at the march. Their life was cut short.

## *Jesus Christ Superstar (1973)*

Director: Norman Jewison. Screenwriter: Melvyn Bragg and Norman Jewison. Country: USA. Production Company: Universal Pictures. Length: 107 minutes. Length of Last Supper scene: 6:46 minutes. Color: Technicolor. Language: English. Musical score: Andrew Lloyd Webber (music) and Tim Rice (lyrics). Filming locations: Negev Desert, Capernaum, Dead Sea, Israel. Cast: Judas (Carl Anderson), Jesus (Ted Neeley).

### *Lens One*

*Jesus Christ Superstar*, according to Andrew Lloyd Webber, was simply a work attempting to ask a couple of questions, the chief of which was asked by Bob Dylan some years ago: "Did Judas Iscariot have God on his side?"[10] In an interview with Dennis Polkow, Webber explains:

10. The American folk singer expresses "confusion" in his 1964 song "With God on Our Side." Although Dylan lives in a country that has "God on its side," he wonders why former wartime enemies also had God on their side. Citing each military conflict involving the USA since its colonization, Dylan denies responsibility

> *Superstar*…was never really intended to be anything more than a piece examining the story of Jesus from the point of view of Judas Iscariot. In that sense it is a dramatic work and not specifically a religious work at all. I mean, clearly Iscariot was not an unintelligent man, and how much was the whole thing in the end an accident of what was necessary given the politics of the day? That's really what we were asking in *Superstar.*[11]

*Jesus Christ Superstar* introduced a new genre to Jesus films: the rock-opera and a new type of Jesus, one who sings and who might be characterized as a "hippy." *Superstar* originated as a double record album in 1968, followed by a stage production in 1970, and then, in 1973, was made into a film. The rock-opera depicts a version of the last seven days of Jesus. It is a creative reworking of the Jesus story, imitating "the episodic plotting of the Gospels,"[12] and harmonizing events from the four Gospels. The libretto, considered contemporary in reaching 1970s audiences, still attracts audiences today.

The most noticeable historical feature of the film is that it was shot on location in Israel, utilizing the ruins of Avdat in the Negev, the ruins at Caesarea and the Bell Caves at Beit Guvrin. Screenwriters Norman Jewison and Melvyn Bragg replaced traditional and typical images from characters, settings and costumes that had been vital for classical Jesus films. In their place, scaffolding becomes the province of the Jewish priests, tanks and military jets invade the screen and the Temple becomes a tourist bazaar! The most effective and evocative inclusion in the film is that of a montage of medieval and renaissance paintings of the Passion. This occurs when Jesus, contemplating his painful fate, sings: "See how I die; just watch me die."[13] During the song, twenty-three images, which include Grunewald's, *The Crucifixion* (1515), flash onto the screen. The twenty-six-second sequence "dissolves into a close-up of Judas' face, making the connection between Jesus' uncertainty and Judas' betrayal."[14]

and ignorance because "you never ask questions / when God's on your side." If God is on the side of all people, good and bad, as the song infers, one assumes Judas too has God on his side.

11. Dennis Polkow, "Andrew Lloyd Webber: From Superstar to Requiem," *Chr Century* (March 18–25, 1987). http://www.religion-online.org/showarticle.asp?title=1011.

12. Staley and Walsh, *Jesus, the Gospels*, 63.

13. "Gethsemane (I only want to say)." Music by Andrew Lloyd Webber; lyrics by Tim Rice. Lyrics for all the songs quoted are from the *Jesus Christ Superstar* libretto insert for the MCA Records/Astor Records film soundtrack album.

14. Forshey, *American Spectaculars*, 109.

Pamela Grace explains:

> images from an extra-diegetic era produce a shock... Suddenly before us are pictures that convey a depth of religious feeling that we virtually never encounter in film, everyday life, or modern art. The old painters' excruciating empathy for Jesus' suffering catches us off guard, leaving us somewhat undefended as the film moves toward the crucifixion.[15]

The three key characters in *Jesus Christ Superstar* are Jesus (Ted Neeley), Judas Iscariot (Carl Anderson) and Mary Magdalene (Yvonne Elliman). The latter is a combination of the woman taken in adultery (John 8:1–11) and the woman who anoints Jesus with costly perfume (Luke 7:36–50). However, it is Judas who steals the show: the story is told almost completely from his perspective with one-seventh of the libretto devoted to him.

Costuming is important in defining characters. Jesus is separated from the other characters in that he wears a long white caftan, whereas the rest are in the fashion of the 1970s. Contrasted against Jesus' white attire are the priests' long black flowing capes, black trousers and bare chests. As a group standing on scaffolding, they strike both an imposing and threatening image; like that of the crows sitting on overhead powerlines in Alfred Hitchcock's thriller, *The Birds* (1963). The religious status of the group is marked by the wearing of the priestly breastplate (Exod 28:15–19) and bizarre-shaped headgear similar to the design used by Pasolini in *Il Vangelo Secondo Matteo*. The size and shape of the hat defines the priest's position in the religious hierarchy. To differentiate between the biblical Jesus story and that of modern times, Jewison has the scribes holding scrolls and not note-pads as the "reporters" do in the cleansing of the marketplace scene. Annas and Caiaphas swap their black capes for red ones in the trial before Pilate scene, adding emphasis to their petition that although they want Jesus crucified, they have no authority to execute a man and must turn to Rome for sentencing. The red capes symbolize their appeal for Jesus' death. In contrast, Pilate, his guards and even the women of his "palace" wear different shades of purple—a regal color. The implication is that the Romans are in charge and in control.

*Jesus Christ Superstar* turns the emotional trajectory of the conventional musical on its head and purposely breaks with most of the formularies of earlier Jesus films. There is no authoritative voiceover at the beginning to draw the audience into a closed historical past nor does

15. Grace, *Religious Film*, 96.

the film end with reassuring words from the same extra-diegetic god-like source. What Jewison achieves through his direction, setting, filming and interpretation of the text is an intentional disorientation of the viewer: a continuous changing between ancient and modern scenes.

*Lens Two*

Jewison intended the Last Supper to be a picnic and went to extraordinary lengths to ensure there would be a suitable grassy picnic spot.[16] An area in an olive grove in the Negev Desert was fenced off, grass seed planted and watered twice a day for four months. The lush green is in stark contrast to the dry and dusty desert, which borders the area. The image almost corroborates Jesus' declaration, "If anyone is thirsty, let him come to me and drink. Whoever believes in me, as the Scripture has said, streams of living water will flow from within him" (John 7:37–39). This Last Supper location also doubles for the Garden of Gethsemane.

By basing the Last Supper tableau on da Vinci's painting, Jewison was able to give the actors playing the disciples specific character names. An obvious mistake in the scene is that Peter (Paul Thomas) is situated incorrectly. He is at the left end where da Vinci positioned Bartholomew. Similarly, in the painting, Peter is considered the one whispering to John, the disciple seated immediately to Jesus' right. The reason for Jewison's change in placements is unknown but I would suggest that Peter's place at the end of the table affords him more space to stand and declare his loyalty to Jesus. Bartholomew, who like Judas is an African American, is situated on the other side of the table far away from Judas. It is only when Jewison freezes the frame that his reasoning for using the da Vinci image becomes evident. The painting is so easily recognizable that secular people in the audience would be able to make the link and therefore appreciate the significance of the scene. Jewison follows historical/religious convention by having only males present at the meal. Even Mary Magdalene, who has developed a close relationship with Jesus, is excluded from the gathering.

The structure of the libretto in this Last Supper scene is like that of a Greek tragedy. The song begins as a conversation between a single actor (Jesus) and a very important chorus (the disciples.) The role of the chorus is to observe and comment on the action of the actors and may seem as an interlude between the main actions. A second actor is then added (Judas).

16. Feature Commentary with director Norman Jewison and actor Ted Neeley on *Jesus Christ Superstar*, Special Edition DVD, Universal Studios, 2001.

The scene opens with a shepherd leading his flock and the disciples singing, "Look at all my trials and tribulations…"[17]

The frame changes to show a stream and the reflection of sheep walking past. The scene changes again to show the reflection of the disciples walking in the opposite direction to the sheep. The procession of disciples arrives at the picnic site where Jesus waits with a jug of water to wash their hands. After Jesus pours water over their hands, they each take their place at the "table." The chorus continues: "Always hoped that I'd be an apostle…" Jesus begins singing, "The end is just a little harder when brought about by friends." The disciples, stunned by this statement, look questioningly at each other. Jesus continues, "For all you care this wine could be my blood." Jesus takes the large round matzot, breaks it, and gives half to the disciples on either side of him. He continues, "For all you care this bread could be my body." These statements about the bread and wine are not an act of generosity but an accusation.[18] They undercut any claim to Jesus' superiority in "kind" as in the early Church debates over whether Jesus was "wholly God' or 'wholly man." Jesus takes a pottery jug and pours wine into a glass and continues with the traditional words, "This is my blood you drink / This is my body you eat." One could interpret these lyrics as Jesus thinking out loud. That he does not appear to be addressing the comments to anyone in particular gives credibility to this interpretation. Jesus continues expressing his hope that the disciples would remember him when they eat and drink but doubts that he will be remembered. The camera cuts to a close-up of Judas who appears curious as to why Jesus is questioning himself. The disciples are shocked and become defensive when Jesus declares, "One of you denies me / One of you betrays me." Judas is silent and scrutinizes the group. Jesus continues to predict what is about to happen. He tells Peter that he will deny him three times and that one of the "twelve chosen" will betray him.

Judas screams at Jesus, "Cut out the dramatics! You know very well who…," and there follows a heated exchange where Jesus provokes Judas into betraying him. Judas declares that he no longer admires Jesus but despises him. The apostles move closer toward Jesus as though protecting him. Jesus shouts, "You liar—you Judas."[19] Judas defends himself by claiming that Jesus wanted him to betray Jesus, then threatens not to, thus ruining Jesus' "ambition" and finally shouts, "Christ you deserve it!"

17. "The Last Supper." Music by Andrew Lloyd Webber; lyrics by Tim Rice.
18. Grace, *Religious Film*, 95.
19. "You Judas" is an interesting inclusion of a metaphor for betrayal.

The rage in which Judas sings "Christ" suggests not a title but a curse. An angry Jesus, no longer wanting to hear Judas' "speeches," orders Judas to go.

Judas runs off through the olive grove and then suddenly stops. A crosscut shows Jesus picking up the dark cloak Judas had left behind, and walking in the direction of Judas. The apostles, gathering their composure, do not notice Jesus leaving, and begin to sing the chorus. Jesus approaches Judas and holds out the cloak but Judas shakes his head and refuses this act of kindness. With anger in his eyes and contempt in his voice, Judas calls Jesus a "sad pathetic man" who ruined all their ideals. Someone has to turn in Jesus. Tension, dread and fear overcome Jesus. He screams at Judas, "Get out! They're waiting!" Jesus is aware of Judas' meeting with Caiaphas.

Judas is the embodiment of despair. His open hands stretch out towards Jesus who gently takes them. Drawing nearer to Jesus, Judas tenderly holds Jesus' hand against his cheek. Judas attempts to explain his disillusionment. He turns to run but a flock of sheep are in his way. Startled, they scatter and then follow him. A crosscut shows a close-up of a somber Jesus. In the background, we hear the disciples singing their chorus for the final time.

*Lens Three*

*Jesus Christ Superstar* emerged in an era of significant social upheaval. There are many scenes within the film that correspond to the turmoil unfolding within Western culture. Casting an African American as the Judas character is a response to the American Civil Rights Movement and Afro-centrism (focus on Africa or African peoples). Larry Marshall, who played Simon Zealotes in the film, identified Jesus as a first-century equivalent of the 1960s "Black Power" leader Stokeley Carmichael (1941–1998). *The Telegraph* (July 6, 2012) reports Marshall commenting, "it was all politics and manipulation then, and that's what it's at today." The inclusion of military tanks pursuing Judas in the desert allegorizes the military conflicts of the Vietnam War (1959–1975) and the Israeli/Egyptian Six Day War (June 5–10, 1967), as well as illustrating the political desperation and personal conflict which drove Judas to consult the priests about betraying Jesus. It is also probable that the air-force jets and military tanks represent the authorities going to arrest Jesus. The cleansing of the Temple and Jesus' rage are directed against "the abuses of modernity" and "the symbols of human weaknesses."[20] An angry and frustrated Jesus voices the tenets of liberation theology while the "resurrection" of Judas reinforced

20. Forshey, *American Spectaculars*, 110.

economic, political or social conditions of Black Americans. Thus, the Jesus story of the Gospels is turned into a kind of *midrash* on the social and racial problems plaguing Western society in the 1970s.

The 1971 stage production of *Jesus Christ Superstar*, directed by Tom O'Horgan, received unfavorable reviews, as Stephen Prothero notes:

> *Superstar* offended so many kinds of people when it premiered in October 1971 that the opening-night picket line was a model of interfaith comity. Protestants and Catholics claimed the show portrayed Jesus as insufficiently divine and Judas as insufficiently demonic. Jews objected to yet another portrait of them as Christ killers.[21]

The film was criticized by Christians, African Americans and Jews. Rabbi Marc Tanenbaum, the director of inter-religious affairs on the American Jewish Committee who in 1973, commissioned a line-by-line analysis of Rice's lyrics, led Jewish criticism. It concluded that *Jesus Christ Superstar* was a singularly damaging setback in the struggle against the religious sources of anti-Semitism and even went as far as to suggest that as an anti-Semitic product, *Jesus Christ Superstar* "ought to be abandoned voluntarily."[22] Likewise, Benjamin R. Epstein, national director of the Anti-Defamation League of B'Nai Brith, commented: "Even the casting is of the most primitive type. Anyone who has ever seen cowboy films knows that the good guys wear white hats and the bad guys wear black. Here the actor portraying Jesus is blond; Judas is black; the priests and rabbis are dark-haired, foreboding, and garbed in black."[23]

Jewison and the Webber/Rice partnership were castigated for perpetuating the myth that the Jews collectively killed Jesus, and for ignoring the new, ecumenical interpretation of the crucifixion as set out in the 1965 papal encyclical *Nostra Aetate*. The irrefutable proof of the film's anti-Semitic thrust, according to Norman Finkelstein, is the biased rendering of the biblical protagonists.[24] With Pilate portrayed as a weakling whose power is possibly based on fear and superstition, and Herod portrayed

21. Stephen Prothero, *American Jesus: How the Son of God Became a National Icon* (New York: Farrar, Straus & Giroux, 2003), 133.

22. Marc Tanenbaum, "Passion Plays and Vilification of Jews," *Christian Century* 90, no. 31 (1973): 859.

23. Linda Greenhouse, review of "Superstar Film Renews Disputes: Jewish Groups Say Opening Could Stir Anti-Semitism Reasons Given Company Issues Statement," *New York Times* (August 8, 1973). http://www.nytimes.com/movie/review?res=9904e3dd103de63abc4053dfbe668388669ede.

24. Norman G. Finkelstein, *Beyond Chutzpah: On the Misuse of Anti-Semitism and the Abuse of History* (California: University of California Press, 2008), 22–23.

as a "pampered child...a kind of harmless pervert," the only possible villains are the Jewish priests.[25] Epstein also complained that "the movie's sharp and vivid emphasis on a Jewish mob's demand to kill Jesus can feed into the kind of disparagement of Jews and Judaism which has always nurtured anti-Jewish prejudice and bigotry, and the American Jewish Committee expressed concerns about the effect the film might have when distributed overseas."[26]

The claim of anti-Semitism was only one objection to *Jesus Christ Superstar*. Tanenbaum laid an additional complaint against the film: the casting of an African American actor as Judas equated blackness with sin. A committee of African American Baptist ministers who protested to Universal Pictures reinforced this. Racism based on skin color had been the basis for discrimination and stereotyping throughout history as Claud Anderson explains:

> [W]hite Americans have devalued black skin color. Blackness in general has been associated with discouragement, despair, depression, coldness, the unknown, the haunting shadow, and the nightmare. This negative blackness concept, no doubt originating from the associations with day and night, has fused with skin color devaluation.[27]

Hence, the complaints against *Jesus Christ Superstar* were issues of religion, color and racial identity.

Figure 9. Jesus and Judas are talking in the Garden of Gethsemane.
© Universal Studios.

25. Forshey, *American Spectaculars*, 114.

26. Kendall R. Phillips, *Controversial Cinema: The Films That Outraged America* (Westport: Praeger, 2008), 142.

27. Claud Anderson, "Black Is Beautiful and the Color Preferences of Afro-American Youth," *JNE* 46, no. 1 (1977): 76.

*The Portrayal of Judas*

Pamela Grace observes that in the first few minutes of *Jesus Christ Superstar*, Judas articulates more critical analysis of Christianity than most Jesus films do in two hours or more.[28] Carl Anderson's portrayal of Judas is perhaps the most controversial of all the portrayals of Judas Iscariot in Jesus films. This controversy has been fueled by a variety of reasons.

First, Judas as the black performer is the prophet who comments on the history of African Americans. One of Judas' early warnings to his friend Jesus is rooted in the African American experience of being subjugated and subservient.[29] However, the most powerful commentary on the American racial relations and tensions is when Judas commits suicide. The camera pulls back, revealing a disturbing image: Judas' body hangs like the victim of a racist lynching. Despite the passing of the Civil Rights Act in 1964 when lynching was outlawed by government decree, racist attitudes were still ingrained in the minds of Americans.

Second, Judas is the hero in *Jesus Christ Superstar*. He is the only one of Jesus' disciples who is conscious of the Roman threat to destroy the Jesus movement. Judas is also the only disciple who is prepared to point out the dangers of Jesus' delusion of grandeur—his messiahship—and who has a legitimate concern about Jesus' popularity. By blurring the lines between actor and role, and between the first and twentieth century, Judas' sophisticated understanding of oppression and violence is subtly linked to the blackness of Carl Anderson.[30] It is only when the oppressed speak out that their plight is noticed.

Third, Judas is the voice for the poor and oppressed and for economic justice, thus mirroring the rise of liberation theology, especially in South America; and echoing the emergence of black liberation in theologians such as James Cone.[31] Judas questions Mary's use of costly oil in the anointing of Jesus. The gospel account cites that Judas' criticism of the use of the oil was "not because he cared for the poor, but because he was a thief; he kept the common purse and used to steal what was put into it" (John 12:6). In the film, Judas states that the hungry matter more than Jesus' feet and hair. A defensive Jesus responds by brushing off Judas'

28. Grace, *Religious Film*, 93.

29. See "Heaven on Their Minds." Music by Andrew Lloyd Webber; lyrics by Tim Rice.

30. Grace, *Religious Film*, 97.

31. James Cone, *A Black Theology of Liberation* (Maryknoll, NY: Orbis Books, 1970).

concern for the poor and criticizing his naiveté.[32] Judas empathizes with the poor because as an African American he has experienced poverty and oppression. An empathetic Judas, contrary to what John's Gospel tells us, wants to give the thirty pieces of silver to the poor. His liberation is tied up with liberation of the poor.

Fourth, Judas prophesies the future with its demonization of Jews and Judaism. In his meeting with Caiaphas and Annas, Judas foreshadows that if Jesus is allowed to continue, it will bring a great tribulation to the Jews, especially with a ruler like Pilate who had a reputation of responding to religious/civil unrest with brutality. Judas calls this "the sad solution."[33] Could this be a subtle reference to the "Final Solution," Hitler's response to ridding the world of Jews? Later in the meeting with Caiaphas and Annas, Judas claims that he did not come on his own accord, nor did he think of his own reward. His main concern is that he will be "damned for all time."[34] Judas does not betray Jesus for monetary gain yet for his actions he *is* "damned for all time."

In the opening scene of the film, Judas expresses his inner conflict about Jesus' mission and where it will lead the disciples. Judas wants to strip the "myth from the man" and see where they all will be. He fears that Jesus is caught up in the euphoria of public recognition that he is the Messiah.

Judas' insight comes from sharing a close relationship with Jesus. Judas' commitment is to free the people from Roman oppression. He interprets Jesus' mission as a political overthrow of the Roman Empire. The songs declare "a Judas who wants to warn Jesus about the irresistible direction that events are taking ('Heaven on their Minds'), who does not want to take 'Blood Money', and who feels abused by God, chosen for a fate that ends with his own 'murder' by God ('Judas' Death')."[35]

It is significant that the film begins and concludes with Judas. The final scene is of a resurrected Judas realizing that he is the victim of an act of betrayal rather than its perpetrator. Judas protests that God chose him to betray Jesus and that God murders him. God exploited Judas for

32. See "Everything's Alright." Music by Andrew Lloyd Webber; lyrics by Tim Rice.

33. See "Damned for All Time/Blood Money." Music by Andrew Lloyd Webber; lyrics by Tim Rice.

34. Ibid.

35. Mark Goodacre, "Do you think you're what they say you are? Reflections on *Jesus Christ Superstar*," *JRF* 3, no. 2 (1999). http://www.unomaha.edu/jrf/jesuscss2.htm.

God's own ends and at the cost of Judas' reputation and life. *Jesus Christ Superstar* presents to a wide and diverse audience another interpretation of the Judas gospel character. The African American Judas Iscariot discards the stereotypical traits of Blacks and Jews. Judas is not greedy but generous. He is not self-absorbed but speaks out for the voiceless. He does not hate but loves to the point of frustration. He is not the villain in *Jesus Christ Superstar*: Judas is the hero. The damned disciple is signaling his redemption.

### *Godspell: A Musical Based on the Gospel According to St. Matthew (1973)*

Director: David Greene. Screenwriter: David Greene and John-Michael Trebelak. Country: USA. Production Company: Columbia. Length: 103 minutes. Length of Last Supper scene: 4:24 minutes. Color: Color (TVC). Language: English. Musical score: Stephen Schwartz. Filming locations: Manhattan, New York. Cast: Judas/John the Baptist (David Haskell), Jesus (Victor Garber).

*Lens One*

A dour Easter service at the Trinity Episcopal Cathedral in Pittsburgh, a lackluster liturgy and being accosted for his "hippy" appearance, left John-Michael Trebelak "with the feeling that, rather than rolling the rock away from the tomb, they were piling more on."[36] Trebelak's response to this uninspiring worship experience was to write the rock-musical *Godspell*. Originally presented as a stage rock-musical, *Godspell* is set in New York in the 1970s, and presents an "interpretative reading of the Gospel."[37] The story is told in two acts. The first is a series of life-lessons and parables, while the second follows the Passion story interspersed with stories and teachings.[38] The narrative focuses mainly on six of the best-known Matthean parables, which are not narrated by Jesus but by his disciples. Trebelak's inspiration for many of the songs in *Godspell* originated with the Episcopalian hymnal. Psalm 137 is the basis of the song "On the Willows" while Matt 5 provides the theme for "Light of the

36. Joseph Barton, "The Godspell Story." http://www.geocities.com/Broadway/Lobby/4209/america.html.

37. Peter Malone, *Movie Christs and Antichrists* (Sydney: Parish Ministry Publications, 1988), 34.

38. Stephen Schwartz, "*Godspell* Script Notes and Revision 1999." http://www.oocitoes.org/cugodspell/scriptnotes.html.

World," and Matt 23 is transformed into "Alas for you." Through these songs, Trebelak is concerned to affirm "the divinity of Jesus, and the truth of the resurrection."[39]

There are often misconceptions about the disciples cast as "hippies" or "flower children" and Jesus as a clown in *Godspell*. Trebelak took the idea of Jesus the clown from Harvey Cox's[40] *The Feast of Fools: A Theological Essay on Festivity and Fantasy*, especially the chapter, "Christ the Harlequin."[41] The Feast of Fools was a late-Middle Ages celebration marked by much excess and buffoonery, which in many parts of Europe, and particularly in France, took place every year on or about the Feast of the Circumcision (1st January).[42] Cox's book is an examination of contemporary culture and theology, analyzing both the loss and re-emergence of festivity and fantasy in Western civilization. *Godspell* incorporates "buffoonery," with the solemn words associated with Jesus and the Gospels being replaced with quirky songs.

*Lens Two*

The major emphasis in *Godspell* is about the formation of community.[43] It is at the Last Supper that we see how close-knitted the group has become. The Supper scene takes place in an empty allotment, replete with old car, a cart laden with props, two tall lockers, a pinball machine and a seesaw. A cyclone fence surrounds the allotment. The group enter in high spirits. Jesus (Victor Garber) and Judas (David Haskell) pick up a red door that is leaning against a fake brick-wall painted with a window at either end. In the center is a rising orange and yellow sun with white stars in its rays. They carry the door and place it on the concrete floor. This is probably intended to evoke the metaphor "I am the gate; if anyone enters through me, he shall be saved, and shall go in and out, and find

39. Prothero, *American Jesus*, 134. Stephen Schwartz is the composer and lyricist for all the *Godspell* songs. The librettist is John-Michael Trebelak.

40. Harvey Cox is one of the most celebrated theologians of this era. His *Secular City*, published in 1965, was selected by the University of Marburg as one of the most influential books of Protestant theology in the twentieth century.

41. Stephen Schwartz, "Stephen Schwartz Answers Questions About the *Godspell* Movie." *stephenschwartz.com.* http://www.stephenschwartz.com/wp-content/uploads/2010/08/godspell-movie.pdf.

42. Max Harris, *Sacred Folly: A New History of the Feast of Fools* (Ithaca: Cornell University Press, 2011), 23.

43. Stephen Schwartz, "*Godspell* Notes for Directors and Musicians, Producers," *stephenschwartz.com.* http://www.stephenschwartz.com/wp-content/uploads/2010/08/Godspell-notes-for-directors-and-musicians-pdf.

pasture" (John 10:9). The color of the door is symbolic as Jennifer Eblin explains:

> In early colonial America, a red door was a symbol of a safe haven. Travelers often kept a look out for red doors on homes as signs of welcome and safety. In Catholicism, a red door symbolizes the blood of Christ, which meant once you passed through the door, you were on holy ground. In Scotland, people paint their doors red to indicate they've paid off a mortgage.[44]

Moreover, according to the Hebrew Scriptures, the Jewish slaves in Egypt smeared their doors with lamb's blood as a sign that the required sacrifice had already been made, and those homes would be passed over by the Angel of Vengeance (Exod 12:13). Therefore, the red door as the table/altar in *Godspell*'s Last Supper scene could represent one or all of the following: a sacred space, the pending sacrifice Jesus will make for humankind on the cross and the payment of the debt of humanity's sins.

Judas has taken tissues and make-up remover from the cart. Jesus joins him and holds a mirror in front of Judas' face. Judas does not like what he sees and yet Jesus nods approval and begins to remove the painted red lightning strike from Judas' cheek. Jesus continues to remove the distinctive face paintings from the other disciples. This action not only alludes to the foot-washing event in John's Gospel (John 13:1–11) but Jesus is saying that the group have "assimilated his teaching into themselves and no longer need the outward trappings that brand them as disciples."[45] They are about to take on a new role and return to society to proclaim the gospel.

Jesus goes to the props cart and takes a flagon of red wine and two paper cups. He returns to the gathering and sits at the center of the table. A painted sun is behind him. The long shot embraces the group sitting behind the table and at either end. Judas reclines in front and at the right of the table. In a light-hearted manner Jesus declares, "I tell you this, one of you among us will betray me." Jesus is not taken seriously and each of the disciples asks jokingly, "Could it be me Lord?" The camera moves to a close-up of Judas who is pointing to himself and smiling, "Rabbi, do you mean me?" It then crosses to a close-up of Jesus who nods and answers, "The words are yours. Do quickly what you have to do." The camera cuts to a close-up of Judas: he is looking somewhat confused. He stands,

44. Jennifer Eblin, "What Is the Significance of a Red Door on a Home?" *eHow.com*. http://www.ehow.com/facts_7201516_significance-red-door-home_.html.

45. Schwartz, "*Godspell* Notes for Directors."

and as a parting gesture takes the hand of fellow disciple, Gilmer, and then runs out of the vacant lot, slamming shut the gate behind him. This action could be interpreted as Judas imprisoning Jesus and ensuring his easy capture by the authorities, but the anger expressed in Judas' actions suggests that Judas is shutting out Jesus and all that he represents.

The scene returns to a mid-shot of Merrell, Jesus and Jerry. Jesus takes matzot and begins to pray the *Hamotzi*, "*Baruch atah Adonai eloheinu melech ha-alom ha-motzi lechem min ha-aretz*" (Blessed are You, O Lord our God, Ruler of the universe, who brings forth bread from the earth). As Jesus begins the prayer, Jerry removes his cap. According to Emily Post, an American authority on etiquette, a man should remove his hat at mealtimes, at the table and in a house of worship. Jewish custom however requires a man to have his head covered. Jerry's removal of his hat is ambiguous. Although the meal is set within a Jewish context—the Jewish blessings—the disciples, about to partake of the meal, are Christians, followers of Jesus.

Jesus breaks off pieces of matzot, gives them to his disciples, and says, "Take this and eat. For this is my body." Jesus then takes two paper cups and from a large flagon pours red wine into each. He prays the *Kiddush*, "*Baruch atah, Adonai Eloheinu, Melech Haolam, borei p'ri hagafen*" (Blessed are You, O Lord our God, Ruler of the universe, Creator of the fruit of the vine). Jesus says, "Take this and drink, for this is my blood of the covenant shed for the forgiveness of sins. And I tell you I shall never again drink of the fruit of the vine until I drink it again with you in the kingdom of my father." The camera pans to show each of the disciples drinking from the cup.

The Last Supper ends with the song "On the Willows (Matt 26:20–30)—the Institution of the Lord's Supper." The lyrics to this song echo the sentiments of Ps 137, a lament over the destruction of Jerusalem, prayed by Jews of the Diaspora. Although in keeping with the Matthean text, "On the Willows" seems out of place and even anachronistic in this film's Last Supper scene. It signifies the hymn sung by Jesus and the disciples after the meal and before they went out to the Mount of Olives (Matt 26:30).

*Lens Three*

*Godspell* is a "feel-good" film whose "forced cheerfulness and theological vagueness"[46] fed the spiritual needs of the Jesus Movement—young Christians classically characterized by their long hair, bell-bottom trousers, tract delivering and finger to the sky pointing. The film endorsed

46. Grace, *Religious Film*, 91.

the belief that the only way to survive in the world was to "drop out" of it and form alternative "loving" Christian communities (communes). Jesus and his disciples sang, played, danced and listened to each other, in a city (New York) devoid of inhabitants; but that did not matter, as all they needed to survive was their special group of friends. Their world was an alternative happy and democratic Jesus-centered lifestyle, which was free from the constraints of money, wealth and power. *Godspell* is an example of merging the narrative with the historical context: "a hippy Jesus would be expected to be found in a community of equals who would carry on his work, not a hierarchy with himself at the top."[47]

The omission of the resurrection of Jesus raised criticisms. Stephen Schwartz explains the reasoning behind the omission:

> The ending is meant to be ambiguous. *Godspell* is about the formation of a community that is going to carry on the teachings of Jesus and spread his messages, and that is what they are rejoicing about. Regardless of whether or not one believes in the divinity of Jesus, the gift of his messages is something everyone has cause to celebrate… [T]he end of *Godspell* has always left it up to the individual viewer to decide whether or not Jesus rises from the dead. I would argue that it can be interpreted either way.[48]

Just as the lack of a resurrection scene can be interpreted ambiguously, so too is the character of Judas open to multiple interpretations.

*The Portrayal of Judas*

The portrayal of John the Baptist and Judas as a "dual character" by one actor who wears the same costume throughout the film is unique in the Jesus film genre. Schwartz explains that John the Baptist/Judas "has attributes of both Biblical figures: he is both Jesus' lieutenant and most ardent disciple and the doubter who begins to question and rebel."[49] His costume supports this. Designer Susan Tsu describes the costume as including tails with felt stripes, rosette, buttons, fringe trim, striped T-shirt, striped pants, work scarf, and painted tennis shoes. The dual character has the qualities of a circus ringleader and a politician.[50]

47. Paffenroth, "Film Depictions of Judas."
48. Schwartz, "Answers Questions About *Godspell.*"
49. Schwartz, "*Godspell* Script Notes and Revision."
50. Susan Tsu, "Costume Notes." http://itsayskeds.bravehost.com/costumenotes.htm.

The defining and identifying prop for John the Baptist is the shofar, an instrument made from the horn of a ram or other kosher animal. The shofar in ancient Israel announced the New Moon (*Rosh Chodesh*) and rallied people together. It was also blown on *Rosh Hashanah*, marking the beginning of the Jewish New Year, signifying both the need to wake up to the call to repentance, and in connection with the Scripture read on the second day of *Rosh Hashanah*, the Binding of Isaac (Gen 22) in which Abraham sacrifices a ram in place of his son, Isaac. It is appropriate that John the Baptist wears a shofar, as he is the character responsible for calling together the disciples.

In the opening scene, John walks across Brooklyn Bridge whilst pulling a cart. A close up of the cart shows a shofar resting on the top of it. Later we see John blowing the shofar to gather the disciples and Jesus. At their baptism in the Bethesda Fountain, the shofar is in John's belt. Having baptized the disciples and Jesus, John's mission is completed and the character assumes the role of Judas.

An interpretative reading of Matthew's Gospel is evident in this film's portrayal of Judas. Contrary to traditional representations, in *Godspell* Judas is often Jesus' stage manager, making sure that the stage is appropriately set for the next event, parable or game. Judas is presented as Jesus' only obedient disciple. His obedience is evident when at the Last Supper Judas leaves after Jesus has commanded Judas to betray him. Judas returns with police cars. The police officers never appear which could suggest that blame could not be afforded to any particular group or person. At Gethsemane Judas cannot bring himself to kiss Jesus so Jesus takes the initiative, kissing him not the once but twice. Judas singularly chains Jesus to the fence symbolizing his sole responsibility in the handing over of Jesus. Judas does not commit suicide but is willing, along with the other disciples, to be crucified with Jesus. He helps the other apostles to carry the dead Jesus through the city streets. The film's message is "forgiveness for all," even and including Judas.[51]

The most evocative and prophetic lyric in this musical is from the scene where the disciples and Jesus are saying the Beatitudes antiphonally. Towards the end of it we hear Katie speaking of those who are persecuted for righteousness' sake. Jesus confirms that the Kingdom of heaven is theirs. Judas, shouting from the distant stage, adds, "Blessed are you when men shall persecute you and revile you and say all manner of evil against you"—he pauses and then calms down—"falsely."

51. Walsh, *Reading the Gospels*, 78.

Judas is not foretelling his future but is recalling the past. For two thousand years false accusations made against Judas Iscariot and the Jews encouraged their persecution. Judas traditionally bore the brunt of anti-Semitism. Now for the first time in this twentieth-century setting, he identifies with it.

Although this "elevated, Christ-like depiction of Judas and the other disciples"[52] may cause concern for some members of the audience, director David Greene has made a convincing attempt in capturing Jesus' teaching that is "meant to free his disciples from what limits them and to allow them to free one another."[53] Judas Iscariot, in his handing over of Jesus to the authorities, is the one who is instrumental in bringing about this freedom. He is redeemed with the rest of the disciples at the end of the film and there are no overtones of anti-Semitism. The tide is turning for Judas.

### *Gospel Road: A Story of Jesus (1973)*

Director: Robert Elfstrom. Screenwriter: Johnny Cash and Larry Murray. Country: USA. Production Company: Twentieth Century Fox Film Corporation. Length: 93 minutes. Length of Last Supper scene: 3:40 minutes. Color: Color. Language: English. Musical score: Johnny Cash, John Denver, Kris Kristofferson. Filming locations: Israel. Cast: Judas (Thomas Leventhal), Jesus (Robert Elfstrom).

#### *Lens One*

American Country and Western singers Johnny Cash and his wife June Carter Cash produced *Gospel Road: A Story of Jesus*. This low budget film is targeted at a very different audience from *Godspell* and *Jesus Christ Superstar*. It represents Johnny Cash's personal faith testimony and his attempt at evangelism having converted to Christianity in late 1968 after years of drug and alcohol abuse. The film's message of sin, forgiveness, redemption and salvation echoes the plan of salvation outlined by conservative Christianity.

The film is part documentary, part dramatic re-construction and part travelogue on the Holy Land. The script is based on the King James Version of the Bible. Matt Page explains that scriptural quotes are seemingly used in a random way:

52. Paffenroth, "Film Depictions," 4.
53. Baugh, *Imaging the Divine*, 45.

> [m]ainly one or two verses without much in the way of context—aphorisms, particularly those snippets of Jesus' teaching which are most beloved by the (Christian) community that the film is primarily aimed at. Most of it is extracted from its original context. And it is reported by a well-known, colorful, Christian character [Johnny Cash], with many sayings introduced by the words "Jesus said."[54]

Cash's intention was not to make a "little big movie" or "to make a Cecil B. DeMille film," but to "make as good a film and spend whatever it took, for the month that [they] had to spend over there [Israel]."[55] The filming, like its use of Scripture, was relatively *ad hoc*. For example, the decision to cast blue-eyed, blonde-haired director Robert Elstrom as Jesus was not made until the day before the beginning of the shoot. Cash explains the constraints of a small of budget:

> We used as few extras as we could, and at the times when there should have been a multitude of people, we didn't use anybody. We used sound effects, to try to make it seem like there was a multitude of people. Well, when we came back and started editing the film and putting it together, we saw the need of a song to help tell the story here and there.[56]

Cash and other Country and Western singers including John Denver, Kris Kristofferson and Larry Gatlin, composed ten songs, which were performed in Cash's rhythmic travelling train signature style.

However, budgetary limitations did not have to have an entirely negative effect on filming. If anything, they promoted creativity and inventiveness. For example, the three trials of Jesus are depicted at the same time. Jesus stands before the three men who represent all his worldly opposition: Caiaphas, the chief priest who condemns Jesus, Herod, the puppet king, and Pilate, the Roman procurator who sentences Jesus. They are located in adjacent arches with Jesus moving from one to the other. The benefit of depicting Jesus' trials in this manner is that it "crystallises the often confusing sequence of events into a single moment."[57] However, the disadvantage is that it not only negates the biblical story and any pretense at historical accuracy but also stretches the audience's credibility.

54. Matt Page, "Thomas on the Road: A Comparison of the Gospels of Cash and Thomas," *Bible Films Blog*. http://biblefilms.blogspot.com.au/search?q=%22Gospel+Road%22.

55. Interview with *Country Music Magazine*, cited by Matt Page, "Thomas on the Road."

56. Matt Page, review of "*Gospel Road* (1973). http://biblefilms.blogspot.com.au/2006/05/gospel-road-1973.html.

57. Ibid.

Robert Elfstrom had the additional responsibility of cinematographer together with Tom McDonough. The use of natural light and its effect is emphasized by the low camera angles and inclusion of the rising or setting sun in many scenes. By not relying on a large cast and impressive sets, the viewer is absorbed into the scene, no longer an onlooker, but a participant. In addition, voiceless characters give the film a naturalistic cine-camera feel and enable the audience to relate more freely to them.

*Lens Two*

The narrator, Johnny Cash, sets the scene: "They sat down to share in a little room upstairs, the Passover feast of the unleavened bread." The table is long with a bench seat on either side and is covered with a white cloth, a variety of dishes, bowls of food, cups and flasks of wine. A *Hanukkah* menorah, without its candles, is in the center of the table. Although this menorah is out of place on a Seder table, it does identify the gathering as Jewish. Jesus sits at one end of the table, facing the setting sun. Judas sits at his left. There does not appear to be any order to the meal, with the disciples randomly helping themselves to the dishes in front of them.

The narrator continues, "And Jesus said, 'Verily I say one of you will betray.'" The camera cuts to a mid-shot of Judas rising from the table and walking out of the room. At the same time as Judas' departure the narrator's voice adds "and the friends of Jesus answered and said, 'Lord, is it I?'" Jesus interrupts the flow of the meal by taking bread and wine. The narrator explains, "Jesus said, 'This bread is my body. I am the bread of life, and this cup is my blood of the new testament, which is shed for the remission of sins. This do in remembrance of me'." A number of close-shots shows the disciples drinking from the cup. There is no interaction between Jesus and the disciples, and no sense that this is a sacred moment. The narrator informs that when the cock crows someone will deny knowing Jesus. Jesus stands, followed by the disciples. They question Jesus in the song "Lord is it I?"[58] The camera focuses on Peter as the disciples continue to sing, "Will one of us be ashamed to mention your sweet name?"

Johnny Cash changes from being the narrator to the voice of Jesus and sings the "Last Supper" song. The message is about sharing a meal, loving one another, overcoming fear and Jesus loosening "the chains that set the captives free."[59] An extreme close-up of Jesus crosses to an image of a suffering Jesus on the cross. The Supper ends and they all leave the room and head towards Gethsemane.

58. "Lord, Is It I?" Written and sung by Harold Reid and Don Reid.
59. "Last Supper." Written by Larry Gatlin; sung by Johnny Cash.

*Lens Three*

*Gospel Road* focuses on the "gospel" road of faith. It is not concerned with historical reconstruction or with being faithful to the biblical events. It emerged at a time when public profession of Christian faith and "commitment to evangelism"[60] was sweeping America. The film was popular at Christian crusades and was used by Billy Graham as a primary source of educating young people. His son, Franklin Graham, recounts the impact of *Gospel Road*. "The movie became one of the most popular films distributed by the Billy Graham Evangelistic Association. Johnny Cash often sang at my father's crusades, bringing in countless people who otherwise might never have heard the Gospel [the Good News]."[61]

In the film's climax—the crucifixion—Jesus dies in close-up, and the camera pulls back to reveal a modern yet unidentified American city—an unusual but powerful payoff, indicating that Christ died not only for the sins committed up to his time but for the ones still being committed today.

*The Portrayal of Judas*

In the calling of the disciples, Judas (Thomas Leventhal) is the second last to be identified. Simon Peter is last. This echoes Jesus' response to Peter who questions having left everything to follow Jesus, "But many who are first will be last, the last will be first" (Matt 19:30). What is striking is that having seen individual shots and close-ups of the previous ten disciples (all white, Anglo-Saxon Americans), when Judas is introduced, he is noticeably different to the others. The initial response is that Judas' facial features are similar to those of an Ashkenazic Jew—an Eastern European Jew. It is as though Cash wanted to distinguish Judas from the other disciples—without using the gospel descriptor, "the one who betrayed Jesus." When Judas is named, the narrator pauses slightly between the names Judas and Iscariot enabling the audience to make the necessary connection.

Unlike most other Jesus films, Judas in *Gospel Road* is very subdued and thinly drawn. There is no reference to betrayal or involvement with Jewish religious authorities, no identifying kiss at Gethsemane and no suicide. All the disciples are recognized as "betraying" Jesus. In describing Jesus in Gethsemane, the narrator states: "And now [Jesus] is all alone, completely alone. And the ones who loved him and stood behind are now in the background out of the way of those who cry for his death."

60. Prothero, *American Jesus*, 143.

61. "Johnny Cash and Billy Graham Through the Years," *Billy Graham Evangelistic Association*. http://billygraham.org/gallery/the-cashes-and-the-grahams-through-the-years/.

So, why would an overtly Christian evangelistic film not identify Judas as "betrayer"? The reason is revealed in Cash's autobiography. Even though he was committed to evangelism, Cash never forgot his own dramatic conversion. Acknowledging that he too had deeply sinned, Cash believed that God forgave him unconditionally. Moreover, Jesus died for all sinners—Judas included.[62]

### *Jesus of Nazareth (1977)*

Director: Franco Zeffirelli. Screenwriter: Anthony Burgess, Suso Cecchi d'Amico. Country: Italy/United Kingdom. Production Company: ITC Entertainment. Length: 371 minutes. Length of Last Supper scene: 5:57 minutes. Color: Color. Language: English. Musical score: Maurice Jarre. Filming locations: Morocco and Tunisia. Cast: Judas (Ian McShane), Jesus (Robert Powell).

*Lens One*

The 1970s saw the introduction of a new film genre: the television miniseries. Usually based on successful novels of an established writer, the miniseries afforded the film director and producer a number of advantages. These included:

- Offering a unique tele-visual experience; often dealing with harrowing and difficult material of the life-story in a changed context.
- The time lapse between episodes allows occasion for the audience to assimilate, discuss and come to terms with the difficulties of the narrative.
- The extended narrative time offered by serialization makes possible the in-depth exploration of characters, their motivations and development, and the analysis of situations and events.
- There is a clearly defined beginning, middle and end, enabling characters to change, mature or die as the serial proceeds.
- The clear link between these two adaptations (novel and miniseries) is their implied autobiographical character.[63]

62. See Johnny Cash, *The Autobiography* (San Francisco: HarperCollins, 2003) and the Cash biopic, *Walk the Line* (2005).

63. Margaret Montgomerie, "Miniseries," *The Museum Broadcast Communications*. http://www.museum.tv/eotvsection.php?entrycode=miniseries.

The first television miniseries was screened in 1974. It was an adaptation of Leon Uris' *QB VII* and had a running time of 390 minutes. This was followed in 1976 by Irwin Shaw's novel *Rich Man, Poor Man,* and adapted to twelve fifty minutes episodes. In January 1977 *Roots* (600 minutes), the saga of African American life based on Alex Haley's family and tracing six generations, was screened over eight consecutive nights and had 80 million viewers for its final episode. *Jesus of Nazareth* (371 minutes) was released in the same year.

With the success of television miniseries well established, Franco Zeffirelli accepted Sir Lew Grade's offer to make a miniseries based on the life of Jesus. Two factors prompted Zeffirelli's decision: he envisaged the series progressing his directing career, and the additional running-time would enable him to develop his own interpretation of Jesus' story. Zeffirelli's life-long dream of portraying Jesus was as "a Jew, a prophet, who grew out of the cultural, social, and historical background of the Israel of the time."[64] Collaborating with Anthony Burgess as scriptwriter, Zeffirelli's concern was to highlight how Jesus responded to the political machinations of his day: the Zealot resurgence, the tension of Roman occupation and the Herodian "puppet" government.

To meet the miniseries format, and to accommodate the commercial breaks, the narrative is carefully structured into brief, self-contained scenes. These follow in rapid succession with each scene carefully connected by narrative and thematic bridges. To replicate first-century Palestine, filming took place in Morocco and Tunisia. Intriguingly, the "extras" used in synagogue scenes were members of an ancient Jewish community who lived on the Isle of Djerba off the coast of Tunisia.[65]

Filming for television is dictated by the size of the television screen. The popular use of long shots in other Jesus films was not favored as television vastly reduces the effect of the extreme long shot while making the close-shot more powerful. To accommodate the changes in adapting from big screen to small, Zeffirelli settled for a middle distance, emphasizing the relationships between the people. He also favored the low angle where the camera looks up at the figure of Jesus, which in the opinion of one reviewer evoked a "phony reverence, at an over-divine, almost docetic Jesus (Robert Powell)."[66]

64. Franco Zeffirelli, *An Autobiography* (New York: Weidenfeld & Nicholson, 1986), 275.

65. Tatum, *Jesus at the Movies*, 138.

66. Goodacre, "Do you think you're what they say you are?"

Zeffirelli admits he had been a typical lazy Italian Catholic who performed the minimum religious observance to remain in the Church. However, recovering in hospital from a car accident, Zeffirelli had a religious experience. It was a dream involving his patron saint, Francis of Assisi. From that, he vowed to dedicate his work to God whenever possible.[67] However, his Roman Catholicism and his familiarity with the Jesus story were not sufficient for the producer Lew Grade who covered all bases by consulting scholars from the Vatican, the Leo Baeck Rabbinical College of London and the Koranic School at Meknes, Morocco.

The script for *Jesus of Nazareth* draws from the four Gospels, with particular emphasis on John's Gospel. There are minor divergences and additional non-scriptural events such as the death of Jesus' father Joseph and the burial of John the Baptist. Notable exclusions from the biblical story include the temptations of Jesus in the desert, the wedding at Cana, the transfiguration, the storm on the lake and Jesus walking on the water—very rarely depicted in Jesus films—and much of the physical suffering of Jesus during the crucifixion. Baugh posits, "some of these omissions suggest Zeffirelli's desire to avoid representing Jesus as too divine, too transcendental, what in theology is called too-high Christology."[68]

As in previous Jesus films, traditional masterpieces of Christian artwork provided a valuable source of information. Just as the makers of films of the silent era used Doré's and Tissot's famous paintings for inspirational purposes, the artwork used in *Jesus of Nazareth* "simultaneously invest the film with an aura of authenticity and an acceptance as real, through the unconscious and subliminal manipulation of images."[69] Examples of artwork include works of Rembrandt, Michelangelo, Botticelli and Raphael. Although the filmmakers went to extraordinary lengths to ensure that it was historically and culturally representative of first-century Palestine, Hyam Maccoby considered the "much-vaunted 'authenticity' as largely a sham":

> The Old Testament background, with its Arab head-dresses, its anachronistic prayer shawl, *etc*., was about as inauthentic as it could get, being a mixture of 'Oriental' mumbo-jumbo, and medieval Jewishness displaced by 1500 years from its true setting. Some of the Biblical characters in the film spoke

67. Zeffirelli, *An Autobiography*, 238.

68. Baugh, *Imaging the Divine*, 74.

69. Diane Apostolos-Cappadona, "From Eve to the Virgin and Back Again: The Image of Woman in Contemporary (Religious) Film," in May, ed., *New Image of Religious Film*, 114.

> in a Jewish accent so redolent of Yiddish and its wry shoulder-shrugging resignation to persecution that they seemed as out of place in first-century Palestine as *borscht*-circuit comics… Jewish characters were even depicted singing Hassidic melodies from 18th century Poland![70]

*Lens Two*

The Last Supper is set within the Jewish Passover. This is evident by the two large Seder-plates at each end of the table. The scene commences with much merriment. A disciple arranges the table, while others dance, sing and play musical instruments. The room is mud brick with exposed wooden columns supporting the ceiling and is quite cramped. It is divided into two sections—an area for entertainment and an area for eating—and is poorly lit by a few open flames, which emanate a golden glow.

The meal begins with Peter (James Farentino) saying to Jesus that they are happy to eat this Passover with him. Jesus responds, "I have longed with all my heart to share it with you. It is for this Passover that I came into this world." The celebratory atmosphere is squashed with Jesus' declaration that he won't be with them for much longer. A mid-shot shows Peter and Jesus, and the back of a reclining disciple in the lower right of the screen. A lengthy conversation follows with Peter declaring his loyalty and Jesus telling Peter that he will deny him three times and that the sheep will scatter once the shepherd is taken. The camera pans to the right and reveals Judas (Ian McShane) drinking wine and oblivious to, or disinterested in the discussion. Jesus stares at Judas and reveals, "Truly I tell you one of you is about to betray me." The camera cuts to a close-up of Peter, then cuts to a mid-shot of three disciples, and finally zooms in to Judas who stops drinking and looks up at the others. John (John Duttine) rises, approaches Jesus and asks who it is who will betray him. Jesus replies, "He who dips his bread in the dish when I dip mine; he shall be the one." The camera zooms to the hand of Jesus as he takes a morsel of bread and dips it into a bowl. At that moment, another hand comes into frame. That hand also takes and dips a piece of bread. The camera follows the rising hand and cuts to a close-up of Judas putting the bread into his mouth. He seems unaware of Jesus' identification of the betrayer even though Judas was within earshot of the discussion. Judas sits back, leans against the wall, and turns to look at Jesus who tells him, "What you are going to do, do it quickly." Judas looks puzzled, tears well in his eyes, and he quickly sits up. It is as though Judas has suddenly realized what Jesus was saying to him. Nothing more is said between them, but Judas shows signs of

70. Hyam Maccoby, "Jesus on the Small Screen," *Encounter* 49 (July 1977): 43.

relief that the opportunity has come for Jesus to declare himself. Judas leaves the room with the disciples wondering where he is going and Judas enters the darkness of the night (John 13:30).

A long shot from the camera's point-of-view looks on those gathered and seated on the floor. Some disciples have their back to the camera. Jesus is sitting to the right of the screen. The Last Supper commences with the disciples covering their heads when Jesus begins to pray: "Blessed be thou O Lord who has blessed us with thy laws and made bread to issue from the earth." A camera cuts to a close-up of Jesus. He continues, "From now on this will no longer be the bread of the passage of our fathers from bondage to freedom. This Passover is for you the passage from the bondage of death to the freedom of life." There is a cut to close-up of Jesus' hands holding bread and breaking it in two. The camera draws back, showing Jesus giving a half to the disciple on either side of him. Without looking at the disciples, Jesus continues, "This is the bread of life. Whoever eats of this bread shall have eternal life. Eat it, for this is my body. Do this in remembrance of me." A long shot shows the disciples eating the bread in silence and with reverence. Jesus takes a cup filled with wine and states, "From now on this cup will not only be a memorial and sacrament to the covenant of God made with our fathers on Mount Sinai." Jesus lifts his head, opens his eyes and continues, "This is my blood, the blood of the new covenant which is poured out for many. I shall not drink again the fruit of the vine until the day I drink it with you in my father's kingdom."

The words of institution bear the taint of supersessionism and anti-Judaism. Reinhartz notes "Jesus redefines the central ritual of symbols of bread and wine."[71]

> Zeffirelli himself remarked that "the Last Supper was set up according to traditional Jewish ritual and marked the moment when Jesus *superseded* the ancient rite and gave his disciples and all humanity the Eucharistic mystery."[72] Here, as in his film, Zeffirelli is expressing a straightforward *supersessionist* theology, implying that the Passover rituals do not retain the meaning they had for Jews once they have been *superseded* by Jesus' Eucharistic interpretation.[73]

71. Reinhartz, *Jesus*, 50.

72. Franco Zeffirelli, *Franco Zeffirelli's Jesus: A Spiritual Diary*, trans. Willis J. Egan (San Francisco: Harper & Row, 1984), 101.

73. Reinhartz, *Jesus*, 51. My emphasis.

After consuming the bread and wine, Jesus continues instructing his disciples. He gives them a new commandment to love one another as he has loved them and explains the virtues of one giving his life for another. The camera continues to zoom to a close-up of Jesus. Closing his eyes and lowering his head, he begins to pray: "Father, the hour has come; glorify thy Son so that the Son may glorify thee. Keep in thy name those thou hast given. I do not pray for these only but also for those believing me through their words" (John 17). Jesus raises his head and has tears in his eyes. He looks around at those gathered and says, "I am the way, the truth and the life" (John 14:6). The scene fades to black.

Ending the Last Supper scene with this statement is both powerful and provocative. Jesus was declaring himself as the great "I am," the only path to righteousness, the only measure of righteousness, and the source of both physical and spiritual life. Zeffirelli has chosen not to include the second part of that statement: "No one comes to the Father except through me"—the basis for exclusive claims in later Christian history. With this omission, Zeffirelli makes Jesus accessible to all: to sinners, to non-believers, to people of other faiths and to Judas Iscariot.

*Lens Three*

The production of *Jesus of Nazareth* as a miniseries gained a new viewing audience who would not necessarily go to the cinema to watch a religious movie, but would sit and view it at home. Indeed the evangelistic qualities of the miniseries was recognized by Pope Paul VI who gave his imprimatur in his 1977 Palm Sunday address to the crowds in St Peter's Square: "Tonight you are going to see an example of the fine use which can be made of the new means of communication that God is offering man." Moreover, unlike *Jesus Christ Superstar* and *Godspell*, Zeffirelli's film was truly ecumenical, pleasing both Catholics and evangelical viewers.[74]

Likewise, it addressed the issue of anti-Semitism in a unique way. In dealing with the culpability of the Jews for Jesus' crucifixion, the film makes a non-biblical event that divides the Sanhedrin. At his trial before the Sanhedrin, two fair-minded men, Nicodemus (Laurence Olivier) and Joseph of Arimathea (James Mason), speak on Jesus' behalf because they are followers of Jesus. Nicodemus is also given the role of theological commentator. Tatum suggests that this explains why in the film the Roman centurion beneath the cross does *not* utter those familiar biblical words: "Truly, this man is the Son of God" (Mark 15:39).[75]

74. Lang, *Bible on the Big Screen*, 218.

75. Tatum, *Jesus at the Movies*, 143. Emphasis in the original.

Although the film is not anti-Semitic, it is anti-hierarchy and this is nowhere more evident than in the roles played by the priests and other Jewish leaders. Most of the wickedness of the Jewish hierarchy is centered in the fictional character Zerah (Ian Holm), a scribe who negotiates with Judas for Jesus' betrayal. At the trial before the Sanhedrin, Zerah is the one who gives the actual order to turn Jesus over to Pilate. The burden of guilt is taken from the priests and the Sanhedrin, and placed onto one man, Zerah. As Richard Walsh accurately notes, "Zeffirelli displaces Judas somewhat by inventing Zerah. With Zerah, Zeffirelli offers a Passion play in which none of the traditional characters—Judas, Jews or Romans—are culpable. Thereby, Zeffirelli sanitizes the apostolic church's story for a pluralist age."[76] Zeffirelli circumvents Christian tradition, rearranging the narrative to be acceptable to all viewers.

*The Portrayal of Judas*

Judas in *Jesus of Nazareth* is significantly different to the traditional Judas. Writer Anthony Burgess decided that Judas would have to be remade from scratch because he considered that the traditional descriptions of the betrayal—greed, ambition, jealousy, fear—did not give him enough reason to betray Jesus.[77] What Burgess creates is a Judas who is an exemplary disciple.

Judas enters the story at the burial of John the Baptist. At the graveside, he talks with a group of Zealots about Jesus. Judas believes that, "If one day the people of Israel do find the messiah, it will be [Jesus]." Judas seeks out Jesus to ask if he can be his disciple. Judas believes he has qualities that will be of use to Jesus: he is "a scholar who reads and writes Hebrew, Greek, and Latin." He translates documents, which is very useful in "a country of many tongues." Judas acknowledges that he is different to the other disciples who are artisans and fishermen, explaining, "My father is a prosperous builder who said my son must never have calluses on his hands nor brick dust in his hair." He asks if Jesus has any need of a man like him. Jesus covers his face with his hands and tells Judas, "The tree will be known by its fruit," and invites Judas to come and stay.

Prior to Jesus' triumphal entry into Jerusalem, Judas meets with Zerah and tries to convince him to have the Sanhedrin proclaim Jesus the king of Judea because he is the "only one who can bring peace to Israel." The scheming Zerah bolsters Judas' hopes by saying, "I think I can promise you that he shall have that opportunity."

76. Walsh, *Reading the Gospels*, 38.
77. Zeffirelli, *Franco Zeffirelli's Jesus*, 104.

When Judas next meets with Zerah, he is unsure of himself and lacks the confidence he had in his previous dealings with Jesus. He admits to Zerah that he "always believed political action could always solve everything. I thought it was enough to think clearly and act clearly but I fear my master does not agree with me. He says the heart is more important." Judas continues with his confession, self-doubt and questioning whether he is fit to be one of Jesus' disciples. Zerah takes advantage of Judas' vulnerability and recognizes that Judas no longer believes that Jesus is the Messiah. Zerah then attempts to convince Judas to hand Jesus over to the Sanhedrin. The scene abruptly ends leaving the audience in suspense as to what Judas will decide to do.

It is not until Gethsemane that the audience is made aware that Judas has succumbed to Zerah's persuasion. Judas, Zerah and temple guards arrive at the garden. Judas makes his way to Jesus and both pause, looking at each other. Jesus breaks the silence. "This is your hour, Judas: the hour of shadows." Judas sighs, "Oh Master" and kisses Jesus on the cheek. Jesus responds with a cold, "You betray your master with a kiss?" Judas shakes his head in disagreement. Jesus moves towards the guards. Zerah points and orders the guard to "Arrest him!" When the disciples wake up, chaos ensues. Peter calls Judas a traitor, but Judas defends his actions saying, "The only way the master can save himself is by speaking to the Sanhedrin." Andrew spits in the face of Judas letting us know he thinks Judas' action is despicable. In the confusion, we hear one of the disciples shout, "Brothers, let us save ourselves."

Judas runs off in search of Zerah, hoping to be a part of the planned meeting with Caiaphas. However, when he finds Zerah, he is informed that there is to be no meeting but a trial for blasphemy. Zerah adds, "You have been an invaluable help to us Judas. Come and see me when all this is over." As an after-thought, he hands a bag of coins to a servant who passes it on to Judas. The stunned Judas does not know what to make of the purse, and leaves.

It is early morning and the camera pans the countryside. It stops at the figure of a man hanging from a tree. The camera zooms to the grass beneath the tree and stops at an open money purse, scattered silver coins filling the screen. Staley and Walsh suggest that although the Judas character was somewhat rehabilitated in the narrative, his anguish leading him to suicide and the disheveled coins beneath his feet "returns Judas to his traditional status."[78] I would argue that Judas was so overcome with remorse and shame because of Zerah's deception that he kills himself after

78. Staley and Walsh, *Jesus, the Gospels*, 198 n. 20.

that meeting. That Judas did not return the money to Zerah, and that he killed himself before Jesus had even begun his walk to Calvary, support my argument. Judas' suicide is the action of a defeated man, not the action of a sinner. Judas' suicide evokes sympathy, not condemnation.

### *Karunamayudu (1978)*

Directors: A. Bheem Singh, Christopher Coelho. Screenwriters: Christopher Coelho, Johnson Modukuri. Country: India. Production Company: Dayspring International. Length: 160 minutes. Length of Last Supper scene: 8:37 minutes. Color: Color. Language: Telugu, Hindi, English. Musical score: Joseph Krishna, Boddu Gopalam. Filming locations: Bhairava Palem, Calcutta, Mumbai. Cast: Judas (actor unknown), Jesus (Vijaya Chandra).

*Lens One*

*Karunamayudu* was produced to educate ordinary folk in rural India about Jesus. The makers of *Karunamayudu* (pronounced kah-roon-ah-my-u-du; Telugu for "Man of Compassion" or "Embodiment of Mercy" or "The Merciful One") had to overcome an obstacle not faced by Western filmmakers: a long-standing perception that Jesus is a foreigner who cannot be identified with Indian culture. Filmic portrayals of Jesus generally depict him as white Anglo Saxon, but in this film, an Indian actor plays Jesus. Moreover, directed and produced in India, with all-Indian actors, the film circumvents some of the cultural barriers to the Gospels. Although not technically a "Bollywood" film, just as not all American films are "Hollywood" productions, there are obvious similarities in *Karunamayadu* to this Indian filmic genre. Thus one will find classical drama and musical traditions using humorous diversions, formulaic songs and choreographed dances, mythology, allusions and flashbacks, "which are used to remind, reinforce and explain."[79]

*Karunamayudu* reflects the influence of Roman Catholicism by including in the film Catholic iconography, hymns and Taizé meditative chants. Matthew's Gospel is the prominent text, and the central theme is "Jesus' teaching about a new kingdom and a new way of seeing and responding to a broken world."[80] Jesus' identification with the poor and oppressed dominates the narrative.

79. Dwight H. Friesen, "An Analysis of the Production, Content, Distribution, and Reception of *Karunamayudu* (1978), an Indian Jesus Film" (PhD diss., University of Edinburgh, 2009), 143.

80. Ibid., 132.

*Lens Two*

The disciples walk in single file into the room where the Last Supper is to take place. A long inverted U-shaped table is set with a white cloth, dishes of food, jugs and cups. Two male servants stand by the wall ready to assist when needed. The room is poorly lit even though there are two large burning torches on the wall. Additional lighting in provided by a large open flame situated in the middle of the floor.

Judas (actor unknown) is standing waiting for Jesus to enter the room. One of the disciples comes up to him and claims, "Judas, I am the first disciple. Let me sit next to Jesus." Judas replies, "No. This day is special. I want to know something. I want to clarify my doubts. You go." John then approaches Judas and explains that Jesus loves him very much and that he should sit next to Jesus. Peter joins in the seating squabble. "The Lord appointed me as the leader. I should sit next to him." Another disciple suggests that no one is better than the other is and that lots should be cast. They all agree with this solution.

Jesus (Vijaya Chandra) appears in the doorway and asks, "Peter, why do you do this? Sit down." The disciples sit at the place nearest to them. Judas sits next to Jesus. What follows is Jesus washing the feet of the disciples. He can be heard humming the Taizé chant "Ubi Caritas et amor, Deus ibi est" (Where love and charity are, there God is). Jesus explains that the reason for washing their feet is that they are fighting among each other about who is the greatest. As Jesus is about to pour water over Judas' feet, Judas asks, "Teacher, after the supper, are we going to Gethsemane?" The camera cuts to a close-up of Jesus showing his mental processing of the question. Smiling slightly, Jesus replies "Don't be in a hurry, Judas." Cutting back to Judas, a close-up shows him ill at ease.

A long shot shows Jesus and the disciples, about to begin the meal. Jesus sits higher than the others who are reclining around the table. There is no mention of Passover or Seder meal. Jesus simply says, "Disciples, we will have supper like this in the kingdom of my Father." A disciple questions the meaning but Jesus ignores him. The use of close-ups and Jesus speaking directly to the camera convey an atmosphere of intimacy. The audience is drawn to the table. Nothing else seems to be happening except for Jesus speaking "personally" to the viewing audience. Jesus continues, "The time is near to fulfil the prophecy about me. One of you is going to betray me." Various close-ups and mid-shots show anxious disciples asking, "Is it me?" Judas watches, listens to the questions and then asks Jesus, "Surely you don't mean me, Lord?" A close-up of Judas shows his utter despair when Jesus tells him, "What you are about to do, do quickly!" Judas rises from the table and departs from the room.

The disciples and Jesus watch him leave, and when asked where Judas is going, Jesus replies, "This is to fulfil the passage of Scripture. Unless I shed my blood there can be no salvation for this world. To fulfil the Scriptures this must happen to me." It is evident that Judas is to be that "agent of salvation."

The Supper scene cuts to a room in the temple. A large Star of David decorates a wall. Judas, Caiaphas and another temple official are in discussion. Caiaphas slaps Judas on the shoulder and expresses his delight that Judas has realized his mistake and agreed to betray Jesus. He asks Judas what they can offer him for catching Jesus. The answer is laced with sarcasm, "Don't you know Caiaphas? Only you can decide the price."

The scene changes back to the Supper. A mid-shot shows Jesus holding flat bread. He elevates it, looks heavenward and says, "This is my body given for you." He breaks the bread in two and gives half to the apostle on either side of him. A long shot shows Jesus pouring wine from a pottery jug into a metal cup. Again, a mid-shot shows Jesus elevating the cup and raising his head and eyes in prayer. "This is my blood given for you. Do this in remembrance of me." A long shot captures the single cup being passed to each disciple followed by a mid-shot of Jesus. He tells his disciples, "I am giving you my love. Take it!"

A crosscut to the temple room shows a close-up of a golden cloth moneybag being handed to Judas with the directive, "Take it! Thirty pieces of silver." Judas expresses a slight concern over the amount and hints that a larger amount would be more suitable. "Caiaphas, the age of Jesus is thirty-three." The second priest interjects, "You are right Judas but Jesus did not trouble us until he reached thirty years. [This refers to when Jesus began his public ministry, supposedly at the age of thirty.] That's why there are thirty pieces of silver." Caiaphas, not wanting to look as though he had cheated Judas out of money adds, "Not only that, the cost of a slave is thirty pieces of silver. Judas be satisfied with this and tell me what you have planned." Judas juggles the moneybag as though attempting to gauge the weight of the coins and a possible deception by Caiaphas.

Caiaphas' comparison between the thirty pieces of silver, the age of Jesus and the cost of a slave is non-biblical and is unique in Jesus films. The allusion is to the sum of compensation for a slave that had been killed (Exod 21:32) and the price at which a slave could be purchased (Hos 3:2). Caiaphas' statement has three inferences: (1) Judas is now bound to Caiaphas and his commands; (2) Judas has chosen to serve wealth over serving God (Matt 6:24); and (3) Caiaphas' statement pre-empts the fulfilling of Zechariah's prophecy of the Lord, where Zechariah is paid thirty shekels of silver, throws them into the treasury, to be used later to buy land at the Potter's Field (Zech 11:12–13; Matt 26:15; 27:3–10). Each of the three inferences is valid and contributes to Judas' participation in and his entanglement in a web of conspiracy.

A cut shot to Jesus shows him telling his disciples that he is giving them a new commandment: "Love one another as I have loved you. Also, love your neighbor. Love those who hate you." Again, Jesus looks straight at the camera. His new commandment is for all who hear it. Jesus continues with his farewell discourse and his prediction of Peter's denial. Interestingly, this prediction is juxtaposed with the scene of Judas telling Caiaphas to prepare the soldiers. "It is time to catch Jesus."

*Lens Three*

Production took place between 1974 and 1978. This was a turbulent time in Indian history. The nation's first atomic bomb was detonated in 1974. Indira Gandhi declared a state of emergency from 1975–1977 after she was found guilty of earlier electoral malpractice in the 1971 elections, and had to resign.[81] It was during this period that compulsory birth control was introduced. Nearly one thousand political opponents of this draconian approach to family planning were imprisoned. The 1970s was also a period of close relationships between the film industry and regional politics in the south of India, which was at the forefront of "resistance to the hierarchical control of the Brahmins, the caste system, suppression of women and the domination of Hindi as the national language."[82]

The initial reception for *Karunamayudu* was muted: there was no buyer for the film. To increase its audience and selling power, versions were made in Telegu, Tamil and Malayalam dialects. The film was released on December 21, 1978 but it was not until December 26 that the cinema experienced a full house and maintained that status for the next 100 days.[83]

*Karunamayudu* is not the most successful box-office Jesus film but it is one of the most viewed Jesus films. Reasons for the film's wide reception are that it continues to be screened in rural villages throughout India

81. Ranbir Vohra, *The Making of India: A Historical Survey*, 2nd ed. (New York: M. E. Sharpe, 2001), 232.

82. Robert L. Hargrave, *The Dravidian Movement* (Bombay: Popular Prakasham, 1965), 10, 26, 35, 43.

83. Interview by Sri Sathavahana with Vijaychander, "Vijaychander, Born to Perform Jesus," trans. SVL Narasimha Swamy. http://ilovehyderabad.com/interviews/interviews-vijaychander-born-to-perform-jesus.html.

and has been dubbed into sixteen languages: Telugu, Tamil, Malayalam, Hindi, Urdu, Arabic, Oriya, Marathi, Punjabi, Assamese, Bengali, Kannada, Gujarathi, Nepali, Sindhi and English. According to John Gilman, the founder of Dayspring International, an evangelical Christian organization, the success of the film is that "all the dramatic, action-packed, entertaining, and emotional events of Jesus' life, from birth to ascension, are portrayed by their own people, in their own spoken dialect, with the very music and sound effects that stir their Indian hearts."[84]

The film adheres closely to the biblical story, and as a result, "the Jewish leaders are cast as conniving villains and their machinations overdone."[85] As there appears to be no evidence of anti-Semitism in India, Friesen questions whether the villainous portrayal is a "remnant of a long-standing [Passion play] tradition" or whether the Jewish leaders' portrayal is meant to be a caricature of religious leaders in general.[86] It would seem that the portrayal is based on the Christian tradition given that the director/screenwriter is a Roman Catholic priest.

*The Portrayal of Judas*

Judas has a substantial role in this film. He introduces Jesus to Barabbas and Caiaphas, he is the protagonist whose actions move the story along and he is the disciple who has the most screen time. Although his role bears similarities to Judas in *Day of Triumph* (1954) and *King of Kings* (1961), particularly the Barabbas/Judas liaison, *Karunamayudu* offers unique interpretations of this disciple.

Judas is Barabbas' right-hand man and is held in high-esteem by the leader of the Jewish freedom fighters. Barabbas explains that Judas is "the greatest, the mightiest and most intelligent" and because he is with the freedom fighters they will be victorious. Judas is not swayed by this flattery but remains levelheaded. He considers that the fall of Jerusalem is near but warns Barabbas, "Freedom will not come unless some of us die for it." Thus, he is willing to die for the Jewish cause.

However, he knows that Jesus can offer an alternative non-violent way. At the news of the death of John the Baptist, Barabbas believes that the followers of John will now join with the Zealots. Judas is not so convinced. He knows that the people are following Jesus because the Nazarene offers

84. John Gilman, "*Dayasagar* and the Life of Christ in India," *Lausanne World Pulse* (September 2006). http://www.lausanneworldpulse.com/worldreports/470/09-2006?pg=all.

85. Friesen, "Analysis," 149.

86. Ibid.

a better way. Judas explains to Barabbas that using swords frightens the people whereas Jesus attracts them with words. Where the Zealots are trying to establish a Kingdom with blood, Jesus is using love. People fear the Zealots and love Jesus. Judas is confident that having seen and heard Jesus, with Jesus as leader they could easily conquer Rome. For these reasons, Judas decides to leave the Zealots and become a disciple of Jesus.

It is after Jesus delivers his teaching "on the mount" (Matt 5:1–12; Luke 6:20–26) that Judas introduces himself and Barabbas to Jesus. No interest is shown by Jesus in Barabbas' request for Jesus to join them. Judas tries to mediate but Jesus simply tells Judas to go. Judas rides away but struggles with what he should do. The use of soliloquy exposes Judas' thoughts and emotions: "His words are pulling me back. Jesus is no ordinary man. He can fulfil my heart's desire. I must join him."

Judas finds Jesus and declares that he wants to become the Teacher's disciple. Judas' request is met with skepticism and animosity from the disciples. Comments include, "Lord, he is not good," "He only desires power," "Your name will be ruined" and "Lord, he is corrupt." We are not told how the disciples know of these negative traits of Judas' character. The atmosphere is tense. A disciple asks Jesus to speak, suggesting that his silence is a show of acceptance. Jesus replies, "Disciples. Is not the sun giving the same light to good and bad? You and Judas are the same for me. Judas, you are one of my disciples from today." With that acknowledgment Jesus approaches Judas, kisses him on the cheek and they embrace each other. Jesus is putting into action his directive, "Love those who hate you."

The disciples saw in Judas negative traits that Jesus chose to ignore. Judas, according to Scripture, had a role to fulfil. Jesus was facilitating that fulfilment. The high priests on the other hand exploited Judas' desire for power and predicted that there could be no "alliance between sword and kindness." For these reasons, they sought Judas' help in capturing Jesus.

Judas' belief that Jesus is the expected Messiah is confirmed when the group arrive at Jerusalem. In a scene that is similar to DeMille's *The King of Kings*, Jesus "cleanses" the Temple and declares that he will destroy it and re-build it in three days. Judas interprets this as a messianic claim. Holding a crown of leaves, Judas stands next to Jesus and asks the crowd, "Do you understand? Jesus can destroy the Roman government in three days and can become king. We need your co-operation for that to happen." Facing Jesus, the ecstatic Judas declares, "Lord, take this crown." Judas tries to place the crown on Jesus' head but he holds fast Judas' hand and then turns away. Judas is angry and tosses down the crown. His humiliation amplifies upon hearing the Temple leaders' laughter. As he leaves, the authorities stop Judas and inform him that Caiaphas wants to meet him. Having little respect for the Jewish authorities, he ignores them and continues on his way.

Judas considers re-joining Barabbas' fighters but Barabbas tells him that he would be more useful joining with Caiaphas, and betraying Jesus. The suggestion sits well with Judas so he meets with Caiaphas. Judas asks what is expected of him. Their expectation is articulated: "Kingdoms come and go but God and religion will not change. Join hands with us Judas. We will finish Jesus." Judas shows little interest in their plan.

When we next see Judas, he is wandering in the wilderness: a scene, which parallels Jesus' earlier temptation by Satan. Breaking Judas' solitude is a man running towards him, shouting that Barabbas had been arrested by the Romans. What follows is an inner conflict of thoughts in which Judas struggles to discern what is right and just. Judas hears Barabbas coaxing him, "Betray Jesus for the sake of my friendship." He then hears Caiaphas' prompting, "Give us a hint where Jesus stays at night. You will get what you didn't get with Barabbas and Jesus." The distinct sound of a ticking clock punctuates each thought: time is of the essence. Judas is a walking time bomb. Realizing that he failed Barabbas and that Jesus did not consider his hopes, Judas declares, "I will betray Jesus."

That betrayal comes to fruition in the Garden of Gethsemane. Judas, carrying a blazing torch, leads the soldiers. He walks up to Jesus, says "Greeting Rabbi" embraces and kisses Jesus on the cheek, and then steps back. He is unperturbed by Jesus' question, "Judas, are you betraying the Son of Man with a kiss?" Judas seems resigned to the fact that he is the necessary force behind this part of the Jesus story.

From a distance, Judas watches Jesus' trek to Calvary. Barabbas, who had been released in place of Jesus and who now recognize Jesus as Messiah, is also seen running along the route and shouting "Lord." Jesus breathes his last with "It is finished." A multitude of natural disasters fills the screen: erupting volcano, earthquake, tsunami, typhoon, flooding and a total eclipse. A centurion standing near the cross removes his helmet and declares, "Surely this was a righteous man." The crucifixion scene cuts to Judas hanging from a tree. His head is uncovered and his feet are bare: Judas is prepared to enter sacred ground. The moneybag and thirty pieces of silver lay scattered at his feet. Judas' earlier warning to Barabbas that "freedom will not come unless some of us die for it" has come true.

Judas does not wear a distinguishing costume, nor does he carry a moneybag. His clothing is similar to that of the other disciples and indeed to that of the rest of the male cast. This consists of a long sleeved, knee-length tunic, a three-quarter sleeve knee-length coat, a waist sash and a headscarf held in place by a black rope band. The costumes are colorful and look like something out of a children's Sunday school pageant. Judas has twelve-costume changes in *Karunamayudu*. Jesus by comparison has two: his white tunic with either a red or a white cloak. Costume changes may have some significance for the scene but analysis does not support this notion. However, Judas wore the same costume in a number of scenes involving Barabbas and the Jewish priests, suggesting that these scenes were filmed out of sequence. Another observation is that when he becomes a disciple, Judas wears a headscarf like the other disciples. Perhaps the scarf is simply a means of identifying the disciples. When Judas hangs himself, his head is again uncovered. This has probably more to do with expediency than a possible hidden implication that Judas no longer considered himself a disciple.

### *Summary*

The revival of Jesus films in the 1970s and the innovative representations of Jesus provided an environment for reinterpreting Judas. In the six films analyzed, each of the Judas characters introduces different traits to traditional filmic portraits of the twelfth disciple. In the Mexican film *Jesús, Nuestro Señor*, Judas is elevated to Jesus' right-hand man. When his liberationist ideals do not eventuate, he hangs himself but not before declaring that he does not deserve pity. In *Jesus Christ Superstar*, Judas is no longer representative of the Jews but of oppressed Black Americans. His suicide is the act of a martyr. Although Judas is the hero, he does not achieve sainthood but he is resurrected! Judas in *Godspell* takes on dual roles, those of John the Baptist and of Judas Iscariot. He is Jesus' alter ego. Where Jesus is patient and compassionate, Judas is somewhat intolerant and impulsive. Judas is the character that is most like us. Johnny Cash's interpretation of Judas in *Gospel Road* amounts to identifying him by name, accompanied by a brief-close up and a hurried exit from the Last Supper. By not expanding on Judas' character, Cash reinforces his message that all the disciples (and hence us!) were responsible for Jesus' death but might be redeemed. It is in Zeffirelli's *Jesus of Nazareth* that Judas is portrayed as one who can speak three languages, is an exemplary disciple and is fully rehabilitated. The Indian production

*Karunamayudu*, although clinging to traditional traits such as greed and untrustworthiness, gives Judas a leading role and makes him the protagonist. Judas epitomizes the struggle that many face in their decision to follow Jesus and the Christian way.

## Chapter 6

# Moving Towards the New Millennium

### *The 1980s*

The title of Bobby McFerrin's song "Don't Worry Be Happy" became a slogan for the late 1980s. Awarded the best song of the year at the 1988 Grammy Awards, it was a carefree response to a volatile decade and a seriously minded populace. Global events were marred by the assassinations of Egypt's president Anwar Sadat, India's Indira Gandhi, San Salvador's Archbishop Oscar Romero and the attempted assassinations of Pope John Paul II and the US President, Ronald Reagan. Zimbabwe (formerly Rhodesia) gained independence; Lech Walesa's Polish non-government trade union *Solidarity* was born; Cyprus was divided between Greece and Turkey; martial law was declared in South Africa; and many countries in Europe faced domestic or international terrorism. The discovery of the AIDS virus, development of an abortion pill and an increase in the use of illicit drugs with a corresponding rise in cases of addiction raised concerns and fears.

The 1980s was characterized by similar socio-religious instability: increasing secularism, easing of censorship and religious relativism. In 1983, Roman Catholicism was abolished as Italy's state religion and Italy became secular. John Paul II (Karol Józef Wojtyła), the first non-Italian pope since 1523, denounced liberation theology, birth control and the ordination of women. He wanted priests out of politics and attempted to silence those, like Hans Kung and Edward Schillebeeckx, whom he considered theologically liberal. In America, the visibility and political awareness of the evangelical right wing greatly increased, despite the failures of flamboyant tele-evangelists Jim and Tammy Bakker's Praise the Lord (PTL) ministry, which came under scrutiny after sex scandals and tax evasion. Some American conservative States passed laws permitting the teaching of "creation science" to counter science taught in public schools, which negated the Genesis account of creation.

Michael Medved acknowledges the inability of moviemakers to stay away from religious themes

> because of their deep-seated desire to be taken seriously; religion offers one subject which everyone acknowledges as fundamentally serious. If writers and directors take a swipe at religion in one of their films, no matter how clumsy or contrived that attack may be, they can feel as if they've made some sort of important and courageous statement.[1]

Martin Scorsese's *The Last Temptation of Christ* is one such courageous statement.

### *The Last Temptation of Christ (1988)*

Director: Martin Scorsese. Screenwriter: Paul Schrader, Country: USA/ Canada. Production Company: Universal Pictures, Cineplex Odeon Films. Length: 164 minutes. Length of Last Supper scene: 4:25 minutes. Color: Technicolor. Language: English. Musical score: Peter Gabriel. Filming locations: Morocco. Cast: Judas (Harvey Keitel), Jesus (Willem Dafoe).

#### *Lens One*

Despite being a modern film, *The Last Temptation of Christ* opens almost like a throwback to the "Silent Era" with a black screen and a scrolled text that outlines the purpose of the film.[2]

> The dual substance of Christ—the yearning, so human, so superhuman, of man to attain God…has always been a deep inscrutable mystery to me. My principle [*sic*] anguish and source of all my joys and sorrows from my youth onward has been the incessant battle between the spirit and the flesh…and my soul is the arena where these two armies have clashed and met. This film is not based upon the Gospels but upon this fictional exploration of the eternal spiritual conflict.[3]

The words are from Nikos Kazantzakis' novel *The Last Temptation of Christ*[4] and Scorsese's film "follows the bold revisionism" of that story of Jesus' life, which had been "placed on the (Catholic) church's index

1. Michael Medved, "Hollywood vs Religion," *SMR* 142 (Winter 1990): 10–11.
2. Adele Reinhartz, "History and Pseudo History in the Jesus Film Genre," *BI* 14 (2006): 3.
3. *The Last Temptation of Christ*. DVD. The Criterion Collection. The film will be referred to as *Last Temptation*.
4. Nikos Kazantzakis, *The Last Temptation of Christ*, trans. P. A. Bien (New York: Simon & Schuster, 1998).

of forbidden books."[5] So, within the opening scene the film is deeply confrontational on three counts. First, it is not based on the biblical story. Second, it explores not only the spiritual but also the sexual tension between "flesh" and "spirit" in Jesus, who according to Christian tradition is "sinless" and did not succumb to any "sins of the flesh." Third, it flies in the face of Roman Catholicism as it challenges their decision to forbid the faithful reading Kazantzakis' interpretation of the life of Jesus.[6]

The lack of reliance on Scripture has led film critics such as Forshey to claim that, "because [Scorsese] was using a Greek novel rather than the Bible as text, the usual research was so insignificant that the traditional dating of Holy Week is compressed into what appears to be three days."[7]

However, Forshey's observation is invalid for two reasons. First, the film is an adaptation of a fictional novel and so comparison with Gospel texts becomes redundant. Second, and perhaps more importantly, it must be acknowledged that Scorsese and his production staff carried out extensive biblical and historical research using a wide variety of sources to ensure the film's authenticity.[8] Apart from written sources such as *The Jewish Encyclopaedia* and the *Biblical Archaeology Review*, the production staff drew inspiration from Renaissance paintings such as Bosch's *Christ Carrying the Cross* and Messina's *Crucifixion*. Although references to Renaissance art do not equate to historical accuracy in the depiction of biblical subjects, they do provide images, which are familiar to audiences. Researchers also made use of Rembrandt's *chiaroscuros* technique, which contrasts and manipulates light and shadow, to achieve three specific effects that have become trademarks of his style: dramatic intensity, rhythmic visual harmony and psychological depth. This technique informed the film's Passover montage.

Moreover, Scorsese was not a slave to the novel, altering it in many places and rendering it more sensitive to modernity's ideas.[9] The image of the devil was changed from that of the novel's "negro boy" to that

5. Roger Ebert, *Scorsese by Ebert* (Chicago: University of Chicago Press, 2008), 102.

6. Margaret Bald, *Literature Suppressed on Religious Grounds* (New York: Infobase, 2006), 180.

7. Forshey, *American Spectaculars*, 175.

8. "Scorsese's Visual Research," Bonus Features on DVD version of *The Last Temptation of Christ*. It is possible that Forshey did not have access to the DVD version.

9. Miles, *Seeing and Believing*, 38.

of a blonde girl in order to avoid any overtones of racism.[10] There is no inclusion in the film of Caiaphas or the bloodthirsty Jewish crowd although the novel mentions Pilate's hand washing and the crowd saying "His blood be on us and our children." Thus, Scorsese dispels any charges of anti-Semitism.

Unlike the silent masterpiece, *The King of Kings*, Scorsese's film does not attempt either to recreate the historical Jesus or to evangelize.[11] Scorsese claims the aim of the film is "to make the life of Jesus immediate and accessible to people who haven't really thought about God in a long time."[12] The result is "the first truly subjective cinematic interpretation" of the life of Jesus.[13] The film was originally scheduled to be produced by Paramount and shot on location in Israel with a budget of about US$14 million but the studio, influenced by the many letters of protests from religious organizations, got cold feet and withdrew support. Universal Pictures rescued the project and *Last Temptation*, set in Morocco with its "vast, hostile expanses of hard soil, distant mountains, and struggling vegetation,"[14] was shot in fifty-five days, with a budget of a mere US$7 million.

Contrary to what might be expected, the film actually follows in broad outline the Gospel stories. Tatum identifies three parts to the film. The first begins with Jesus (Willem Dafoe) working in his carpentry shop and shows the development of the relationships between Jesus, Mary Magdalene (Barbara Hershey) and Judas (Harvey Keitel). The second draws on familiar Gospel pericopes, which include the woman caught in adultery, the Sermon on the Mount, the call of the disciples and several miracles and healings. The divinity of Jesus is highlighted. The third and most controversial part is the "vision sequence"—Jesus' "last temptation"—which takes place between the second and third of Jesus' last words from the cross.[15]

Martin Scorsese is one of the few modern directors who openly talks about his religious upbringing and religious experiences in his films. Raised in an Italian Roman Catholic household, Scorsese embraced a

10. Peter Bien, "Nikos Kazantzakis' Novels on Film," *JMGS* 18 (2000): 169 n. 5.

11. Reinhartz, "History and Pseudo History," 3.

12. Martin Scorsese, *Scorsese on Scorsese*, ed. David Thompson and Ian Christie (London: Faber & Faber, 1989), 124.

13. Peter Chattaway, "Come and See," *Chr Tod* (March 16, 2012). http://www.christianitytoday.com/ct/2005/februaryweb-only/comeandsee2.html?start=2.

14. Ebert, *Scorsese by Ebert*, 101.

15. Tatum, *Jesus at the Movies*, 182–84.

Catholicism, which in pre-Vatican II days was "a seductive labyrinth of logic, ritual, vision, and guilt"[16] with its powerful elements of "[f]aith and sacrifice, guilt and redemption, sin and atonement."[17] These features are evident in the protagonists' role in Scorsese's earlier films—Johnny Boy (Robert De Niro), a hood from New York city's Little Italy in *Mean Streets* (1973), Travis Bickle (Robert De Niro), a mentally ill taxi driver in *Taxi Driver* (1976) and Jake Lamotta (Robert De Niro), the violent middle-weight boxer of the 1940s in *Raging Bull* (1980). From these films and *Last Temptation*, another Scorsese stylish cinematic hallmark is easily recognizable; the blood leitmotif.[18]

Scorsese explains that the prevalence of blood in his films is because of his faith: "Blood is very important in the church… Blood is the life force, the essence, the sacrifice."[19] The blending of Scorsese's Catholic beliefs and the blood leitmotif are embodied in a remarkable scene. Jesus demonstrates his personal struggle with his divinity by physically pulling his heart out of his chest, holding it in his hand, and inviting the astonished disciples to follow him. This is clearly a reference to the Sacred Heart of Jesus iconography indicating Jesus' love for humanity. In this instance, however, the meaning is "destruction rather than love."[20] Scorsese, explaining the apparition, said, "[I]t could be in the minds of the apostles, it could be a mass hallucination, but engendered by Him, divinely."[21]

The portrayals of miracles can be problematic for filmmakers. Scorsese, however, decided that the way to approach miraculous occurrences was to be "very straight and very simple"[22] and to treat them as though they are an everyday occurrence. Jesus' turning of water into wine at the wedding at Cana did not see Jesus leave the meal to go and stand in front of the

16. Ebert, *Scorsese by Ebert*, 101.

17. Caryn James, "Fascination with Faith Fuels Work by Scorsese," *New York Times* (August 8, 1988). http://www.nytimes.com/1988/08/08/movies/fascination-with-faith-fuels-work-by-scorsese.html?scp=1&sq=last+temptation+of+christ&sst=nyt&pagewanted=print.

18. Lloyd Baugh, "Martin Scorsese's The Last Temptation of Christ: A Critical Reassessment of Its Sources, Its Theological Problems and Its Impact on the Public," in *Scandalizing Jesus? Kazantzakis's* The Last Temptation of Christ *Fifty Years On*, ed. Darren J. N. Middleton (New York: Continuum, 2005), 176.

19. Richard Corliss, "Body and Blood: An Interview with Martin Scorsese," *FC* 24, no. 5 (1988): 42.

20. Flesher and Torry, *Religion and Film*, 145.

21. James, "Fascination With Faith."

22. Ibid.

water jars. There were no attempts at piety or looking towards heaven to invoke God's blessing. Instead, one of the disciples approaches Jesus announcing that the wine has run out. Jesus responds, "No, it hasn't. Go and see." The disciple reluctantly checks and finds that the water has indeed turned into wine.

During the 1980s and 1990s, the role of film music came under scrutiny as "identity formations such as race, ethnicity, sexuality, and gender"[23] were considered important, and inappropriate musical settings received negative reviews. Neither Scorsese nor Peter Gabriel—composer of the musical score—was concerned with "ethnomusicological accuracy."[24] Papanikolaou notes that the film's soundtrack "is not subordinate to the narrative" but becomes "a third voice that acts as a bridge between Kazantzakis and Scorsese. It not only comments on the drama; it also acts as an interpretive voice."[25] Although Peter Gabriel's musical score received an Oscar nomination for best original score and two years later won a Grammy for best New Age recording, many critics disapproved of Gabriel's blatant mixing of racial, ethnic and cultural borders. In order to adapt Kazantzakis' Greek novel to an American context, Scorsese adopted a number of techniques and to celebrate American pluralism the film has a multicultural setting: "Israel pulses with cosmopolitanism [and] cultural syncretism,"[26] and Gabriel's music complements this.

*Lens Two*

A mid-shot of a Jewish priest blowing a shofar introduces the preparation for Passover. The sacrifice of sheep follows with graphic close-ups of cutting their throats, blood dripping into brass bowls and the splashing of blood onto the altar. The music is frenetic. Groups clapping hands, singing and playing musical instruments, suggest a celebratory atmosphere.

The camera cuts to Jesus stepping into a steaming bath. Another crosscut shows the sandaled feet of a priest stepping through puddles of blood. The bloodied hem of his caftan draws the viewer's attention to the sacrificial killing of sheep. The camera cuts back to Jesus in the bath and the disciples making their way into the warm water.

23. Anahid Kassabian, *Hearing Film: Tracking Identifications in Contemporary Hollywood Film Music* (New York: Routledge, 2001), 4.

24. Eftychia Papanikolaou. "Identity and Ethnicity in Peter Gabriel's Sound Track for *The Last Temptation of Christ*," in Middleton, ed., *Scandalizing Jesus?* 222.

25. Ibid., 218 and 224.

26. Christine Hoff Kraemer, "Wrestling with Flesh, Wrestling with Spirit: The Painful Consequences of Dualism in *The Last Temptation of Christ*," *JRPC* 8 (2004). http://www.usask.ca/relst/jrpc/art8-lasttemptation-print.html.

An extreme close-up of a lit menorah fills the screen and signifies the beginning of the Last Supper scene. A change to an overhead shot—a favorite Scorsese camera technique—shows an inverted U-shape configuration of those gathered. There is no table: food and utensils rest on long rectangular mats. Large bowls, clay and woven, hold matzot and a variety of foods. Four lit menorahs, strategically placed, provide muted lighting.

The meal takes place on a semi-enclosed balcony. This is not a clandestine meal, nor is there any hint of hiding away from the community. This is evidenced by the steady stream of people carrying lit torches and wandering past during the meal.

Figure 10. Judas, left, shares a Passover meal. © The Criterion Collection.

A long shot reveals Judas, Peter (Victor Argo), Jesus and John (Michael Been) seated at the left of the screen. Judas and Peter (reclining) are both deep in thought while Jesus and John are talking to each other. Mary (Verna Bloom), the mother of Jesus, and another woman descend some stairs and enter the room. Mary carries a pottery jug of wine and approaches Jesus. She interrupts Jesus and John's conversation by placing her hand on Jesus' shoulder. When he turns towards her, she hands him the jug of wine. Although there are other jugs on the mats, their body language and silence suggest that this jug of wine is significant. Placing the jug in front of him, Jesus leans over, takes round matzot in both his hands, and interrupts the celebration with, "Listen to me." The camera pans down. Jesus commands, "Take this bread." A close-up shot shows Jesus' hands holding the bread. He continues, "Share this bread. This is my body." The camera pans up. A close-up shows Jesus snapping off a piece of matzot, and, still in close-up, Jesus hands the matzot to John. There is another scene cut and we see a mid-shot of the seated Mary Magdalene, sisters Martha and Mary, and Jesus' mother. To interrupt the monotony of watching each disciple break and eat the bread, the camera follows the action by dipping and rising in a wave-like motion. Before the bread is passed to the other side, the scene cuts to a close-up of wine being poured into a clay-drinking bowl. Jesus orders, "Now drink this wine. Pass the cup." Jesus' hands clasp the cup and the camera follows his raising the cup to his lips. As the cup nears his lips, Jesus declares, "This wine is my blood." He looks up, glances at the group and then drinks. He lowers the cup, looks up again and says, "Do this to remember me." He passes the cup to John who drinks and then hands the cup to the disciple seated next to him.

Judas receives the cup. He looks at the wine trying to comprehend what Jesus might mean by "This wine is my blood." Keeping his eyes open, Judas drinks and then passes the cup to Peter. The camera lingers on Peter while he is drinking. He lowers the cup but places his fingers in his mouth to remove a clot: the wine has turned into blood. An extreme close-up shows him rubbing the clot between his thumb and index finger. He opens his hand revealing a pool of blood in the palm of his hand: a precursor to crucifixion wounds. Peter takes the jug and pours a little wine into his hand. The crosscut shows Judas watching with curiosity. To illustrate the body and blood of Christ, Scorsese cuts to an extreme close-up of Peter's hand and the wine—now blood—dripping through his fingers onto the matzot. Scorsese shows the wine as blood, not because of theological convictions but because "in a movie you have to see it."[27]

The camera cuts to Judas who is looking at Jesus. When their eyes meet, Jesus looks away and towards "the body and blood." This is the signal of what Judas must do. Judas rises, takes his staff, slings his leather bag over his shoulder and leaves the meal. Peter calls, "We're not finished." Jesus places his hand on Peter's arm and says, "Let him go." Jesus watches Judas leave. The camera slowly zooms towards Jesus' face, drawing the audience to him. Jesus, with a sense of urgency in his voice calls, "All of you. I want to tell you something." There is a look of resolve on his face and the Last Supper scene ends.

Scorsese's Last Supper includes three unique features. First, present at the meal and sharing the bread and wine are Mary, Mary Magdalene, Martha and Mary—sisters of Lazarus. The presence and prominence of women at what was traditionally in film an all-male event, not only revises the Christian interpretation of the Supper but also accurately

27. Corliss, "Body and Blood," 42.

reflects first-century Middle-Eastern culture where women shared meals with men. Second, the Roman Catholic doctrine of transubstantiation—the bread and wine changing into the body and blood of Christ—is supported by the appearance of the blood clot when Peter drank the wine. Third, a Senegalese singer, Baaba Maal, intones an Arabic song based on the Islamic profession of faith or creed. Although criticized as "totally inappropriate (and) offensive, and blasphemous, both to Christians and Muslims,"[28] most viewers would not be aware of Scorsese embracing theological pluralism and perhaps intimating that the Holy Land is home to the three major monotheistic faiths. Stern comments, had the viewers been made aware that the music was based on an Islamic creed, it would be an affront to audiences of both Christian and Islamic faiths.[29] I maintain that it would also be offensive to Jewish viewers.

*Lens Three*

The film was released amidst a firestorm of controversy, attracting most criticism from "the so-called American evangelical Bible Belt, with Texas being its buckle."[30] Bill Bright of the *Campus Crusade for Christ* offered to buy the negative and prints in order to destroy them, while several bishops in major Catholic centers discussed banning the film even though they admitted to not having viewed it! Flowers and Middleton summarize opposition to the film. What the fundamentalist Christians opposed "was an irresolute, beleaguered Jesus, one who suffered from peculiar visions and breakdowns, one tempted to the point of giving up the call of the cross. The point is, they rejected *The Last Temptation of Christ* because it demanded too much of them by presenting a Jesus just a shade too human."[31]

Conservative Catholics also were disturbed by Judas kissing Jesus on the mouth at the betrayal in Gethsemane. The concern, according to Forshey, was "partly because one can sense that there is passion in their relationship, though up to this point not identified as 'sexual' passion."[32] Reinhartz notes homoerotic undertones were evident in their body language, such as proximity, tenderness shown toward one another and "the intensity of their relationship."[33] She also considers that although this relationship

28. Baugh, *Imaging the Divine*, 60.

29. Stern, *Savior*, 284.

30. Elizabeth H. Flowers and Darren J. N. Middleton, "Satan and the Curious: Texas Evangelicals Read *The Last Temptation of Christ*," in Middleton, ed., *Scandalizing Jesus?* 148.

31. Ibid.

32. Forshey, *American Spectaculars*, 177.

33. Reinhartz, *Jesus*, 176.

with Judas does not come to sexual fruition, it would be considered more "scandalous" than the lovemaking dream sequence between Jesus and Mary Magdalene.[34]

Judas first appears early in the film, barging into Jesus' carpentry workshop and yelling at him: "You're a Jew killing Jews! You're a coward! How will you ever pay for your sins?" Reinhartz claims the way he speaks to Jesus intimates that they have "a prior relationship marked by both tension and love. Judas cares intensely about Jesus."[35] However, this seems a difficult claim to substantiate, as there is no prior evidence to suggest this, although the actions that follow affirm Judas' friendship with Jesus.

I am not convinced of the "scandalous" nature of the relationship between Judas and Jesus. By the late 1980s in the Western world, close sexual friendships between two males was becoming more accepted and openly discussed. The 1980s saw the release of a number of films dealing with the subject of homosexuality. Films included *Cruising* (1980), *Querelle* (1982), *Maurice* (1987) and *Kiss of the Spider Woman* (1985), for which William Hurt won the Best Actor Oscar and the first Academy Award won by an actor for playing an openly gay character. There is also the matter of viewer response: while one viewer might perceive homoerotic undertones, another might respond that the relationship was merely one of friendship. However, *Last Temptation* was the first film to deal with Jesus' sexuality—and bisexuality. This would offend conservative and fundamental Christians who believe Jesus has to be celibate to confirm his sinless state.

The film performed poorly at the box-office and yet many film-reviewers hailed *Last Temptation* as a masterpiece. Indeed, the Academy of Motion Picture Arts and Sciences nominated Scorsese for the award of best director of the year. Although he was beaten by Barry Levison for his film *Rain Man*, Medved contends that the Academy's response to *Last Temptation*

> represents the film industry's "Circle the Wagons" mentality at its most hysterical and paranoid. Since religious figures across the country were attacking the picture, the members of the Hollywood community felt called to defend it… The movie industry's resounding endorsement of *The Last Temptation of Christ* is only the latest and perhaps the most grotesque illustration of the overt and pervasive hostility that has taken root in Hollywood.[36]

34. Ibid.
35. Ibid., 171.
36. Medved, "Hollywood vs Religion," 9–10.

Medved is arguing that Hollywood defends the film because it views conservative Christianity's criticism of the film as an attack on Hollywood. The implication is that the merits or otherwise of the film are not discussed because of this Hollywood paranoia about being criticized.

*The Portrayal of Judas*

Directors use two main aspects of Judas to depict his character: physical appearance and dialogue. For the portrayal of Judas, Scorsese considered a number of factors. He wanted to create "a stereotypical villain and then make him a hero."[37] Costume and make-up helped him achieve this goal. Scorsese uses wardrobe to symbolically separate Judas from the other disciples. They all wear white or cream colored robes while Judas is dressed in black, symbolizing his connection to violence—his killing of a Roman guard—and his threat to kill Jesus. In order to make actor Keitel look like "a Fagin," the stereotypical Jew in *Oliver Twist*, he wears a short, curly red wig and his nose is made to look larger and to curve outward—stereotypical Jewish features. From the film's opening moments, Judas is referred to as the "red devil." Indeed another disciple, Zebedee, admits to Philip, "I don't like his hair. I've heard that his ancestor Cain had a beard like that." The implication is that Judas is a murderer in the tradition of Cain: the most recognized killer in the Hebrew Bible (Gen 4:1–16).

Judas evolves from murderer to follower then to Jesus' adviser. His role progresses from subordinate to equal and finally surpasses that of Jesus. This progression is possible because of the various functions Scorsese— and Kazantzakis— assign to Judas' character.

The Judas character functions in fifteen different ways in *The Last Temptation*.

- Judas is a "parallel protagonist."[38]
- Judas is a hero with principles who does not give into his "tortured objections."[39]
- Judas is Jesus' "alter ego" with Judas and Jesus in collusion over the divine plan.[40]

37. James, "Fascination With Faith."

38. Shilling, "Servant of the Story."

39. Steven D. Greydanus, "The Last Temptation of Christ: An Essay in Film Criticism and Faith." *Decent Films* http://www.decentfilms.com/articles/lasttemptation.

40. Telford, "The Two Faces of Betrayal," in Christianson, Francis, and Telford, eds., *Cinéma Divinité*, 231.

- Judas is a confessor of profound faith who comes to believe in Jesus "when Jesus turns from the way of love to the way of the axe."[41]
- Judas as a disciple is both a loyal friend and a "voice of challenge." Although a nationalist and the one most opposed to Jesus, Judas is the one disciple who truly understands Jesus' message.[42]
- Judas is "Christ's manager," issuing ultimatums and devising strategies.[43]
- Judas is Jesus' confidant. Jesus tells Judas of his dreams, where Elijah came to him and "showed him a prophecy that he understood to mean that he must be sacrificed on the cross."[44]
- Judas is the link between the Zealots and Jesus. The Zealots ordered Judas to kill Jesus because he makes crosses for the Romans. Judas' ongoing interaction between the rebel group and Jesus clarifies and defines the person and mission of Jesus.[45]
- Judas is a mouthpiece for liberation theology.[46] He argues that "pity for men" and the overturning of an oppressive government should be central to the mission of Jesus. It is only at the end of the film that Judas realizes he has been mistaken and that Jesus' kingdom is a spiritual kingdom.
- Judas is almost exclusively a device to highlight Jesus' struggle.[47]
- Judas' role is to help Jesus overcome "temptation and his weakness in the face of it."[48]
- Judas is Jesus' "beloved disciple" and his "strongest friend."[49]
- Judas is a faithful disciple model. He is stable, dedicated and his "sense of mission never wavers."[50]

41. Reinhartz, *Jesus*, 173.
42. Kraemer, "Wrestling with Flesh."
43. Ebert, *Scorsese by Ebert*, 102.
44. Flesher and Torry, *Religion and Film*, 153.
45. Tatum, *Jesus at the Movies*, 184–85.
46. Miles, *Seeing and Believing*, 38. Stephenson Humphries-Brooks writes, "Judas states the classic social gospel." *Cinematic Savior: Hollywood's Making of the American Christ* (Westport: Praeger, 2006), 86.
47. James Wall calls the film a "buddy" picture, referring to such films as *Butch Cassidy and the Sundance Kid* (1969), where the interest is in the relationship between two male protagonists. James Wall, "The Last Temptation: A Lifeless Jesus," *Christ Century* 105 (August 17–24, 1988): 724. http://www.religion-online.org/showarticle.asp?title=974.
48. Paffenroth, *Judas: Images* 138.
49. Staley and Walsh, *Jesus, the Gospels*, 111.
50. Lang, *Bible on the Big Screen*, 247–48.

- Judas is the informant Jesus needs.[51]
- Judas is an "agent of salvation."[52] Jesus convinces Judas to betray him in order that redemption can take place. Judas does so, reluctantly, not for payment of thirty pieces of silver, "but out of painful responsibility and deep friendship."[53] Judas does not betray Jesus: Jesus demands that Judas betray him.[54]

Roger Ebert in the *Sun Times* review of *Last Temptation* (October 29, 1988) suggests that Judas is Scorsese's autobiographical character: "Certainly not the Messiah, but the mortal man walking beside him, worrying about him, lecturing him, wanting him to be better, threatening him, confiding in him, prepared to betray him if he must. Christ is the film, and Judas is the director." Ebert's suggestion actually intimates something more revealing of the Judas character—Judas has the power to direct Jesus' future and the future of Christianity.

### *The 1990s*

The arrival of the end of the twentieth century was met with excitement, anticipation and fear. The uncertain dangers of the Y2K Bug gripped the world with prophecies of computer failures and even airplanes falling from the skies whilst in flight. The world population reached six billion; India and Pakistan tested nuclear weapons; *Titanic* (dir. James Cameron) became the most successful film to date; US President Clinton was impeached; the Euro became the new European currency; and China restricted Internet use. A killing spree at Columbine High School—the first mass-student shooting on a US campus—left twelve students and one teacher dead and shocked the entire country. NATO launched air strikes in the former Yugoslavia, the first time the military alliance had attacked a sovereign country. The release of the miniseries *Jesus* showed that not even the Jesus story could escape political machinations and criticism of religious influence in war.

51. Kraemer, "Wrestling with Flesh: Wrestling with Spirit."

52. Paffenroth makes a convincing case that Judas is an "agent of salvation." See *Judas: Images*, 135–42.

53. James, "Fascination With Faith."

54. Reinhartz, *Jesus*, 173.

### *Jesus (1999)*

Director: Roger Young. Teleplay: Suzette Couture. Country: Czech Republic, Italy/Germany, USA. Production Company: Antena 3 Televisión, Arbeitsgemeinschaft der öffentlich-rechtlichen Rundfunkanstalten der Bundesrepublik Deutschland (ARD). Length: 240 minutes; International Version. Length of Last Supper scene: 4:20 minutes. Color: Color. Language: English. Musical score: Patrick Williams. Filming locations: Ouarzazate, Morocco and Malta. Cast: Judas (Thomas Lockyer), Jesus (Jeremy Sisto).

*Lens One*

The story begins just before Jesus (Jeremy Sisto) starts his ministry, and takes the viewer through his baptism by John (David O'Hara) to his death, resurrection and ascension. Director, Robert Young, like Scorsese, emphasizes the subjective humanity of Jesus. Therefore, his interpretation of Jesus is of one who laughs, plays and has romantic feelings for Mary, sister of Martha and Lazarus. This Jesus could easily have been modeled on Ralph Kozak's 1976 *Laughing Christ* print. This black and white pencil line portrait drawing of Jesus shows his head thrown back, mouth open wide and heavy laughter lines around his eyes. One can almost hear the laughter!

Suzette Couture's teleplay offers fresh perspectives to the biblical narrative. Women, particularly Mary, mother of Jesus (Jacqueline Bisset) and Mary Magdalene (Debra Messing), play prominent roles, instead of simply adorning the set. Mary Magdalene's transition from prostitute to her role as the first to proclaim Jesus' resurrection is new and credible. It echoes the prevailing rise of feminist theologians such as Elisabeth Schüssler Fiorenza, Kathryn Tanner and Rosemary Radford Ruether and their insistence that women, whose role had often been "forgotten" or "suppressed," were in fact among the first witnesses to the risen Christ.

Instead of using an omniscient narrator, we hear the story through Livio (G. W. Bailey)—Caesar's historian and spy. Livio provides Pilate (Gary Oldman) and the audience background details on significant characters in the story as well as functioning as the film's interpreter of Jewish customs and politics. Satan makes four appearances in the film and in one instance takes on the guise of a woman dressed in red. He (Jeroen Krabbe) strikes an imposing figure as a male. His costume, a modern-day tailored suit, emphasizes that Satan is still with us.[55]

55. Interview between Lorenzo Minoli, producer of the miniseries, and David Bruce, "The Jesus Mini Series." http://hollywoodjesus.com/jesus_min_series.htm.

The film is a prime example of the harmonizing tradition in Jesus films: no single Gospel is given precedence but all four are blended together. Scriptural material is used sparingly and a large proportion of the episodes are fabricated. Matt Page comments that apart from *The Last Temptation of Christ*, the *Jesus* miniseries "imports a greater proportion of non-biblical episodes into its script."[56] This can be seen, as Catherine O'Brien notes, in the use of an apocryphal story in a flashback to Jesus' youth.[57] She does not identify the story but it bears similarities to one in the *Infancy Gospel of Thomas* (1:2–4). There the boy Jesus is throwing rocks at birds; he kills one of them and then miraculously brings it back to life. His mother, later recounting the episode to Jesus, remarks, "I was worried the authorities would hear of it. Your father said that the bird was just stunned but I was so frightened."

The soundtrack complements the contemporary portrayal of the Jesus narrative. Patrick Williams composed and conducted music that moved beyond its typically tired restraints. Included in the soundtrack are "Pie Jésu" from Andrew Lloyd Webber's "Requiem" and American country and pop singer LeAnn Rimes' "I Need You." With an increase in secularism in the Western world, these easily recognizable contemporary songs attempted to make the Jesus story accessible to non-church-going audiences.

*Lens Two*

An extreme long shot shows that the Last Supper is taking place in an alcove. The long rectangular wooden table is quite bare. A large silver goblet is in front of Jesus and near it is a large pottery jug. Individual cups are placed around the table, along with lit terracotta oil-lamps. The lamps are unnecessary because it appears that it is daylight outside! There is very little to suggest that this gathering is part of a meal or that a meal has just ended. There are no utensils or food. One could argue that this Last Supper could have taken place after the meal and the table had been cleared, but this raises the question: Why would a huge bowl and towel (intimating that there had been a foot-washing) still be on the table?

The camera zooms and cuts to an extreme close-up of Jesus' hands breaking bread.

Melodious stringed-background music breaks the silence. Cutting to a cross-angle mid-shot of Jesus, the bread is passed around the table. Jesus says to his disciples, "Take. Eat. This is my body." Although Peter's

56. Matt Page, "*Jesus* (1999–miniseries)," http://ntweblog.com/2004/03/cbs-jesus-to-come-back.html.

57. Catherine O'Brien, *The Celluloid Madonna: From Scripture to Screen* (London: Wallflower, 2011), 119.

position at the table hides Judas (Thomas Lockyer), we can see that Judas lifts the hand holding the bread towards his mouth, although we are uncertain if he eats it.

The camera cuts back to Jesus who takes the jug and pours wine into the silver goblet. The moment is interspersed with mid-shots of the disciples still eating the bread. We now notice that Judas too is eating. A side-view shot shows Jesus looking at the goblet he has cupped in his hands. A tear trickles down his cheek. Peter is looking at Jesus, while Judas is looking at the goblet. Fighting back the tears, Jesus says, "Drink from it all of you for this is my blood of the covenant which is poured out for many for the forgiveness of sins." He continues almost pleading, "Do this is remembrance of me." Peter is looking at the goblet. Judas is neither looking at Jesus nor the goblet: he has a far-away look on his face. Judas willingly drinks when the wine is passed to him.

Jesus interrupts the moment by alerting the group, "One of you will betray me." A mid-shot shows a despondent Jesus, a shocked Peter and an enquiring Judas. After a number of the disciples declare that it would not be them, Judas with a questioning tone in his voice quietly asks, "Not I, Lord?" Jesus looks at Judas and with a heavy heart tells him, "Do what you have to do. Do it quickly." Judas sways from shock and rises from the table to leave. The others wonder where he is going. Philip leans over to ask Peter but instead Jesus answers, "The Kingdom is coming." The words "going" and "coming" are evocative in that they describe a theological event: the Kingdom can only come after Judas has gone to do what he has to do. The Supper scene ends.

*Lens Three*

Two versions (CBS/USA and International) of the miniseries were made to accommodate opposing theological and christological viewpoints. The International version is twenty minutes longer suggesting that the CBS/USA version has been highly edited, or even censored. The CBS/USA version omits eleven scenes that are included in the International version. Included among the deleted scenes are: Jesus and Joseph looking for work; Joseph reading an inscription that forbids non-Jews from entering the temple; Lazarus telling Jesus to "Get out" after Jesus insists to Mary of Bethany that his life is not his own; the hanging of Judas; and an ending which shows Jesus in the 1990s! The latter scene is of Jesus hurrying along an esplanade in Malta towards a large group of excited children who are running towards him. He bends down, gathers one in his arms and they all walk off together.

Staley and Walsh assert that some of these scenes were deleted because they evoke a number of the crises a middle-class American family faced in the late 1990s: "a parent looking for a job and a son, confused about his future and not knowing what to do about the woman who loves him; and a pushy, recently widowed, empty-nester mother."[58] They also suggest that Young's Jesus "is almost the religious equivalent of the male characters in the 1990s television hit comedies *Seinfeld* and *Friends*, which focused on thirty-somethings who could not quite make commitments or decide who they were."[59] The miniseries *Jesus* is another example of film tailoring content to suit a particular audience.

*The Portrayal of Judas*

Judas first appears when the Zealots, led by Barabbas, attack Roman soldiers who are offering protection to a tax collector. A Roman soldier is killed in the melee. Out of compassion, Jesus goes to the body. Judas does not understand why Jesus is weeping over the corpse. Jesus explains that it is a human life but Judas responds, "Romans are not human." Recognizing Judas' hatred, Jesus warns him that it will only harm. Judas argues that hate can be a useful weapon if used correctly. Jesus questions whether Israel is free now the soldiers are dead. He encourages Judas to follow him. "I will show you how to be free. I am the way."

Jesus calls the tax collector, asks him his name—Levi, son of Alphaeus—and gives him a new name, Matthew. Taking hold of Matthew's shoulder Jesus asks Judas, "You wish to kill this collector of Caesar's taxes?" Without waiting for an answer, Jesus tells Matthew, "Follow me." Jesus has decided to eat at Matthew's house. As Jesus walks past Judas, he says to him, "Come Judas, son of Simon Iscariot, your fate is with me." Judas is shocked and asks Peter, "How did he know my name?" to which Peter replied, "Follow him and find out."

This dialogue is significant in that it introduces to the narrative the theological idea of predestination: Judas was pre-ordained by God to hand Jesus over to enable salvation to take place. Jesus did not know the tax collector's name and yet he called Judas by his name and even identified his father. Further, Jesus does not tell Judas that his future or freedom is with him but that Judas' fate is inseparably bound up with his. They are almost "brothers-in-arms."

Jesus' recognition of Judas' role is highlighted again at the public calling of the disciples from a crowd of followers. Jesus calls each disciple by name. Judas is the fifth disciple called and joins Jesus and the other

58. Staley and Walsh, *Jesus, the Gospels*, 130.

59. Ibid., 205 n. 28.

four on the lake's shore. After all the twelve disciples have been chosen, Jesus gathers them into a holy huddle and while moving among them he commissions them to ministry. When Jesus comes to Judas, he places his hand on Judas' shoulder and then kisses him on the cheek. Could Jesus be pre-empting or alluding to the future Gethsemane event, or is the director using this kiss to emphasize Judas' act of "betrayal"? I would suggest that Jesus' kiss is an act of betrayal or deceit. Jesus knows what Judas is being led into—his fate—but Jesus does nothing to change the situation.

Of the twelve disciples, Judas displays the most faith and trust in Jesus' words. Andrew and John, in contrast, only became convinced of the powers of Jesus after the miraculous changing of water into wine at Cana. Peter and James similarly follow Jesus after their miraculous catch of fish. Thomas, who could easily pass as a stereotypical Judas—red hair, antagonistic, an outsider and doubter—follows Jesus after witnessing the healing of a lame boy. Judas, however, joins the group despite Jesus' message that all his followers are to love their enemies, and because Jesus instructed him to follow.

Judas is ambitious and supports the Zealots' fight for freedom. He is constantly trying to rally support from Jesus but fails. On one occasion, Jesus rebukes Judas, who is pleased with his effort of raising thirty pieces of silver to fund Jesus' ministry. Rejecting the money, Jesus tells Judas to give it to the poor. A dejected and angry Judas does just that. Coming across a band of beggars, Judas throws the coins at them, declaring, "A gift from the Messiah."

Judas leaves the Supper to make possible "the coming of the Kingdom." He meets with Seth (Iddo Goldberg), the Sanhedrin's go-between, and arranges to deliver Jesus to him. Seth asks the price. An indignant Judas states he is not a beggar or a thief, but one of the disciples chosen by Jesus himself. Seth is puzzled why Judas is willing to betray Jesus.

Judas offers a clear explanation: "He's not the man I thought he was." As though he is recalling past differences, Judas tells Seth, "You ought to pay me, thirty pieces of silver." This amount would compensate the money Judas was told to give to the poor. The deal is struck and concluded with Seth's emphatic declaration, "Done."

At Gethsemane, when Jesus sees Judas approaching he runs to Judas shouting, "Friend." As they near each other Jesus says, "Do what you are here to do." Judas hesitantly walks up to Jesus and kisses him on the mouth. Jesus responds with, "Betrayed with a kiss." A close-up shot of a speechless Judas shows him staring at Jesus' mouth. Was he recalling the kiss Jesus gave him when Jesus called him to be his disciple?

Judas does not abandon Jesus. We see him following Jesus on his way to Calvary. Peter, also seeing Judas, grabs and pushes him against a wall yelling, "Traitor!" Judas defends himself by repeatedly saying, "It's not what I wanted." Peter accuses Judas of selling Jesus to the Romans for money and claims, "You killed him!" Judas retorts, "You abandoned him! I would have died for him." In this fiery exchange, we hear the reason for Judas' actions. Judas believed that when people saw Jesus as a prisoner of the Romans they would follow Jesus and rise up against Roman oppression. Judas clearly had misjudged Jesus.

Judas watches Jesus being flogged but becomes so distressed that he cannot stay. He exits the scene and our attention is drawn to the crucifixion. Following Jesus' death, an earthquake hits, creating pandemonium. The scene first cuts to a silent image of a large palm frond and then cuts to a mid-shot of Judas dropping from a branch. The effect is startling. The sound of the air escaping from his lungs and the jerking of his body is unsettling. The camera cuts to a long shot of the swinging lifeless body of Judas. It is understandable how viewers would be moved to pity the disciple whose "fate" was sealed the moment he chose to follow Jesus. Pity is not the typical emotion felt for the Judas character that traditionally has borne the wrath and ire of Christians for nearly two thousand years.

Anti-Semitism was carefully circumvented in *Jesus*. The plot and script ensure that the Jews are blameless and all the guilt is placed on the Romans. This is re-enforced by Peter's accusation that Judas "sold out" Jesus to the Romans. Because Judas does all his dealing with the character Seth, the long-established denigration of the Jewish leaders is avoided. Any criticism of the Jews such as Jesus' denunciation of the false piety of the scribes and the Pharisees' hypocrisy (Matt 23:1–36) is absent. Pilate is manipulative, telling Livio, "I could kill this messiah tomorrow or I could see to it that he becomes a problem for some of his own people and they can solve the problem for us." Pilate's cunning results in Caiaphas taking the blame for Jesus' death while Pilate passes himself off as being compassionate.

### *Summary*

Martin Scorsese's *The Last Temptation of Christ* presents both Jesus and Judas in new and unorthodox ways. Jesus is not a leader of disciples but a follower of his own inner voices. Judas has a demanding role in keeping Jesus on the messianic track and being responsible for humankind's salvation more than Jesus is. Judas and Jesus share a close friendship and a passionate relationship. Judas is the "beloved disciple." The Judas character functions in fifteen different ways, including confessing a deep faith, being the model of a faithful disciple and is the agent of salvation. Without Judas' determination and persistence in keeping Jesus focused on his role as Messiah, Jesus would have succumbed to his temptation and not died on the cross.

The Judas character in the miniseries, *Jesus*, is clearly portrayed as being pre-ordained by God to hand over Jesus to the Jewish authorities. Jesus knows Judas' name and lineage before they are introduced to each other. At the naming of the disciples, Jesus kisses Judas, alluding to the betrayal at Gethsemane. Of the twelve disciples, Judas is the most faithful and trustworthy.

Judas Iscariot assumes the traits of a model disciple.

# Chapter 7

# The New Millennium

## *The 2000s*

The 2000s—often referred to as "the Noughties"—continued to be dominated by political upheaval and social change. Pope John Paul II died and his successor, Benedict XVI, warned against "a dictatorship of relativism, which does not recognize anything as for certain and which has as its highest goal one's own ego and one's own desires."[1] Terrorist attacks in the Middle East, America, Asia and London renewed the need for stringent security measures. The year 2000 marked the commemoration of the 60th anniversary of the liberation of Auschwitz while in the Gaza Strip, the Israeli flag was lowered symbolizing the end of thirty-eight years of Israeli occupation of the Palestinian territory.

In the United States, Rosa Parks, the black US civil rights icon, died. Her 1955 protest action in Alabama had marked the start of the modern US civil rights movement. President George W. Bush declared a national emergency after Hurricane Katrina lashed the states of Louisiana, Mississippi and Alabama. Stanley Tookie Williams, co-founder of the Crips gang, anti-violence crusader and nominee for the Nobel Peace Prize, was executed in 2005 by lethal injection. Jennifer Warren reporting for the *Los Angeles Times* on December 13, 2005 wrote, "With its racial overtones and compelling theme—society's dueling goals of redemption and retribution—the case provoked more controversy than any California execution in a generation, and became a magnet for attention and media worldwide." It was in this political, racial and social ferment that *Color of the Cross* was produced.

1. "Benedict XVI Prepares for First Mass as Pope," *CNN International* (Wednesday April 20, 2005). http://edition.cnn.com/2005/WORLD/europe/04/19/pope.wednesday/.

## *Color of the Cross (2006)*

Director: Jean-Claude La Marre. Screenwriter: Jean-Claude La Marre, James Troesh, J. C. Nelson. Country: USA. Production Company: Nu-Lite Entertainment. Length: 108 minutes and 89 minutes. Length of Last Supper scene: 15:02 minutes (edited). Color: Color. Language: English. Musical score: Flexx and J. C. La Marre. Filming locations: Santa Clarita, Los Angeles. Cast: Judas (Johann John Jean), Jesus (Jean-Claude La Marre).

### *Lens One*

*Color of the Cross* is an important Jesus film and is unique in many ways. It is the only Hollywood Jesus film to be directed by an African American (Jean-Claude La Marre) and advertised as "the first film to depict Jesus as a black man." Moreover, it provocatively suggests that racism is the primary motivation for Jesus' crucifixion. The film is also significant in that it endorses Jesus as a Jew. Jesus is called by his Aramaic Jewish name Yeshua, prays to God in his native language, offers Hebrew blessings, refers to the Torah and shares a Jewish Seder meal.

The film focuses on the day before Jesus' crucifixion and omits the drama of both the Sanhedrin and Pilate trials. The narrative jumps from the capture of Jesus at Gethsemane to his dying words on the cross. The director La Marre chose not to focus on "the bloody torture" as in Mel Gibson's *Passion of the Christ* (2004), but on the suffering and human pain endured by Jesus, his disciples and his family.[2] Reviewers, such as IMDb's Mario Gauchi, note that the twenty-minute difference in running time between the original film release and the DVD version is due to the omission or deletion of the Passion scene. Another obvious omission is Jesus' resurrection.[3] La Marre chose to center his script on the events of (Maundy) Thursday because he considered the Gospel narratives to be "tantalizingly thin," allowing him to emphasize the social and political setting of Jesus' ministry.[4]

The film addresses four areas: Jesus and his disciples, the state of mind of the Romans occupying Judea, the issues facing the rabbis in the Sanhedrin and the family life of Joseph, Mary and their remaining children. The use of many flashbacks helps fill in "gaps" in the narrative and enables the viewer to make links between characters and events.

2. Anne Thompson, "Color of the Cross Portrays Jesus as a Black Jew," *Risky Biz Blog* (August 23, 2006). http://reporter.blogs.com/risky/2006/08/color_of_the_cr.html.

3. La Marre made a sequel, *Color of the Cross 2*: *The Resurrection* (2008).

4. Matt Page, "Color of the Cross Interview," October 24, 2006. http://biblefilms.blogspot.com/search/label/color%20of%20the%20Cross.

Stephenson Humphries-Brooks in an interview with Stephen Hooper from CNN states whether a film's plot remains true to biblical and historical facts matters less than the film's relevance to contemporary audiences. He also questions whether an authentic contemporary account of the life of Jesus is cinematically possible, pointing out that the ancient world's concept of race was different to modern racial understanding. He suggests, "The film (*Color of the Cross*) is really translating an American black experience back to the Gospel era."[5] Director/co-writer/co-producer/star, La Marre would counter, "The film was intended as a step towards rehabilitating the portrayal of black characters in Hollywood films after decades of negative stereotyping."[6] In addressing the film as an "evangelistic tool," La Marre explains:

> [T]his film is more than a piece of entertainment, obviously. It is a film which is developing more into a movement. This movie I must add is no way aimed at dismissing the white Jesus. This is a film that merely suggests that black people should worship Jesus in their own image… Black Americans are the only race of people on this planet that worships Jesus outside their own image, and I think there is a connection that can be made between the state of the black people in this country and how they perceive their God. It builds self-esteem, a sense of worth. You know God could very well have looked like me.[7]

La Marre presents then a familiar story of intolerance, betrayal and sacrifice but from a revisionist perspective. Yeshua (Jean-Claude La Marre) is born in a manger because discriminatory lodging laws in Bethlehem denied his black mother a room at the inn. Some members of the Sanhedrin saw Yeshua's actions and messianic prophecies as blasphemous, whereas to Gamaliel, a member of the Sanhedrin, it was the idea of a black messiah that was blasphemy. Here, La Marre is mirroring Albert Cleage's[8] statement: "There never was a white Jesus, and therefore, to portray him as such a color in pictures and other iconography is blasphemy and the work of the Anti-Christ."[9] It could be argued that

5. Stephenson Humphries-Brooks quoted in Simon Hooper, "New Jesus Film Puts Race into Religion," *CNN* (October 30, 2006). http://edition.cnn.com/2006/SHOWBIZ/Movies/10/26/jesus.film/index.html.

6. Ibid.

7. Jean-Claude La Marre in an interview with Cynthia Pope. http://www.youtube.com/watch?v=ai6hJEiw4WM.

8. Albert Cleage (1911–2000) was an early exponent of Black Theology and author of *The Black Messiah* (New York: Sheed & Ward, 1968).

9. David E. Ford with Rachel Muers, eds., *The Modern Theologians: An Introduction to Christian Theology Since 1918*, 3rd ed. (Malden: Blackwell, 2005), 456.

La Marre is not experimenting or telling a revisionist story. The narrative is simply portrayed in a manner that strips the hegemonic influences of racial pretext.

La Marre, as mentioned previously, opined that the film was intended as a step forward towards rehabilitating the portrayal of black characters in Hollywood films after decades of negative stereotyping. In this he succeeds, but unfortunately transfers the guilt to the Jews. They become the racists, making offensive comments, such as when the Pharisees mutter about a "dark-skinned Nazarene" and a "Whites-only" policy for Bethlehem innkeepers. La Marre reinforces Roman hatred for Jews in first-century Palestine with Horatio, the Roman captain, "spitting" out the word Jew and at every opportunity denigrating people by identifying them as "a Jew." When speaking to Caiaphas he reminds him that he (Caiaphas) has no power to arrest and taunts him, "How does it feel, a Jew handing over a Jew, to a Roman authority?" Horatio is critical of having to go to Gethsemane to capture Yeshua complaining, "Roman officers being sent by Jews to capture Jews. What has the Empire become?"

Peter Chattaway makes a compelling observation in that *Color of the Cross*, "serves a valid allegorical purpose, in-so-far as members of an oppressed minority can look to Jesus and believe that he shares their suffering. However, projecting modern racial issues into the ancient story itself could be unnecessarily divisive."[10] Thus by emphasizing too much the color of Jesus, the film deflects from the Gospel message of salvation for all, irrespective of color.

*Color of the Cross* was a small-budget film production, which resulted in some shortcomings in cinematic appeal. Although it was shot on location in Santa Clarita just north of Los Angeles, it made no use of natural backdrops or crowds, and consisted mostly of close-ups. The result was a confusing "succession of eye-straining, candlelit interiors and reliance on stilted exposition."[11]

*Lens Two*

The film shows three Seder meals taking place simultaneously: those of Yeshua's family, a group of Jewish religious leaders and Yeshua, with his twelve disciples. The Last Supper scene takes up a quarter of the film's

10. Peter T. Chattaway, "Ethnicity in Jesus Films—Does It Matter?" *Mennonite Brethren Herald* 45, no. 15 (November 24, 2006). http://www.mbherald.com/45/15/movies.en.html.

11. Jeanette Catsoulis, "Christ, With a Color Change," review of *Color of the Cross* (2006). *New York Times* (November 9, 2008). http://www.nytimes.com/2006/11/09/movies/10cross.html?_r=0.

length. For twenty-three minutes, the audience experiences the final meal, together with some interruptions: a Jewish couple's devious plotting to disclose the location of Yeshua's supper, their subsequent meeting with the rabbis, a debate among the Sanhedrin about Yeshua and the messiah, and Roman soldiers entering two homes searching for "the black Jew." For the sake of simplicity, this analysis of the Last Supper does not include the interruptions but will present a continuous account. This results in the Last Supper scene amounting to fifteen minutes of screen time.

The Supper takes place in a very small and cramped upper room. The stacked boxes and large water jars against the walls suggest that it is some kind of storeroom. There is no space for the disciples to recline at the inverted U-shaped table, which is covered with white cloths, plates, cups, a few candles and food. The cramped room implies that the meal is clandestine.

La Marre has made a good attempt at depicting an authentic Seder meal. The camera settles on bitter herbs, a plate with traditional Seder food and a basket with matzot and four cups, one for each of the four cups of wine to be drunk during the meal. Following a short time of light-hearted banter Yeshua begins the meal by offering the *Kiddush*. Yeshua tells the *Maggid*, the story of Moses and the Jews' escape from Egypt. The atmosphere changes when Yeshua tells the group, "Verily I say unto you, one of you shall betray me." The shot reverts to the disciples who look suitably shocked. They voice their disbelief. Yeshua continues, "Earlier in the garden my Father spoke with me and told me that one of you will betray me." The camera cuts to Judas (Johann John Jean) who is dipping matzot into the sop. Thomas cannot contain his concern and declares, "No, Master. It is impossible. Everyone at this table loves you." This declaration meets with scathing rebuke, "Do you call my Father a liar, Thomas?" All the disciples, except Judas, want to know who the "traitor" is. Yeshua satisfies their curiosity by responding, "His hands are indeed at this table."

What follows is additional material woven into the Gospel account. Peter demands that the traitor reveal himself. Thomas, not silenced by Yeshua's earlier rebuke, asks Peter, "How do we know that the traitor isn't you?" Peter reaches across the table, thrusts a dagger to Thomas' throat, and yells, "I question you Thomas for whom it came so hard to accept the Messiah." Yeshua responds to the disciples' pleas to "Stop this" by stating that his Father "will deal with that later in his own way." There is still tension in the room as the disciples try to resolve the issue of who loves Yeshua more. The argument among them ends when Peter stabs his dagger into the table and declares, "I love him more than any of you." However, the question is then asked of Yeshua and includes a second query, "Who is the greatest?" This leads into the discourse on servitude (Matt 18:1–5; Mark 9:33–37; Luke 9:46–48) and Yeshua washing his disciples' feet.

Judas is uncomfortable at having his feet washed but Yeshua looks up at him and says, "I know you love me Judas." Yeshua does not make this statement about love to any of the other disciples. It is almost as though Yeshua is reassuring Judas of his role in the narrative. When Peter understands the significance of the feet washing he demands Yeshua wash his head and his hands. Yeshua responds, "I only need to wash your feet Peter and you will be clean. But some of you will never be clean."

The camera cuts to Judas who is standing and wiping his hands with a small towel. The image is similar to that of Pilate washing his hands and therefore negating blame in the death of Yeshua. This could be a deliberate ploy by La Marre to confuse the viewer or to allow the audience to draw its own conclusions. Judas' wiping his hands could symbolize the *Urechatz*, a washing of the hands without a blessing, in preparation for eating the *Karpas*, the vegetable (usually parsley) dipped in salt water. Alternatively, it could represent the *Rachtzah*, a second washing of the hands, but which this time includes a blessing and is to prepare for eating the matzot. Perhaps Judas was wiping his hands because they were perspiring: a reaction to feeling nervous and fearful.

The scene changes to them all sitting around the table. Yeshua forewarns his disciples that this may be their last Passover together and that it is only a matter of time before he is captured and killed. Peter threatens, "They will collide with our swords," to which Yeshua responds, "It is too late, Peter."

Unlike other filmic Last Supper scenes, Yeshua begins the meal with wine. He takes the cup that is directly in front of him and says, "This is the cup of my blood. The blood of the everlasting life. It will be given up for you and for all men. Do this in memory of me." He drinks and passes the cup to Peter on his left followed by each disciple drinking from the cup. We hear the words, "I shall not drink again until it is done in my Father's Kingdom." Yeshua takes a large matzot in both his hands and says, "This bread is not just bread; it is my body which shall be given up for you. Share my flesh." He breaks the bread in half, takes some for himself and then passes the halves to Peter and John. Just as Judas breaks off a piece, a loud knocking disrupts the moment. The camera cuts to an extreme-close up of Yeshua's terrified face.

Yeshua and the disciples make their way to a small side-door in order to escape. As Judas is about to make his way through the door, Yeshua puts his hand on Judas' shoulder and asks, "What is wrong Judas?" He turns to face Yeshua and says, "Rabbi, maybe I should pick up some supplies. Where shall you and the rest be so that I can find you?" Yeshua replies,

"At Gethsemane." Without any provocation, Judas declares, "I love you, Master," and turns to exit through the side-door. Yeshua again puts his hand on Judas' shoulder. "Judas, your way is not my way but you go do what you must do." Judas disappears from sight. John turns to Yeshua and asks, "Is it him [the traitor]?" No answer is given but John knows. "Judas! And yet you let him steal all our donations and run off to betray you. We can prevent what must be." The Last Supper scene ends with Yeshua's response, "We cannot stop it."

*Lens Three*

*Color of the Cross* was screened across America and according to La Marre was met with an enthusiastic response from the Black Christian Community.[12] The controversy of having an African American play the part of Jesus/Yeshua did not result in the boycotting of cinemas, nor encourage picket line protests or preachers speaking of blasphemy. Although many called the film controversial, it failed to raise the ire of audiences. With a small budget, estimated at only $2,500,000, limited release and a relatively unknown cast, the film "states a possibility that Christ was a man of color."[13] Reviewer Jeannette Catsoulis acknowledges that "Manufactured controversy can drag audiences into theatres but to keep them there one needs a real movie."[14] Subsequently, *Color of the Cross* failed at the box-office. Apart from the poor production and unknown cast, I would suggest that the film failed to gain attention, positive or negative, because the concept of a black Jesus was not controversial by the time of its production in 2006.

The premises of "Black theology," that began with the publication of a "black power" statement in the *New York Times* newspaper on July 31, 1966,[15] were that it was

> a drama played out between a literal phenotypical black Jesus and the occupying white, colonial presence from Rome (Europe). Jesus became a black-skinned zealot whose sole goal was to wage a national liberation struggle, by any means necessary, to free the oppressed black nation of Israel from the white European colonizers.[16]

12. La Marre, interview with Cynthia Pope.

13. Stephen Hunter, "A Powerful Man of 'Color'," *Washington Post* (October 27, 2006). http://www.washingtonpost.com/wp-dyn/content/article/2006/10/26/AR2006102600401.html.

14. Catsoulis, "Christ, With a Color Change."

15. Ford with Muers, eds., *The Modern Theologians*, 453.

16. Albert Cleage's re-interpretation of the biblical witness from a Black perspective. *Modern Theologians*, 455.

It was now forty years later and the tide of public opinion had turned. The "drama" had unfolded and been played out in many ways in America. Prejudice and racism, if not fully eradicated from American culture, were viewed by most of the populace as unacceptable. Black people had gained positions of authority in many social institutions; and black preachers from Martin Luther King onwards had promoted a black Jesus. La Marre's film was not as groundbreaking as perhaps he imagined. Moreover, his statement that he was the first to film an African American Jesus is false. In 1992, African American Blair Underwood both directed and played the role of Jesus in the thirty-minute short film, *Second Coming*. Similarly, in the 2004 rock opera, *Hero*, African American Michael Tait, the dread-locked one-third of the group dc Talk, played the lead role of Hero, a modern-day Jesus.

*The Portrayal of Judas*

Judas' role in *The Color of the Cross* is striking. Judas is mentioned within the first ten minutes of the film when members of the Sanhedrin are discussing the problem of "the Black Nazarene." Nicodemus believes that capturing him will be possible because one of his disciples has been hired as a spy. This is the first time in any of the Jesus films viewed that Judas is identified as a spy. It raises the question as to whether Judas is spying for the Jews or whether Judas has infiltrated the Jewish court to keep informed of attitudes towards Jesus. Judas' actions and speech suggest that he is in fact the latter: an infiltrator.

We see Judas in the next scene when Yeshua and his disciples are setting up camp for the night. Judas, laughing and enjoying the banter between the disciples, is sharpening his large sword with a stone. The sword is the only indication that Judas is a Zealot. Judas is tall, heavy set, handsome and in his mid-thirties. His distinctive dark robes and turban easily identify him. He is Black. This is not a particularly distinguishing feature because the disciple Peter is also Black, as are Yeshua, Mary, Joseph and a number of other characters.

We know from the events of the Last Supper that Judas holds the common purse and is called a thief by fellow disciple, John. The disciples recognize Judas' love for Yeshua and that Yeshua loves Judas even though he realizes that Judas will betray him. Word that Judas was the traitor must have passed quickly among the disciples because as they are all scattering after the Supper is interrupted, a disciple grabs Judas from behind. Holding a sword to Judas' throat, he threatens "the traitor" not to make a sound and adds, "If it were not for our Master I would open your throat." Judas manages to pull free and escapes.

La Marre, following DeMille, includes a romantic love triangle: Judas loves Mary Magdalyn (Marjan Faritos) who in turn loves Yeshua. Seeing Judas running through the streets, after the Supper had been interrupted, and fearing that Judas is in danger, Mary takes Judas to her home. In the course of the conversation, Mary realizes that Judas was on his way to the Sanhedrin to betray Yeshua. Mary also castigates Judas' support of the Zealots and his reliance on the sword to bring about peace. Judas retaliates by admitting that although he believes Yeshua is the Messiah, he cannot agree with Yeshua's passive ways. Judas, realizing that he is losing the argument, tells Mary, "It is easier to love a messiah than a fisherman." She responds by slapping Judas across the face. Judas continues, "What is it that you see in him that is not in me?" With venom in her voice, Mary states, "The truth." Judas grabs Mary, says, "Here is my truth," forcefully kisses her and pushes her onto the bed. Mary, who, because of her profession—the implication is that she used to be a prostitute—is not a stranger to force. She responds, "Fine. Would you like a feast your master has not yet enjoyed?" Judas again kisses Mary and the screen fades.

This scene is controversial and intriguing. Strangely, a few film reviews simply choose to ignore it. Some argue that Mary is willfully "sacrificing" her body in order to delay Judas' betrayal. Others claim that Judas rapes Mary. Rape is about power, control and dominance. Perhaps this was Judas' display of power. I would suggest that Judas' forcefully "takes" Mary Magdalyn because she has offered herself to him. La Marre's inclusion of the scene raises questions as to his reasoning. If he intended to draw attention to racist attitudes towards Blacks, why would he have an African American rape a non-colored woman?

The Gospels record greed and Satan's influence as motives for Judas' betrayal. In *Color of the Cross* Judas' motivation is disillusionment with Yeshua and the desire to push Yeshua's hand in bringing about a revolution. When the Sanhedrin pays Judas thirty pieces of silver, he reluctantly receives the moneybag. Tears welling in his eyes suggest that Judas is saddened and regrets what he has done.

This unwillingness to betray Yeshua is further evident when Judas leads the Roman soldiers to Gethsemane. He is having second thoughts. Judas cannot bring himself to identify Yeshua but Horatio, the Roman captain, pushes him forward. With his face turned away from Yeshua, Judas slowly makes his way towards the Messiah. Peter, who is standing next to Yeshua, cannot contain his contempt for Judas and spits on the ground. Judas places both his hands around Yeshua's shoulders and tenderly nuzzles his face into Yeshua's neck. Yeshua pulls him closer and whispers in Judas' ear, "Do you betray me with a kiss, Judas?" Yeshua's face is strained with sadness and fear. This is the last time in the film that Judas appears and no other references are made to him or his betrayal.

### *The 2010s*

The first half of the second decade of the twenty-first century gave us a world in turmoil. Earthquakes and tsunamis in Haiti, Chile, Japan, China and Nepal decimated populations. A fire in an eight-story garment factory in Pakistan claimed over eleven hundred lives and the West was shamed into rethinking the use of sweatshops and the exploitation of workers. In 2010, the sovereign-debt crisis in Europe began. The War on Terrorism continued even after the death of Osama Bin Laden in 2011, and in that same year, the "Arab Spring"—a series of anti-government protests, uprisings and armed rebellions—spread across the Middle East. With the shock resignation of Pope Benedict XVI in 2013, the Roman Catholic College of Cardinals elected an Argentinian, Pope Francis. The January 7, 2015 Islamist terrorist attack on the French satirical weekly *Charlie Hebdo* in Paris, left twelve dead and united world leaders who marched in solidarity and protest against the attack. At the same time in the Nigerian town of Baga, the Salafi jihadist group Boko Haram massacred two thousand people. Inexplicably, this act of violence did not receive extensive media coverage. Cyber hacking, leaks and theft of sensitive information became another form of terrorism. The United States of America re-elected President Barack Obama, South Korea elected their first female president and Australia its first female Prime Minister. North Korea, with the fourth largest army in the world, conducted their third nuclear test.

The world appeared to be enveloped by a pall of despondency, uncertainty and fear. Prosperity, hope and peace seemed beyond reach. It is in this atmosphere that five religious films either were in production or released; *Noah*, *Heaven Is for Real*, *Mary the Mother of Christ*, *Exodus* and the Jesus biopic, *Son of God*. Hollywood unofficially declared 2014 the Year of the Bible.[17]

17. Andrew Romano, "Hollywood Declares 2014 the Year of the Bible," *The Daily Beast*. http://www.thedailybeast.com/articles/2014/01/09/hollywood-declares-2014-the-year-of-the-bible.html.

### *Son of God (2014)*

Director: Christopher Spencer. Screenplay: Nic Young, Christopher Spencer, and Colin Swash. Country: United States. Production Company: Lightworkers Media. Length: 138 minutes. Length of Last Supper scene: 6:10 minutes. Color: Color. Language: English. Musical score: Hans Zimmer. Filming locations: Morocco. Cast: Judas (Joe Wredden), Jesus (Diogo Morgado).

*Lens One*

The producers of *Son of God*, Mark Burnett and Roma Downey, decided to make the film because it had been ten years since the release of Mel Gibson's *The Passion of The Christ* and five decades since a Jesus biopic had been screened in American cinemas. Director Christopher Spencer and lead editor Robert Hall took material from five episodes of the television miniseries *The Bible* and edited it into *Son of God* for cinematic release. The film is bookended with the apostle John, beginning and ending with him living in a cave on the Island of Patmos. He appears to be in spiritual distress. Ted Giese, in reviewing the film for *Lutheran Church-Canada* Magazine (March 13, 2014), claims this is "a plot device designed to sling-shot the viewer into the narrative with a little dramatic crisis." What is evident here is speculation regarding John's spiritual life and an example of one of the difficulties filmmakers have in deciding which sources they will use.

One would assume that as John is the film's narrator, the Gospel of John would be the major source, but this is not so. The narrative is marred by deviations from and alterations to the four Gospels and other accounts in Scripture—such as the Acts of the Apostles. This is another difficulty faced by Jesus filmmakers: choosing what to include and what to omit. The decision to delete the Satan character was to avoid controversy. Some observers claimed that the actor cast in the role for the television version bore a resemblance to President Obama. Producer Downey felt that the controversy was a distraction. As *Son of God* is a movie about Jesus, the son of God, "the devil gets no more screen time."[18]

However, that meant eliminating a key element of the Jesus story, the temptation in the wilderness, an important link to understanding the way Jesus saw his role and his sacrifice. A reviewer in *Film Journal International* (February 27, 2014) writes of a "sanitized version" of Jesus. *Son of God* is seen as "the equivalent of a Cliff Notes version of a religious epic, a greatest-hits package that skips all the hard parts. Incidents are

18. Paul Bond, "Bible Producers Cut Satan Scenes from 'Son of God' Following Obama Controversy," *hollywoodreporter.com*. http://www.hollywoodreporter.com/news/bible-producers-cut-satan-scenes-680781.

shown but not examined, and anything that requires more than a superficial explanation is simply ignored."

Spencer has twenty-seven directorial credits for miniseries and television documentaries including, *Ancient Rome: the Rise and Fall of an Empire* (2006) and *The Bible* (2013). *Son of God*, although filmed like a blockbuster epic, with quick cuts, hi-definition photography and a musical score by Hans Zimmerman and Lorne Balfe, has some awkward repetitive computer-generated imagery (CGI) shots. As in Gibson's *The Passion of the Christ*, flashbacks are employed to fill in gaps in the story. Despite modern film devices, the film lacks the grandiose quality of DeMille's *The King of Kings* or Steven's *The Greatest Story Ever Told*. Spencer shoots in close-up to hide sets and locations. His crowd scenes are basically ten to fifteen extras. However, as in Pasolini's *Il Vangelo Secondo Matteo*, Spencer has the Sermon on the Mount taking place in various locations on different occasions throughout the film. This is to convey the concept that Jesus repeated his message.

*Lens Two*

Figure 11. Judas (center) praying at the beginning of the Supper.
© Lightworkers Media.

The next scene is a mid-shot of the apostles and Jesus seated around a rectangular wooden table. Judas sits to screen left of Jesus (Diogo Morgado). An unnamed disciple sits on the right of Jesus.[19] A strip of

19. It is interesting to note that a lobby still of the Last Supper has Mary Magdalene sitting screen right next to Jesus. Perhaps the producers were reluctant to be this creative or even this inclusive. When Jesus and the disciples leave the room for Gethsemane, Mary is present.

white linen covers the middle of the table. Could this represent Jesus' burial shroud? The food on the table does not have elements of a Seder meal nor does the dialogue suggest that either. Two large pottery plates with pita bread, two bowls of grapes, two medium sized pottery jugs, a clay mug, a marble goblet and a single lit candle occupy the table. A large brass bowl is passed around for each to wash their hands. As Jesus washes his hands, he has a premonition of being nailed to the cross. He looks at Judas. The vision continues with Judas surreptitiously walking along a street and then Judas kissing Jesus' cheek in the Garden of Gethsemane. This cinematic technique helps develop the story and builds tension, particularly for those viewers who know the story.

Jesus places his elbows on the table and lifts his arms and hands in prayer. Judas notices this and nods to the others to do the same. He must have some authority and respect because the others comply. The meal begins with Jesus praying, "We thank you Lord, by whose word everything comes to be." All respond, "Amen." As the disciples begin to break bread, Jesus interrupts by telling them, "This is our last meal together before I die." Judas is pensive; the others are confused. A disciple asks, "What do you mean?" Jesus continues, "I am going to be betrayed to my enemies, arrested and condemned to death." A crosscut to Judas shows his concern. Jesus continues, "Don't be afraid. Trust in God. Trust in me also. You know where I am going." Thomas (Matthew Gravelle) interjects, "We don't know where you are going. How can we know the way?" Jesus replies, "I am the way, the truth, and the life." A close-up of Judas shows him looking heavy-hearted, and his eyes are filling with tears.

An extreme close-up shows Jesus picking up a large pita bread. He hands the bread to Peter (Darwin Shaw) with the command, "Take it. Eat. This is my body." Another extreme close-up focuses on Jesus pouring wine into the marble goblet. He drinks and says, "This is my blood." Jesus makes no explanation of the statement and the disciples do not query it. He passes the goblet to Judas who reverently drinks from it. Jesus says, "Remember me by doing this. I am going to the Father." Judas pauses, lowering the goblet when Jesus declares, "Now I must tell you, one of you here will betray me." Peter asks "Who?" Jesus responds, "Whoever eats this. The one I give this to." Jesus tears off a morsel of bread and turns to face Judas. Both their faces fill the screen; both their faces express anguish and they are tearful. Jesus, as the priest does in a Christian communion service, places the bread near Judas' mouth. Judas is reluctant to eat it, stating that he will not betray Jesus. His manner changes when Jesus directs him to "do it quickly." Jesus places the bread in Judas' mouth and then tenderly places his fingers on Judas' cheek. Is this a sign of compassion or is Jesus alluding to the pending betrayal kiss? Distraught Judas rises from the bench and makes his way out of the room. A disciple grabs his arm, but Jesus orders, "Let him go!"

We follow Judas out onto the street where Roman soldiers are marching and we observe Judas coughing up the bread into his hand. Crossing back to the supper, Jesus tells his disciples that they will all fall away and then leaves the room.

*Lens Three*

Even though the primary purpose of films is to entertain, they also educate and can be classified as tools of evangelism.[20] The objective of *Son of God* was to bring the word of God through mass-market entertainment to a secular society. Yet it is decidedly apparent that this movie is made by believers *for* believers. There is an expectation that viewers will be familiar enough with the story to fill in some of the gaps and devout enough to assume the significance of each moment. Hilary Lewis of *The Hollywood Reporter* (February 20, 2014) reported that a week before the film's premiere, faithful audiences secured nearly half-a-million tickets to screenings across the country. Lewis added that the world's largest Christian University, Liberty University, gave away thousands of tickets, and brought out an entire Regal multiplex near the campus, where *Son of God* would be showing on all fourteen screens on the film's opening day. Mark Burnett, in the same article, explained that the movie was designed to be seen in communities and "it's the perfect venue for church groups to band together and watch *Son of God* in community."

*Son of God* had the support of religious leaders. Barbara Vancheri, reviewer for the *Pittsburgh Post-Gazette* (February 20, 2014), reported that Cardinal Donald Wuerl, Archbishop of Washington, DC, called the film "engaging and compelling." According to Heather Alexander of the *Houston Chronicle* (February 14, 2014), popular televangelist Joel Osteen of Lakewood Church in Texas—the largest church in America—claimed Burnett and Downey "have produced an epic work that tells the story of Jesus and touches the heart." Susan Granger of *Entertainment Commentaries* (March 6, 2014) reports that the film also received commendation from Abraham Foxman of the Anti-Defamation League. He called the film "the antidote to the poison that *The Passion of the Christ* became."

20. Catherine M. Barsotti and Robert K. Johnston, *Finding God in the Movies: 33 Films of Reel Faith* (Grand Rapids: Baker Books, 2004), 26.

The producers avoided possible controversies with further omissions from the Gospel narratives. Sensitive to the Islamic religious cleansing and preparation ritual of *Wudu*, Jesus washing the feet of his disciples before the Supper (John 13:1–17) was not included. Were the filmmakers fearful of Islamic reprisals? Considered another potentially controversial incident is Mary using an expensive fragrant oil on Jesus' feet (John 12:3).[21] It is unclear who this may offend, possibly the poor and the needy. Similarly, the decision not to include Jesus' first miracle, the changing of water into wine, at the wedding feast in Cana, is baffling.

The producers have appeased their target audience by covering all the bases—a popular practice in film production—to ensure that the Gospel story is heard and seen by as many audiences as possible. It also helps in box-office revenue.

*The Portrayal of Judas*

The Judas character in *Son of God* is one-dimensional. It is very difficult to define his personality or even his purpose in this film. He is simply one of the disciples, moving from town to town, witnessing Jesus' miracles, and when entering Jerusalem, makes passing comments such as, "We [the disciples] are not ready for this" and "I don't like the look of this." When Jesus overturns the tables of the moneychangers (Matt 21:12; Mark 11:15; John 2:15) Judas pleads, "Jesus! Please!" We recognize Judas—as does the Temple guard, Malchus—by his distinctive maroon-colored costume with a matching hood. Satan in *The Bible* miniseries wore a similar costume, only his was black. The hood is reminiscent of contemporary clothing worn by youths who use this garment for cloaking their identity. The only other distinguishing feature is that he has a van Dyke beard whereas the other disciples have full beards.

Due to the producers' decision to omit the anointing scene, we do not hear Judas' concern for the waste of money and the possibility that it could be sold for three hundred denarii, or that Judas was greedy and was preparing to betray Jesus (John 12:4–6). The only time we witness something akin to greed is when Judas meets with Caiaphas, who attempts to convince Judas that Jesus needs to be brought to the Sanhedrin. Judas grins and asks, "What's in it for me?" The Roman guard Malchus hands the purse to Judas. With the producers casting out Satan to the cutting room floor, Judas' motives for betrayal are also scrapped. In the film, it is Judas' concern that Jesus is going too far—similar to the Judas of *Jesus Christ Superstar*—that drives him to speak with Caiaphas. The iconic

21. "Son of God (2014)," *History Vs Hollywood*. http://www.historyvshollywood.com/reelfaces/son-of-god/.

image of betrayal, Judas kissing Jesus at Gethsemane, is included but the uninformed—those who do not know the Jesus story—are left wondering why.

Betrayal is depicted in the sequence in which Nicodemus (Simon Kunz) visits Jesus (John 3:1–21) at the very same time that Judas visits Caiaphas (Adrian Schiller). This juxtaposition suggests that Nicodemus, by becoming one of the followers of Jesus, is thereby betraying the Sanhedrin, just as Judas is betraying Jesus.

The morning following the Supper, Judas joins the crowd gathered to hear what has become of Jesus. Caiaphas declares Jesus guilty of blasphemy and the penalty is death. Judas, realizing what he has done, is horrified. He throws the silver coins at the priests, runs away and later hangs himself. Judas' death does not evoke pathos, sympathy or much emotion. How can one empathize if one does not have a relationship with the character? It is almost as if Judas' death is included because the "informed" audience would be expecting it.

This "thin" depiction of Judas could be seen as the producers deliberately making him so in order to tone down anti-Semitism and the unjust villain.

## *Additional Judas Filmic Portrayals*

The advanced technology and almost instant world-wide communication of the new millennium allows controversy to sweep the world and there was no film more controversial in this new decade than Mel Gibson's *The Passion of the Christ* (2004.) This film, together with *The Messiah* (2007) and *The Passion* (2008), do not belong in the original study as they do not meet the essential criteria of a Last Supper scene. However, from the perspective of Judas, these additional films support my treatise that Judas has become a person of note—or to take notice of—within theology, and add weight to the argument of the filmic transformation of the character of Judas.

### *The Passion of the Christ (dir. Mel Gibson, Icon Productions, 2004)*

Although largely based on Matthew's Passion narrative, Gibson also draws on the canonical Gospels, apocryphal writings, legends and images from the visions of Anne Catherine Emmerich, narrated in her *Dolorous Passion*. Gibson blends this disparate collection of concepts to carve his Judas character.

This Judas appears an anxious and frightened informer. In Jesus' flashbacks to the Last Supper, we see Judas is present and sits to the left of Jesus. Judas holds the bowl of water but washes only his left hand. Jewish ritual requires that water be poured twice over the right hand and then twice over the left. He looks at his hand. Is Judas reflecting on his imminent meeting with the Jewish priests? Is he trying to wash away the pending act of betrayal and the reception of blood money? Judas is enticed by the devil (John 13:27) but only after the supper. Judas greets Jesus with a kiss (Mark 14:41–42; Matt 26:49) and follows Jesus to the place of the first trial, which takes place in a Sanhedrin court (John 18:25). The one responsible for Jesus' death is announced by Jesus himself, who tells Pilate, "It is he who delivered me to you who has the greater sin" (John 19:11). Judas' guilt is such that he rubs his lips against a stone pillar, to try to remove the kiss of betrayal. Later, in his attempt to return the blood money, Judas' desperate plea of "Release him!" falls on disinterested ears and evokes his admission, "I have sinned by betraying innocent blood" (Matt 27:4).

Judas begins to spiral into madness. He is taunted by two boys, one of whom bites him and takes on grotesque facial features. This incident is reminiscent of an episode in *The Arabic Gospel of the Infancy of the Savior*, where the young Judas, tormented by Satan, would bite either himself or all who came near him. Judas tries to escape from his tormentors—the two boys and Satan—by running through the Valley of Hinnom. It was in this valley that Judah offered its children to the fire god Molech and to Baal (Jer 7:31; 32:35). Early sages, referring to Isa 31:9 interpreted this place to be the gates of hell. It is believed to be the field purchased by the chief priests with Judas' thirty pieces of silver (Matt 27:6–8). Judas cannot rid himself of the ever-present voice of Satan in his ears. He comes across the carcass of a rotting worm-filled donkey, cast away and abandoned on the side of the road. Are we to presume that this was the donkey used for Jesus' triumphant entry into Jerusalem and now a sign of betrayal and rejection? Judas proceeds to hang himself with the rope taken from the rotting carcass. It is with that action that director Gibson fulfils the warning by the prophet Isaiah: "And they shall go out and look at the dead bodies of the people who have rebelled against me; for their worm shall not die, their fire shall not be quenched, and they shall be an abhorrence to all flesh" (Isa 66:24).

By interweaving various sources, Gibson depicts Judas in a somewhat confusing manner. Scot McKnight claims that Gibson's use of Emmerich's *Dolorous Passion* enhances the demonization of Judas and the moral, demonological, dimension of betrayal.[22] Anna Lännström raises the question whether Judas was responsible for his actions and indeed his suicide.[23] If Satan was such a driving influence and the mental state of Judas impaired his reasoning, Judas is not morally responsible. The character of Judas is complex and Gibson introduces another dimension to the more traditional Judas character: his Judas has a conscience. We see a Judas who appears to be a nervous informant, a reluctant betrayer, a tormented soul and a penitent.

*The Messiah aka Jesus, The Spirit of God (dir. Nader Talebzadeh, production company unknown, 2007)*

The making of this Iranian film was an Islamic answer to Mel Gibson's *The Passion of the Christ*. Director, Nader Talebzadeh, wanted to show "common ground" between Muslims and Christians, while also showing two key differences. Islam sees Jesus as a prophet, not the Son of God, and does not believe he was crucified.[24] In making this film, Talebzadeh draws on the Gospels, the Koran and the Gospel of Barnabas, a fourteenth-century Muslim composition. The audience views two endings to the film. The first is based on the Gospels while the second is a "Continuation of events according to Islamic sources and the Gospel of Barnabas." The Judas character is thinly drawn yet plays a significant role in this Jesus film.

The depiction of the calling of the twelve disciples is revealed early in the film. Judas (actor unknown) is called last and is described by the narrator as "Judas Iscariot the son of Simon, who hadn't benefited from the blessing of faith." This lack of faith is evident when Jesus (Ahmad Soleimani-Nia) miraculously provides the hungry disciples with a meal of fish and bread in the desert. Asked why Judas is not eating, he replies, "Don't expect me to fool myself. This is a mirage, not a miracle." With that he runs off. The scene cuts to a supper where Mary Magdalene anoints Jesus. Judas criticizes the waste of money spent on oil claiming, "Thirty people could be fed with the money from the perfume." He is

22. Scott McKnight, "The Betrayal of Jesus and the Death of Judas," in *Jesus and Mel Gibson's* The Passion of the Christ*: The Film, the Gospels and Claim on History*, ed. Kathleen E. Corley and Robert L. Webb (London: Continuum, 2004), 70.

23. Anna Lännström, "Forgiving Judas: Extenuating Circumstances in the Ultimate Betrayal," in *Mel Gibson's Passion and Philosophy: The Cross, the Questions, the Controversy*, ed. Jorge J. E. Gracia (Chicago: Open Court, 2004), 236.

24. Lara Setrakian, "Story of Jesus Through Iranian Eyes," *ABC News* (February 16, 2008). http://abcnews.go.com/Entertainment/story?id+4297085&page+1&single Page+true.

unsettled when Jesus tells him, "I know what is in your heart!" We know the cause of this to be Judas' planned meeting with the Sanhedrin, during which Caiaphas offers Judas thirty silver coins for his service, but we do not see the transaction take place. The narrator informs the viewers that Judas led the Roman soldiers to capture Jesus, yet there is no Gethsemane scene and no betrayal kiss. Jesus is captured in the room where the Supper took place.

In the alternative ending according to the *Gospel of Barnabas*, the angel Gabriel appears to Jesus just before he is about to be captured by the Roman soldiers. The angel informs Jesus, "Now your Lord says: O Son of Mary, I shall take you from this world tonight and raise you to myself." In a blast of light, Jesus ascends into Heaven without dying. Judas has returned to the Supper room and witnesses the light. He screams and writhes in agony. The narrator explains, "Then the wonderful God acted wonderfully. Judas changed amazingly in speech and face into the form of Jesus." The soldiers barge in and arrest Judas who has been transformed to look like Jesus. It is Judas who stands trial, is mocked and scourged, and who is condemned to death. Although guilty of leading the "legion of soldiers" to Jesus, Judas claims his own innocence with his dying words from the cross, "God why have you forsaken me, seeing the malefactor has escaped and I die unjustly?"

Judas is presented as a disciple of little or no faith, a cynic, and concerned with money matters, attributes that could be seen in some twenty-first-century disciples of Christ. What sets this filmic Judas apart from any other portrayal is that Judas is a sacrificial substitution: he dies in place of Jesus. Judas has become the scapegoat.[25] The concept of a substitute victim is not unique. In the *Apocalypse of Peter*—a gnostic scripture—Peter sees two figures involved in the crucifixion: executioners who were striking the feet and hands of one and the other "glad and laughing on the tree." The latter was Jesus.[26]

*The Passion (dir. Michael Offer, British Broadcasting Company, 2008)*
Although Judas (Paul Nicholls) blends in with the disciples, he can be distinguished by his wearing of a turban, and we learn that he is the group's treasurer. His being sent by Jesus (Joseph Mawle) to purchase

25. See René Girard, *The Scapegoat*, trans. Yvonne Freccero (Baltimore: The Johns Hopkins University Press, 1986), 112–24, for an account of the Passion read from the point of view of the innocent victim.

26. James M. Robinson, gen. ed., *The Nag Hammadi Library in English* (New York: HarperSanFrancisco, 1990), 377.

a dove sacrifice and to pay the temple tax evidences this. At Passover, Jesus tells Judas to take a lamb to the Temple for their Passover offering. Responsibility for preparing the Upper Room is placed on Judas. Cautious about money, Judas criticizes the use of expensive anointing ointment. Yet when he is paid thirty pieces of silver for "betraying" Jesus, he spits on those giving him the coins, shouting, "I don't want any of the temple tax." He is forced to take the money because the authorities "won't be in [Judas'] debt" and is told to "throw it away or give it to the poor if [he] is so upset."

Judas has been with Jesus for only one year. Judas is passionate about Judea, and is convinced that he himself is a true believer in what Jesus is doing. The motive for Judas informing Sagan (John Lynch)—"part police, part thug, part rabble-rouser"[27]—as to the whereabouts of Jesus after the Passover meal is unclear. However, it is evident that Judas is reluctant to "point him out" in Gethsemane. Judas does not lead the arresting party, but is pulled along by Sagan, yet Judas informs Sagan, "Jesus will be the one I kiss." What follows is a tender moment. Having greeted Jesus by name, Jesus replies, "My friend." Judas says "Peace be with you." Jesus places his hand on Judas' cheek and encourages Judas, "Do what you have come to do." Judas takes Jesus' head in both his hands. Jesus responds by embracing Judas who then kisses Jesus on the cheek. Judas hurries away.

We next see Judas attempting to deaden his senses in wine. Barabbas tells Judas that Jesus is to be crucified. Judas thoughtfully rolls the coins around in his hands and exclaims, "Blood money! The one who truly loved me; I sold his life." Judas runs onto the street and headlong into the Roman soldiers escorting Jesus carrying the crossbeam. A distraught Judas turns and runs to an empty marketplace. Seeing the well, he undoes the bucket's rope and makes a noose. There is a moment of silence when Judas sits on the edge of the well, contemplating his fate. The silence is broken during a close-up of the rope being dragged down over the wooden beam. The audible crack as it reaches its length limit shocks us that Judas has hanged himself.

Despite the stereotypical characteristics of a filmic Judas that include his preoccupation with money, the identifying kiss of betrayal and a repentant despair that drives him to hang himself, director Offer's Judas portrayal is both significant and unique. Jesus bestows upon Judas the forgiveness Judas asks for. Judas is pardoned.

27. Peter Malone, *Screen Jesus: Portrayals of Christ in Television and Film* (Lanham: Scarecrow, 2012), 176.

Intermittently throughout the film, there are scenes where we are privy to intimate conversations between the two men. Judas tells Jesus that they—all the disciples—believe. They want to. The conversation continues with Jesus asking Judas what he sees when he looks into his heart. Judas does not answer the question but says, "Forgive me Lord." This plea is not recorded in any of the Gospels. Similarly, Jesus' reply, "You are forgiven," is not documented. Jesus again asks what Judas sees "inside." Judas has no answer. Jesus then utters. "I am sorry, Judas."

At the Passover meal, while Jesus is washing the disciples' feet, he tells them they have to let him go. He tells them not to be hard on themselves when their courage fails. Jesus reassures the twelve disciples that there is room for *each* of them in his Father's house, even for the one who *must* betray him. "Betray?" asks John. Jesus instructs them, "Don't hunt for the traitor. Pity him. He'll wish he never was born."

Jesus casually hands Judas a piece of bread without even looking at him. Judas takes the bread and eats. Jesus advises, "Judas you have to go. Things to do!" The obedient Judas, replies, "Yes, Rabbi." Judas leaves. As soon as he closes the door behind him, he vomits up the bread. It would be interesting to hear the response of the audience to this unusual action.

Judas does what he *must* do. For this, he asks forgiveness and we hear the words of Jesus that guarantee a place for the betrayer in his Father's house. Thus is Judas redeemed.

### *Summary*

Although Judas in *Color of the Cross* is identified as having traditional traits—holder of the common purse, a thief and a traitor—he does not resemble or represent the epitome of the evil Jew. Instead, Judas represents Black people and their historical struggle for freedom from oppression. The rebuttal by Mary Magdalyn (a non-Black) and her reference to Yeshua being "your master" instead of "our master" alludes to her superiority and Judas' subservience. His citing his status as "fisherman" intimates a social barrier between himself and Mary. Judas, like Jesus, is a mouthpiece for Black theology.

Filmmakers were able to create interesting Judas depictions by drawing from non-biblical sources. In Gibson's *The Passion of the Christ*, Satan was the driving force behind the demonization of Judas. Whereas, Satan is omitted from *Son of God*. In Talebzadeh's *The Messiah,* Judas is the one who dies on the cross. Michael Offer's film, *The Passion*, through the use of innovative—and non-scriptural—dialogue, presents a very different Judas. He is not to be condemned but pitied.

By the second millennium, the Judas filmic character had undergone many incarnations but the consensus is that he is rehabilitated. Now filmmakers are ready to portray Judas as the one who was pre-destined to hand over Jesus and his role is to ensure that Jesus fulfills God's plan. Jesus sanctions these actions and forgives Judas, therefore freeing him from the torment of hell and eternal damnation. The transformation since the 1902 black and white silent film *La Vie et la Passion de Jésus Christ*, is remarkable: the damned Judas has become the redeemed Judas.

## Chapter 8

# JUDAS AS PORTRAYED IN FILM

### *Introduction*

Jesus—and Judas—films are not just simple adaptations of Gospel narratives. Most films about Jesus have a spiritual agenda. Perhaps it is an act of faith or a sincere attempt to engage with Christianity. Jon Rainey believes Jesus films have come to be understood as "bearers of meaning and theology in their own right. These films also capture the social and cultural concerns of their time, so that the various incarnations of the celluloid Christ [and Judas] stand as artifacts of our pluralistic and diverse society."[1]

The Judas figure became representative of Judaism and an instrument for advancing anti-Semitism. Disregarding the Jewishness of Jesus and the other apostles, filmmakers in the early era of films divorced Judas from the others by portraying him with exaggerated Jewish features, distinctive clothing and carrying a moneybag—a symbol for avarice. By linking the actions of Judas with Judaism, his character came to symbolize the proto-type Jew and Christianity's rejection of Judaism.

The most significant event influencing the changes in the filmic portrayals of Judas is the Holocaust. In *Popular Culture and the Shaping of Holocaust Memory in America,* Alan Mintz writes, "The Holocaust… constituted a 'tremendum,' an event of such awful negative transcendence that it cleaved history into a before and after. That we view the present through a profoundly altered lens goes without saying, but we also cannot escape viewing the past through the medium of this terrible knowledge."[2]

From the analysis of the filmic portrayals of Judas (Chapters 2–7), it is evident that he is different to the Judas of the Christian Gospels. Richard Walsh correctly notes:

1. Jon Rainey, "The Cinematic Savior: Jesus Films and Related Literature," *TL* 3, no. 2 (2010). https://journal.atla.com/ojs/index.php/theolib/article/viewFile/157/448.

2. Alan Mintz, *Popular Culture and the Shaping of Holocaust Memory in America* (Seattle: University of Washington Press, 2001), 36.

> While some films vastly improve the Judas story by adding plot connection and amplifying Judas' character, they testify to the continuing power of Christian discourse. Jesus films retell the gospel, visualize the tradition, modernize Judas, and create new Christian myths.[3]

Viewing the Last Supper scene in the selected films through a theological lens requires an understanding of the significance and ritual of the Jewish commemorative Passover meal. An understanding and knowledge of the theological and doctrinal concepts of the Christian Eucharist is also required. By paying particular attention to dialogue, body language, ritual and liturgical practices, specific actions by both Judas and Jesus, and how the Jews are portrayed, it is evident that two distinct theologies emerge: a "theology of rejection" and a "theology of acceptance."

It is clear that there has been a dramatic shift in focus during the last hundred years in interpreting Judas in film, resulting in the emergence of these two theologies. The eight films from 1902 to 1946 that were analysed follow Christianity's traditional evaluation of Judas as a stereotypical Jewish villain, and reveal a theology of rejection. Between 1946 and 1961 there was what I label a "transition" period when there is a softening of the vitriol against Judas, though he is still viewed with suspicion. This is represented by three films of that period. However, the thirteen films from 1961 to 2014 elevate Judas to a freedom fighter, social mouthpiece, martyr and even a hero: a theology of acceptance becomes the norm.

### *Theology of Rejection (1902–1946)*

There are four examples of rejection as represented in the Last Supper scene in post-Second World War films. These are: (1) rejection of Jesus as Messiah; (2) rejection of Judas at the Institution of the Eucharist; (3) rejection of partaking of bread and wine by Judas; and (4) the rejection of Judaism.

The motif of the rejection of Jesus is a major theme in the Synoptic Gospels. Jews are portrayed as opposing Jesus as the long-awaited Messiah for a variety of reasons. These include Jesus' "attitude toward the Law, toward legal traditions, and toward the sanctity of the Jewish nation."[4] The rejection of Jesus as Messiah is depicted in the filmic Last

3. Richard Walsh, "The Gospel According to Judas: Myth and Parable," *BI* 14 (2006): 37.

4. Scott McKnight, "A Loyal Critic: Matthew's Polemic with Judaism in Theological Perspective," in *Anti-Semitism and Early Christianity: Issues of Polemic and Faith*, ed. Craig A. Evans and Donald A. Hagner (Minneapolis: Fortress, 1993), 72.

Supper by Judas' bargaining with the chief priests, his position at the table, his body language and the manner in which he exits the Supper.

Judas' initial rejection of Jesus is in his making a deal with the chief priests to "betray" Jesus. The Gospels do not agree on the specific motivation for Judas' actions, nor why he became involved with the Temple hierarchy. However, in films up to the 1950s, the motives of Judas are identified as "seeking revenge," "looking for financial gain," "personal greed" and "the influence of Satan."

The silent films, *From the Manger to the Cross* (1912) and *The King of Kings* (1927), accentuate the motivation of greed—not just of Judas but also of the priests. We see Judas and the priests haggling over the fee, their deliberate counting of each coin—neither Judas nor Caiaphas trust each other—and their satisfaction and delight expressed in the stroking of their long beards and rubbing their hands together. *Christus* (1916), through the title card, introduces a new motive: "The Hatred of Judas who now sought the opportunity to betray him [Jesus]." Satan also appears before Judas enters Caiaphas' house and again when he leaves. Satan's goading and Judas' hallucination of the coins turning into droplets of blood condemn Judas as evil and reinforce his complicity in the death of Jesus. The inclusion of the devil figure also underpins "the identification of the Jew with the devil—and of the devil with the Jew."[5] This interaction between Judas and Satan reiterates "the image of the Jews as irredeemably evil: 'Christ-killers,' 'children of the devil,' 'agents of Satan,' ritual murderers, and a menace to Christianity."[6]

The films *From the Manger to the Cross*, *Christus* and *The King of Kings* also include the three main characterizations of anti-Semitism. The first is the accusation of deicide—the belief that Jews rejected and killed Jesus. The second is the suspicion of disloyalty and treachery. The third is "the assumption that Jews have a unique, and uniquely evil, relationship to money—that they will sacrifice all other interests in the pursuit of wealth."[7]

The early Jesus films were tableau shots. Camera immobility and action within the frame restricted where Jesus and his disciples sat at the Last Supper table. Seating Judas in front of the table and across from Jesus was a standard position. By having Judas and Jesus within the frame, the audience could observe their actions and, more importantly, their interactions, simultaneously. Their closeness also made possible the handing of

5. Nicholls, *Christian Antisemitism*, 240.

6. Perry and Schweitzer, eds., introduction to *Anti-Semitic Myths*, xviii.

7. Abraham H. Foxman, *Jews and Money* (New York: Palgrave MacMillan, 2010), 153.

the sop or dipping the bread. By situating Judas in front of the table while the others sit behind it expresses the isolation of Judas and sets him apart from the group. The table acts as a barrier to Judas and implies that Judas is now an "outsider."

Body language, particularly in silent films, is an important component in characterization. The three earliest films, *La Vie et la Passion de Jésus Christ*, *La Vie du Christ* and *From the Manger to the Cross*, have Judas in front of the table and with his back to Jesus. This is clearly a sign of rejection. In *Golgotha*, Judas is sitting next to Jesus but when Jesus begins to speak to him, he quickly turns away and pretends to be in deep conversation with the disciple next to him. Judas' look of disinterest augments rejection. In *The King of Kings*, Judas gives the impression that he does not want to be at the Supper and that he is biding his time to betray Jesus. Similarly, in *Blade af Satans Bog*, his slumped demeanor, nervous crumbling of pieces of matzot and oblivious to what Jesus is saying, suggest that Judas' thoughts are elsewhere.

The most telling example of body language rejection of Jesus as Messiah is in *Christus*. Judas is standing behind Jesus, having taken the bread from him. Jesus reaches out to bless Judas but Judas cowers to avoid Jesus' touch. Judas is willing to take the bread (though not to eat it) yet he refuses this public display of Jesus' affection. The meaning is clear: Judas—that is the Jews— rejects the person of Jesus and all that he stands for.

Apart from John's Gospel, the Synoptic Gospels do not mention Judas' departure from the Last Supper. This gives the film director artistic and creative license. Six of the films show Judas leaving the Last Supper. *From the Manger to the Cross* and *Maria Magdalena, pecadora de Magdala* do not show Judas' departure although it is implied. An extremely dramatic exit is in *La Vie du Christ* where Judas flees in terror after seeing the Suffering Servant vision. His running away represents Christianity's portrayal of the Jewish refusal to accept Jesus as the hoped-for Messiah. While early Christian interpretation applied the Hebrew Scriptures' idea of the "Suffering Servant" to Jesus (Isa 53:4–9; Matt 8:17; Acts 8:32–35; 1 Pet 2:22–25), in *La Vie du Christ* Judas is the one who is "despised and rejected." Judas' reaction to the vision re-affirms what Paul wrote in his second letter to the Corinthians, that God has purposefully blinded the spiritual understanding of the Hebrews whenever they attempt to access the spiritual information in the "old" covenant—the implication of course being that turning to Jesus as the Messiah will cure that spiritual blindness (2 Cor 3:14–16).

In contrast to such a dramatic departure, *Christus* has Judas sneaking out of the room when Jesus elevates the chalice. Not even the extraordinary appearance of a hovering white dove above the chalice halts his departure. We know from the scene following that Judas' exiting at this point in the Last Supper was to meet with the Sanhedrin. The question is why was Judas present for Jesus' proclamation "This is my body," yet he left before Jesus claimed the wine to be his blood? Perhaps the director used this opportunity, while the disciples and Jesus were focused on the chalice, to enable Judas to leave unnoticed. It seems more likely that the reference to blood would be a reminder that Jesus' death was caused by Judas' betrayal. Again, the film condemns Judas as the one who rejected Jesus.

A notable feature of Judas' departure, in both *Blade af Satans Bog* and *The King of Kings*, is the importance placed on Judas closing the door. In both films when Judas departs, he opens the door, looks back at those gathered at the table and closes the door after him. It would seem that Judas' closing the door was to prevent the Messiah from entering. Traditionally those celebrating the Passover would symbolically open a door so the prophet Elijah could enter, heralding the advent of the Messiah. As the door was already shut, the director could also be implying that waiting for the Messiah was futile because the Messiah had arrived in the person of Jesus. Judas' turning to look at Jesus before closing the door could be reinforcing Judas' decision to reject Jesus as the Messiah, thus also bring to an end his own discipleship.

The Gospels are unclear as to when or even if Judas leaves the supper. However, a tradition of Judas' dismissal at the Last Supper developed in Christianity when the institution of the Eucharist was formalized in the last years of the second century.[8] The implication was that the one who betrayed Jesus could not have participated in the most holy sacrament of the Church. Film depictions have Judas leaving before, during or after the institution of the Eucharist. In the Last Supper scene, Judas is the one who is rejected. This rejection takes place when Judas is identified as the one who will betray Jesus, when Jesus expels him from the Last Supper and through the disciples' responses and reactions.

Identifying the betrayer takes different forms and the declaration is made at varying times during the supper. Instead of just pointing to Judas and saying "It is you!," the Gospel writers heighten the tension by having Jesus provide clues as to who is the betrayer. Film directors also apply

8. Kenneth Hein, "Judas Iscariot: Key to the Last-Supper Narratives?" *NTS* 17 (1970–71): 228.

the same ploy but they have the advantage of being able to utilize the clues provided in all four Gospels. Therefore, in film versions of the Last Supper, the following statements identify Jesus' betrayer: "The one who is eating with me" (Mark 14:18); "It is one of the twelve, one who is dipping bread into the bowl with me" (Mark 14:20); "The one who has dipped his hand into the bowl with me" (Matt 26:23); "The one who betrays me is with me, and his hand is on the table" (Luke 22:21). The vagueness of the clue may well mean that the betrayer might be any of the disciples as each of the clues could have been applied to each of them. Regardless of which statement is used to identify Judas, pinpointing this betrayer at the Last Supper "illuminates the abrupt shift from table fellowship to enmity."[9] This animosity is verbalized in Jesus' following condemnation: "For the Son of Man goes as is written of him, but woe to that one by whom the Son of Man is betrayed! It would have been better for that one not to have been born" (Mark 14:21; Matt 26:24). Judas' role as betrayer is demonized even further by Jesus' claim that this person is utterly damned.

The change from fellowship to enmity is apparent in *La Vie et la Passion de Jésus Christ*. This silent film had no intertitles and yet the manner in which Jesus glares at Judas leaves no doubt in the viewers' minds that Jesus is incensed. What follows is the most dramatic filmic representation of Judas' expulsion from the Supper. Jesus stands, points to Judas, extends his arm and then points to the door. Judas cannot ignore this command. He reluctantly rises from his seat but then defiantly turns his back on Jesus and leaves the room. Similarly, *From the Manger to the Cross* has Jesus rising to his feet and staring at Judas. Although there are no words, or exaggerated arm gestures, Judas realizes that he is condemned. He stoops to pick up his sandals, with the scene changing as he is about to leave the room.

Judas' shock at being identified as the betrayer is intensified by Jesus' command to him, "That thou doest, do quickly!" (John 13:27). This command, given in three of the films—*Blade af Satans Bog*, *The King of Kings* and *Golgotha*—is significant in that Judas acts only when instructed to do so by Jesus.

George Steiner argues that Judas' speedy departure from the Last Supper and into the night sealed the fate of the Jews in Christian history:

> Judas goes into a never-ending night of collective guilt. It is the sober truth to say that his exit is the door to the Shoah. The "final solution" proposed, enacted by National Socialism in this twentieth century is the perfectly

9. Gerd Theissen, *The Gospels in Context: Social and Political History in the Synoptic Tradition*, trans. Linda M. Maloney (Minneapolis: Fortress, 1991), 168.

> logical, axiomatic conclusion to the Judas-identification with the Jew... That utter darkness, that night within night, into which Judas is dispatched and commanded to perform "quickly," is already that of the death ovens. Who, precisely, has betrayed whom?[10]

Jesus is not the only one at the Last Supper to reject Judas: the eleven disciples do too. This rejection however is not verbal but is expressed in their body language. When Judas exits the room in *Blade af Satans Bog*, Jesus and all the disciples watch him leave. Some stand on stools to ensure a better view; some crane their necks. Even as Judas turns to close the door behind him, a point-of-view shot shows the disciples still watching him. What is revealing is that not one of the disciples speaks or attempts to prevent Judas from going to betray Jesus. The reason for this could be that they are portrayed as being the righteous in contrast to Judas as the sinner. However, Gordon Allport argues that Judas is being set up as a "scapegoat," with the disciples' own frustrations and failures being heaped upon him:

> prejudice grows out of personal *frustration*, which in turn generates aggressive feelings. When this *aggression* cannot be directed against the real cause of the frustration, the aggression is *displaced* onto relatively defenseless "scapegoats." This displaced hostility is then rationalized and justified by blaming, projecting, and stereotyping.[11]

In Duvivier's *Golgotha*, Judas is clearly no longer part of the group: he is an outsider. His rejection at the Last Supper is made more pitiable by his watching the group from outside the room. Judas becomes the exemplar for "closed reception" and "worthy reception" and the Christian belief that only the faithful are welcome at Holy Communion. This belief had its origin in the first century *Didache*, the Teaching of the Twelve Apostles: "(And) let no one eat or drink from your eucharist except those baptized in the name of [the] Lord, for the Lord has likewise said concerning this: 'Do not give what is holy to the dogs'" (*Did.* 9.5). Setting apart believers from non-believers came to be known as closed communion with non-believers, identified as:

10. George Steiner, *No Passion Spent: Essays 1978–1996* (London: Faber & Faber, 1996), 417.

11. Gordon Allport, "The Meaning of Scapegoat," in *Can It Happen Again? Chronicles of the Holocaust*, ed. Roselle K. Chartock and Jack Spencer (New York: Black Dog & Levanthal, 2001), 109–11. Emphasis in original.

> heretics, catechumens, those not in fellowship with the church, those who were mentally incompetent, and those under church discipline were dismissed from the sanctuary. The doors were closed, and then, and only then, the Sacrament was celebrated. The call went out to the faithful, "The holy things for the holy ones."[12]

Judas as portrayed in early Jesus films was a non-believer because he aligned himself with Jewish religious leaders, refused Jesus' blessing and betrayed the Messiah.

One way in which to convince the viewing audience of Judas' duplicity and his mockery of Holy Communion is to have Judas present during the institution of the Eucharist but not partaking of the bread and wine. This occurs in six of the films—*La Vie et la Passion de Jésus Christ*; *La Vie du Christ*; *From the Manger to the Cross*; *Christus*; *The Kings of Kings*; and *Maria Magdalena, pecadora de Magdala*.

These films show Judas going to extraordinary lengths to avoid eating the bread. He craftily places it next to him on the seat. He slides the bread into his cloak and pretends to eat it when he returns to his place at the table. He lets the bread slip between his fingers—first having checked that no one is watching him. He uses similar tactics when he is passed the cup. Judas' pretense in drinking the wine is deliberate. In *La Vie et la Passion de Jésus Christ*, Judas reaches across the table to take the cup, holds it to his lips and then tips the contents onto the floor. The audience is able to see this because Judas is in front of the table. However, the table blocks the view of Jesus and of the disciples. In an era when Roman Catholic priests "were required to keep the fingers that touched the host joined (lest a particle drop unnoticed) until they were rinsed after communion,"[13] pre-Vatican II Christian viewers would have considered Judas' actions sacrilegious. Likewise, echoing the words of Paul in 1 Cor 11:27–29, Judas brings judgment against himself because he receives communion in an "unworthy manner." He does not acknowledge the sacredness of the bread and wine. He came to the Last Supper without "true faith" and with knowledge that he had sinned and that he was going to sin again.

12. Paul McCain, *Communion Fellowship—A Resource for Understanding, Implementing, and Retaining the Practice of Closed Communion in the Lutheran Parish* (Waverly, Iowa: The International Foundation for Lutheran Confessional Research, 1992), 19.

13. John Martos, *Doors to the Sacred: A Historical Introduction to Sacraments in the Catholic Church*, rev. and updated ed. (Liguori: Liguori/Triumph, 2001), 237.

In *The King of Kings*, DeMille juxtaposes the actions of Judas with those of Peter, illustrating the differences between "worthy" and "unworthy" reception. Whereas Judas reluctantly takes the matzot from Jesus, snaps off a piece and casually passes the remainder onto the disciple next to him, Peter cradles the matzot, then carefully and reverently breaks off a small piece for himself before gently passing the rest on, keeping his eyes fixed on the bread. Judas chooses not to eat but lets the matzot drop from his fingers and onto his lap. Peter hesitates before piously placing the piece in his mouth. By fixing his gaze on Jesus, Peter seems to have gained an understanding of the significance of eating the bread. When Judas is passed the chalice, panic overcomes him. The chalice in his hand is like a cup of poison and rather than drink from it he rebelliously places it on the table. Peter on the other hand takes hold of the chalice as though it is a precious object, careful not to spill the sacred wine. Again, his gaze is fixed on Jesus. Having drunk from the chalice, Peter holds it close against his breast and then passes it on, ensuring it does not get spilled. DeMille has transformed onto film the teaching of Saint Augustine that "Peter was the biblical exemplar for the church, while Judas, the betrayer, represented the Jews."[14]

The unworthiness of Judas to receive communion is confirmed by early Christian theologians. John Chrysostom uses the example of "the blindness of the traitor" Judas to warn congregations against receiving Christ's body and blood in an unworthy manner or under the guise of being part of the faithful. Chrysostom cautions those gathered:

> Let no one communicate who is not of the disciples. Let no *Judas* receive, lest he suffer the fate of Judas. This multitude also is Christ's body. Take heed, therefore, you that ministerest at the mysteries, lest you provoke the Lord, not purging this body. Give not a sword instead of meat. (Homily 82 on Matt 26:26–28)

Chrysostom in this warning removes Judas from the list of the disciples, uses his name metaphorically to describe "traitors" and considers that Judas is an exemplar of how Christians ought not to act.

As Judas is the perceived representative of the Jews, it is important to comment on how rejection of Judaism is represented in the Last Supper scenes. Christianity originated in a Jewish environment and inherited many of its liturgical practices from Judaism.[15] According to the Synoptic

14. Larry B. Stammer, "New Look at Ancient Betrayer," *Los Angeles Times* (April 21, 2000). http://articles.latimes.com/2000/apr/21/news/mn-22024.

15. Paul F. Bradshaw, *The Search for the Origins of Christian Worship: Sources and Methods for the Study of Early Liturgy*, 2nd ed. (London: SPCK, 2002), 23. The

Gospels, the Last Supper was a Jewish Passover or Seder meal. Christianity reinterprets the Passover meal as a Christian Eucharist, Jesus becomes a pseudo-Christian priest and the focus is on a *new Christian* covenant. Early filmmakers, in most cases, followed the Christian tradition, choosing to ignore that Jesus was Jewish and that the Last Supper was originally a Seder or Passover meal.

Jewish Passover meals are family celebrations. In the early Jesus films, only Jesus and his disciples shared the meal. The table resembles a Christian altar with its white cloth and focus on bread and cup/chalice. The Passover ritual revolved around the body and blood of the sacrificial Passover lamb. Only *Blade af Satans Bog* and *Golgotha* includes a whole roasted lamb for the meal. Because there is no mention in the Gospels of the lamb, the focus shifts to Jesus' own body and blood.[16] Jesus' actions, notably in *Christus* and *The King of Kings*, are similar to those of a priest's during the consecration of bread and wine in the Mass. The appearance of a white dove at the epiclesis—invoking the Holy Spirit to consecrate the bread and wine—stamps the meal with a Christian imprimatur. The Passover meal concludes with the singing of a hymn (Matt 26:30; Mark 14:26) but *Blade af Satans Bog* is the only early film to include this.

The Passover celebrates God's covenant with Abraham, the exodus from Egypt and the entry into the promised land of Canaan. The Gospel writers at the Last Supper adopt the language of "New Covenant" (Luke 22:20 and 1 Cor 11:25). The King James Bible and the Book of Common Prayer translated this as "New Testament." In *From the Manger to the Cross* and *The King of Kings*, the term "New Testament" is used. The inference is that Jesus/Christianity supersedes Judaism: an overt rejection of Judaism.

### *The Transition Stage (1950s)*

The 1950s can be described as a transitional stage where filmmakers began to be conscious of the negative portrayal of Judas and the Jews. Images of the horrors of the concentration camps and the disturbing reports of genocide against the Jewish race prompted filmmakers to be reticent in portraying Judas, Jews and Judaism in a negative light.

recognition that liturgical practices are inherited from Judaism can be traced back to the late seventeenth century and to Dutch Protestant theologian, Campegius Vitringa (1659–1722).

16. See Chapter 3, "The New Passover" in Brant Pitre, *Jesus and the Jewish Roots of the Eucharist: Unlocking the Secrets of the Last Supper* (New York: Doubleday, 2011), 48–76.

Therefore, in this decade, the portrayal of Judas became problematic for film producers. The 1950s films show considerable evolution of the Judas character. At first, he was almost omitted from the story. In *I Beheld His Glory* (1952), Judas is identified as Judas of Kerioth (distancing this character from the traditional villain identified as Judas Iscariot) and is mentioned by name only twice. He only speaks one word, "Master!," and his sole purpose in the film is to identify Jesus at Gethsemane. No motive for Judas' actions is given. He is not an outsider, a betrayer, nor a villain; but simply the person who makes possible what God has determined—Jesus' death on the cross.

The role of Judas evolves further in *Day of Triumph* (1954). Again, he is not the villain but a leading member of the Zealots. As the narrative focusses on the forthcoming religious uprising, Judas' part is significantly larger than that of Jesus'. Stereotypical Jewish traits are not evident in Judas' character. His loyalty to Jesus may have been questionable but his concern for Jesus' safety is commendable. Although surrounded by an angry crowd calling for Jesus' crucifixion, Judas calls for the release of the Nazarene. This act results in a fellow Zealot attacking him. Judas in this film represents the vociferous protestor representing innocent victims of oppression in a world and time of political intrigue.

Similarly, in the 1952 Mexican film *El mártir del Calvario*, Judas also plays the part of a Zealot who believes that Jesus is the Messiah come to bring about social revolution to an oppressed people under a tyrannical ruler, Rome. Judas, ignoring his own safety, is the only disciple to attend Jesus' trial by the Sanhedrin and is the only person to defend Jesus' actions. Director Miguel Morayta Martinez presents Judas as paralleling the Passion and death of Jesus by juxtaposing the events of their last day. In *El mártir del Calvario*, Judas is the heroic figure.

In these three films of the 1950s, we witness a change in the role and portrayal of Judas. He is no longer the stereotypical greedy villain, but a victim who displays heroic traits. His actions, words and even his physical appearance and costume support this transition. Filmmakers in the 1950s were making attempts to exonerate the disciple who betrayed Jesus and who was synonymous with Judaism.

Filmmakers' enthusiasm to exonerate Judas did not extend to their portrayals of all Jews and Judaism. There still needed to be a villain in the story: film narratives need an antagonist. This role was placed on the Sanhedrin. This Jewish religious group became the collective villains, the ones to blame for the death of Jesus. Although filmmakers of the 1950s were alert to the dangers of anti-Semitism and to this end made dramatic changes to the way in which Judas was portrayed, it appears that they were not prepared to making sweeping changes to the traditional story of Jesus of Nazareth. In this light, the 1950s can be considered a transition stage.

### *Theology of Acceptance (1961–2014)*

Jesus films made after the Second World War portray Judas, Jews and Judaism in a more positive light. There begins to emerge a theology of acceptance. In the thirteen films in this period, six expressions of acceptance are identified. They are; acceptance of Jesus as Messiah; acceptance of Judas, betrayer and sinner; acceptance of the presence of Judas at the Institution of the Eucharist; acceptance that Judas was forgiven; acceptance of Jewish religious traditions; and acceptance that Judas was acting out his pre-destined role.

In *King of Kings* (1961), Jesus does not call Judas to follow him. Rather, Judas asks to become his disciple after Judas is stirred by Jesus' compassion and authoritative nature when a woman accused of adultery is brought before him. Judas is baptized by John in the Jordan River (*The Greatest Story Ever Told*, 1965). This unique filmic portrayal presents Judas preparing for the coming of the Messiah by repentance and being baptized (Matt 3:1–12; Mark 1:1–8; Luke 3:1–20). When Jesus returns to the Jordan River, Judas is the first to ask to follow Jesus and is the first person Jesus accepts as his disciple. Judas is no longer the last disciple to be called. Similarly, in *Jesus Neustro Señor* (1972), Judas actively pursues Jesus and asks to join the other disciples after he hears Jesus speaking in the synagogue and his declaration, "Today this scripture has been fulfilled in your hearing." Recognizing Jesus as the Messiah, Judas in the miniseries *Jesus of Nazareth* (1977) seeks out Jesus to offer him his services. In *Karunamayudu* (1978), Judas leaves the Zealots and seeks out Jesus because Jesus offers a way of love and peace.

Jesus' recognition of Judas' part in his life is highlighted at the public calling of the disciples from a crowd of followers in the miniseries *Jesus* (1999). Although Jesus knew that Judas would betray him, he publicly shows his acceptance of Judas. He even commissions Judas as a disciple by kissing Judas on the cheek, thus reversing the kiss of betrayal at Gethsemane. The inference is that if Jesus displays such benevolence towards Judas, then should not we also do the same? Although Christianity espouses Jesus' message and second great commandment, "You shall love your neighbor as yourself" (Matt 22:39), two thousand years of tradition show that Judas and the Jews had not been until then afforded this love.

Judas is present throughout the Supper in *Il Vangelo Secondo Matteo*, *The Greatest Story Ever Told*, *Jesus Christ Superstar*, *The Last Temptation of Christ*, *Jesus*, *Color of the Cross* and *Son of God*.

In *The Greatest Story Ever Told*, Jesus gives Judas the bread and the wine even though he knows that Judas has been to see Caiaphas. Although we can tell from Judas' body language that he desired to share the bread and the wine, he accepts that he is not worthy to eat and drink. An obedient Judas leaves the Last Supper to do what he has to do—betray Jesus to the Jewish authorities. Jesus validates the actions of Judas by announcing, "Now is the Son of Man glorified" (John 13:26–30). Judas leaves to fulfil God's plan. Jesus is aware of Judas' betrayal and puts the process in motion that will lead to his death and glorification. Judas' presence at the Last Supper was not only a sign of his acceptance: it was a God-given necessity.

That Judas was pre-destined to betray Jesus is evident in *Jesus*—the miniseries (1999). Although Judas was a stranger to Jesus, when Jesus asked him to follow him, Jesus called Judas by his name and named his father as well. This event showed Jesus' determination to carry out God's will as well as his embracing Judas as the one to make that possible.

It is in the two Jesus musicals that Judas is portrayed as forgiven for betraying Jesus. In *Godspell* (1973) instead of Judas kissing Jesus in the Gethsemane scene, Jesus kisses Judas. The reason for this change in roles according to Stephen Schwartz is that "Jesus is forgiving Judas in advance for what he is about to do. This forgiveness is the hardest thing of all to bear."[17] At the end of the film, Judas, along with the other disciples, is seen carrying Jesus' body through a deserted street of New York. This suggests that Judas is forgiven and restored to the company of the disciples.

In *Jesus Christ Superstar*, the audience is encouraged to sympathize with Judas who hated what Jesus had become but still loved him and wanted to help him. We join with a heavenly choir affirming Judas' decision to betray Jesus ("Blood Money") and again when the same choir laments his death ("Judas' Death"). There is a euphoric atmosphere when Judas re-appears after he has killed himself. He is resurrected! The dazzling white jumpsuit with long fringes that Judas wears in this scene symbolizes purity and transformation. Hence, Judas carries no guilt for his actions. The long fringes hanging from the sleeves are reminiscent of the fringes or tassels on the Jewish prayer shawl. I would suggest that Judas could now fully celebrate his Jewishness without fear of reprisal because he has been redeemed.

17. Schwartz, "*Godspell* Notes for Directors."

Jesus confirms his forgiveness of Judas in *The Passion* (2008). Judas, aware that Jesus knows what is in his heart, says, "Forgive me Lord." Jesus states, "You are forgiven." Jesus even reassures Judas that there is room in his Father's house for him.

Although the Last Supper scene in *Son of God* is a shallow representation of a Passover meal, Judas stays to the end. He eats the bread and drinks the wine, genuinely denies that he would betray Jesus and is tearful when Jesus commands him to do what he needs to do.

The Last Supper scenes in post-Holocaust Jesus films attempt to depict a Passover meal as opposed to a Christian Mass. There are varying degrees of commitment to this sensitivity towards Judaism. It could simply be Jesus praying in Hebrew the *Hamotzi* and *Kiddush* as in *Godspell*. The table or mat could be set with a Seder dish, with traditional herbs, lamb shank, lettuce and other ingredients as shown in *King of Kings* and *Jesus of Nazareth*. The recounting of the story of Moses and the Jewish Exodus could be included at the beginning of the meal as in *Color of the Cross*. The most inclusive and authentic setting of a Passover meal is depicted in *The Last Temptation of Christ*. In the preparation for the Passover, we witness the blowing of the shofar, sacrificing of sheep, singing and dancing, and ritualistic bathing by Jesus and the disciples. At the meal, there are very few "Eucharistic" words although inclusion of the blood clot and subtle reference to transubstantiation link it to a Christian Eucharist. In adherence to Jewish practice, women are present at the meal.

The portrayals of Judas in film have progressively mellowed during the last hundred years. However, an obvious and important question still needs to be answered: "Why has there been such a dramatic shift from damnation to redemption in the filmic portrayals of Judas?"

## Chapter 9

# JUDAS, THE HOLOCAUST AND SHOAH THEOLOGY

### *Introduction*

The costume the Judas character wears in the 1961 epic film, *King of Kings*, can be likened to the striped uniform worn by concentration camp prisoners. This could be viewed as a subtle link between Judas and Jewish Holocaust victims. There is a metamorphosis from the biblical Judas as betrayer, evil and representative of Judaism and Jews, to a post-Holocaust representation of Judas. Susan Gubar explains:

> The Nazi's exploitation of the twelfth apostle and the Aryanization of Christ precipitated a crisis in Christendom that issued in the illegitimacy of the Jewish pariah. Widespread recognition of the betrayal of the Jewish people in the Holocaust stripped Judas of stereotypical traits, as he grew into a revered savior, splitting to incarnate either omniscient but vulnerable good or omnipotent evil.[1]

Film is a powerful medium and nowhere more so than in facilitating the changing of attitudes towards the Jewish race after the liberation of Nazi concentration camps in 1945. The public release of documentary footage showing this barbarism on such a huge scale shook people to the core and informed the world of the true meaning of Adolf Hitler's Final Solution. It also dramatically affected how Christians both related to their Jewish neighbor and how Christian anti-Judaism and anti-Semitism might have contributed towards the murder of six million European Jews. In particular, Christian theologians and scholars began to re-examine those Gospel "texts of terror" that vilified the Jews. They also re-considered the role of Judas Iscariot as the betrayer or the representative of *all* Jews who were tainted with killing the founder of Christianity.

1. Susan Gubar, *Judas: A Biography* (New York: W. W. Norton & Co., 2009), 259.

Film in itself will not establish change and Boggs and Petrie correctly note that "film does not create *new* truths for society for it cannot reshape a society that is not ready for change."[2] The Holocaust was that catalyst for change and film followed by amending its portrayal of Judas, Jews and Judaism in new and enlightened ways.

There are a number of reasons for this change in Judas portrayals in post-Holocaust films: (1) sympathy/guilt for the Holocaust; (2) filmmakers' fear of accusations of anti-Semitism; (3) heightened sensitivity towards Judaism; and (4) a more critical understanding of the Scriptures. The post-Holocaust camera, or cinema, became one of the main contributors to the documenting of the history of the destruction of European Jewry.[3] Moreover, at the same time there emerged a theological response to the Holocaust, which was to be vital in transforming attitudes towards Judaism. Indeed, as Roman Catholic theologian, Johann-Baptist Metz, succinctly put it: "What Christian theologians can do…is…: Never again to do theology in such a way that its construction remains unaffected, or could remain unaffected by Auschwitz."[4] It became essential for theology to break silence and embrace the horror that was the Holocaust in order to redefine its understanding of God as well as question those attributes of dogma and doctrine that may have aided the continued vilification of the Jews.

## *Anti-Semitism, Anti-Judaism and Christian Supersessionism*

To appreciate the vitriol that surrounds Judas, those issues of anti-Semitism and anti-Judaism, together with Christian supersessionism, have been addressed more fully in previous chapters. Christianity has used Judas to advance its demonization of the Jews and to justify Christianity's claim of superseding Judaism.

Demonization and the subsequent dehumanization of the Jew was the foundation of anti-Semitism. Marvin Perry and Frederick Schweitzer write of a "theology of victimization,"[5] asserting that the Jews as a race were eternally cursed for rejecting Jesus as the Christ. A number of the films

2. Boggs and Petrie, *Art of Watching Films*, 516. My emphasis.

3. Judith E. Doneson, *The Holocaust in American Film*, 2nd ed. (Syracuse: Syracuse University Press, 2002), 220.

4. Johann-Baptist Metz, *Emergent Church: Future of Christianity in a Post-bourgeois World* (London: SCM-Canterbury, 1981), 28.

5. Perry and Schweitzer, eds., *Antisemitic Myths*, 6.

analyzed exemplify how the Judas Iscariot character is demonized (*From the Manger to the Cross*, 1912), where he is a victim (*Blade af Satans Bog*, 1921), and where he represents the Jewish people and Judaism (*Christus*, 1916).

Gabriel Wilensky suggests the Christian Church, through its "acts of commission or omission,"[6] may have contributed to the Holocaust. William Nicholls lays the blame on the Christian Church claiming that not only did the Church perpetuate the anti-Semitic myth in the past but also continues to be responsible for it. He comments that an end to anti-Semitism must begin with theology and that the Church should undertake a "theological repentance" for its teaching about the Jews.[7] Similarly, Dan Cohn-Sherbok argues that the roots of modern anti-Semitism are in Christianity itself. He claims that it is primarily the New Testament writings that have "sowed the seeds of contempt" for Jewish people and Judaism.[8] Joel Marcus agrees with this sentiment, maintaining that history shows that "the use and mis-use"[9] of the New Testament have fueled anti-Semitism.

Christian supersessionism is related to anti-Semitism and anti-Judaism for "anti-Jewish Christian theology is at its core supersessionist."[10] According to Daniel Joslyn-Siemiatkoski there are three key components in Christian supersessionism:

> First is the understanding that Jews are no longer in covenant with God. Second, the church has fulfilled the spiritual longings of Israel by entering into full relations with God through the person of Jesus Christ... Third, since the Jews rejected Jesus of Nazareth as the Messiah and actively participated in his crucifixion, God has ended the covenant with the historical people of Israel.[11]

Indeed, even such a distinguished theologian as Karl Barth (1886–1968)—described by some as being the last great supersessionist thinker—believed the Holocaust was a form of divine punishment, that

6. Gabriel Wilensky, *Six Million Crucifixions: How Christian Teachings About Jews Paved the Road to the Holocaust* (San Diego: QWERTY, 2010), 19.

7. Nicholls, *Christian Antisemitism*, 413, 416.

8. Cohn-Sherbok, *Crucified Jew*, 235.

9. Joel Marcus, "Epilogue," in *Anti- Semitism and Early Christianity*, 291–96.

10. Daniel Joslyn-Siemiatkoski, "Moses Received the Torah at Sinai and Handed It On (Mishnah *Avot* 1:1): The Relevance of the Written and Oral Torah for Christians," *ATR* 91, no. 3 (2009): 444.

11. Ibid.

God's covenant with the Jewish people was null and that Christianity was now the true Israel, the community truly chosen by God.[12]

The impact of Christian supersessionist beliefs has been a determining factor in the demonization of the Jewish race. It might be argued that this provided the necessary theological justification for not only the rise of anti-Semitism in Mediaeval Europe but also the rationale for Christians to avert their eyes when the Jews became a scapegoat for all the ills that beset Germany in the 1930s. National Socialism could easily tap into Christian supersessionism.

By claiming that election was transferred from the people of Israel to the community of the new covenant, Christians have engaged in a process of spiritual genocide. The step from such spiritual genocide to physical genocide—from "you have no right to exist as Jews" to "you have no right to exist"—is a step prepared by Christian *religious* anti-Judaism and carried out under Nazi *secular* anti-Semitism.[13]

Acknowledgment of Christian supersessionism is important because it is a key to understanding many of the differing interpretations and representations of the Last Supper scenes in Jesus films.

### *The Holocaust, the Shoah and the Tremendum*

History shows that while the word genocide is new, the concept is ancient.[14] The Holocaust, however, is unparalleled in that, under the order of one political party (the Nazis), Jewish people from all over Europe were systematically transported to death camps and murdered because of their race and religion. In order to comprehend the Holocaust, it has to be seen in its various contexts. Yehuda Bauer explains these contexts: "One is that of Jewish history and civilization, another is that of anti-Semitism, a third is that of European and world history and civilization. There are two other important contexts: that of World War II and that of genocide, which are interconnected."[15]

12. Emil Fackenheim, *To Mend the World: Foundations of Future Jewish Thought* (New York: Shocken, 1982), 284.

13. Darrell J. Fasching, *Narrative Theology After Auschwitz: From Alienation to Ethics* (Minneapolis: Fortress, 1992), 21. Emphasis in the original.

14. Leo Kuper, *Genocide: Its Political Use in the Twentieth Century* (Harmondsworth: Penguin, 1981), 9.

15. Yehuda Bauer, "Reviewing the Holocaust Anew in Multiple Contexts," *JCPA*. http://jcpa.org/article/reviewing-the-holocaust-anew-in-multiple-contexts/.

That the genocide of six million Jews in Europe in the Second World War is given three different designations—Holocaust, Shoah and *Tremendum*—suggests that genocide is a "challenge to human meaning and understanding."[16] It also shows that the meaning given to this act against humanity is a function of the needs and interests of different groups.[17] Consider the Stalinist, Maoist and Pol Pot regimes and the systematic murder of people of Russia, China and Kampuchea. The most common term in use for the murder of European Jewry is the Holocaust.[18] The term was rarely used before the end of the 1950s, although in the 1943 Hollywood film, *Gung Ho!*, the character Lt. Col. Evary Carson (Randolph Scott) describes the pending "sacrifice of our brothers… This holocaust will be a just and equitable peace." Another Hollywood film, *The Keys of the Kingdom* (1944), has a Chinese military officer ask Father Chisholm (Gregory Peck) if he wants to witness the holocaust—the necessary burning of a typhus infested village. It was not until 1968 that the American Library of Congress created a major entry card "Holocaust—Jewish, 1939–1945."[19] "Holocaust" is an Anglicization of the Greek translation of the Hebrew word *'olah*, the burnt offering or sacrifice made to God. Shoah, a biblical word which has been used to mean "destruction," "desolation" or "time of desolation" since the Middle Ages, became the standard Hebrew term for the genocide from the early 1940s. However, since the 1980s, Shoah has come to be widely accepted as more suitable and preferable as the word has no sacrificial connotation.[20] The *Tremendum* is a term coined by Arthur A. Cohen (1928–1986) and is used to describe "the liquidation of the Jewish People."[21] It is derived from German phenomenologist Rudolf Otto's (1869–1937) Latin phrase "*mysterium tremendum et fascinans*"

16. Fasching, *Narrative Theology*, 22.

17. Mintz, *Popular Culture*, 173.

18. I use the term "Holocaust" when describing the "event," because it dominates academic and popular discourse and because I acknowledge that five million non-Jews were also murdered along with six million Jews. When referring to theological implications of the Holocaust I use the term Shoah as a mark of respect for Judaism and Jewish theologians.

19. Michael R. Marrus, "Holocaust Research and Scholarship Today," in *The Holocaust: Voices of Scholars*, ed., Jolanta Ambrosewicz-Jacobs (Cracow: Auschwitz-Birkenau State Museum, 2009), 78.

20. John T. Pawlikowski, "Christian Ethics and the Holocaust: A Dialogue with Post-Auschwitz Judaism," *TS* 49, no. 4 (1988): 651; Fasching, *Narrative Theology*, 22.

21. Arthur Cohen, "In our Terrible Age: The *Tremendum* of the Jews," in *The Holocaust as Interruption*, ed. Elisabeth Schüssler Fiorenza and David Tracy (Edinburgh: T. & T. Clark, 1984), 12.

(fearful and fascinating mystery) to name the awesome mystery that was the object common to all forms of religious experience.[22] Cohen's "*Tremendum*" is an evocative term because it not only expresses immensity, terror and incomprehensibility, but also God's presence.

It was as a response to this calamitous event—Hitler's Final Solution and the extermination of European Jews, which "initiated a hermeneutical rupture" in both Judaism and Christianity—that Shoah theology emerged.[23]

## *Shoah Theology*

In considering God's role in the Holocaust, John Roth sets out the usual responses. Was it "Rejection? Protest? Faithful waiting? Repentance? Martyrdom? Justification of God's way—theodicy? Silence?"[24] For Jews, the Shoah and its central issue was theodicy. How could God permit such evil to occur? Where was God in the suffering of God's people? The Jews believed that they were God's chosen race and their Hebrew Scriptures confirmed it (Gen 12:1–3; 22:17–18 et al.). So what had gone wrong? Intriguingly Alice Eckhardt argues:

> [T]he *Shoah* raises no *new* religious questions. The questions had all been raised before about evil. God's presence or absences, the covenant's continuing existence or its abrogation, repentance or impenitence, forgiveness, martyrdom, and self-sacrifice. And, above all, questions about suffering—especially suffering of the essentially innocent and righteous.[25]

That might be so, but Eckhardt has surely missed the crucial point: that all these religious questions were centered in one dramatic event that affected one religious tradition at a particular time in history. Moreover, it was not caused by a natural disaster, nor something that was self-inflicted, but it was a systematic attempt by a political leader to eradicate a religion and a race of people. It is that consideration of the value of Judaism that is at the heart of Shoah theology. In particular, what fuelled this anti-Semitism, and how can it be avoided in the future?

22. See Rudolf Otto, *The Idea of the Holy*, 2nd ed., trans. John W. Harvey (New York: Oxford University Press, 1958), 12–24.

23. Fasching, *Narrative Theology*, 26.

24. Ibid., 14; Richard L. Rubenstein and John K. Roth, *Approaches to Auschwitz: The Holocaust and Its Legacy*, rev. ed. (Louisville: Westminster John Knox, 2003), 327.

25. Alice Lyons Eckhardt, "Suffering, Theology and the Shoah," in *Contemporary Christian Religious Responses to the Shoah*, ed. Steven L. Jacobs, Studies in the Shoah 6 (Lanham: University Press of America, 1993), 36.

Shoah theology is "the search for meaning between text and context, between Sinai and Auschwitz."[26] Shoah theology was not an immediate response to the Holocaust. Indeed, for nearly two decades after the end of the Second World War, there was virtual silence from theologians, Jewish or Christian. Rosemary Ruether suggests, "Perhaps this was because, before there could be *Shoah* theology, the *Shoah* had to be articulated as story."[27] Although the Holocaust had little meaning for Americans, it did have an impact on America's attitudes towards the Jews. While filmmakers dealt with the issues of "the universalization of the Holocaust, the cinematic image of the Jew, and the questions of historical accuracy,"[28] theologians considered God's role in the genocide. John Roth explains: "No example of mass murder other than the Holocaust has raised so directly or so insistently the question of whether it was an expression of *Heilsgeschichte*, that is, God's providential involvement in history."[29]

George Ginzburg, a survivor of the concentration camp at Auschwitz, asks:

> Where was the G-d in whom we so believed? How could G-d tolerate such injustice and horrors? The German soldiers had, *Gott mit uns* (G-d be with us) and *Unsere Ehre ist Treue* (Our honour is faithfulness), engraved on their belt buckles! If G-d was with them, then he certainly was not with us! And if there was honour in murdering millions of innocents, we certainly didn't understand G-d the way they did.[30]

Ginzburg's dual plea as to where God was when six million Jews were systematically murdered and what is the correct God to worship are theological questions that haunt Jewish and Christian theologians when reflecting on the Holocaust. Indeed, Perry and Schweitzer correctly assert that any research "calls for a 'moral and religious memory' and, particularly among Christians, a very serious reflection on what gave rise to it [the Shoah]."[31]

26. James F. Moore, *Toward a Dialogical Community: A Post-Shoah Christian Theology* (Lanham: University Press of America, 2004), 6.

27. Rosemary Radford Ruether, "Theological and Ethical Reflections on the *Shoah*: Getting Beyond the Victim–Victimizer Relationship," in Jacobs, ed., *Contemporary Christian Responses*, 169.

28. Doneson, *Holocaust*, 61.

29. John K. Roth, "If God Was Silent, Absent, Dead, or Nonexistent, What About Philosophy and Theology?" in *After the Holocaust: Challenging the Myth of Silence*, ed. David Cesarani and Eric J. Sundquist (London: Routledge, 2012), 139.

30. George Ginzburg, *A Will to Live: A Story About Hope and Strength of the Human Spirit*, 2nd rev. ed. (Richmond, VIC: Cycle Press, 2007/2010), 202.

31. Perry and Schweitzer, *Antisemitic Myths*, 230.

A key aspect of Shoah theology is "to remember." The Hebrew Bible is replete with commands "to remember," with the word *sakhor/zakhar* in its various forms occurring no fewer than 169 times.[32] The command "to remember" is directed to Israel, specifically to events that they had every reason to wish to forget. Jewish theology, as explained by Marc Ellis,

> arises out of and is accountable to the experience of the people. Its function is threefold: to articulate significant moments in Jewish history; to become a guide for direction and choice in the present; and to provide the resources necessary to create a future for the Jewish people. The present incorporates the past as a guide and witness. Memory serves as an anchor to those who have gone before us and as a critical reminder of the difficult path of fidelity.[33]

The theological dialogue gave rise to numerous texts and theories, which Dan Cohn-Sherbok, in *Holocaust Theology*, explores in the writings of eight Jewish theologians. He reveals that because of the absence of "an appeal to the Hereafter in which Jews will be compensated for their earthly travail," none of the eight theologians has been able "to reconcile the belief in a loving and just God" with the shocking plight of the Jews at the hands of the Nazis.[34] In brief:

1. Ignaz Maybaum argues that Jews died in the camps for the sins of humankind as God's Suffering Servant and that Hitler was "an instrument to cleanse, to purify, and to punish a sinful world."[35]
2. Emil Fackenheim contends that in Auschwitz, God issued the 614th commandment: "Jews are forbidden to grant posthumous victories to Adolf Hitler."[36]

32. Jonathan Sacks, *Tradition in an Untraditional Age: Essays on Modern Jewish Thought* (London: Valentine Mitchell, 1990), 141. Examples of remember commands are, "Remember that you were a slave in the land of Egypt" (Deut 5:15; 15:15; 16:12; 24:18; 24:22); "Remember what Amalek did to you" (Deut 25:17).

33. Marc H. Ellis, *Toward a Jewish Theology of Liberation* (Maryknoll, NY: Orbis Books 1987), 110.

34. Dan Cohn-Sherbok, preface to *Holocaust Theology* (London: Lamp, 1989), xi.

35. Ignaz Maybaum, *The Face of God After Auschwitz* (Amsterdam: Polak & Van Gennep, 1965), 66–67.

36. Emil Fackenheim, "Jewish Faith and the Holocaust: A Fragment," *Commentary* 46, no. 2 (August 1968): 32.

3. Eliezer Berkovits believes God was present during the Holocaust, but hidden. God did not intervene because at creation God had bestowed free-will on humanity.[37]
4. Arthur A. Cohen redefined God's nature and, like Berkovits, believed that God does not intervene because of human free-will. Therefore, it is a mistake to hold God responsible for the Holocaust.[38]
5. Richard Rubenstein argues that after the Holocaust, it is impossible to believe in God and believes Jews should abandon the traditional belief of the God of history.[39]
6. Marc Ellis developed a post-Holocaust liberation theology and "a call to *teshuvah* [repentance]: commitment and solidarity in all their pain and possibility."[40]
7. Bernard Maza argues that the Holocaust was the result of divine providence.[41]
8. Elie Wiesel traces the erosion of his faith from fascination with God's mystery to questioning God and cessation of prayer.[42]

Jonathan Sacks, in *Tradition in an Untraditional Age*, comments that it is not rabbis, theologians or philosophers whose writing about the Holocaust is the most compelling, but novelists like Elie Wiesel. Sacks explains, "A novel is a vehicle for unresolved tension and ambiguity, and is evidence that a problem still disturbs and bewilders us."[43] Film is also an effective vehicle for this disruption and filmmakers have used films to express that "unresolved tension and ambiguity." Scorsese's *The Last Temptation of Christ* (1988) is an example.

### *The Holocaust: The Seelisberg Conference—Ten Points*

The horrors of the Holocaust, Christian complicity in the denigration of Jews and combating anti-Semitism were the prime motives behind the Seelisberg Conference—International Conference of Christians and Jews. Held from July 30 through August 5, 1947, sixty-five representatives (Jews, Protestants, Roman Catholics and Orthodox) from seventeen

37. Eliezer Berkovits, *Faith After the Holocaust* (New York: KATV, 1973), 63–64.

38. Arthur A. Cohen, *Tremendum* (New York: Crossroad, 1981), 1–8.

39. Richard L. Rubenstein, *After Auschwitz* (Indianapolis: Bobbs Merrill, 1966), 151–53.

40. Ellis, *Toward a Jewish Theology*, 111–12.

41. Bernard Maza, *With Fury Poured Out* (New York: KTAV, 1986), 124–27.

42. Elie Wiesel, *Night* (New York: Bantam Books, 1982), 61–66.

43. Sacks, *Tradition*, 153.

countries met in Switzerland and proposed "The Ten Points of Seelisberg."[44] These ten points focused on Christianity's roots in Judaism and became an important cornerstone in Jewish–Christian dialogue. This document marked the beginning of a revision in Christian attitudes to Judaism and the Ten Points could be considered another Decalogue, another set of Ten Commandments (Exod 20:1–17). Apart from having ten directives, the language also bears similarity: the introductory words of "Remember" and "Avoid" can be likened to commands.

The concept of Ten Points flowed into the film industry and particularly into the production of Jesus films and the portrayals of Judas. Each of these ten points provided an impetus for a theology of acceptance for the filmic Judas, Judaism and Jewish people. The way in which each point is pertinent to film and to Shoah theology is best illustrated by citing each Seelisberg point; including a Shoah theology explanation; and providing examples of how post-Holocaust Jesus films integrate the point.

*1. "Remember that One God speaks to us all through the Old and the New Testaments."*

*Shoah Theology*. In Judaism, the fundamental relationship in which the Jew stands is covenant. Eugene Borowitz explains that throughout Scripture and rabbinic literature, the terms of the covenant are repeated, again and again, and that their fulfilment is historical record.[45] The covenant has not been broken by God, nor has God permitted the people to "shake it off."[46] It is therefore out of necessity that the notion of *brith* or covenant must now be redefined. Steven Jacobs states, "A violated but never abrogated biblical understanding of covenant only makes sense in relation to the God-who-acts-in-history."[47] Ruether adds that in post-Holocaust Christian theology, "Israel's election has been elevated as a powerful symbol of the Jewish people's intimacy with God, and as proof of the continuing efficacy of the covenant."[48]

44. Christian Rutishauser, "The 1947 Seelisberg Conference: The Foundation of the Jewish–Christian Dialogue," *SCJR* 2, no. 2 (2007): 34–53. http://escholarship.bc.edu/scjr/vol2/iss2.

45. Eugene Borowitz, *Choices in Modern Jewish Thought* (New York: Behrman House, 1983), 281.

46. David Weiss, "The Holocaust and the New Covenant," in *Holocaust: Religious and Philosophical Implications*, ed. John K. Roth and Michael Berengaum (New York: Paragon House, 1989), 74–75.

47. Steven L. Jacobs, *Rethinking Jewish Faith: The Child of a Survivor Responds* (Albany: State University of New York Press, 1994), 120.

48. Ruether, *Faith and Fratricide*, 272.

Ruether notes:

> Everything in Judaism becomes "Old Testament" in relation to the Christian "New Testament." The relationship between the two testaments becomes a triple supersession: supersession ontologically, morally, and historically. Everything Jewish is, at best, an outward "shadow," which symbolizes on a bodily level the spiritual meaning realized in the Christian dispensation.[49]

*Film*. Christian supersessionism—although a major contributor to anti-Judaism—is no longer overtly promoted in Jesus films. For instance, in over half of the films studied, the Last Supper is part of a Jewish Passover meal and not a Christian Mass. Jesus introduces the meal by telling the *Maggid*, the story of the Passover, of Moses and the Jews' escape from Egypt. When blessing the bread and the wine, Jesus prays the *Kiddush* and the *Hamotzi.* Jesus does not include the word "new" when describing covenant.

*2. "Remember that Jesus was born of a Jewish mother of the seed of David and the people of Israel, and that His everlasting love and forgiveness embraces His own people and the whole world."*

*Shoah Theology*. The Christian Church is rooted in the life of the people of Israel. Christians look upon Abraham as both their spiritual ancestor and father of their faith. The ministry of Jesus and the life of the early Christian community were thoroughly rooted in the Judaism of their day. Michael McGarry identifies Christ as being "the link…enabling Gentiles to be numbered among Abraham's 'offspring' and therefore fellow-heirs with the Jews according to God's promise."[50] Jesus submitted himself to the Law (Gal 4:4), extolled respect for it (Matt 5:17–20) and invited obedience to it (Matt 8:4).[51]

Karl Barth preached, "Jesus Christ was a Jew." Barth explains that "anyone who believes in Christ, who was himself a Jew, and died for Gentiles and Jews: simply cannot be involved in the contempt for Jews and ill-treatment of them which is now the order of the day."[52]

49. Ibid., 164.

50. Michael McGarry, *Christology After Auschwitz* (New York: Paulist, 1977), 57–58.

51. Eugene J. Fisher, "The Bible, the Jews, and the Passion," *America* 190, no. 5 (2004): 7–9.

52. Letter to E. Steffens, January 10, 1934, cited in Eberhard Busch, *Karl Barth: His Life from Letters and Autobiographical Texts*, trans. John Bowden (Philadelphia: Fortress, 1976), 223.

*Film*. Post-Holocaust Jesus films stress Jesus' Jewishness. He is named Yeshua in *The Color of the Cross.* The rite of circumcision (*brit milah*) is shown in *Jesus of Nazareth*. He is called "Rabbi" in *Godspell*. In *The Passion*, Jesus observes payment of Temple taxes, the Jewish custom of a dove offering and Passover lamb sacrifice.

*3. "Remember that the first disciples, the apostles, and the first martyrs were Jews."*

*Shoah Theology*. Memory is inextricably connected with the issue of identity that transcends history. Shalom Rosenberg claims that before he remembers, he must know himself and his identity: what is his and what is not.[53] Christians need to remember that Christianity is rooted in Judaism. Taking Scripture literally, ignorance or lack of consideration of the *Sitz im Leben* (situation in life or setting), and the lack of historical investigation, have been factors in the misinterpretation of the New Testament and the resulting anti-Semitic claims. One needs to be cognisant of the prejudices of the competing claims of the Gospel writers and their relationship to Jesus who was a Jew.

Stephen Haynes notes: "While Holocaust theologians argued that renewed Christian–Jewish relations would never be realized as long as Christians dogmatically clung to their Scriptural traditions, many biblical scholars now concern themselves with the importance of the New Testament for a positive understanding of Israel."[54] Alan Davies, for example, writes that anti-Judaism is "inherent in any ideology which regards the New Testament as sacrosanct after the fashion of Protestant biblicalism."[55]

*Film*. Portraying the Jewish cultural and religious identity of these first-century people has been achieved by the inclusion of Jewish costumes, the wearing of prayer shawls, untrimmed beards and *payots* (side curls). Hebrew language is used. Jewish rituals include blessings, sharing a Passover meal—clearly identified by the narrator as "Passover of the

53. Shalom Rosenberg, "The Holocaust: Lessons, Explanation, Meaning," in *The Impact of the Holocaust on Jewish Theology*, ed. Steven T. Katz (New York: New York University Press, 2005), 83.

54. Stephen Haynes, *Prospects for Post-Holocaust Theology* (Atlanta: Scholars Press, 1991), 21.

55. Alan T. Davies, ed., *Anti-Semitism and the Foundations of Christianity* (New York: Paulist, 1979), 12.

unleavened bread"—ritual bathing and showing Jesus and the disciples at prayer in the synagogue. Use of Jewish songs such as "Kol Nidre" also promotes Jewishness and Judaism. In a post-Crucifixion scene in *Son of God*, the disciples say *Kaddish*, the Jewish mourning prayer.

*4. "Remember that the fundamental commandment of Christianity, to love God and one's neighbor, proclaimed already in the Old Testament and confirmed by Jesus, is binding upon both Christians and Jews in all human relationship, without any exception."*

*Shoah Theology*. How could the Holocaust take place when Christians are commanded to love "your neighbor as yourself"? Frank Littell states, "The moral claims of religion-in-general died at Auschwitz. The pretensions of the Christian intellectuals to a love of humanity—quite divorced from love, even compassion, toward specific persons and groups—floundered on the mechanical precision of the Nazi extermination of European Jewry."[56]

It must be noted that during the chaos there were instances where Christians saved and rescued Jews. "Not all German Christians followed a false messiah or the political preacher of hatred and division. A faithful remnant resisted actively and publicly the rise of National Socialism and Adolf Hitler. Some created and signed the Theological Declaration of Barmen, while others preached against idolatry, falsehood, and folly of nationalism."[57]

The rescuers of Jews embodied the practice of a Christian faith called for in the fourth Seelisberg Point and grounded in the biblical teachings "to love your neighbor" (Mark 12:31) and "care for the sojourner in your midst" (Prov 25:21–22). Their actions answered in the affirmative Cain's question, "Am I my brother's keeper?" (Gen 4:9) and removed the limitations or barriers to the lawyer's question in the Gospel of Luke, "Who is my neighbor?" (Luke 10:29).[58]

*Film*. Post-Second World War filmic portrayals of the relationships between Judas, Jews and Jesus encourage tolerance and understanding. Jesus, at the Last Supper, gives his disciples a new commandment "to

56. Franklin H. Littell, "Church Struggle and the Holocaust," in *The German Church Struggle and the Holocaust*, ed. Franklin H. Littell and Hubert G. Locke (Detroit: Wayne State University Press, 1975), 19.

57. Steven Jacobs, ed., *Contemporary Religious Responses to the Shoah*, Studies in the Shoah 6 (Lanham: University Press of America, 1993), 94.

58. Ibid.

love one another" (John 13:34–35) and offers a peace blessing. The film *Godspell* expands on this directive with the focus on building loving communities and on forgiveness for all.

*5. "Avoid distorting or misrepresenting biblical or post-biblical Judaism with the object of extolling Christianity."*

*Shoah Theology*. A major contributor to anti-Semitism and anti-Judaism is the wrongful and ill-informed perceptions of the Jewish people. Steven Jacobs contends that "the foundational Jewish and Christian scriptural texts can no longer be read, understood, and either interpreted or reinterpreted the way they were" prior to the Second World War.[59] James F. Moore posits, "any post-*Shoah* theology must be constructed in dialogue and focused on dialogue, not on received traditions."[60] Nora Levin asserts, "The fundamental problem seems to lie in the very nature of theological discourse."[61] Jews exist only in terms defined by the tensions and conflicts between the Old and the New Testaments—"as witness, rejected by God, doomed to suffer, to wander, to be denied salvation until they accept Jesus as Christ."[62] What Levin is describing is Christian supersessionism and holds this belief responsible for the plight of Jewish people.

Steven Jacobs proposes that Christians re-think

> (1) the whole notion of God the Father and His Son Jesus the Redeeming Christ in an unredeemed world that could and did countenance the *Shoah*; (2) the very "mission" of the church specifically toward the Jewish people and generally towards all non-Christian peoples in the aftermath of the *Shoah*, as well as toward each other; (3) the proper relationship between the "parent" Judaism and the "child" Christianity, between Jews and Christians, given the long, sad, and tragic history of that relationship, or, rather, nonrelationship; and (4) a long, hard look at the historical realities and implications of the relationship between Jews and Christians, beginning with the birth of Christianity and the person of Paul and including the rise of Nazism, all *before* turning to our contemporary world.[63]

59. Steven Leonard Jacobs, "Toward the Construction of a Post-*Shoah* Interfaith Dialogical Universal Ethic," *Zygon* 38, no. 3 (2003): 735.

60. James F. Moore, "Re-Envisioning Christianity: A New Era in Christian Theological Interpretation of Christian Texts," *Cross CURR* 50, no. 4 (2000/2001): 437.

61. Nora Levin, "Whither Christian–Jewish Dialogue," *Judaism* 33, no. 2 (1984): 235.

62. Ibid.

63. Jacobs, *Rethinking Jewish Faith*, 90. Emphasis in the original.

Haynes advises that "careful theological reflection" be given to the relationship between Jewish Monotheism as opposed to Christian Trinitarianism, and questions whether it is necessary or useful to refer to Jesus as the Messiah of Israel, and whether "the identity of Jesus as Israel's Messiah [is] an essential part of Christian faith."[64]

*Film.* Most post-Holocaust filmmakers avoid exaggerating Jewish legalism and negative portrayals of the Jewish priesthood and Judaism. Denigration of the Jewish leaders is avoided, as is Jesus' denunciation of the false piety of the scribes and of the Pharisees' hypocrisy (Matt 23). Jewish Passover rituals such as the blowing of the shofar, and sacrificing of sheep and splashing their blood over altars are shown. While miracles and Jesus' transfiguration were popular in the silent film era, post-Holocaust Jesus films were reluctant to portray the divinity of Jesus. If viewers of *Last Temptation* were unfamiliar with the story of changing the water into wine at the marriage in Cana (John 2:1–11) they would not have realized that it was Jesus who performed that miracle.

*6. "Avoid using the words 'Jews' in the exclusive sense of the enemies of Jesus, and the words 'the enemies of Jesus' to designate the whole Jewish people."*

*Shoah Theology.* Jew and Judaism have held generally negative connotations in Christian theology since the second century. Israel has found a more ambitious function in Christian thought. One reason for this stems from Scripture itself. The formula "the Jews" is used in the New Testament to represent those who oppose Jesus, Paul, or the early church, while "Israel" is often adopted to refer to those Jews who believe in Jesus as the Messiah.[65]

Ruether alerts us to the differing interpretation of Messiah as "the core of anti-Judaism."[66] Its meaning as reinterpreted by Christians was so radically separated from what it meant in Jewish tradition that it hindered communication between Judaism and Christianity. Ruether has coined a metaphor to describe anti-Judaism, claiming that this developed

64. Haynes, *Prospects for Post-Holocaust Theology*, 277.

65. Ibid., 12–13.

66. Rosemary Radford Ruether, "Anti-Semitism and Christian Theology," in *Auschwitz: Beginning of a New Era?*, ed. Eva Fleischner (New York: KTAV, 1977), 80.

theologically in Christianity "as the left-hand of Christology"—anti-Judaism was "the negative side" of the Christian claim that Jesus was the Messiah.[67] Ruether admonishes the Christian Church claiming it was "imbued with a self-image of infallible righteousness resulting from its doctrine of Messianic fulfilment, and has typically displaced evil upon outside enemies, the unredeemed world and the godless forces without its walls, rather than take responsibility for its own sins."[68]

*Film.* In 1947, the Hollywood Motion Picture Project, later to be known as the Jewish Film Advisory Committee, was formed in Los Angeles. The Project sought, not always successfully, to work closely with Hollywood filmmakers, not as censors but as advisors, in order to avoid negative portrayals of Jews in film and television and further to improve the image of the Jews in the minds of Americans. Jewish characters, Jewish names and the word Jew itself were edited out of films. In Philip Saville's *The Gospel of John* (2004), whenever the Johannine term "the Jews" is used in his Gospel, the film changed the words to "the Jewish leaders." In latter Jesus films, efforts were made to ensure that the Jews were not blamed for the death of Jesus and all guilt was transferred to the Romans. This is evident in Roger Young's miniseries *Jesus* (1999) where anti-Semitism was circumvented, with the plot and script ensuring that the Jews were blameless.

*7. "Avoid presenting the Passion in such a way as to bring the odium of the killing of Jesus upon all Jews or upon Jews alone. It was only a section of the Jews in Jerusalem who demanded the death of Jesus, and the Christian message has always been that it was the sins of mankind which were exemplified by those Jews and the sins in which all men share that brought Christ to the Cross."*

*Shoah Theology*. The threat of anti-Judaism re-appears every time the Passion narratives are read. Amy-Jill Levine offers six strategies to overcome difficult texts: "excision; retranslate; romanticize; allegorize; historize; and admit the problem."[69] For centuries, clergy and theologians have solidified their power by distorting the historicity of the crucifixion.

67. Ibid.

68. Ibid., 92.

69. Amy-Jill Levine, "Holy Week and the Hatred of the Jews," *ABC Religion and Ethics*" (April 4, 2012). http://www.abc.net.au/religion/articles/2012/04/04/3470618.htm.

It is not surprising then that Hitler concluded that the Jews sealed Jesus' fate on the cross.[70] Jacobs is correct in stating, "The only faithful response to suffering is to oppose and transform it. It is faithless and cynical to exalt the humiliation and suffering of Jesus to legitimate violence against Jews and attacks on Judaism."[71] The same can be said about the treatment of Judas Iscariot.

*Film.* As early as 1927, sole responsibility for the death of Jesus was placed on Cecil B. DeMille's Caiaphas in *The King of Kings*. Mel Gibson's *The Passion of the Christ* also had Caiaphas claim sole responsibility. In *King of Kings* and *Godspell*, significant elements of the Passion narrative are omitted. Jewish religious authorities have no involvement in persecuting Jesus during his ministry, in the conspiracy to arrest him and for his death. It is Pilate who bears that responsibility. In *The Greatest Story Ever Told*, the Dark Hermit (Satan) carries the blame. The consensus now is that the Romans are responsible for Jesus' crucifixion. Post-Holocaust films emphasize the political status of crucifixion rather Jewish religious needs.

*8. Avoid referring to the scriptural curses, or the cry of a raging mob: His blood be upon us and our children, without remembering that this cry should not count against the infinitely more weighty words of our Lord: Father forgive them, for they know not what they do.*

*Shoah Theology*. The deicide accusation (John 19:6) records that the Jewish authorities and those who followed their lead pressed for the death of Christ by shouting out, "Crucify him! Crucify him!" This theological construct provided the cornerstone of Christian anti-Semitism.[72] Jacobs argues correctly that the starting point for the re-examination of Christianity and Jewish–Christian relations is with the New Testament text and its supposed anti-Semitism.[73] He notes that a "more accurate understanding of that negative depiction would be to see the controversy as 'in-house, intra-family Jewish debate and dispute,' with the Gospel of John excepted, being an attack on the Jews by one outside the family."[74]

70. Adolf Hitler, *Mein Kampf*, trans. Ralph Manneheim (Boston: Houghton Mifflin, 1971), 307.

71. Jacobs, *Contemporary Christian Responses*, 101.

72. Edward Flannery, *The Anguish of the Jews* (New York: Paulist, 1985), 288.

73. Jacobs, *Rethinking Jewish Faith*, 90.

74. Ibid.

Ellis Rivkin, in considering Jesus' response to his fate, concludes, "And Jesus understood. Twisted in agony on the cross—the symbol of imperial Roman cruelty and ruthless disregard of the human spirit—Jesus lifted his head upward toward God and pleaded, 'Father, forgive them; for they know not what they do.' "[75]

*Film*. This "blood curse" and the resultant accusation of deicide was the most damning of all claims against the Jews. It is now omitted from films. It is noted, however, that while the curse was not included in the English subtitles of Gibson's *The Passion*, it could be heard in the Aramaic being spoken.[76]

*9. "Avoid promoting the superstitious notion that the Jewish people are reprobate, accursed, reserved for a destiny of suffering."*

*Shoah Theology*. Jacobs posits Christians who subscribe to the belief that Jews are reprobates, "have taken God's place, and substituted their own moral and eternal judgment on Jews for God's more compassionate quest to be re-united with the covenant people."[77]

In coming to terms with the Holocaust, a person must not only consider why this genocide took place but also attempt to empathize with the victims. Clark Williamson believes

> Christian theology has to go beyond the emphasis on historical consciousness and historicity as those were stressed in the Liberal and Neo-Reformation eras. It must move into the actual history of suffering and oppression, which it cannot do without facing the awful ways in which it has contributed to that history, particularly in the case of the praxis of the teaching and contempt for the Jews and Judaism and the reality of the *Shoah*.[78]

*Film*. Judas portrayals, particularly in the Silent Era, presented a stereotypical Jew, easily identified by his appearance, his dark clothes and his sinister interaction with the camera. Judas was clearly the villain who was deceived by the devil. Post-Holocaust films rarely use the demonic motivation for Judas' actions as it is perceived as being anti-Semitic. Similarly, the traditional greed motivation is also now avoided.

75. Ellis Rivkin, *What Crucified Jesus?* (Nashville: Abingdon, 1984), 124.

76. Cohen, *Christ Killers*, 249.

77. Jacobs, *Contemporary Christian Religious Responses*, 100.

78. Clark Williamson, *A Guest in the House of Israel: Post-Holocaust Church Theology* (Louisville: Westminster John Knox, 1993), 14.

*10. "Avoid speaking of the Jews as if the first members of the Church had not been Jews."*

*Shoah Theology*. Edward Kessler states that it was the Shoah, "first and foremost," which provoked an intense desire among many Christians and Jews to learn about the history, theology and other aspects of Jewish–Christian relations, resulting in Christianity's reassessment of its relationship with Judaism.[79] The 1965 Papal Encyclical *Nostra Aetate* opened the way to interreligious dialogue. This key work focused on the ways the Roman Catholic Church had traditionally viewed Jews and Judaism. Relevant to Point 10 is *Nostra Aetate's* recognition that "the apostles, the pillars on which the church stands, are of Jewish descent, as are many of those early disciples who proclaimed the Gospel of Christ to the world."[80]

*Film*. The story of Judas as a villain was to accentuate the difference between Christian and Jew. Biblical scholarship during the past few decades has revised this notion and Judas is viewed in a more positive light. This is evident in Jesus post-Holocaust films as well. Judas is a supportive, faithful and committed disciple of Jesus who does as his Master tells him. His action of handing Jesus over to the Jewish religious leaders was pre-ordained and was to fulfil God's will.

### *Summary*

Academic research on anti-Semitism rarely makes reference to the Seelisberg Conference. Christian Rutishauser believes "this might be understood from the fact that the conference set forth few theoretical statements focusing instead on recognized practical solutions for fighting anti-Semitism. Its theoretical contributions lay instead in the realm of Jewish–Christian relationship."[81] Haynes suggests:

> Many Jews and Christians doubt the Christian theology has come far enough to provide a basis for genuine dialogue and mutual acceptance between "average" Christians and Jews... If such prospects for post-Holocaust

79. Edward Kessler, "The Future of Jewish–Christian Relations," in *The Future of Jewish-Christian Dialogue*, ed. Dan Cohn-Sherbok (Lewiston: Edwin Mellen, 1999), 150–52.

80. Paul VI, "Declaration On the Relation of the Church to Non-Christian Religions—*Nostra Aetate*" (October 28, 1965). http://www.vatican.va/archive/hist_councils/ii_vatican_council/documents/vat-ii_decl_19651028_nostra-aetate_en.html.

81. Rutishauser, *Seelisberg Conference*, 35.

> theology are to become an effective part of the history of the church–Israel relationship which has been so poisoned in the past, courage and imagination will be required in the future, as well as the grace of the God whom Jews and Christians serve.[82]

The Seelisberg Ten Points present a way forward in ensuring that anti-Semitism is never permitted to flourish again. Film is a powerful educational teaching tool and has been instrumental in helping to assimilate the Holocaust in popular consciousness.[83] If used effectively, film can counter the claims of Christian supersessionism and combat anti-Judaism and anti-Semitism, perhaps leading to a more open Jewish–Christian dialogue and reconciliation.

82. Haynes, *Prospects for Post-Holocaust Theology*, 287–88.
83. Doneson, *The Holocaust*, 5.

# Conclusion

We began this journey with a description of the manufactured Jew—Judas Iscariot—and the question was posed, "Jewish enough for you?" Christendom's traditional regard of Judas with deep loathing and suspicion is based on the Gospels that identify him as "the one who betrayed Jesus." Judas became synonymous with Judaism, the Jewish people and anti-Semitism. The development, exaggerated embellishment and impact of the Judas story and anti-Semitism can be mapped through three stages: demonization, isolation and elimination. These stages reflected Christianity's attitudes towards Jews from post-biblical times to the present. With the arrival of "moving pictures," these predominantly Christian interpretations were promoted through the production of Jesus films.

Throughout this film study, I sought answers to these three questions. (1) How is Judas portrayed in film? (2) Why does the Judas character change? (3) What are the theological implications of these changes?

Questions one and two can be briefly answered through the chosen films, which are graphic in their interpretations of the Judas character. The archetypal "Judas-as-Jew" is common to most of the films, as are the negative traits and indicators we have learned to define Judas with art, doctrine and misguided interpretations of text. It is with an historical and social background linked to the era of each film presented, that we are able to appreciate the changes that the filmic Judas undergoes as the viewing audience become more educated and (perhaps) more tolerant to competing perspectives, and, not ignoring or forgetting the intentional bias of the film's director. Film has been an important medium in shaping and reflecting societal attitudes and beliefs. This is nowhere better seen than in the depiction of Judas in Jesus films.

At the beginning of the twentieth century when Jesus films were first screened, Judas was the epitome of evil: the villainous Jew. Filmmakers cast Judas in this way as this was the Judas audiences recognized and *expected*! In the following three decades, filmmakers, as a result of critical biblical study, were more circumspect about accepting the alleged historicity of the Gospel accounts. Filmmakers granted Judas a more nuanced and significant role in the narrative. His motive for betrayal—if indeed it is such an action—became a sub-plot, and by the middle of the twentieth century, filmmakers moved away from type-casting Judas, as well as the Jewish religious members and people, as the villain. Another significant factor for modifying the Judas–Jewish perspective was the catastrophe of the Nazi Holocaust, with the fear of accusations of anti-Semitism also contributing to change. Judas was relegated to a cameo role so that filmmakers could focus on the ministry of Jesus. It was during the 1960s that Judas became the protagonist. His role in the film was as important as that of Jesus. Judas is no longer seen as the betrayer of Jesus but as the facilitator of Jesus' sacrifice on the cross. Judas becomes the "agent of salvation."

With such dramatic changes made to the filmic Judas character, one presumes there would be concurrent theological changes. Films from the silent era and the thirties promoted Christian supersession or replacement theology, the mistaken medieval idea that Christianity (*Ecclesia*) has replaced Judaism (*Synagoga*). What is evident, particularly in the Last Supper scene, is a theology of rejection; rejection of Jesus as Messiah, rejection of Judas at the Institution of the Eucharist, Judas' rejection of partaking of the bread and wine and rejection of Judaism. In contrast, Jesus films produced post-Holocaust espouse a theology of acceptance. This is seen in the acceptance of Jesus as Messiah, acceptance of Judas, betrayer and sinner, acceptance of Judas' presence at the institution of the Eucharist, acceptance that Judas was acting out his pre-destined role, acceptance that Judas is forgiven and acceptance of Jewish religious traditions.

Filmmakers have developed the portrayal of Judas and Judaism even if viewers did not always recognize this. Directors utilizing camera shots, dialogue, choice of actors and other equally important elements of film have been able to shape their own interpretation and understanding of the Judas character. Although directors/filmmakers do not reflect changing societal attitudes in their films, they may be shaping those attitudes more than they are reflecting them.

The critical discovery of this comprehensive film study was a visible rehabilitation of the Judas character together with an implied restoration of Judaism. Through this varied sample of Jesus films we are witness to the evolution of Judas from damnation to redemption.

In the closing scene of the film *Sorry, Judas* (1993/2004), Judas is in a public telephone box. He is phoning the Vatican. However, he has to leave a message because the pope is unavailable to answer his call.

> This is Judas Iscariot, Blood Acre, a couple of millennia too late. My only sin as I understand it is that I facilitated Christianity. My message is therefore this: Isn't it about time you said, "Thank you"?

# BIBLIOGRAPHY


Abel, Richard. *The Ciné Goes to Town: French Cinema 1896–1914.* Updated and expanded ed. Berkeley: University of California Press, 1998.

———. *The Red Rooster Scare: Making Cinema American 1900–1910.* Berkeley: University of California Press, 1999.

Aichele, George. "Translation as De-canonization: Matthew's Gospel According to Pasolini." *Cross CURR* 51, no. 4 (Winter 2002): 524–34.

Aichele, George, and Richard Walsh, eds. *Screening Scripture: Intertextual Connection Between Scripture and Film.* Harrisburg, PA: Trinity Press International, 2002.

Allport, Gordon. "The Jew as Scapegoat." Pages 109–11 in *Can It Happen Again? Chronicles of the Holocaust.* Edited by Roselle K. Chartock and Jack Spencer. New York: Black Dog & Levanthal, 2001.

Anderson, Claud. "Black Is Beautiful and the Color Preferences of Afro-American Youth." *Journal of Negro Education* 46, no. 1 (Winter 1977): 76–88.

Apostolos-Cappadona, Diane. "From Eve to the Virgin and Back Again: The Image of Woman in Contemporary (Religious) Film." Pages 111–27 in May, ed., *New Image of Religious Film.*

Armes, Roy. "Images of France." *The Movie: The Illustrated History of the Cinema* 16 (1980): 301–4.

Atkinson, Michael. "Time Regained: Remembering Julien Duvivier, a Casualty of Auteurism." *Moving Image Source.* http://www.movingimagesource.us/articles/time-regained-20090504.

Babington, Bruce Francis, and Peter William Evans. *Biblical Epics: Sacred Narrative in the Hollywood Cinema.* Eugene: Wipf & Stock, 1993.

Bald, Margaret. *Literature Suppressed on Religious Grounds.* New York: Infobase, 2006.

Barsotti, Catherine M., and Robert K. Johnston. *Finding God in the Movies: 33 Films of Reel Faith.* Grand Rapids: Baker Books, 2004.

Barton, Joseph. "The Godspell Story." http://www.geocities.com/Broadway/Lobby/4209/america.html.

Bauer, Yehuda. "Reviewing the Holocaust Anew in Multiple Contexts." *Jerusalem Center for Public Affairs.* http://jcpa.org/article/reviewing-the-holocaust-anew-in-multiple-contexts/.

Baugh, Lloyd. *Imaging the Divine: Jesus and Christ-Figures in Film.* Franklin: Sheed & Ward, 1997.

———. "Martin Scorsese's *The Last Temptation of Christ*: A Critical Reassessment of Its Sources, Its Theological Problems, and Its Impact on the Public." Pages 229–30 in Middleton, ed., *Scandalizing Jesus?*

Baum, Paul Franklin. *The Mediaeval Legend of Judas Iscariot (1916)*. Reprinted from the *Publications of the Modern Language Association of America* 31, no. 3. Kessinger Legacy Reprints. Whitefish, MT: Kessinger, n.d.

Bazin, André. *What Is Cinema?* Berkeley: University of California Press, 1968.

Benofy, Susan. "Communion by Intinction: A 'New' Way of Receiving Communion in Both Kinds." *Adoremus Bulletin* 9, no. 6 (September 2003). http://www.adoremus.org/0903Intinction.html.

Berkovits, Eliezer. *Faith After the Holocaust*. New York: KTAV, 1973.

Bertolucci, Giuseppe. "Pier Paolo Pasolini's Anger." *New Ways* 36 (September 6, 1962), *WUZ*. http://www.wuz.it/articolo-film/2498/rabbia-pasolini-bertolucci.html.

Beuken, Wim., Seán Freyne and Anton Weiler, eds. *Messianism Through History*. Concilium. London: SCM, 1993.

Bien, Peter. "Nikos Kazantzakis' Novels on Film." *Journal of Modern Greek Studies* 18. 1 (2000): 161–69.

Blaising, Craig A. "The Future of Israel as a Theological Question." *Journal of Evangelical Theological Studies* 44. 3 (2001): 435–450.

Boggs, Joseph M., and Dennis W. Petrie. *The Art of Watching Films*. 7th ed. Boston: McGraw-Hill, 2008.

Bond, Paul. "Bible Producers Cut Satan Scenes from 'Son of God' Following Obama Controversy." *hollywoodreporter.com*. http://www.hollywoodreporter.com/news/bible-producers-cut-satan-scenes-680781.

Bondanella, Peter. *A History of Italian Cinema*. New York: Continuum, 2009.

Borowitz, Eugene. *Choices in Modern Jewish Thought*. New York: Behrman House, 1983.

Bradshaw, Paul F. *The Search for the Origins of Christian Worship: Sources and Methods for the Study of Early Liturgy*. 2nd ed. London: SPCK, 2002.

Brocker, Frances L. and J. Nasgowitz. "Interview of James Kempe Friedrich—Collection 327." *Billy Graham Center Archives*, Wheaton, IL. Accession 85-100, July 30, 1986. http://www2.wheaton.edu/bgc/archives/GUIDES/327.htm.

Brockman, Stephen. *A Critical History of German Film*. Suffolk: Camden House, 2010.

Brunetta, Gian Piero. *The History of Italian Cinema: A Guide to Italian Film from Its Origins to the Twenty-first Century*. Translated by Jeremy Parzen. Princeton: Princeton University Press, 2003.

Bultmann, Rudolf. "Prophecy and Fulfillment." Pages 50–75 in *Essays on Old Testament Hermeneutics*. Edited by Claus Westermann. Translated by James J. C. Greig. London: SCM, 1963.

Busch, Eberhard. *Karl Barth: His Life from Letters and Autobiographical Texts*. Translated by John Bowden. Philadelphia: Fortress, 1976.

Campbell, Richard H., and Michael R. Pitts. *The Bible on Film: A Checklist: 1897–1980*. Metuchen: Scarecrow, 1981.

Cane, Anthony. *The Place of Judas Iscariot in Christology*. Aldershot, Hampshire: Ashgate, 2005.

Caron, Vicki. *Uneasy Asylum, France and the Jewish Refugee Crisis: 1933–1942*. Stanford: Stanford University Press, 1999.

Carr, William. *A History of Germany 1815–1985*. 3rd ed. London: Edward Arnold, 1987.

Cash, Johnny. *The Autobiography*. San Francisco: HarperCollins, 2003.

Cassidy, Edward Idris, Pierre Duprey and Remi Hoeckman. "We Remember: A Reflection On The Shoah." *Commission for Religious Relations with the Jews* (March 16, 1998). http://www.vatican.va/roman_curia/pontifical_councils/chrstuni/documents/rc_pc_chrstuni_doc_16031998_shoah_en.html.

*Catechism of the Catholic Church*. Dublin: Veritas, 1994.

Catsoulis, Jeanette. “Christ, With a Color Change.” Review of *Color of the Cross* (2006). *New York Times* (November 9, 2008). http://www.nytimes.com/2006/11/09/movies/10cross.html?_r=0.

Chattaway, Peter T. “Come and See.” *Christianity Today* (February 4, 2005). http://www.christianitytoday.com/ct/2005/februaryweb- only/comeandsee2.html?start=2.

———. “Ethnicity in Jesus Films—Does It Matter?” *Mennonite Brethren Herald* 45, no. 15 (November 24, 2006). http://www.mbherald.com/45/15/movies.en.html.

Christianson, Eric C., Peter Francis and William R. Telford, eds. *Cinéma Divinité: Religion, Theology and the Bible in Film.* London: SCM, 2005.

Clark, Jim. “The Films of Pier Paolo Pasolini.” *Jim's Reviews/Pasolini.* http://jclarkmedia.com/pasolini/pasolini05.html.

Cleage, Arthur. *The Black Messiah.* New York: Sheed & Ward, 1968.

Coerver, Don M., Suzanne B. Pasztor and Robert Buffington. *Mexico: An Encyclopedia of Contemporary Culture and History*. Santa Barbara: ABC-CLIO, 2004.

Cohen, Arthur. “In Our Terrible Age: The *Tremendum* of the Jews.” Pages 11–18 in *The Holocaust as Interruption.* Edited by Elisabeth Schüssler Fiorenza and David Tracy. Edinburgh: T. & T. Clark, 1984.

———. *Tremendum*. New York: Crossroad, 1981.

Cohen, Jeremy. *Christ Killers: The Jews and the Passion from the Bible to the Big Screen.* Oxford: Oxford University Press, 2007.

Cohn-Sherbok, Dan. *The Crucified Jew: Twenty Centuries of Anti-Semitism.* London: Harper Collins, 1992.

———. *Holocaust Theology*. London: Lamp, 1989.

———. ed. *Holocaust Theology: A Reader*. New York: New York University Press, 2002.

Cone, James. *A Black Theology of Liberation.* New York: Orbis Books, 1970.

Corliss, Richard. “Body and Blood: An Interview with Martin Scorsese.” *Film Comment* 24, no. 5 (September/October 1988): 36–42.

Cowie, Peter. “Silents of the North.” *The Movie: The Illustrated History of the Cinema.* 113 (1982): 2241–45.

Crowther, Bosley. “The Life of Jesus: Pasolini's Film Opens at the Fine Arts.” *New York Times* (February 18, 1966). http://movies.nytimes.com/movie/review?_r=1&res=9800E2D9143CE53BBC4052DFB466838D679EDE.

Dashiell, Chris. “Loaves and Fishes: Pasolini's Gospel and the Depiction of Jesus on Film.” *CineScene.com.* http://www.cinescene.com/dash/gospel.htm.

Davies, Alan T., ed. *Anti-Semitism and the Foundations of Christianity*. New York: Paulist, 1979.

Deacy, Christopher. “Faith in Film.” Pages 306–11 in *The Religion and Film Reader*. Edited by Jolyon Mitchell and S. Brent Plate. New York: Routledge, 2007.

Deacy, Christopher, and Gaye Williams Ortiz. *Theology and Film: Challenging the Sacred/Secular Divide.* Malden: Blackwell, 2008.

de la Vega Alfaro, Eduardo. “The Decline of the Golden Age and the Making of the Crisis.” Pages 165–81 in Hershfield and Maciel, eds., *Mexico's Cinema*.

DeMille, Cecil B. *The Autobiography of Cecil B. DeMille.* Edited by Donald Hayne. Englewood Cliffs: Prentice-Hall, 1959.

Doherty, Thomas. “A Code is Born.” *Reason* (December 4, 2007). https://reason.com/archives/2007/12/04/a-code-is-born.

Donahue, John R., and Daniel J. Harrington. *The Gospel of Mark Sagra*. Pagina Series 2. Collegeville: Liturgical Press, 2002.

Doneson, Judith E. *The Holocaust in American Film*. 2nd ed. Syracuse: Syracuse University Press, 2002.

Douchet, Jean, and Jacques Joly. "*Nouvel entretien avec* Nicholas Ray." *Cahiers du Cinéma* 2, no. 27 (January 1962): 1–17.

Doyle, Kate. "The Tlatelolco Massacre: US Documents on Mexico and the Events of 1968." *The National Security Archive*, George Washington University. http://www.gwu.edu/~nsarchiv/NSAEBB/NSAEBB99/.

Drane, James. *A New American Reformation*. New York: Philosophical Library, 1973.

Durgnat, Raymond. "*The Greatest Story Ever Told*: Raymond Durgnat on the Images of Jesus." *Films and Filming* 11, no. 9 (1965): 25–26.

Ebert, Roger. *Scorsese by Ebert*. Chicago: University of Chicago Press, 2008.

Eblin, Jennifer. "What is the Significance of a Red Door on a Home?" *eHow.com*. http://www.ehow.com/facts_7201516_significance-red-door-home_.html.

Eckhardt, Alice Lyons. "Suffering, Theology and the *Shoah*." Pages 34–57 in Jacobs, ed., *Contemporary Christian Religious Responses*.

Ehrman, Bart D. *The Lost Gospel of Judas Iscariot: A New Look at Betrayer and Betrayed*. Oxford: Oxford University Press, 2006.

———. *Misquoting Jesus: The Story Behind Who Changed the Bible and Why*. New York: HarperSanFrancisco, 2005.

Ehrman, Bart D., and Zlatko Pleše. *The Apocryphal Gospels: Texts and Translations*. Oxford: Oxford University Press, 2011.

Eichenberger, Ambros. "Approaches to Film Criticism." Pages 3–10 in May, ed., *New Image of Religious Film*.

Ellis, Marc H. *Toward a Jewish Theology of Liberation*. Maryknoll, NY: Orbis Books, 1987.

Evans, Craig A., and Donald A. Hagner, eds. *Anti-Semitism and Early Christianity: Issues of Polemic and Faith*. Minneapolis: Fortress, 1993.

Fackenheim, Emil. "Jewish Faith and the Holocaust: A Fragment." *Commentary* 46, no. 2 (August 1967): 30–36.

———. *To Mend the World: Foundations of Future Jewish Thought*. New York: Schocken, 1982.

Fasching, Darrell J. *Narrative Theology After Auschwitz*: *From Alienation to Ethics*. Minneapolis: Fortress, 1992.

Fein, Seth. "From Collaboration to Containment: Hollywood and the International Political Economy of Mexican Cinema after the Second World War." Pages 123–63 in Hershfield and Maciel, eds., *Mexico's Cinema*.

Fiedler, Maureen, and Linda Rabben, eds. *Rome Has Spoken: A Guide to Forgotten Papal Statements and How They Have Changed Through the Centuries*. New York: Crossroad, 1998.

Finkelstein, Norman G. *Beyond Chutzpah: On the Misuse of Anti-Semitism and the Abuse of History*. California: University of California Press, 2008.

Fiorenza, Elisabeth Schüssler. *In Memory of Her: A Feminist Theological Reconstruction of Christian Origins*. 10th Anniversary ed. New York: Crossroad, 1994.

Fisher, Eugene J. "The Bible, the Jews, and the Passion." *America* 190, no. 5 (2004): 7–9.

Flannery, Edward. *The Anguish of the Jews*. New York: Paulist, 1985.

Flesher, Paul V. M., and Robert Torry. *Religion and Film: An Introduction*. Nashville: Abingdon, 2007.

Flowers, Elizabeth H., and Darren J. N. Middleton. "Satan and the Curious: Texas Evangelicals Read *The Last Temptation of Christ.*" Pages 147–55 in Middleton, ed., *Scandalizing Jesus?*

Ford, David E., with Rachel Muers, eds. *The Modern Theologians: An Introduction to Christian Theology Since 1918*. 3rd ed. Malden: Blackwell, 2005.

Forshey, Gerald E. *American Religious and Biblical Spectaculars.* Westport: Praeger, 1992.

Foster, Gwendolyn Audrey. "Performity and Gender in Alice Guy's *La Vie du Christ.*" *Film Criticism* 23. 1 (Fall 1998): 6–17.

———. *Performing Whiteness: Postmodern Re/Construction in the Cinema.* Albany: State University of New York Press, 2003.

Foxman, Abraham H. *Jews and Money.* New York: Palgrave MacMillan, 2010.

Friedman, Saul S. *The Oberammergau Passion Play: A Lance Against Civilization.* Carbondale: Southern Illinois University Press, 1984.

Friesen, Dwight H. "An Analysis of the Production, Content, Distribution, and Reception of *Karunamayudu* (1978), an Indian Jesus Film." PhD diss. University of Edinburgh, 2009.

———. "*Karunamayudu*: Seeing Christ Anew in Indian Cinema." Pages 165–88 in *Images of the Word: Hollywood's Bible and Beyond.* Edited by David Shepherd. Atlanta: Society of Biblical Literature, 2008.

Gerstendfeld, Manfred. "Anti-Israelism and Anti-Semitism: Common Characteristics and Motifs." *Jewish Political Studies Review* 19 (Spring 2007): 1–2. http://jcpa.org/article/anti-israelism-and-anti-semitism-common-characteristics-and- motifs/.

Gilman, John. "*Dayasagar* and the Life of Christ in India." *Lausanne World Pulse* (September 2006). http://www.lausanneworldpulse.com/worldreports/470/09-2006?pg=all.

Ginzburg, George. *A Will to Live: A Story About Hope and Strength of the Human Spirit.* 2nd rev. ed. Richmond, VIC: Cycle Press, 2007/2010.

Girard, Rene. *The Scapegoat.* Translated by Yvonne Freccero. Baltimore: The Johns Hopkins University Press, 1989.

Goodacre, Mark. "Do you think you're what they say you are? Reflections on *Jesus Christ Superstar.*" *Journal of Religion and Film* 3, no. 2 (October 1999). http://www.unomaha.edu/jrf/jesuscss2.htm.

Grace, Pamela. *The Religious Film.* Chichester: Wiley-Blackwell, 2009.

Greene, Naomi. *Pier Paolo Pasolini: Cinema and Heresy*. Princeton: Princeton University Press, 1990.

Greenhouse, Linda. Review of "Superstar Film Renews Disputes: Jewish Groups Say Opening Could Stir Anti-Semitism Reasons Given Company Issues Statement." *New York Times* (August 8, 1973). http://www.nytimes.com/movie/review?res=9904e3dd103de63abc4053dfbe668388669ede.

Greydanus, Steven D. "From the Manger to the Cross (1912)." *Decent Films*. http://decentfilms.com/reviews/fromthemangertothecross.

———. "The Last Temptation of Christ: An Essay in Film Criticism and Faith." *Decent Films*. http://www.decentfilms.com/articles/lasttemptation.

Griffen, Danel. "Film as Art." *Danel Griffin's Guide to Cinema.* http://uashome.alaska.edu/~dfgriffin/website/golgotha.htm.

Gubar, Susan. *Judas: A Biography*. New York: W. W. Norton & Co., 2009.

Halivni, David Weiss. *Breaking the Tablets: Jewish Theology After the Shoah.* Lanham: Rowman & Littlefield, 2007.

Hargrave, Robert L. *The Dravidian Movement*. Bombay: Popular Prakasham, 1965.

Harrington, Daniel J., ed. *The Gospel of Matthew.* Sacra Pagina 1. Collegeville: Liturgical Press, 1991.

Harris, Max. *Sacred Folly: A New History of the Feast of Fools*. Ithaca: Cornell University Press, 1969.

Hasenberg, Peter. "The 'Religious' in Film: From *King of Kings* to *The Fisher King*." Pages 41–56 in May, ed., *New Image of Religious Film*.

Hawkins-Dady, Mark. *Speeches That Changed the World.* London: Quercus, 2010.

Haynes, Stephen R. *Prospects for Post-Holocaust Theology.* Atlanta: Scholars Press, 1991.

Hebron, Carol Anne. "Judas Iscariot: From Villain to Saint: The Representation of Judas Iscariot in the Creative Arts from the Late First Century CE to the Present." Masters' Thesis. Brisbane College of Theology, Brisbane, 2009.

———. "Judas, Sinner or Saint: A Critical Examination of the Portrayal of Judas Iscariot in Jesus Films (1902–2006) and Its Implications for Christian Theology." PhD diss. Charles Sturt University, Bathurst, 2013.

Hein, Kenneth. "Judas Iscariot: Key to the Last-Supper Narratives?" *New Testament Studies* 17 (1970–71): 227–32.

Henderson-Bland, R. *Actor–Soldier–Poet.* London: Heath Cranton, 1939.

———. *From the Manger to the Cross: The Story of the World Famous Film of the Life of Jesus*. London: Hodder & Stoughton, 1922.

Henriksen, A. D. Review of "Blade af Satans Bog" in *Arbedjet*, cited by Lisbeth Richter Larsen, "Reception." *Carl Th. Dreyer—The Man and His Works.* http://english.carlthdreyer.dk/Films/Blade-af-Satans-Bog/Reception.aspx.

Herman, Felicia. "The Most Dangerous Anti-Semitic Photoplay in Filmdom: American Jews and *The King of Kings* (DeMille, 1927)." *Velvet Light Trap* 46 (2000): 12–25.

Hershfield, Joanne, and David R. Maciel, eds. *Mexico's Cinema: A Century of Film and Filmmakers.* Wilmington: Scholarly Resource, 1999.

Higham, Charles. *Cecil B. DeMille.* New York: Da Capo, 1973.

Hitler, Adolf. *Mein Kampf.* Translated by Ralph Manneheim. Boston: Houghton Mifflin Company, 1971.

Hoberman, J. "First Lady of Film Alice Guy Blaché at the Whitney." *Village Voice* (November 3, 2009). http://www.villagevoice.com/2009-11-03/film/first-lady-of-film-alice-guy-blanch-eacute-at-the-whitney/.

Humphries-Brooks, Stephenson. *Cinematic Savior Hollywood's Making of the American Christ.* Westport: Praeger, 2006.

Hunter, Stephen. "A Powerful Man of 'Color'." *Washington Post* (October 27, 2006). http://www.washingtonpost.com/wp-dyn/content/article/2006/10/26/AR2006102600401.html.

Interview by Sri Sathavahana with Vijaychander, "Vijaychander, born to perform Jesus." Translated by SVL Narasimha Swamy. http://ilovehyderabad.com/interviews/interviews-vijaychander-born-to-perform- jesus.html.

Jacobs, Lewis. *The Rise of the American Film: A Critical History*. New York: Teachers College Press, 1968.

Jacobs, Steven L., ed. *Contemporary Christian Religious Responses to the Shoah.* Studies in the Shoah 6. Lanham: University Press of America, 1993.

———. *Rethinking Jewish Faith*: *The Child of a Survivor Responds*. Albany: State University of New York Press, 1994.

———. "Toward the Construction of a Post-*Shoah* Interfaith Dialogical Universal Ethic." *Zygon* 38, no. 3 (September 2003): 735–42.

James, Caryn. "Fascination with Faith Fuels Work by Scorsese." *New York Times* (August 8, 1988). http://www.nytimes.com/1988/08/08/movies/fascination-with-faith-fuels-work-by-scorsese.html?pagewanted=all.

Jenkins, Bill. "Jesus Christ Superstar? Why the Gospels Don't Make Good Movies." *Journal of Religion and Film* 12, no. 2 (October, 2008). http://www.unomaha.edu/jrf/vol12no2/Jenkins_Passion.htm.

"Johnny Cash and Billy Graham Through the Years." *Billy Graham Evangelistic Association*. http://billygraham.org/gallery/the-cashes-and-the-grahams-through-the-years/.

Johnston, Robert K. "Introduction: Reframing the Discussion." Pages 15–26 in Johnston, eds., *Reframing Theology and Film*.

———, ed. *Reframing Theology and Film: New Focus for an Emerging Discipline*. Grand Rapids: Baker Academic, 2007.

Joslyn-Siemiatkoski, Daniel. "Moses Received the Torah at Sinai and Handed It On (Mishnah *Avot* 1:1): The Relevance of the Written and Oral Torah for Christians." *Anglican Theological Review* 91, no. 3 (2009): 443–66.

"Julien Duvivier 1896–1967." *filmsdefrance.com*. http://www.filmsdefrance.com/biography/julien-duvivier.html.

Kassabian, Anahid. *Hearing Film: Tracking Identifications in Contemporary Hollywood Film Music*. New York: Routledge, 2001.

Kasser, Rudolphe, Marvin Meyer and Gregor Wurst, eds. *The Gospel of Judas*. Washington: National Geographic, 2006.

Kazantzakis, Nikos. *The Last Temptation of Christ*. Translated by P. A. Bien. New York: Simon & Schuster, 1998.

Kessler, Edward. "The Future of Jewish–Christian Relations." Pages 149–68 in *The Future of Jewish–Christian Dialogue*. Edited by Dan Cohn-Sherbok. Lewiston: Edwin Mellen, 1999.

Kierkegaard, Søren. *Journals and Papers*. Vol. 2, *F–K*. Translated and edited by Howard V. Hong and Edna H. Hong. Bloomington: Indiana University Press, 1970.

Kinnard, Roy, and Tim Davis. *Divine Images: A History of Jesus on the Screen*. New York: Carol Publishing Group, 1992.

Klassen, William. *Judas: Betrayer or Friend of Jesus?* Minneapolis: Fortress, 1996.

Klien, Maury. "Laughing Through Tears: Hollywood Answers to the Depression." Pages 87–92 in Mintz and Roberts, eds., *Hollywood's America*.

Komar, George. "*King of Kings:* Rediscovering the Film and Score." *Pro Musica Sana* 60, Series 2, 4, no. 2 (Winter 2002): 3–39. http://www.mrs.miklosrozsa.info/pmsfiles/PMS60.pdf.

Koppes, Clayton R., and Gregory D. Black. "What to Show the World: The Office of War Information and Hollywood, 1942–1945." Pages 157–68 in Mintz and Roberts, eds., *Hollywood's America*.

Kraemer, Christine Hoff. "Wrestling with Flesh, Wrestling with Spirit: The Painful Consequences of Dualism in *The Last Temptation of Christ*." *Journal of Religion and Popular Culture* 8 (2004). http://www.usask.ca/relst/jrpc/art8-lasttemptation-print.html.

Krauskopf, Joseph. *A Rabbi's Impressions on the Oberammergau Passion Play*. Philadelphia: E. Stern, 1901.

Kuper, Leo. *Genocide: Its Political Use in the Twentieth Century*. Harmondsworth: Penguin, 1981.

Lang, Stephen J. *The Bible on the Big Screen: A Guide from Silent Films to Today's Movies*. Grand Rapids: Baker Books, 2007.

Lännström, Anna. "Forgiving Judas: Extenuating Circumstances in the Ultimate Betrayal." Pages 234–45 in *Mel Gibson's Passion and Philosophy: The Cross, the Questions, the Controversy*. Edited by Jorge J. E. Gracia. Chicago: Open Court, 2004.

Larsen, Lisbeth Richter. "Reception." *Carl Th. Dreyer—The Man and His Works.* Danish Film Institute. http://english.carlthdreyer.dk/Films/Blade-af-Satans-Bog/Reception.aspx.

———. "Shoot." *Carl Th. Dreyer—The Man and His Works*. Danish Film Institute. http://english.carlthdreyer.dk/Films/La-Passion-de-Jeanne-dArc/Shoot.aspx.

Levin, Nora. "Whither Christian-Jewish Dialogue." *Judaism* 33, no. 2 (1984): 233–39.

Levine, Amy-Jill. "Holy Week and the Hatred of the Jews." *ABC Religion and Ethics* (April 2, 2012). http://www.abc.net.au/religion/articles/2012/04/04/3470618.htm.

Linder, Douglas O. "State v. John Scopes ('The Monkey Trial')." Speech on the occasion of the 75th anniversary of the Scopes Trial, July 10, 2000. http://law2.umkc.edu/faculty/projects/ftrials/scopes/scopes.htm.

Lindvall, Terry. "Hollywood Chronicles: Toward an Intersection of Church History and Film History." Pages 126–42 in Johnston, eds., *Reframing Theology and Film.*

Lindvall, Terry, and Andrew Quicke. *Celluloid Sermons: The Emergence of the Christian Film Industry 1930–1986.* New York: New York University Press, 2011.

Littell, Franklin H. "Church Struggle and the Holocaust." Pages 11–29 in *The German Church Struggle and the Holocaust*. Edited by Franklin H. Littell and Hubert G. Locke. Detroit: Wayne State University Press, 1975.

Lodge, Jack. "Carl Theodor Dreyer." *The Movie: The Illustrated History of the Cinema* 113 (1982): 2252.

Luther, Martin. *On the Jews and Their Lies, 1543*. Translated by Martin H. Bertram. http://reactor-core.org/jewish-lies.html.

Lynch, Joseph H. *The Medieval Church: A Brief History*. London: Longman, 1992.

Lysik, David, ed. *The Liturgy Documents: A Parish Resource*, Vol. 1. 4th ed. Chicago: Liturgy Training Publications, 2004.

Maccoby, Hyam. "Jesus on the Small Screen." *Encounter* 49 (July 1977): 42–47.

———. *Judas Iscariot and the Myth of Jewish Evil*. New York: Free Press, 1992.

Malone, Peter. *Movie Christs and Antichrists.* Sydney: Parish Ministry Publications, 1988.

———. *Screen Jesus: Portrayals of Christ in Television and Film*. Lanham: Scarecrow, 2012.

Maltby, Richard. "*The King of Kings* and the Czar of All the Rushes: The Propriety of the Christ Story." Pages 60–86 in *Controlling Hollywood: Censorship and Regulation in the Studio Era*. Edited by Matthew Bernstein. London: Athlone, 2000.

Marcus, Joel. "Epilogue." Pages 291–96 in Evans and Hagner, eds., *Anti-Semitism and Early Christianity*.

Marrus, Michael R. "Holocaust Research and Scholarship Today." Pages 73–82 in *The Holocaust: Voices of Scholars*. Edited by Jolanta Ambrosewicz-Jacobs. Cracow: Auschwitz-Birkenau State Museum, 2009.

Marrus, Michael R., and Robert O. Paxton, *Vichy France and the Jews.* Stanford: Stanford University Press, 1995.

Marsh, Clive. *Cinema and Sentiment: Film's Challenge to Theology.* Waynesboro: Paternoster, 2004.

———. *Theology Goes to the Movies: An Introduction to Critical Christian Thinking.* London: Routledge, 2007.

Marsh, Clive, and Gaye Ortiz, eds. *Explorations in Theology and Film: Movies and Meaning.* Malden: Blackwell, 1997.

Martos, John. *Doors to the Sacred: A Historical Introduction to Sacraments in the Catholic Church*. Revised and updated ed. Liguori: Liguori/Triumph, 2001.
Marx, Karl. "The Jewish Question." Page 79 in Perry and Schweitzer, eds., *Antisemitic Myths*.
Matts, Peter. "Showman of Piety." Pages 7–10 in *The King of Kings*. The Criterion Collection DVD booklet.
May, John R. "Contemporary Theories Regarding the Interpretation of Religious Film." Pages 17–37 in May, ed., *New Image of Religious Film*.
———, ed. *New Image of Religious Film*. Franklin: Sheed & Ward, 1997.
Maybaum, Ignaz. *The Face of God After Auschwitz*. Amsterdam: Polak & Van Gennep, 1965.
Maza, Bernard. *With Fury Poured Out*. New York: KTAV, 1986.
McCain, Paul. *Communion Fellowship—A Resource for Understanding, Implementing, and Retaining the Practice of Closed Communion in the Lutheran Parish*. Waverly, Iowa: The International Foundation for Lutheran Confessional Research, 1992.
McGarry, Michael. *Christology After Auschwitz*. New York: Paulist, 1977.
McKnight, Scott. "The Betrayal of Jesus and the Death of Judas." Pages 63–70 in *Jesus and Mel Gibson's* The Passion of the Christ*: The Film, the Gospels and Claim on History*. Edited by Kathleen E. Corley and Robert L. Webb. London: Continuum, 2004.
———. "A Loyal Critic: Matthew's Polemic with Judaism in Theological Perspective." Pages 55–79 in Evans and Hagner, eds., *Anti-Semitism and Early Christianity*.
McMahan, Alison. *Alice Guy Blaché: Lost Visionary of the Cinema*. New York: Continuum, 2002.
Medved, Harry, and Michael Medved. *The Hollywood Hall of Shame: The Most Expensive Flops in Movie History*. New York: Perigree Books, 1984.
Medved, Michael. "Hollywood vs Religion." *St Mark's Review* 142 (Winter 1990): 6–11.
Metz, Johann-Baptist. *The Emergent Church: Future of Christianity in a Post-bourgeois World*. Translated by P. Mann. London: SCM-Canterbury, 1981.
Meyer, Marvin. *Judas: The Definitive Collection of Gospels and Legends About the Infamous Apostle of Jesus*. New York: HarperOne, 2007.
"Mexican Cinema." *Mexico Explorando*. http://www.explorandomexico.com/about-mexico/5/105/.
Middleton, Darren J. N., ed. *Scandalizing Jesus? Kazantzakis's* The Last Temptation of Christ *Fifty Years On*. New York: Continuum, 2005.
Miles, Margaret R. *Seeing and Believing: Religion and Values in the Movies*. Boston: Beacon, 1996.
Mintz, Alan. *Popular Culture and the Shaping of Holocaust Memory in America*. Seattle: University of Washington Press, 2001.
Mintz, Steven, and Randy Roberts, eds., *Hollywood's America: United States History Through its Films*. 2nd ed. St. James: Brandywine, 1999.
Mitchell, Jolyon, and S. Brent Plate, eds. *The Religion and Film Reader*. New York: Routledge, 2007.
Montgomerie, Margaret. "Miniseries." *The Museum Broadcast Communications*. http://www.museum.tv/eotvsection.php?entrycode=miniseries.
Moore, James F. "Re-Envisioning Christianity: A New Era in Christian Theological Interpretation of Christian Texts." *Cross Currents* 50, no. 4 (2000/2001): 437–47.
———. *Toward a Dialogical Community: A Post-Shoah Christian Theology*. Lanham: University Press of America, 2004.

Morgan, Michael, ed., *The Jewish Thought of Emil Fackenheim*. Detroit: Wayne State University Press, 1987.

Moro, Carl J. *Mexican Cinema: Reflections of a Society 1896 to 2004*. 3rd ed. Jefferson: McFarland & Co., 2005.

"Motion Pictures classified by National Legion of Decency." 1959 version. https://archive.org/stream/motionpicturescl00nati/motionpicturescl00nati_djvu.txt.

Nicholls, William. *Christian Antisemitism: A History of Hate*. Lanham: Rowman & Littlefield, 1993.

Noakes, Jeremy, and Geoffrey Pridham. *Documents on Nazism 1919–1945*. New York: Viking, 1974.

Noble, Andrea. *Mexican National Cinema*. London: Routledge, 2005.

Nysten, Jes. "An Unrealized Lifelong Dream—Dreyer's Jesus Film." *Carl Th. Dreyer—The Man and His Work*. Danish Film Institute. http://english.carlthdreyer.dk/AboutDreyer/Themes/An-Unrealized-Lifelong-Dream.aspx.

O'Brien, Catherine. *The Celluloid Madonna: From Scripture to Screen*. London: Wallflower, 2011.

O'Connor, Edward. "King of Kings." *Films* 12, no. 9 (November 1961): 546–49.

Origen. *Contra Celsum*. Translated by Henry Chadwick. Cambridge: Cambridge University Press, 1980.

Ortiz, Gaye Williams. "World Cinema: Opportunities for Dialogue with Religion and Theology." Pages 73–87 in Johnston, eds., *Reframing Theology and Film*.

Otto, Rudolf. *The Idea of the Holy*. 2nd ed. Translated by John W. Harvey. New York: Oxford University Press, 1958.

Pacatte, Rose. "Shaping Morals, Shifting Views: Have the Rating Systems Influenced How (Christian) America Sees Movies?" Pages 261–86 in Johnston, eds., *Reframing Theology and Film*.

Paffenroth, Kim. "Film Depictions of Judas." *Journal of Religion and Film* 5, no. 2 (2001). https://www.unomaha.edu/jrf/judas.htm.

———. *Judas: Images of the Lost Disciple*. Louisville: Westminster John Knox, 2001.

Page, Matt. Review of *Golgotha*, "One of the Finest Films Ever Made." *Golgotha. IMDb* http://www.imdb.com/title/tt0025191/?ref_=fn_tt_tt_2.

———. "Thomas on the Road: A Comparison of the Gospels of Cash and Thomas." *Bible Films Blog*. http://biblefilms.blogspot.com.au/search?q=%22Gospel+Road%22.

Pagels, Elaine, and Karen L. King, *Reading Judas: The Gospel of Judas and the Shaping of Christianity*. New York: Viking Penguin, 2007.

"Papal Encyclicals." *Papal Encyclicals Online*. http://www.papalencyclicals.net/all.htm.

Papanikolaou, Eftychia. "Identity and Ethnicity in Peter Gabriel's Sound Track for *The Last Temptation of Christ*." Pages 217–28 in Middleton, ed., *Scandalizing Jesus?*

Paranaguá, Paulo Antonio, ed. *Mexican Cinema*. Translated by Ana M. López. London: British Film Institute, 1995.

———. "Of Periodizations and Paradigms: The Fifties in Comparative Perspective." *Neuvo Texto Critico* 10, no. 21/22 (1998): 31–44.

Paul VI, "Declaration On the Relation of the Church to Non-Christian Religions—*Nostra Aetate*." (October 28, 1965). http://www.vatican.va/archive/hist_councils/ii_vatican_council/documents/vat-ii_decl_19651028_nostra-aetate_en.html.

Pawlikowski, John T. "Christian Ethics and the Holocaust: A Dialogue with Post-Auschwitz Judaism." *Theological Studies* 49, no. 4 (1988): 649–69.

Pereboom, Maarten. *History and Film: Moving Pictures and the Study of the Past*. Boston: Prentice Hall, 2011.

Perry, Marvin, and Frederick M. Schweitzer, eds. *Antisemitic Myths: A Historical and Contemporary Anthology.* Bloomington: Indiana University Press, 2008.

Phillips, Kendall R. *Controversial Cinema: The Films that Outraged America.* Westport: Praeger, 2008.

Piekow, Herbert W. "The Golden Age of Mexican Cinema." *El Ojo del Lago.* http://www.chapala.com/elojo/index.php?option=com_content&view=article&id=77:mexcinema&catid=59:aprilissue.

Pitre, Brant. *Jesus and the Jewish Roots of the Eucharist: Unlocking the Secrets of the Last Supper.* New York: Doubleday, 2011.

Pius X, "*Vehementer Nos*" Encyclical of Pope Pius X on "The French Law of Separation" (February 11, 1906). http://w2.vatican.va/content/pius- x/en/encyclicals/documents/hf_p-x_enc_11021906_vehementer-nos.html.

Polkow, Dennis. "Andrew Lloyd Webber: From Superstar to Requiem." *Christian Century* (March 18–25, 1987). http://www.religion-online.org/showarticle.asp?title=1011.

Prothero, Stephen. *American Jesus: How the Son of God Became a National Icon.* New York: Farrar, Straus & Giroux, 2003.

Quijano, Julio Alejandro. "Murió Miguel Zacarías el creador de estrellas." *El Universal* (April 21, 2006). http://www.eluniversal.com.mx/espectaculos/69505.html.

Rainey, Jon. "The Cinematic Savior: Jesus Films and Related Literature." *Theological Librarianship* 3, no 2 (2010): 22–26. https://journal.atla.com/ojs/index.php/theolib/article/viewFile/157/448.

Regaldo, Antonio. "Miguel Morayta: A Forgotten Film." *ABC.es* (October 30, 2009). http://www.abc.es/hermeroteca/historico-30-10-2009/abc/Toledo/miguel-moroayta-un-olvido-de-cine_1131083948429.html.

Reinhartz, Adele. *Bible and Cinema: Fifty Key Films.* London: Routledge, 2013.

———. "History and Pseudo History in the Jesus Film Genre." *Biblical Interpretation* 14, no. 1 (2006): 1–17.

———. "Jesus in Film: Hollywood Perspectives on the Jewishness of Jesus." *Journal of Religion and Film* 2, no. 2 (1998). http://www.unomaha.edu/jrf/JesusinFilmRein.htm.

———. *Jesus of Hollywood.* Oxford: Oxford University Press, 2007.

———. *Scripture on the Silver Screen.* Louisville: Westminster John Knox, 2003.

Reynolds, Herbert. "From the Palette to the Screen: The Tissot Bible as Source-book for *From The Manger to the* Cross." Pages 275–310 in *An Invention of the Devil? Religion and the Early Cinema: Une Invention du Diable? Cinéma des Premiers et Religion.* Edited by Roland Cosandey, Andre Gaudreault and Tom Gunning. Sainte Foy, Canada: Les Presses de l'Université Laval, 1992.

Rivkin, Ellis. *What Crucified Jesus?* Nashville: Abingdon, 1984.

Robinson, David. *From Peep Show to Palace: The Birth of American Film.* New York: Columbia University Press, 1996.

Robinson, James M., gen. ed. *The Nag Hammadi Library in English.* New York: HarperSanFrancisco, 1990.

Romano, Andrew. "Hollywood Declares 2014 the Year of the Bible." *The Daily Beast.* http://www.thedailybeast.com/articles/2014/01/09/hollywood-declares-2014-the-year-of-the-bible.html.

Rosenberg, Shalom. "The Holocaust: Lessons, Explanation, Meaning." Pages 82–109 in *The Impact of the Holocaust on Jewish Theology.* Edited by Steven T. Katz. New York: New York University Press, 2005.

Roth, John K. "If God Was Silent, Absent, Dead, or Nonexistent, What About Philosophy and Theology?" Pages 139–51 in *After the Holocaust: Challenging the Myth of Silence*. Edited by David Cesarani and Eric J. Sundquist. London: Routledge, 2012.

Rubenstein, Richard L. *After Auschwitz*. Indianapolis: Bobbs Merrill, 1966.

Rubenstein, Richard L., and John K. Roth, *Approaches to Auschwitz: The Holocaust and its Legacy*. Revised edition. Louisville: Westminster John Knox, 2003.

Ruether, Rosemary Radford. "Anti-Semitism and Christian Theology." Pages 79–92 in *Auschwitz: Beginning of a New Era?* Edited by Eva Fleischner. New York: KTAV, 1977.

———. "Christology and Jewish–Christian Relations." Pages 125–35 in *Messianism Through History*. Edited by Wim Beuken, Seán Freyne and Anton Weiler. London: SCM, 1993.

———. *Faith and Fratricide: The Theological Roots of Anti- Semitism*. Eugene: Wipf & Stock, 1997.

———. "Theological and Ethical Reflections on the *Shoah*: Getting Beyond the Victim–Victimizer Relationship." Pages 168–93 in Jacobs, ed., *Contemporary Christian Religious Responses*.

Rutishauser, Christian. "The 1947 Seelisberg Conference: The Foundation of the Jewish–Christian Dialogue." *Studies in Christian–Jewish Relations* 2, no. 2 (2007): 34–53. http://ejournals.bc.edu/ojs/index.php/scjr/article/view/1421/1310.

Sacks, Jonathan. *Tradition in an Untraditional Age: Essays on Modern Jewish Thought*. London: Valentine Mitchell, 1990.

Samuels, Stuart. "The Age of Conspiracy and Conformity: *Invasion of the Body Snatchers* (1956)." Pages 221–30 in Mintz and Roberts, eds., *Hollywood's America*.

Schwartz, Stephen. "*Godspell* Notes for Directors, Music Directors and Musicians, Producers." *stephenschwartz.com*. http://www.stephenschwartz.com/wp-content/uploads/2010/08/godspell-notes-for-directors-and-musicians1.pdf.

———. "*Godspell* Script Notes and Revision 1999." http://www.oocitoes.org/cugodspell/scriptnotes.html.

———. "Stephen Schwartz Answers Questions About the *Godspell* Movie." *stephenschwartz.com*. http://www.stephenschwartz.com/wp-content/uploads/2010/08/godspell-movie.pdf.

Scorsese, Martin. "On Appreciating Kazantzakis." Pages 229–30 in Middleton, ed., *Scandalizing Jesus?*

———. *Scorsese on Scorsese*. Edited by David Thompson and Ian Christie. London: Faber & Faber, 1989.

Scoville, Chester N., and Kimberley M. Yates. "The Cordwainers' Play: The Agony in the Garden and Betrayal." *The York Plays: A Modernization*. http://www.rhaworth.myby.co.uk/pofstp/REED/York28.html.

———. "The Cutlers' Play: The Conspiracy." *The York Plays: A Modernization*. http://www.rhaworth.myby.co.uk/pofstp/REED/York26.html.

Setrakian, Lara. "Story of Jesus Through Iranian Eyes." *ABC News* (February 16, 2008). http://abcnews.go.com/Entertainment/story?id+4297085&page+1&single Page+true.

Shilling, Kaille. "Servant of the Story: Judas as Tragic Hero in Film." *Journal of Religion and Film* 8, no. 2 (October 2004). http://www.unomaha.edu/jrf/Vol8No2/servant.htm.

Sklar, Robert. *Movie-Made America: A Cultural History of American Movies*. New York: Vintage Books, 1994.

Slide, Anthony, ed. *The Memoirs of Alice Guy Blaché*. Lanham: Scarecrow, 1986.

Solomon, Jon. *The Ancient World in the Cinema.* Revised and expanded edition. New Haven: Yale University Press, 2001.

Soulen, R. Kendall. *The God of Israel and Christian Theology.* Minneapolis: Fortress, 1996.

Stack, Oswald, and Pier Paolo Pasolini. *Pasolini on Pasolini: Interviews with Oswald Stack.* London: Thames & Hudson, 1969.

Staley, Jeffrey L., and Richard Walsh. *Jesus, the Gospels, and Cinematic Imagination: A Handbook to Jesus on DVD.* Louisville: Westminster John Knox, 2007.

Stammer, Larry B. "New Look at Ancient Betrayer." *Los Angeles Times* (April 21, 2000). http://articles.latimes.com/2000/apr/21/news/mn-22024.

Steiner, George. *No Passion Spent: Essays 1978–1996.* London: Faber & Faber, 1996.

Stern, Richard, Clayton N. Jefford, and Guerric Debona. *Savior on the Silver Screen.* New York: Paulist, 1999.

Strick, Philip. "The Greatest Stories Ever Told." *The Movie: The Illustrated History of the Cinema* 103 (1981): 2050–53.

Studer, Seth. "*Il Vangelo Secondo Matteo.*" *Vagrant Café.* http://www.vagrantcafe.com/christiancinema/2004_02_24_archive.htm.

Tanenbaum, Marc. "Passion Plays and Vilification of Jews." *Christian Century* 90, no. 31 (1973): 859.

Tatum, W. Barnes. *Jesus at the Movies: A Guide to the First Hundred Years.* Salem, OR: Polebridge, 1997. 3rd ed., 2013.

———. *Jesus at the Movies: A Guide to the First Hundred Years.* Santa Rosa, CA: Polebridge, 1997. Revised and expanded ed., 2004.

———. "The Novel, the Four Gospels, and the Continuing Historical Quest." Pages 19–33 in Middleton, ed., *Scandalizing Jesus?*

Taylor, Barry. "The Colors of Sound: Music and Meaning Making in Film." Pages 51–69 in Johnston, ed., *Reframing Theology and Film.*

Telford, William R. "The Two Faces of Betrayal: The Characterization of Peter and Judas in the Biblical Epic or Christ Film." Pages 214–35 in Christianson, Francis, and Telford, eds., *Cinéma Divinité.*

———. "Through a Lens Darkly: Critical Approaches to Theology and Film." Pages 15–43 in Christianson, Francis, and Telford, eds., *Cinéma Divinité.*

"The Jesus Film Project." http://www.jesusfilm.org/.

"The Jesus Mini Series." Interview between Lorenzo Minoli, producer of the mini-series and David Bruce. http://hollywoodjesus.com/jesus_min_series.htm.

"The Pledge of the Legion of Decency." *Catholic Apologetics.* http://www.catholicapologetics.info/morality/general/decent.htm.

Theissen, Gerd. *The Gospels in Context: Social and Political History in the Synoptic Tradition.* Translated by Linda M. Maloney. Minneapolis: Fortress, 1991.

Thomas, Gordon. Review of *The King of Kings*, "A Tale of Two *Kings*." *BLFJ* 51 (February 2006). http://brightlightsfilm.com/51/51king.php.

Thompson, Anne. "Color of the Cross Portrays Jesus as a Black Jew." *Risky Biz Blog* (August 23, 2006). http://reporter.blogs.com/risky/2006/08/color_of_the_cr.html.

Thomson, David. *Europe Since Napoleon.* Harmondsworth: Penguin, 1982.

Trotter, F. Thomas. "The Church Moves Toward Film Discrimination." *Religion in Life* 38, no. 2 (Summer 1969): 264–76. http://www.religion-online.org/showarticle.asp?title=3474.

Tsu, Susan. "Costume Notes." http://itsayskeds.bravehost.com/costumenotes.htm.

Vaux, Sara Anson. “Unforgiven: The Sentence Death and Radical Forgiveness.” *Christianity and Literature* 47, no. 4 (1998): 443–58.

Viano, Maurizio. *A Certain Realism: Making Use of Pasolini’s Film Theory and Practice*. Berkeley: University of California, 1993.

Vohra, Ranbir. *The Making of India: A Historical Survey.* 2nd ed. New York: M. E. Sharpe, 2001.

Wall, James. “The Last Temptation: A Lifeless Jesus.” *Christian Century* 105 (August 17–24, 1988). http://www.religion-online.org/showarticle.asp?title=974.

Walsh, Moira. “Christ or Credit Card?” *America* 106, no 3 (October 21, 1961): 71–74.

Walsh, Richard. *Three Versions of Judas*. London: Equinox, 2010.

———. “The Gospel According to Judas: Myth and Parable.” *Biblical Interpretation* 14 (2006): 37–63.

———. *Reading the Gospels in the Dark: Portrayals of Jesus in Film.* Harrisburg, PA: Trinity Press International, 2003.

Wanamaker, Marc. “The Kalem Trailblazers.” *The Movie: The Illustrated History of the Cinema* 102 (1981): 2032–33.

Weiss, David. “The Holocaust and the New Covenant.” Pages 74–75 in *Holocaust: Religious and Philosophical Implications*. Edited by John K. Roth and Michael Berengaum. New York: Paragon House, 1989.

Wells, Jeffrey. “Red and White.” *Hollywood Elsewhere.* http://www.hollywood-elsewhere.com/2008/07/five_things.php.

Wiesel, Elie. *Night.* New York: Bantam Books, 1982.

Wilensky, Gabriel. *Six Million Crucifixions: How Christian Teachings About Jews Paved the Road to the Holocaust.* San Diego: QWERTY, 2010.

Williamson, Clark. *A Guest in the House of Israel: Post-Holocaust Church Theology.* Louisville: Westminster John Knox, 1993.

Wright, Melanie J. *Religion and Film: An Introduction.* London: I. B. Tauris, 2007.

Wright, N. T. *The New Testament and the People of God.* Minneapolis: Fortress, 1992.

Zeffirelli, Franco. *An Autobiography.* New York: Weidenfeld & Nicholson, 1986.

———. *Franco Zeffirelli’s Jesus: A Spiritual Diary.* Translated by Willis J. Egan. San Francisco: Harper & Row, 1984.

Zwiep, Arie W. *Christ, the Spirit and the Community of God: Essays on the Acts of the Apostles*. Wissenschaftliche Untersuchungen zum Neuen Testament 2/293. Tübingen: Mohr Siebeck, 2010.

# Filmography

*42nd Street* (1933), Dir. Lloyd Bacon, USA: Warner Bros.

*Ancient Rome: The Rise and Fall of an Empire* (2006), Dirs. Tim Dunn, Nick Green, Andrew Grieve, Nick Murphy, Arif Nurmohamed, and Christopher Spencer, UK: British Broadcasting Company.

*Ben-Hur* (1959), Dir. William Wyler, USA: Metro-Goldwyn-Mayer.

*Bible, The* (2013), Dirs. Crispin Reece, Tony Mitchell and Christopher Spencer, USA: Lightworkers Media.

*Big Lebowsky, The* (1998), Dir. Joel Coen, USA: Polygram Filmed Entertainment.

*Birds, The* (1963), Dir. Alfred Hitchcock, USA: Universal Pictures.

*Blade af Satans Bog* (1921), Dir. Carl Theodor Dreyer, DK: Nordisk Film.

*Brokeback Mountain* (2005), Dir. Ang Lee, USA/CA: Focus Features.

*Butch Cassidy and the Sundance Kid* (1969), Dir. George Roy Hill, USA: Twentieth Century Fox Film.

*Christus* (1916), Dir. Giulio Antamoro, IT: Società Italiana Cines.

*Color of the Cross* (2006), Dir. Jeane-Claude Le Marre, USA: Nu-Light Entertainment.

*Color of the Cross 2: The Resurrection* (2008), Dir. Jeane-Claude Le Marre, USA: Nu-Light Entertainment.

*Creature from the Black Lagoon* (1954), Dir. Jack Arnold, USA: Universal International Pictures.

*Cruising* (1980), Dir. William Friedkinder, USA/DE: United Artists.

*David Golder* (1931), Dir. Julien Duvivier, FR: Les Films Marcel Vandal et Charles Delac.

*Day of Triumph* (1954), Dirs. John T. Coyle and Irving Pichel, USA: Century Films Inc.

*Destry Rides Again* (1939), Dir. George Marshall, USA: Universal Pictures.

*Die Gezeichneten* (1921), Dir. Carl Theodor Dreyer, DE: Primus Film GbmH.

*Donnie Darko* (2001), Dir. Richard Kelly, USA: Pandora Cinema.

*El Hombre sin Patria* (1922), Dir. Miquel Contreras Torres, MX: Producciones Contreras Torres.

*El mártir del Calvario* (1952), Dir. Miguel Morayta, MX: Oro Films.

*El Pecado de Adán y Eva* (1969), Dir. Miguel Zacarías, MX: Aztec Films.

*Exodus: God and Kings* (2014), Dir. Ridley Scott, USA: Chemin Entertainment.

*Fargo* (1996), Dir. Joel Coen, USA: Polygram Filmed Entertainment.
*Forbidden Planet* (1956), Dir. Fred M. Wilcox, USA: Metro-Goldwyn-Mayer.
*Fountainhead, The* (1949), Dir. King Vidor, USA: Warner Bros.
*From the Manger to the Cross* (1912), Dir. Sidney Olcott, USA: Kalem.

*Gangs of New York* (2002), Dir. Martin Scorsese, USA/IT: Miramax Films.
*Gentleman's Agreement* (1947), Dir. Elia Kazan, USA: Twentieth Century Fox.
*Gli ultimo giorni di Pompeii* (1913), Dirs. Mario Caserini and Eleuterio Rodolfi, IT: Societá Anomina Ambrosio.
*Godspell: A Musical Based on the Gospel According to St. Matthew* (1973), Dir. David Greene, USA: Columbia Pictures.
*Golgotha* (1935), Dir. Julien Duvivier, FR: Ichtys Film.
*Gospel Road: The Story of Jesus* (1973), Dir. Robert Elfstrom, USA: Twentieth Century Fox.
*Gran Torino* (2008), Dir. Clint Eastwood, USA: Matten Productions.
*Great Commandment, The* (1939), Dir. Irving Pichel, USA: Cathedral Films.
*Greatest Story Ever Told, The* (1965), Dir. George Stevens, USA: United Artists.
*Gung Ho! The Story of Carlson's Maikin Island Raid* (1943), Dir. Ray Enright, USA: Universal Pictures.

*Hawaii* (1966), Dir. George Roy Hill, USA: United Artists.
*Heaven is for Real* (2014), Dir. Randall Wallace, USA: TriStar Pictures.
*How The West Was Won* (1962), Dirs. John Ford and Henry Hathaway, USA: Metro-Goldwyn-Mayer.

*I Beheld His Glory* (1952), Dir. John T. Coyle, USA: Cathedral Films.
*Il figlio dell'uomo* (1954), Dir. Virgilio Sabel, IT: Parva.
*Il Messia* (1975), Dir. Roberto Rossellini, IT: Orizzonte 2000.
*Il Vangelo Secondo Matteo* (1964), Dir. Pier Paolo Pasolini, IT/FR: Arco Film.
*Intolerance* (1916), Dir. D. W. Griffith, USA: Triangle Film Corporation.
*It Happened One Night* (1934), Dir. Frank Capra, USA: Columbia Picture Corporation.

*Jesus* (1999), Dir. Roger Young, CZ/IT/DE/USA: Antena 3 Television.
*Jesus Christ Superstar* (1973), Dir. Nowman Jewison, USA: Universal Pictures.
*Jesús el Niño Dios* (1970), Dir. Miguel Zacarías, MX: Panorama Films.
*Jesús, Maria y José* (1970), Dir. Miguel Zacarías, MX: Laguna Films.
*Jesús, Nuestro Señor* (1972), Dir. Miquel Zacarias, MX: Panorama Films.
*Jesus of Nazareth* (1977), Dir. Franco Zeffirelli, IT/UK: Incorporated Television Company.
*Judas* (2004), Dir. Charles Robert Carner, USA: Paramount Network Productions.

*Karunamayudu* (1978), Dirs. A. Bheem Singh and Christopher Coelho, IN: Dayspring International.
*Keys to the Kingdom, The* (1944), Dir. John N. Stahl, USA: Twentieth Century Fox.
*King of Kings* (1961), Dir. Nicholas Ray, USA: Metro-Goldwyn-Mayer.
*Kings of Kings, The* (1927), Dir. Cecil B. DeMille, USA: DeMille Pictures Corporation.
*Kiss of the Spider Woman* (1985), Dir. Héctor Babenco, BR/USA: Film Dallas Pictures.

*La Passion* (1897), Dir. Albert Kircher (a.k.a. Léar), FR: Léar Production Company.
*La Vie du Christ* (1906), Dir. Alice Guy, FR: Société des Etablissments L. Gaumont.
*La Vie et la Passion de Jésus Christ* (1902/1905), Dirs. Ferdinand Zecca and Lucien Nouquet, FR: Pathé Frères.
*Last Days of Pompeii, The* (1935), Dir. Ernest B. Schoedsack, USA: RKO Radio Pictures.
*Last Temptation of Christ, The* (1988), Dir. Martin Scorsese, USA/CA: Universal Pictures.
*Life of Brian, The* (1979), Dir. Terry Jones, UK: HandMade Films/Warner Bros.
*Little Caesar* (1930), Dir. Mervyn Leroy, USA: First National Pictures.
*Los Tres Garcia* (1946), Dir. Ismael Rodríguez, MX: Producciones Rodríguez Hermanos.
*Lost Weekend, The* (1945), Dir. Billy Wilder, USA: Paramount Pictures.

*Maria Magdalena, pecadora de Magdala* (1946), Dir. Miguel Contreras Torres, MX: Hispano Continental Films.
*Mary: Mother of Christ* (2015), Dir. Alister Grierson, USA: Lionsgate.
*Maurice* (1987), Dir. James Ivory, USA: Cinecom Pictures.
*Mean Streets* (1973), Dir. Martin Scorsese, USA: Warner Bros Pictures.
*Messiah, The* (2007), Dir. Nader Talebzadeh, IR: Production Company unknown.

*Noah* (2014), Dir. Darren Aranofsky, USA: Paramount Pictures.

*Oliver Twist* (1948), Dir. David Lean, UK: Rank Organisation.

*Passion of Joan of Arc, The* (1928), Dir. Carl Theo. Dreyer, DK: Société générale des films.
*Passion of the Christ, The* (2004), Dir. Mel Gibson, USA: Icon Productions.
*Passion Play, The* (1898), Dir. Henry C. Vincent, USA: Edision Manufacturing Company.
*Passion, The* (2008), Dir. Michael Offer, UK: British Broadcasting Company.

*Q B VII* (1974), Dir. Tom Gries, USA: Douglas S. Cramer Company.
*Querelle* (1982), Dir. Rainer Werner Fassbinder, DE/FR: Gaumont (France).
*Quo Vadis* (1912), Dir. Enrico Guazzoni, IT: Societá Italiana Cines.
*Quo Vadis* (1925), Dir. Gabriellino D'Annunzio and Georg Jacoby, IT: Unione Cinematografica Italiona.
*Quo Vadis* (1951), Dir. Mervyn Leroy, USA/IT: Metro-Goldwyn-Mayer.
*Quo Vadis* (1985), Dir. Franco Rossi, IT: RAI Radiotelevisione.

*Raging Bull* (1980), Dir. Martin Scorsese, USA: United Artists.
*Rain Man* (1988), Dir. Barry Levison, USA: United Artists.
*Reina de Reinas: La Virgen María* (1948), Dir. Miguel Contreras Torres, MX: Hispano Continental Films.
*Rich Man, Poor Man* (1976), Dirs. David Greene and Boris Sagal, USA: Universal Television.
*Robe, The* (1953), Dir. Henry Koster, USA: Twentieth Century Fox.
*Roots* (1977), Dirs. David Greene, Marvin J. Chomsky, John Erman, and Gilbert Moses, USA: David L. Wolper Productions.

*Sand Pebbles, The* (1966), Dir. Robert Wise, USA: Robert Wise Productions.
*Scarface* (1931), Dirs. Howard Hawks and Richard Rosson, USA: The Caddo Company.
*Second Coming* (1992), Dir. Blair Underwood, USA: Quiet Fury Productions.

*Shawshank Redemption, The* (1994), Dir. Frank Darabont, USA: Castle Rock Entertainment.
*Snow White and the Seven Dwarfs* (1937), Dirs. William Cottrell, David Hand, Wilfred Jackson, Larry Morey, Perce Pearce, and Ben Sharpsteen, USA: Walt Disney Productions.
*Son of God* (2014), Dir. Christopher Spencer, USA: Lightworkers Media.
*Son of Man* (2005), Dir. Mark Dornford-May, ZA: Spier Films.
*Sorry, Judas* (1993/2004), Dir. Celia Lowenstein, UK Channel Four.
*Spartacus* (1913), Dir. Giovanni Enrico Vidali, IT: Pasquali e C.
*Spartacus* (1960), Dir. Stanley Kubrick, USA: Bryna Productions.

*Taxi Driver* (1976), Dir. Martin Scorsese, USA: Columbia Pictures.
*Titanic* (1997), Dir. James Cameron, USA: Twentieth Century Fox Film.
*To Kill A Mockingbird* (1962), Dir. Robert Mulligan, USA: Universal International Pictures.

*Untel Pére et Fil* (1940), Dir. Julien Duvivier, FR: Transcontinental Films.

*Visual Bible, The: The Gospel of John* (2004), Dir. Philip Saville, CA/UK: Gospel of John Ltd.

*Walk the Line* (2005), Dir. James Mangold, USA: Twentieth Century Fox.

# Index of References

# Index of Authors

# Index of Subjects